11/20/13

To Carol Watson

Best Wishes
Leonard Dennito
&

Nataliya Shoner

"...in my 36 years in law enforcement fields (chief of police, retired) and now, working with American Military University as a senior law enforcement coordinator, I believe this book should be required reading for anyone working on human trafficking crimes or working to combat this modern day slavery. The book provides a clear understanding of how this crime occurs and entraps its victims that has not been clearly understood before now."

Dave Malone
Senior Law Enforcement Education Coordinator,
American Military University-Midwest

Excellent!! *"Criminal Investigations of Sex Trafficking in America is the only textbook that I am aware of that is a comprehensive collection of sex trafficking information and investigative techniques that will assist law enforcement investigators.* Criminal Investigations of Sex Trafficking in America *is the only book that sex trafficking investigators will need to keep on their desk. Professors of criminal justice will certainly appreciate such a comprehensive textbook that includes the necessary information and resources to teach within the university environment. I wish I had this textbook to use when I was the commander of a human trafficking task force."*

George Koder
Former Lt.

"I would consider this as a valuable tool for those engaged in human trafficking investigations and training. The book provides the necessary material needed to effectively set out for practitioners directions and processes for effective detection, knowledge and prosecution. It also provides the same for NGOs to learn and develop their processes and protocols that intersect with law enforcement."

Kim Derry
Retired Deputy Chief of Police, Toronto Police, Chair of FBINAA
World-Wide Human Trafficking Coordination Center Initiative,
Co-Chair of the International Police Training Center (IPTI),
Budapest, Hungary

Criminal Investigation of Sex Trafficking in America

Leonard Territo
Saint Leo University

Nataliya Glover
Saint Leo University

CRC Press
Taylor & Francis Group
Boca Raton   London   New York

CRC Press is an imprint of the
Taylor & Francis Group, an **informa** business

CRC Press
Taylor & Francis Group
6000 Broken Sound Parkway NW, Suite 300
Boca Raton, FL 33487-2742

© 2014 by Taylor & Francis Group, LLC
CRC Press is an imprint of Taylor & Francis Group, an Informa business

No claim to original U.S. Government works

Printed on acid-free paper
Version Date: 20130827

International Standard Book Number-13: 978-1-4665-5422-1 (Hardback)

Library of Congress Cataloging-in-Publication Data

Territo, Leonard, author.
    Criminal investigation of sex trafficking in America / Leonard Territo, Nataliya Glover.
      pages cm
    Summary: "Human trafficking is the third largest business for organized crime worldwide, next to illegal weapons trading and drugs. Written by well-respected criminal justice scholars, this book covers the criminal investigation of sex trafficking. Focusing on multidisciplinary criminal investigation--specifically in the United States--it also examines psychological damage and treatment and the prosecution of offenders. Full ancillary materials are also available"-- Provided by publisher.
    Includes bibliographical references and index.
    ISBN 978-1-4665-5422-1 (hardback)
    1. Human trafficking--United States. 2. Criminal investigation--United States. 3. Human trafficking. 4. Criminal investigation. I. Glover, Nataliya, author. II. Title.

HQ281.T47 2013
306.3'620973--dc23
                                           2013034920

Visit the Taylor & Francis Web site at
http://www.taylorandfrancis.com

and the CRC Press Web site at
http://www.crcpress.com

Dedication

For my wife, Elena, the kindest and sweetest woman I have ever known, and our children, Lorraine, Kseniya, and Ilia, and our grandchildren, Matthew, Branden, and Alexander.

Leonard Territo

For my late husband, Barry, who inspired me to become who I am now, and my daughter, Anastasia, who gave me the strength and reason to live and fight; for my parents, Tatyana and Vladimir, who loved and supported me every step of the way, and my mentor, Larissa Nossova, who changed my life forever and showed me the way.

Nataliya Glover

Contents

Chapter 8: Crime Scene Examination and Physical Evidence in Sex-Trafficking Cases 287

Preface

A number of years ago, when the authors first became involved in both teaching and attending sex-trafficking training courses, it became quite apparent that many of the local law enforcement officers in attendance had little or no knowledge about the topic. For example, in one memorable case, a vice squad supervisor from a large West Coast law enforcement agency spoke to us after the completion of a sex-trafficking course we were teaching and informed us that, up to that point, he had been involved in the arrest of over 3,000 prostitutes, but until attending this course never realized that many of these women may have been trafficked and were possibly being forced into prostitution. He had always assumed they were engaged in prostitution voluntarily. Fortunately, however, because of the increasing number of sex-trafficking training courses being taught around the country, this lack of awareness on the part of local law enforcement officials has diminished somewhat, but we still have a long way to go. For example, recent studies funded by the National Institute of Justice (NIJ) have revealed a need to better understand the problem. One study found that, in general, officers, prosecutors, and service providers could not:

- identify types of trafficking (e.g., trafficking in sexual exploitation or trafficking in general laborers)
- list the elements of trafficking
- differentiate between severe and nonsevere forms of trafficking
- distinguish trafficking from smuggling
- differentiate between domestic and international trafficking

The same study also found serious communication gaps between local law enforcement and victim service agencies.[1]

As we started our research for this book, it became abundantly clear to us that there was a great deal of information available about sex trafficking that had been published in trade journals and scholarly journals as well as governmental and nongovernmental studies. Also, as we attended numerous sex-trafficking lectures given by highly experienced federal, state, and local law enforcement investigators and prosecutors, it became apparent that they had developed their own specialized lesson plans with accompanying PowerPoint® and photo files. Most of their presentations were based on their own experiences as sex-trafficking investigators and actual cases they had prosecuted. In an effort to maximize and expand upon the amount of information we would be able to draw upon to write this book, we also conducted numerous interviews with highly experienced sex trafficking investigators and prosecutors. All of the sources of information alluded to thus far, in combination, provided us with valuable insights into what the final content of this book should include.

Upon completion of our comprehensive information-gathering process, we concluded that there was a virtual treasure trove of information on the topic of the criminal investigation of sex trafficking in America, but it was widely dispersed. Thus, in order to maximize the usefulness of the voluminous amount of information, we realized that we had to organize it into a consolidated, cohesive, and manageable format. We believe we have accomplished these objectives in this book, which has been divided into the following 10 chapters and an appendix.

In Chapter 1, *Introduction to Sex Trafficking in America: A Current and Historical Overview*, we provide the reader with an international and a national perspective of sex trafficking, a brief overview of sex trafficking in early 20th century America, a discussion about the need to train law enforcement officers in sex-trafficking investigations and, last, what the reader can expect to learn from the book.

In Chapter 2, *Legal Aspects of Sex Trafficking in America*, we have summarized the major federal and state laws that are most applicable in sex-trafficking investigations.

In Chapter 3, *Domestic Sex Trafficking of American Children*, we discuss the sexual exploitation of American children (mostly girls under the age of 18), because they are the ones who are the most vulnerable to predatory traffickers.

In Chapter 4, *Sex Trafficking of Foreign Women and Children into America*, we focus primarily on women and children who are trafficked into the United States from foreign countries and then forced into prostitution.

In Chapter 5, *The "John" Factor in Sex Trafficking*, we examine the role of the customers (johns) in commercialized prostitution without whom the profits generated in sex trafficking could not exist.

In Chapter 6, *Child Sex Tourism and the American Male*, we discuss the profile of the male American child sex tourist, how they go about finding local children in foreign countries, and the extreme and long-lasting damage done to their victims by them.

In Chapter 7, *Interrogation of Sex-Trafficking Suspects*, we discuss those aspects of the interrogation process that are essential for investigators to understand in order to maximize their effectiveness and to be certain that any statements or confessions they obtain will meet the legal standards for admissibility into United States courts.

In Chapter 8, *Crime Scene Examination and Physical Evidence in Sex-Trafficking Cases*, we focus on the identification, collection, and preservation of the main types of physical evidence likely to be present at sex-trafficking crime scenes, namely, biological materials, fingerprints, documents, and communication technology.

In Chapter 9, *Building a Multiagency Task Force*, we discuss the most effective ways to develop and maintain a strategic, well-planned, and collaborative relationship among federal, state, and local law enforcement agencies.

In Chapter 10, *The Prosecution of Sex-Trafficking Cases*, we first discuss the responsibilities and role of prosecutors in general, the role of federal prosecutors in sex-trafficking cases, and how law enforcement officers can assist them in the prosecutorial process.

In the Appendix, titled *Nongovernmental Organizations and U.S. Government Agencies Available to Assist Sex Trafficking Victims and National Service Providers for Commercially Sexually Exploited Individuals*, we have provided the reader with a state-by-state listing of many organizations that can be called upon to assist in providing services to sex-trafficking victims as well as U.S. government agencies available to assist sex-trafficking victims.

Focus on Four Groups

In the final analysis, this book is intended for four different groups. The first group is law enforcement administrators who are in the early stages of redirecting their agency's enforcement efforts to the investigation and prevention of sex trafficking in their communities. The second group is law enforcement officers who may have an interest in this topic, or perhaps have found themselves responsible for conducting sex-trafficking investigations, but have had little or no previous experience. The third group is police instructors/trainers who are developing specialized training modules in sex-trafficking investigations both for recruit officers and veteran officers. Last, this book will be of value to instructors who are teaching in applied criminal justice, community college, and university programs, and who have been interested in teaching an entire college course on the topic of sex-trafficking investigations, but heretofore did not have available a single comprehensive book on this topic.

Learning Aids

The learning aids in this book are:

- **Chapter-opening photographs**, learning objectives, and outlines that draw readers in and serve as a road-map to the chapter.
- **Chapter-opening overviews** provide readers with a snapshot of the entire chapter.
- **Detailed captions accompany photographs and tables,** which enhance and support the discussions of specific topics.

- **Widely acclaimed cases (both legal and investigative) and current news items** are in every chapter, ensuring that this book is not only the most current and definitive text on conducting sex trafficking investigations, but also a practical, relevant, and interesting source of information.
- **End-of-chapter glossaries and review questions** to assist students in preparing for exams.

For the Instructor

The following material has been incorporated into a comprehensive Instructor's Manual:

- *PowerPoint slides:* Complete chapter-by-chapter slide shows with tables, graphs, and photos
- Answers to the end-of-chapter review questions
- A comprehensive test bank of more than 100 multiple-choice questions
- A list of audiovisual materials available dealing with sex trafficking
- A list of websites dealing with sex trafficking

CRC Press will provide the Instructor's Manual free of charge to instructors. For more information, contact the publisher directly at: www.**crcpress**.com or 800-272-7737.

Endnote

1. Karen J. Bachar, "Combating Human Trafficking at the State and Local Levels," a sidebar to the article by Robert Moossy. (2009). Sex trafficking: Identifying cases and victims, *National Institute of Justice*, 262 (March 23). Online at: http://www.nij.gov/nij/journals/262/sex-trafficking.htm

Acknowledgments

Writing a book is a solitary endeavor. However, as a process, writing is highly interactive; anything that makes the transition from an idea to a published work requires considerable goodwill and support from families, friends, colleagues, reviewers, editors, and production staff. Although it is insufficient compensation, we wish to recognize those organizations and individuals who helped to sustain us in our writing endeavors.

When we first had the idea for writing this book, one of the first people we called upon for advice and guidance was our good friend and colleague, Lt. George Koder (Ret.), Special Investigations Division, Clearwater, Florida, Police Department. George agreed to serve as a consultant on this book and has made numerous positive recommendations for improving it, in addition to providing us with research material and photos. However, because he is also a highly experienced sex-trafficking investigator, he was able to provide us with specific information on sex-trafficking cases he had personally investigated. In a number of instances, we were able to incorporate some of his vignettes into the narrative of the book, which helped make it more interesting and informative. It also turns out that he is an outstanding editor. For his considerable efforts, we are very appreciative.

Another person whose guidance and advice we sought was our good friend Tom Gillan, executive director of The National Institute for Human Trafficking Research and Training© in Orlando, Florida. Tom identified important topics that absolutely needed to be covered in this book. He also provided us with relevant written material on sex trafficking and recommended we read certain important books for background information before we started writing this book. We took his advice and read numerous books that provided us with very valuable insights into this important topic. For his generous time, advice, and support, we thank him very much.

Robert E. O'Neill, U.S. attorney for the Middle District of Florida, a highly experienced federal prosecutor, was kind enough to review the first drafts of Chapter 2 (Legal Aspects of Sex Trafficking in America) and Chapter 10 (The Prosecution of Sex Trafficking). His comments and suggestions were most helpful.

We also called upon Detective James McBride, human trafficking investigator, for the Clearwater, Florida, Police Department; and Special Agent William Williger, who is in charge of Homeland Security investigations in Tampa, Florida, to review our chapters. Their recommendations and the additional material they provided were most helpful and we appreciate their time and efforts.

One of the most important nongovernmental organizations in the United States that helps minors who are sex trafficked is Shared Hope International. The president of this association, Linda Smith, and her communications director, Taryn Mastrean, were kind enough to let us use material from one of their outstanding publications. This material was extremely valuable in providing insights and suggestions as to how law enforcement officers can best assist young American girls who are being sexually exploited and trafficked in the United States.

Special Agent Joe Navarro, FBI (Ret.), an internationally recognized expert on the detection of deception in interviews and interrogation, was kind enough to share his work with us. His contributions appear in Chapter 7 (Interrogation of Sex-Trafficking Suspects). We have called upon Joe a number of times to assist us with projects and he has never let us down. He is an incredibly generous, bright, and outstanding writer whose books on the topic of detection of deception have deservedly received international acclaim.

Our colleague, Dr. Jalika Rivera Waugh, formerly a highly experienced crime scene technician and now an assistant Professor in the Department of Criminal Justice at Saint Leo University, was most helpful in providing a thorough review of Chapter 8 (Crime Scene Examination and Physical Evidence in Sex-Trafficking Cases). Her numerous suggestions were very useful and assured us that we were technically correct on all points.

We wish to thank our good friend Chief Deputy Jack Jordan (Ret.), Sumter County, Florida, Sheriff's Office for providing us with the most current U.S. Supreme Court rulings as they relate to a suspect's right to remain silent under the provisions of *Miranda v. Arizona* 1966.

We wish to thank Sal and Maryellin Territo, who spent many hours reviewing, critiquing, and editing our final chapters. Their dedication and thoroughness are very much appreciated.

Regardless of the pressures of time constraints we were up against, our secretary, Sharon Ostermann, was unbelievable, and completed every task expeditiously and with good humor. She was also an invaluable editor, researcher, and friendly, constructive critic. It has always been a pleasure working with her, but this time her services were truly exceptional and well above and beyond the call of duty. Her trusty assistant, Shari Allen, was also part of the "911" typing rescue team when we were up against tight deadlines. She, too, was great in helping us.

It is also important to acknowledge that some material used in this book was inspired by the presentations of those sex-trafficking investigators and prosecutors who taught with us in many sex-trafficking courses and whose lectures we had the opportunity and pleasure to sit through. To them we say, "Thank you."

We also wish to thank our project coordinator, Marsha Pronin, and our project editor, Jay Margolis, for their great work and invaluable assistance. Last, we want to thank our acquiring editor at Taylor & Francis Group, Carolyn Spence, for sharing our conviction that this book would make a significant contribution toward the investigation, understanding, and prevention of sex trafficking in America.

About the Authors

Leonard Territo, EdD, is a distinguished professor in the Department of Criminal Justice at Saint Leo University, Saint Leo, Florida, as well as professor emeritus in the Department of Criminology at the University of South Florida, Tampa. He has for the past five years been teaching a university class titled International Sex Trafficking of Women and Children and also has been involved as both an instructor and coordinator in the training of in-service police officers at Saint Leo University each summer in a course titled International Sex Trafficking. He previously served first as a major and then as chief deputy (undersheriff) with the Leon County Sheriff's Office, Tallahassee. As chief deputy, he was responsible for the daily operation of the department. While serving in the sheriff's office, he was a major homicide investigative advisor on the Chi Omega murders committed by Theodore Robert (Ted) Bundy on the Florida State University campus in Tallahassee. This investigation eventually led to the arrest, conviction, and execution of Ted Bundy. He also served for almost nine years with the Tampa Police Department and had assignments as a patrol officer; motorcycle officer; homicide, rape, and robbery detective; internal affairs detective; and member of the police academy training staff. Dr. Territo is the former chairman of the Department of Police Administration and director of the Florida Institute for Law Enforcement at St. Petersburg Junior College (now St. Petersburg College), St. Petersburg, Florida.

Dr. Territo is a graduate of the U.S. Secret Service "Dignitary Protection Seminar," the nationally recognized University of Louisville "National Crime Prevention Institute," and the Saint Leo University Institute for Excellence in Criminal Justice Administration "Non-Verbal Communications/ Detecting Deception."

He has co-authored some of the leading books in the law enforcement profession including *Criminal Investigation* (11th ed.) (McGraw Hill, 2011), which is by far the bestselling book of its kind in the United States and has recently been translated into Chinese for use by the Chinese police and Chinese criminal justice students.

Other co-authored books are:

Stress Management in Law Enforcement (3rd ed.) (Carolina Academic Press, 2013)

The International Trafficking of Human Organs: A Multidisciplinary Perspective (CRC Press, 2012)

Police Administration (8th ed.) (Prentice Hall, 2012)

International Sex Trafficking of Women and Children: Understanding the Global Epidemic (Looseleaf Law Publications, 2010)

Crime and Justice in America (6th ed.) (Prentice Hall, 2003)

College Crime Prevention and Personal Safety Awareness (Charles C Thomas Publishers, 1989)

Hospital and College Security Liability (Hanrow Press, 1987)

Police Civil Liability (Hanrow Press, 1984)

The Police Personnel Selection Process (Macmillan Publishing, 1980)

Stress and Police Personnel (Allyn & Bacon, 1980)

Dr. Territo also wrote a novel with Dr. George Kirkham titled *Ivory Tower Cop* (Carolina Academic Press, 2009), which is a mystery crime novel based on a true story.

His books have been used in more than 1,000 colleges and universities in all 50 states and he has had numerous articles published in nationally recognized law enforcement and legal journals. His books have been used and referenced by both academic and police departments in 16 countries including Australia, Barbados, Belarus, Canada, Chile, China, Czechoslovakia, England, France, Germany, Israel, the Netherlands, Poland, Saudi Arabia, South Korea, and Spain.

He was selected for inclusion in *Who's Who in American Law Enforcement*; selected as Florida's Outstanding Criminal Justice Educator by the Florida Criminal Justice Educators Association; cited for 10 years of Meritorious Service by the Florida Police Chiefs Association; given the Outstanding

Teacher Award by the College of Social and Behavioral Sciences, University of South Florida, Tampa; and cited for 25 years of teaching and meritorious service to the Tampa Florida Police Academy and awarded the Saint Leo University Outstanding Publication Award.

He also has been qualified as a police policies and procedures expert in both federal and state courts in the following states: Alaska, Arizona, Florida, Georgia, Illinois, Iowa, Kansas, Kentucky, Louisiana, Michigan, New Jersey, Ohio, Oregon, Pennsylvania, Tennessee, Virginia, Washington, and Wisconsin as well as the District of Columbia.

Dr. Territo has served as a lecturer throughout the United States and has instructed a wide variety of police subjects to thousands of law enforcement officials.

Nataliya Glover, MA, MS, was born and raised in the Ukraine (part of the former USSR), which is a country notorious for human sex-trafficking activity. She studied at the State University of Foreign Languages and earned her undergraduate and graduate degrees in English and German.

Upon graduation from the State University, Professor Glover began teaching English and German as second languages at the same university. She also taught specialty courses, such as basic English and communications. In addition, Professor Glover lectured in the School of Foreign Languages, specializing in Russian history and the history of terrorism. As a supplement to her career in education, Professor Glover worked as an interpreter for a company that was involved in the preparation and translation of documents for individuals who wanted to receive work visas and work abroad. The majority of these applicants were young women wanting to leave the Ukraine for a chance of a better life in another country. After spending much of her adult life in the Ukraine and experiencing the devastating effects of the collapse of the Soviet Union, Professor Glover decided in 2003 to relocate to the United States to further her education and continue teaching at the university level. During her time in the Ukraine, she was concerned about the sex trafficking taking place; however, due to the involvement of corrupt officials, there was nothing she or any other citizen could do to prevent these crimes.

Glover's passion for teaching was the driving force for continuing her education at Saint Leo University and earning a graduate degree in criminal justice administration. Professor Glover is currently an adjunct professor in the Department of Criminal Justice at Saint Leo. While pursuing her advanced degree in criminal justice, she attended numerous specialized courses and holds certificates in the following areas: counterterrorism, hostage negotiation, school violence, nonverbal communications, detecting deception, and international sex trafficking. Professor Glover has co-taught a course on hostage negotiation/school violence with retired NYPD (New York Police Department) hostage negotiator, Dominick Misino, a nationally recognized expert in the field.

She also teaches an international and domestic sex-trafficking course for the Institute of Police Technology and Management. Professor Glover is a frequent lecturer on the topic of terror at Beslan (a town in the North Ossetian Republic in Russia, where 186 children and 148 adults were massacred in 2004) and has recently lectured on international sex trafficking to more than 250 criminal justice practitioners in Salt Lake City, Utah and also recently participated in the sex-trafficking retraining session at the FBI National Academy Associates Annual Conference.

Professor Glover's academic expertise and her personal experience living in the Ukraine offer a unique perspective and insight that allow her to provide a wealth of information to those interested in expanding their knowledge regarding sex trafficking worldwide.

1
Introduction to Sex Trafficking in America
A Current and Historical Overview

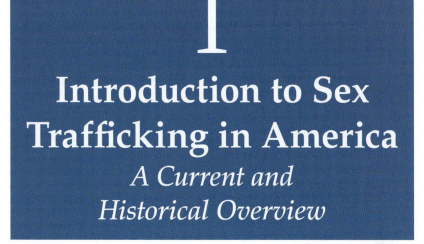

The Asian women depicted in this photo were trafficked into the United States and were engaging in prostitution in a massage parlor in San Francisco when they were arrested. Law enforcement officers can be seen in the mirrors guarding the women. (Photo courtesy of Lt. George Koder (retired), Clearwater, Florida, Police Department.)

Chapter Objectives

1. Be familiar with the statistical trends of sex trafficking both internationally and in the United States.
2. Discuss the various forms of sex trafficking.
3. Understand the difference between trafficking and smuggling.
4. Be familiar with factors contributing to international sex trafficking.
5. Understand the reasons why sex trafficking is such a lucrative business.
6. Explain why sex trafficking is so difficult to stop.
7. Understand why the supply of victims is seemingly endless.
8. Discuss why sex-trafficking victims are often "invisible" in the United States.
9. Be familiar with the ways a modern sex-trafficking operation works.
10. Discuss the history of sex trafficking in early 20th century in America.
11. Understand why it is so important to train law enforcement officers in the various aspects of sex trafficking.
12. Be aware of what can be learned from this book.

Introduction

When the topic of sex trafficking is discussed, it is usually done within the larger context of "human trafficking," which includes not only sex trafficking but forced labor, involuntary servitude, peonage,[1] and the illegal trafficking of human organs and body parts.[2] However, in this book we will be focusing exclusively on the criminal investigation of sex trafficking because it is to this aspect of human trafficking that local law enforcement agencies tend to direct the lion's share of their investigative personnel resources, and time.

It is indisputable that sex trafficking has reached epidemic proportions worldwide, and the United States is no exception. For example, it has been estimated by the U.S. State Department that between 700,000 and 2,000,000 people are trafficked each year worldwide, and 80% of them are being exploited as sexual slaves. Of this number, it is estimated that 14,000 to 17,500 are trafficked into the United States every year. The majority of sex-trafficking victims are being taken from economically depressed locations in Southeast Asia, the former Soviet Union, Central and South America, and other less developed areas. They are then trafficked to the more developed areas of Asia, the Middle East, Western Europe, and North America.

Sex trafficking is often fueled by the enormous pressure on people to leave the economic struggles of their home country and seek opportunities abroad. The sex-trafficking crisis has recently been exacerbated by factors that include a global economy, increased travel, inadequate law enforcement and legislation, treating of trafficking cases as illegal immigration, and the potential criminalization of trafficking victims. It also includes easing restrictions on travel (particularly to and from former Soviet bloc countries), and the increasing availability and use of high-speed communication tools, such as the Internet. These have all contributed to an atmosphere that makes sex trafficking more likely to occur and more difficult to deter.

Unfortunately, the United States not only faces an influx of international sex-trafficking victims, but also has its own homegrown problem of the interstate sex trafficking of American girls, almost all of whom are minors[3] (Figure 1.1).

Although comprehensive research to document the number of children engaged in prostitution in the United States is lacking, it is estimated that 293,000 American youths currently are at risk of becoming victims of commercial sexual exploitation.[4] The majority of these victims are runaway or throw-away youths who live on the streets and become victims of prostitution.[5] These children generally come from homes where they have been abused or are from families that have abandoned them. Often, they become involved in prostitution

Figure 1.1 Underage teenage prostitutes working the streets. These teenage prostitutes were working the streets when they were confronted by uniformed patrol officers. However, unless these officers have been trained to ask the right questions and be familiar with the various aspects of sex trafficking, they may mistakenly believe these girls were engaging in prostitution voluntarily. (AP photo courtesy of L. M. Otero.)

to support themselves financially or to get the things they feel they need or want (like drugs).

In this chapter, we will discuss the need for local law enforcement officers to redefine the way they have traditionally viewed sex crimes, especially those involving young girls engaged in prostitution and also assist them in identifying the differences between commercial and noncommercial forms of sex trafficking (Figure 1.2). We also will discuss the distinctions between trafficking and smuggling and how smuggling can easily turn into trafficking, the major contributing factors to the sex trade, why it is such a lucrative business, and why the supply of victims is seemingly endless. We also will provide a brief discussion as to why modern-day sex-trafficking operations are so difficult to stop, and why the victims are so vulnerable. We will provide a brief discussion of the history of sex trafficking in early 20th century America, the need to provide specific training for law enforcement officers in order to assist them in identifying and investigating sex-trafficking offenses, and lastly, what the reader can expect to learn from this book.

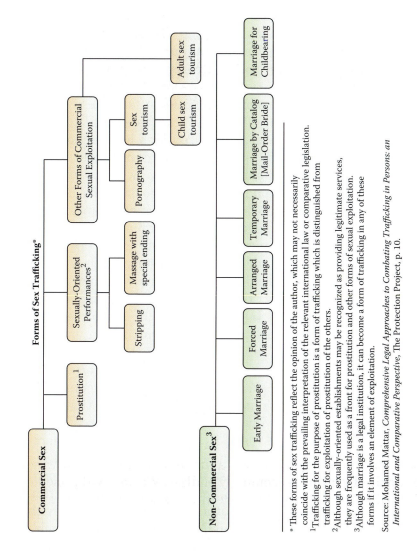

Forms of Sex Trafficking*

Commercial Sex
- Prostitution[1]
- Sexually-Oriented Performances[2]
  - Stripping
  - Massage with special ending
- Other Forms of Commercial Sexual Exploitation
  - Pornography
  - Sex tourism
    - Child sex tourism
    - Adult sex tourism

Non-Commercial Sex[3]
- Early Marriage
- Forced Marriage
- Arranged Marriage
- Temporary Marriage
- Marriage by Catalog [Mail-Order Bride]
- Marriage for Childbearing

* These forms of sex trafficking reflect the opinion of the author, which may not necessarily coincide with the prevailing interpretation of the relevant international law or comparative legislation.
[1] Trafficking for the purpose of prostitution is a form of trafficking which is distinguished from trafficking for exploitation of prostitution of the others.
[2] Although sexually-oriented establishments may be recognized as providing legitimate services, they are frequently used as a front for prostitution and other forms of sexual exploitation.
[3] Although marriage is a legal institution, it can become a form of trafficking in any of these forms if it involves an element of exploitation.

Source: Mohamed Mattar, *Comprehensive Legal Approaches to Combating Trafficking in Persons: an International and Comparative Perspective*, The Protection Project, p. 10.

Figure 1.2 Forms of sex trafficking.

Definition and Identification

Unlike the unique challenges associated with identifying emerging crimes, such as computer crimes, cyber crimes, and identity theft, where officers must learn the elements and indicators of completely new types of criminal activity,[6] trafficking cases require law enforcement to recategorize and reprioritize behavior that has long existed as its own crime type. Part of the challenge of increasing police identification of newly prioritized crimes is that officers on the street tend to solve problems based on routines. These routines are particularly important for helping officers navigate circumstances where legal definitions may be ambiguous.[7] For example, law enforcement is familiar with and has established routines for investigating crimes like prostitution, assault, or kidnapping. When new priorities arise in agencies, either through federal pressure to investigate and interdict certain types of crimes or through local community-driven requests for police response, officers must learn to redefine old problems with new labels and enhanced priorities. This process goes beyond giving behaviors new names; it is about seeing the same elements of a crime (e.g., young girls involved in prostitution, missing children, or abuse) and reframing the old definition of certain behavior as a new, more problematic crime worthy of a heightened level of attention. Concern over sex trafficking now requires officers to reevaluate whether or not a case that looks like prostitution actually involves the elements of force, fraud, or coercion, which would make it sex trafficking and, therefore, necessitate very different types of responses. Trafficking is unique because it is an offense that combines a traditional crime category, such as prostitution, with status as a victim. As such, many victims may initially come into contact with law enforcement as offenders and need to be redefined as more information about their case becomes available. Creating effective working definitions of such crimes is essential, just as we have learned from our inexperience understanding the reporting dynamics of hate crimes.[8]

Looking for Sex-Trafficking Crimes

While local law enforcement officers may be more likely to come into contact with sex-trafficking victims in the course of their regular activities,[9] they also are less likely than many federal law enforcement agents to be looking for these crimes.[10] Effectively responding to sex trafficking additionally requires officers to notice and potentially provide services to victims who have historically been underserved by or had poor relationships with law enforcement (e.g., women in prostitution, migrants, immigrant community members, and poor women). In addition to victim reluctance to self-identify, law enforcement may be reluctant to define individuals as victims when they are perceived as partially responsible for their own victimization. These problems are exacerbated when the victim is a member of a group that historically has not been a priority for law enforcement protection, a member of a "hidden" population, or a member of an ethnic or cultural group that historically has not trusted law enforcement. Preliminary research on local law enforcement responses to sex trafficking indicates they are often reluctant to intervene in these situations due to a belief that victims were complicit in their own victimization.[11] Law enforcement response is further complicated when dealing with foreign women and children because of immigration-related issues. Many local law enforcement agencies have made a decision to not inquire about citizen status during routine policing activities as a means of building trust and confidence in the local immigrant community. These kinds of complicated mixed messages often cause frontline patrol officers to hesitate to intervene in potentially challenging situations.[12]

The Differences between Trafficking and Smuggling

As it relates to the sex trafficking of foreign women and children, it is important to understand the differences between trafficking and smuggling. **Smuggling** occurs when someone is paid to

TABLE 1.1
Difference Between Trafficking and Smuggling

Trafficking	Smuggling
• Is not voluntary; one cannot consent to being trafficked or enslaved	• Is voluntary; an individual typically contracts to be taken across border
• Entails forced exploitation of a person for labor or services	• Ends after the border crossing
• Need not entail the physical movement of a person	• Fees are usually paid in advance or upon arrival
• Can occur domestically, where citizens are held captive in their own country	• Is always international in nature
• Is a crime against the right of each person to be free from involuntary servitude	• Is a crime against the nation's sovereignty

Source: International Association of Chiefs of Police. (2006). *The Crime Of Human Trafficking: A Law Enforcement Guide to Identification and Investigation.* Alexandria, VA, p. 4.

assist another in the illegal crossing of borders. This relationship typically ends after the border has been crossed and the individual has paid the smuggler a fee for assistance. If the smuggler sells or "brokers" the smuggled individual into a condition of servitude, or if the smuggled individual cannot pay the smuggler and is then forced to work that debt off (called debt bondage), the crime has now turned from smuggling into human trafficking. The key distinction between trafficking and smuggling lies in the individual's freedom of choice. A person may choose and arrange to be smuggled into a country, but when a person is forced into a situation of exploitation whereby their freedom is taken away, he/she is then a victim of human trafficking. Central to the distinction is the denial of the victim's liberty (Table 1.1).

Factors Contributing to International Sex Trafficking

Poverty increasingly has acquired a young—and feminine— face. The vast majority of the world's refugees are women and children and this is especially true in the sex-trafficking industry. Sex trafficking falls under the umbrella of human slavery and, amazingly, it is estimated that more people are being held as sex slaves at the outset of the 21st century than at any other time in human history. It is also a very lucrative business. For example, current estimates of the profits obtained from sex trafficking each year come to $9.5 billion with many of these profits supporting other criminal activities, such as money laundering, drug trafficking, and document forgery.

Until recently, criminal penalties in many countries were less severe for sex trafficking than for arms or drug trafficking. Given this reality, sex trafficking has fast become a "growth industry" for criminal syndicates. Many criminal groups appear to be collaborating in the sex-trafficking industry, with different cartels responsible for the various phases (e.g., recruiting, initial transport, and sale/resale of victims).[13]

Criminal activities related to trafficking (money laundering, creation of false passports and identity documents, alien harboring, etc.) also increasingly appear to be "subcontracted" to a variety of international criminal syndicates. Use of the Internet, especially for recruiting purposes, likewise is becoming a hallmark of the sex-trafficking industry. U.S. government sources identify sex trafficking as the fastest-growing criminal industry in the world.[14]

Unlike arms or drug traffickers, whose control over their contraband ceases after the initial point of sale, sex traffickers can continue to exploit their victims. The ongoing control exercised by traffickers over their victims affords traffickers the capability of reaping enormous profits from the resale of their victims. Sex trafficking provides a classic example of the "resale" value of "human contraband" because the victims can be sold over and over again. In some cases, a girl or woman can be forced to have sex with thousands of men each year. Also, sex-trafficking rings prosecuted to date in the United States utilize the American highway system in furtherance of their crimes. Pimps and traffickers typically move their victims from city to city, sometimes as frequently as once every two weeks. The women and girls moved in this fashion are sold to different brothels on a regular basis providing repeated profits for the traffickers. It also results in constant uncertainty for the victims as to their exact location and reduces the possibility of their finding a sympathetic client who would be willing to help them escape or contact the police.[15]

Why the Supply of Victims Is Seemingly Endless

Slaves in the pre-Civil War American South cost more in relative terms to buy and maintain than those currently enslaved through human trafficking practices. However, unlike slaveholders in the pre-Civil War South, those who currently profit from sex trafficking typically do not see their victims as long-term investments, but rather as a low-cost and easily replaceable commodity. This lack of concern for basic needs of victims leads to greater exploitation as well as to greater turnover in the supply of victims.

Kidnapping and the use of force to initially recruit foreign victims have been reported in some U.S. trafficking cases. More often, however, these victims are deceived into believing that job opportunities await them in the United States, and they willingly travel here unaware that forced prostitution awaits them.[16]

Sex Trafficking as a Criminal Continuum

Sex trafficking thrives in areas where prostitution or sexually oriented businesses are legal or are at least tolerated. This would include strip clubs, exotic dancing, massage parlors, and delivery services that would actually bring prostitutes to customers' homes, businesses, or hotels (Figure 1.3). Sex trafficking is best understood not as a crime that occurs at a single moment in time but rather as a criminal continuum. It involves source countries (where victims are recruited or lured), transit countries (through which victims pass), and destination

Figure 1.3 This billboard is an example of the conspicuous advertising of women for the sex trade in one city in the United States in which women are delivered to customers' homes, businesses, or hotels. (Photo courtesy of Abraham Norwitz/Corbis.)

countries (where victims are ultimately exploited). Countries like the United States are primarily destination countries, but many nations experience all aspects of sex trafficking.[17]

Why Sex-Trafficking Victims Are Often "Invisible" in the United States

Many immigrant victims of sex trafficking come from countries where law enforcement officials are corrupt and/or abusive. Such victims bring to the United States both a fear of law enforcement and a general distrust of government. Traffickers find both tendencies easy to exploit and repeatedly tell their victims that American police and the U.S. court system will put the victims in jail should they try to escape their traffickers. The fact that many trafficking victims are illegal aliens provides another mechanism of exploitation for the traffickers. Traffickers will threaten to turn victims over to immigration officials for deportation or imprisonment if they do not cooperate.[18]

The Trafficking Victims Protection Act to the Rescue

The Trafficking Victims Protection Act of 2000 (TVPA) (discussed in much greater detail in Chapter 2) provides victims with the possibility of obtaining legal immigration status through T-Visas or "Continued Presence" if they are willing to assist law enforcement with the prosecution of their traffickers. This is a major legal change. Prior to the passage of the TVPA, trafficking victims had few rights under U.S. immigration law, and the threat of deportation served to make U.S. authorities "unwitting co-conspirators" in sex-traffickers' efforts to keep their victims compliant. The TVPA also recognizes that the coercion used to reduce people to slaves or maintain them as such need not be physical. Prior laws focused on the use or threat of physical force against victims; the TVPA now criminalizes the broader forms of psychological coercion that traffickers increasingly employ against their victims (i.e., threats of deportation, threats against family members in the victim's home country, or confiscation of a victim's identity documents or personal property).

Modern Day Sex-Trafficking Operation

Today, the business of sex trafficking is much more organized than at any time in the past. Women and young girls are easily transported by plane, car, truck, boat, and sometimes even on foot to a destination where they are sold to traffickers, locked up in rooms or brothels for weeks or months, drugged, terrorized, and raped repeatedly.[19] These continual abuses make it easier for the traffickers to control their victims. The captives are so afraid and intimidated that they rarely speak out against their traffickers. This may be so because sometimes the abusive methods used by these traffickers (pimps) impact the victim both physically and mentally and, strangely enough, over an extended period of time, she begins to feel an attachment to the perpetrator.[20] This paradoxical psychological phenomenon is known as the Stockholm syndrome and develops in a group of psychological symptoms in some people in a captive or hostage situation. It also is known as Survival Identification Syndrome. When it occurs, victims develop negative feelings toward police and positive feelings toward their captors, thus making it difficult for law enforcement to breach the bond of control, albeit abusive, the trafficker holds over the victim.

A Brief History of Sex Trafficking in Early 20th Century America

Those who are unfamiliar with the history of sex trafficking in America may well be under the impression it is a late 20th century and early 21st century phenomenon. However, nothing can be further from the truth. For example, in 1910 G. S. Ball, a social and religious activist published a book titled *Fighting the Traffic in Young Girls or War on the White Slave Trade* (Figure 1.4). This book contained a collection of 33 articles written by experts in the field of sex trafficking involving young white girls. White slavery is defined as the practice of forcing a female or male to engage in commercial prostitution; however, when the term was used during the early part of the 20th century, it literally meant the sex trade involving white girls only. One of the things that makes this book so fascinating is that sex traffickers operating over 100 years ago were employing basically the same identical tactics that sex traffickers employ today. These include deceit, deception, exploitation of vulnerable young girls, the seasoning process (a combination of physical and verbal abuse meant to break a girl's will and separate her from her previous life so she does not know where to turn for help), debt bondage, methods of physical confinement, and forced drug use resulting in addiction and dependency. The end results of sex trafficking back then also had many of the same unfortunate consequences seen today, such as psychological and physical trauma, enormous shame as well as the transmission of sexually transmitted diseases,

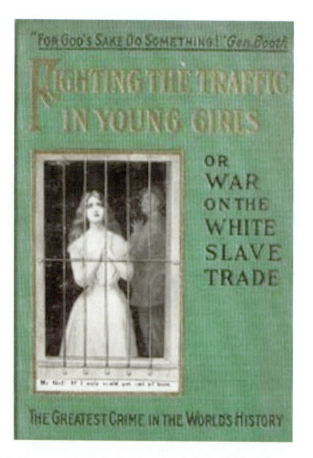

Figure 1.4 The cover from the book published by G. S. Ball in 1910. (From G. S. Ball, *Fighting the Traffic in Young Girls or War on the White Slave Trade* (Chicago: 110), cover.)

and unwanted pregnancies. The following has been excerpted from this 1910 book.

> The evidence obtained from questioning some 250 girls taken in federal raids on Chicago houses of ill repute leads me to believe that not fewer than fifteen thousand girls have been imported into this country in the last year as white slaves.[21] Of course this is only a guess—an approximation—it could be nothing else—but my own personal belief is that it is a conservative guess and well within the facts as to numbers. Then please remember that girls imported are certainly but a mere fraction of the number recruited for the army of prostitution from home fields, from the cities, the towns, the villages of our own country. There is no possible escape from this conclusion.

Another significant fact brought out by the examination of these girls is that practically every one of them who admitted having parents who were still living begged that her real name be withheld from the public because of the sorrow and shame it would bring to her parents. One said, "My mother thinks I am studying in a stenographic school;" another stated, "My parents in the country think I have a good position in a department store—as I did for a time—and I have sent them a little money from time to time; I don't care what happens, so long as they don't know the truth about me." In a word, the one concern of nearly all those examined who have homes in this country was that their parents—and in particular their mothers—might discover, through the prosecution of the "white slavers," that they were leading lives of shame instead of working at the honorable callings which they had left their homes and come to the city to pursue. There are, to put it mildly, hundreds—yes, thousands—of trusting mothers in the smaller cities, the towns, villages and farming communities of the United States who believe that their daughters are getting on fine in the city, and too busy to come home for a visit or "to write much," while the fact is these daughters have been swept into the gulf of white slavery—the worst that can befall a woman.

Again, there is, in another particular, a remarkable and impressive sameness in the stories related by these wretched girls. In the narratives of nearly all of them is a passage describing how some man of their acquaintance had offered to "help" them, and to "take an interest" in them. After listening to this confession from one girl after another, hour after hour until you have heard it repeated perhaps fifty times, you feel like saying to every mother in the country: Don't trust any man who pretends to take an interest in your girl if that interest involves her leaving her own roof. Keep her with you. She is far safer in the country than in the big city, but if go to the city she must, then go with her yourself; if that is impossible, place her with some woman who is your friend, not hers; no girl can safely go to the great city to make her own way who is not under the eye of a trustworthy woman who knows the ways and dangers of city life. Above all, distrust the "protection," the "good offices" of any man who is not a family friend known to be clean and honorable and above all suspicion (Figure 1.5).

Whether these hunters of the innocent ply their awful calling at home or abroad their methods are much the same—with the exception that the foreign girl, who once she leaves her country is more hopelessly at their mercy. Let me take the case of a little Italian peasant girl who helped her father till the soil in the vineyards and fields near Naples. Like most of the others taken in the raids, she stoutly maintained that she had been in this country more than three years and that she was in a life of shame from choice and not through the criminal act of any person. When she was brought into what the sensational newspapers would call the "sweat box"

Figure 1.5 A 1910 artist's depiction of a trafficker attempting to deceive a young and trusting naïve girl. Meeting young girls at railway depots was one of the locations that early 20th century slave traders preferred. The trafficker was almost always nicely dressed and would meet a naïve young girl as she was getting off the train by herself. In a genial and nonthreatening manner he would approach her and tell her that he would be able to provide her with living accommodations and a job if she accompanied him. Once in the trafficker's possession, she was taken to an isolated area where she would be beaten and raped into submission (now called the seasoning process). (Interestingly, today, bus stations are among the most favored places for domestic traffickers (pimps) to pick up American girls who are runaways, many of whom are without money or job skills.) (From G. S. Ball, *Fighting the Traffic in Young Girls or War on the White Slave Trade* (Chicago: 1910), after p. 34.)

it was clear that she was in a state of abject terror. Soon, however, Assistant United States District Attorney Parkin, having charge of the examination, convinced her that he and his associates were her friends and protectors and that their purpose was to punish those who had profited by her ruin and to send back to her little Italian home with all her expenses paid; that she was under the protection of the United States and was as safe as if the king of Italy would take her under his royal care and pledge his word that her enemies should not have revenge on her.

Then she broke down and with pitiful sobs related her awful narrative. That every word of it was true no one could doubt who saw her as she told it. Briefly this is her story: A "fine lady" who wore beautiful clothes came to her where she lived with her parents, made friends with her, told her she was uncommonly pretty (the truth, by the way), and professed a great interest in her. Such flattering attentions from an American lady who wore clothes as fine as those of the Italian nobility could have but one effect on the mind of this simple peasant girl and on her still simpler parents. Their heads were completely turned and they regarded the "American lady" with almost adoration.

Very shrewdly the woman did not attempt to bring the girl back with her, but held out hope that someday a letter might come with money for her passage to America. Once there she would become a companion of her American friend and they would have a great time together.

Of course, in due time, the money came—and the $100 was a most substantial pledge to the parents of the wealth and generosity of the "American lady." Unhesitatingly she was prepared for the voyage which was to take her to the land of happiness and good fortune. According to the arrangements made by letter, the girl was met at New York by two "friends" who were two of the most brutal of all the white slave traders who are in the traffic business. At this time she was sixteen years old, innocent and rarely attractive for a girl of her class, having the large, handsome eyes, the black hair and the rich olive skin of a typical Italian.

Where these two men took her she did not know—but by the most violent had brutal means they quickly accomplished her ruin. For a week she was subjected to unspeakable treatment and made to feel that her degradation was complete and final.

And here let it be said that the breaking of the spirit, the crushing of all hope for any future save that of shame is always a part of the initiation of a white slave. Then the girl was shipped on to Chicago, where she was disposed of to the keeper of an Italian dive of the vilest type. On her entrance she was furnished with gaudy dresses and wearing apparel for which the keeper of the place charged her $600. As is the case with all new white slaves she was not allowed to have any clothing which she could wear upon the street.

Her one object in life was to escape from the den in which she was held a prisoner. To "pay out" seemed the surest way, and at length from her wages of shame, she was able to cancel the $600 account. Then she asked for her street clothing and her releases only to be told that she had incurred other expenses to the amount of $400.

Her Italian blood took fire at this and she made a dash for liberty. But she was not quick enough and the hand of the oppressor was upon her. In the wild scene that followed she was slashed with a razor, one gash straight through her right eye, one across her cheek and another slitting her ear. Then she was given medical attention and the wounds gradually healed, but her face was horribly mutilated, her right eye is always open and to look upon her is to shudder.

When the raids began she was secreted and arrangements made to ship her to a dive in the mining regions of the west. Fortunately, however, a few hours before she was to start upon her journey, the United States marshals raided the place and captured her as well as her keepers. To add to the horror of her situation she was soon to become a mother (Figure 1.6). The awful thought in her mind, however, was to escape from assassination at the hands of the murderous gang which oppressed her.

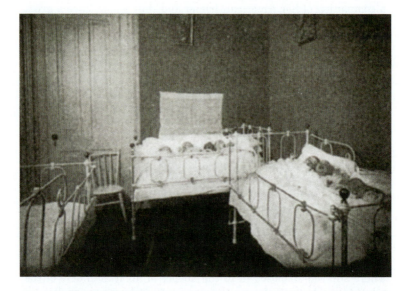

Figure 1.6 Children born from the sex trafficking of girls and women who were forced into prostitution. This photo, taken around 1910, depicts a nursery with numerous babies that were born from prostitutes who were forced into the white slave trade. (From: G. S. Ball, *Fighting the Traffic in Young Girls or War on the White Slave Trade* (Chicago: 1910), after p. 194.)

One recital of this kind is enough, although instances by the score might be cited which differ only in detail and degree.

The white slave traffic is a system operated by a syndicate which has its ramification from the Atlantic seaboard to the Pacific ocean, with "clearing houses" or "distributing centers" in nearly all of the larger cities; that in this ghastly traffic the buying price of a young girl is $15 up and that the selling price is from $200 to $600—if the girl is especially attractive the white slave dealer may be able to sell her for as much as $800 or $1,000; that this syndicate did not make less than $200,000 last year in this almost unthinkable commerce; it is definite that these traffickers send its hunters regularly to scour France, Germany, Hungary, Italy and Canada for victims.

Also the evidence shows that the hirelings of this traffic are stationed at certain ports of entry in Canada, where large numbers of immigrants are landed, to do what is known in their parlance as "cutting out work." In other words, these watchers for human prey scan the immigrants as they come down the gang plank of a vessel which has just arrived and "spot" the girls who are unaccompanied by fathers, mothers, brothers or relatives to protect them. The girl who has been spotted is a desirable and unprotected victim, is properly approached by a man who speaks her language and is immediately offered employment at good wages, with all expenses to the destination to be paid by the man. Most frequently laundry work is the bait held out, sometimes housework or employment in a candy shop or factory.

The object of the negotiations is to "cut out" the girl from any of her associates and to get her to go with him. Then the only thing to accomplish is to ruin her by the shortest route. If they cannot be cajoled or enticed by promises of an easy time, plenty of money, fine clothes and the usual stock of allurements—or a fake marriage— then harsher methods are resorted to. In some instances the hunters really marry the victims. As to the sterner methods, it is of course impossible to speak explicitly, beyond the statement that intoxication, drugging and physical imprisonment are often used as a means to control the victim and to reduce her to a state of helplessness, and sheer physical violence is a common thing (Figure 1.7).

When once a white slave is sold and landed in a house or dive she becomes a prisoner. The raids disclosed the fact that each of these places is a room having but one door, to which the keeper holds the key. In here are locked all the street clothes, shoes, and the ordinary apparel of a woman.

The finery which is provided for the girl for house wear is of a nature to make her appearance on the street impossible. Then added to this handicap, is the fact that at once the girl is placed in debt to the keeper for a wardrobe of "fancy" clothes which are charged to her at preposterous prices. She cannot escape while she is in debt to the keeper—and is never allowed to get out of debt—at

Figure 1.7 Examples of similar imprisonment tactics employed in the past 100 years. The photo on the left depicts a brothel used by traffickers around 1910 to imprison sex-trafficking victims. Occasionally, the women would be allowed to step outside for fresh air, but there was always a trusted female who was nearby to be certain that the girl did not attempt to escape. Note the bars on the windows. The photo on the right, which is a modern-day brothel also has bars on the window. In both cases, these bars were intended to keep the victims locked up and minimize the possibility of escape. (From: (left) G. S. Ball, *Fighting the Traffic in Young Girls or War on the White Slave Trade* (Chicago: 1910), after p. 82. (Right) Courtesy of Brian Crandall, NBC 10, Providence, RI, November 23, 2010. Online at: http://www2.turnto10.com/news/2010/nov/23/5/police-raid-providence-brothel-ar-300669; (accessed November 2, 2012).

least until all desire to leave the life is dead within her. Or she has contracted a debilitating, incurable and fatal sexually transmitted disease (Figure 1.8 through Figure 1.10).

Training for Law Enforcement Officers

Increasingly, local law enforcement agencies have begun to expand the opportunities for their officers to attend training courses on the topic of sex trafficking. This is typically done by sending them to national conferences or regional training centers, which focus on the topic of sex trafficking. These programs, taught by highly experienced federal, state, and local law enforcement officers and prosecutors, are designed to help police identify sex-trafficking activity that may be "masquerading" as other crimes (e.g., alien smuggling, organized crime, forced pornography, prostitution) as well as how to conduct sex-trafficking investigations.

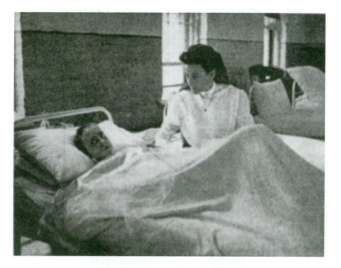

Figure 1.8 This photo taken around 1910 depicts a sex-trafficking victim under 20, dying in the poor house. In less than three years after leaving her home, this young girl, named Daisy, who was forced into prostitution, was found in a poor house, forgotten by family and friends, dying of a fatal sexually transmitted disease. (From: G. S. Ball, *Fighting the Traffic in Young Girls or War on the White Slave Trade* (Chicago: 1910), no page number provided, located after p. 146.)

Many states also have added a mandatory training module on the topic of sex trafficking in their police academies for recruit officers.

What the Reader Can Expect to Learn from This Book

Thus far in this chapter, we have provided a very brief overview of sex trafficking in America. All of these topics and many more will be discussed in much greater detail in this book. Following is a brief description of each chapter.

In Chapter 2, *Legal Aspects of Sex Trafficking in America*, we discuss the major federal and state laws that law enforcement officers will be called upon to utilize in the investigation and arrest of suspects as well as those laws that are most

Figure 1.9 Daisy at 14. The picture shows a pure, winsome girl of 14 going to school in a little country town. (From: G. S. Ball, *Fighting the Traffic in Young Girls or War on the White Slave Trade* (Chicago: 1910), no page number provided, located before p. 98.)

Figure 1.10 Daisy at 17—"young and so fair." This is the same girl who left her home town to take a position in the city. The man she trusted deceived her. (From: G. S. Ball, *Fighting the Traffic in Young Girls or War on the White Slave Trade* (Chicago: 1910), no page number provided, located before p. 98.)

commonly used at both the federal and state level in the prosecutorial process of sex traffickers.

In Chapter 3, *Domestic Sex Trafficking of American Children*, we focus on the sexual exploitation of American children (mostly girls under the age of 18) because, in most cases, they make up the bulk of individuals who are sexually exploited; the factors in their lives that make them so vulnerable to traffickers and pimps, as well as the lifelong consequences to their physical, psychological, and social development; the relationship between drug use and prostitution, gang activity; and the need for shelters and services for these domestically trafficked minors.

In Chapter 4, *Sex Trafficking of Foreign Women and Children into America*, we focus primarily on women and children who are trafficked into the United States from foreign countries, and who upon arrival are forced into prostitution; the various ways they are recruited and transported into the United States, and the methods used for marketing them once they arrive, and the role of organized crime in the sexual exploitation of these women and children; a comprehensive list of suggested questions is provided that will assist sex-trafficking investigators in locating, identifying, and interviewing women and children who have been trafficked into the United States; we also discuss the important role that governmental and non-governmental organizations play in assisting sex-trafficking survivors.

In Chapter 5, *The "John" Factor in Sex Trafficking*, we focus primarily on the role of customers (johns) of commercialized prostitution, without whom the profits generated in sex trafficking could not exist; demand reduction as a primary approach to prevention; police tactics known as "stings" or "reverse stings," as well as other tactics employed to reduce demand; and John schools, intended to both educate and treat men arrested for soliciting illegal commercial sex.

In Chapter 6, *Child Sex Tourism and the American Male*, we discuss the profile of the American child sex tourist and how they go about finding local children in foreign countries, and the extreme and lasting damage done to the victims. We focus primarily on three countries, namely, Cambodia, Mexico, and Guatemala, simply because they provide good examples of why certain countries are so attractive to child sex tourists. Lastly, we discuss the enforcement role of the U.S. Immigration and Customs Enforcement (ICE) Cybercrime Center and what it is doing to decrease child sex tourism by American men.

In Chapter 7, *Interrogation of Sex-Trafficking Suspects*, we discuss those aspects of interrogation in sex-trafficking cases which are essential for investigators to fully understand in order to maximize their effectiveness; the most effective ways for law enforcement officers to obtain voluntary confessions; the limitations set forth by the U.S. Supreme Court cases that affect the admissibility of confessions and admissions; and those behaviors on the part of suspects being interrogated that would suggest they are attempting to be deceptive.

In Chapter 8, *Crime Scene Investigation and Physical Evidence in Sex-Trafficking Cases*, we focus on the main types of physical evidence likely to be present in sex-trafficking cases, namely, biological materials, fingerprints, documents and communication technology; specific features that are unique to sex trafficking crime scenes and how best to preserve and protect evidence found at the scene; and we examine the elements necessary to obtain a search warrant in the quest to retrieve DNA evidence in sex trafficking cases.

In Chapter 9, *Building a Multiagency Task Force*, we discuss the most effective ways to develop and maintain strategic, well-planned, and collaborative relationships among federal, state, and local law enforcement agencies; how best to assess the feasibility of forming a sex trafficking task force in a given area; and, if created, the methods to be employed to be certain it is strategically and tactically efficient and successful.

In Chapter 10, *The Prosecution of Sex-Trafficking Cases*, we examine the role of prosecutors in general, and then examine the specific role of the federal prosecutor in sex-trafficking cases; and the role of the Federal Bureau of Investigation (FBI), Immigration and Customs Enforcement (ICE), and the Human Smuggling and Trafficking Center (HSTC) in assisting in the prosecutorial process. We also discuss how federal and state prosecutors ultimately decide whether a case will be prosecuted in federal or state court, and how to conduct legal searches and seizures in sex-trafficking cases.

In the Appendix, *Nongovernmental Organizations and U.S. Government Agencies Available to Assist Sex-Trafficking Victims and National Service Providers for Commercially Sexually Exploited Individuals*, we have provided the reader with a state-by-state listing of many organizations that can be called upon to assist in providing services to sex-trafficking victims.

Glossary

Commercial sex act: These include prostitution, sexually oriented performances, and other forms of commercial sexual exploitation.

Cutting out work: A turn of the 20th century term used by traffickers to describe the process by which they would visit ports of entry, where they attempt to identify young girls for potential sex trafficking. These would typically involve girls who were unaccompanied by fathers, mothers, brothers, or relatives to protect them. The trafficker, typically a man who spoke their language, would immediately offer employment and good wages with all expenses to the destination to be paid by him.

Debt bondage: When a person provides a loan to another who uses his or her labor or services to repay the debt, where the value of the work, as reasonably assessed, is not applied toward the liquidation of the debt.

Human trafficking: This includes sex trafficking, forced labor, involuntary servitude, peonage, and the illegal trafficking of human organs.

Money laundering: This entails taking criminal profits and moving them in a prohibited manner, specifically, criminals or persons acting on their behalf generate proceeds in the form of money or property as a result of committing a crime designated as a specified unlawful activity (SUA).

Noncommercial sex: This includes early marriage (child marriage), forced marriage, arranged marriage, temporary marriage, marriage by catalog (mail order bride), and marriage for childbearing.

Seasoning process: A combination of physical and verbal abuse meant to break a girl's will and separate her from her previous life so she does not know where to turn for help.

Smuggling: This occurs when someone is paid to assist another in the illegal crossing of the border.

Trafficking: Trafficking involves taking away the individual's freedom of choice whereupon he/she is forced into a situation of exploitation and denied his/her liberty.

Trafficking Victims Protection Act (TVPA): This federal law, passed in 2000, made human trafficking a federal crime and established resources to combat human trafficking and issued measures for the protection of victims, thus squarely targeting human trafficking for federal criminal prosecution.

Stockholm syndrome: A group of psychological symptoms that occur in some persons in a captive or hostage situation. It is also known as Survival Identification Syndrome. Victims develop negative feelings toward police and positive feelings toward their captors.

White slavery: The practice of forcing a female or male to engage in commercial prostitution. However, when this term was coined at the turn of the 20th century, it meant precisely what it said, which was the sex trafficking of white girls without any consideration of girls from other races.

Review Questions

1. What are three types of commercial sex?
2. What are six types of noncommercial sex?
3. What are the differences between trafficking and smuggling?
4. What other criminal activities are being supported by the profits from sex trafficking?
5. Why is sex trafficking often characterized not as a crime that occurs at a single moment in time, but rather as a criminal continuum?
6. Why are sex-trafficking victims in the United States often characterized as being invisible?

7. What tactics were employed by sex traffickers in the early part of the 20th century that are identical to the ones being employed today?
8. What are the most common ways that law enforcement officers are being exposed to sex-trafficking training today?

Endnotes

1. Trafficking victims can be either foreign nationals or natives. Under U.S. law, persons are placed in conditions of **forced labor** if they are forced to work against their will through actual or implied threats of serious harm, physical restraint, or abuse of the law. If they are forced to work through physical force or threats of physical force, they are victims of *involuntary servitude*. A person is subjected to **peonage** if that person is compelled by force, threat of force, or abuse of the law to work against his/her will in order to pay off a debt. If the value of a person's work is never reasonably applied toward payment of the debt, the person has been subjected to *debt bondage*. The term *forced labor* is also often used to describe all of these forms of modern slavery.
2. For a more detailed discussion on this topic, see L. Territo & R. Matteson (eds.). 2012. *The International Trafficking of Human Organs: A Multidisciplinary Perspective.* Boca Raton, FL: CRC Press.
3. Federal law on the exploitation and prostitution of children. Online at http://www.justice.gov/criminal/ceos/prostitution.html (accessed July 19, 2010).
4. Richard J. Estes & Neil Alan Weiner, *Commercial Sexual Exploitation of Children in the U.S., Canada, and Mexico* (Philadelphia: University of Pennsylvania, Executive Summary, 2001).
5. Ibid.
6. D. Carter, "Computer Crime Categories," *Law Enforcement Bulletin* 64 (7) (1995): 21–37.
7. Jerome H. Skolnick, *Justice Without Trial* (New York: John Wiley & Sons, 1966); E. Bittner, "The Police on Skid Row: A Study of Peace Keeping," *American Sociological Review* 32 (1967): 699–

715; J. Nolan et al., "Learning to See Hate Crimes: A Framework for Understanding and Clarifying Ambiguities in Bias Crime Classification," *Criminal Justice Studies* 17 (1) (2004): 91–105.

8. J. McDevitt et al., *Bridging the Information Disconnect in Bias Crime Reporting* (Washington, D.C.: Bureau of Justice Statistics, United State Department of Justice, 2003).

9. L. De Baca & A. Tisi, "Working Together to Stop Modern-Day Slavery," *The Police Chief* (August 2002): 78–80.

10. D. Wilson, W. Walsh, & S. Kleuber, "Trafficking in Human Beings: Training and Services Among U.S. Law Enforcement Agencies," *Police Practices and Research* 7 (2) (2006): 149–160.

11. H. Clawson et al., *Needs Assessment for Service Providers and Trafficking Victims* (Washington, D.C.: ICF International, 2003).

12. For a more detailed discussion of this issue, see C. R. Swanson, Leonard Territo, & Robert Taylor, *Police Administration,* 8th ed. (Upper Saddle River, NJ: Pearson, 2012), 163.

13. Florida Regional Community Policing Institute, *Introduction to Human Trafficking, Student Guide*, p.10. Online at: http://cop.spcollege.edu/Training/HumanTrafficking/EN/HTstudent8hour.pdf (accessed November 17, 2012).

14. Ibid.

15. Ibid., 12.

16. Ibid., 14.

17. Ibid., 15.

18. Ibid., 16.

19. For a description of what constitutes human trafficking, see: http://www.womenshealth.gov/violence/types/human-trafficking.cfm (accessed July 19, 2010).

20. For additional information, see Nathalie De Fabrique et al., "Understanding Stockholm Syndrome," *FBI Law Enforcement Bulletin*, July 2007, 10–15.

21. Edwin W. Sims, "The White Slave Trade of Today," in *Fighting the Traffic in Young Girls or War on the White Slave Trade,* ed. G. S. Ball (Chicago: Dodo Press, 1910), 49–60.

2
Legal Aspects of Sex Trafficking in America

President George W. Bush signing the 2005 Trafficking Victims Protection Reauthorization Act, which expanded the provisions of the original 2000 Trafficking Victims Protection Act. (Reprinted with permission from the March 2006 issue of *New Jersey Municipalities Magazine*.)

Chapter Objectives

1. Discuss the major legal provisions of the Mann Act and the Travel Act.
2. Understand the reasons for the creation of the special status T visa and U visa.
3. Describe the differences between the four Trafficking Victims Protection Acts passed by the U.S. Congress between 2000 and 2008.
4. Explain the rationale behind "The Tier System."
5. Become familiar with the federal laws relating to Domestic Minor Trafficking.
6. Discuss how the Racketeer Influenced and Corrupt Organizations Act (RICO) can be used in the prosecution of sex-trafficking cases.
7. Discuss why the U.S. Congress included the criminal forfeiture provision in the Racketeer Influenced and Corrupt Organizations Act.
8. Understand how money laundering is accomplished and what law enforcement can do to apprehend those engaged in the practice.
9. Become familiar with some examples of state statutes dealing with the sex trafficking of adults and minors.

Introduction

It is very important for law enforcement officers engaged in the investigation of sex-trafficking cases to have a basic working knowledge of the laws they will be called upon to enforce. In this chapter we will not, nor could we realistically, address all of the state and federal laws on sex trafficking that law enforcement officers may have at their disposal, but we can familiarize them with the laws most commonly used in the enforcement and prosecutorial process. However, in the final analysis, law enforcement officers will always be guided by the advice and recommendations of the state or federal prosecutors as to which law(s) can best be applied in a specific case in order to maximize the possibility of a successful prosecution.

In this chapter we will first discuss one of the oldest U.S. laws regarding sex-trafficking prevention, namely the Mann Act. We also will be discussing the Travel Act, the special status visa, and the various trafficking victim's protection acts passed by the U.S. Congress between 2000 and 2008, federal laws related to domestic minor sex trafficking. as well as the major provisions of the Racketeer Influenced and Corrupt Organizations (RICO) Act. In addition, we will examine the use of asset forfeiture and money laundering laws to break the power of organized crime. Lastly, we will provide some examples of state statutes that deal with sex trafficking of adults and minors.

The Mann Act

The Mann Act, passed on June 25, 1910 (also known as the White Slave Traffic Act), was named after Representative James Robert Mann (R-IL) (Figure 2.1) and is one of the oldest U.S. laws relating to sex trafficking prohibitions. This law prohibits the transportation of individuals across state lines for purposes of engaging in prostitution or other criminal sexual activity.[1,2] The Mann Act has separate provisions relating to adult and minor "transportees." These are distinguished as:

Adults
Whoever knowingly transports any individual in interstate or foreign commerce, or in any territory or possession of the United States, with intent that such individual engage in prostitution, or in any sexual activity for which any person can be charged with a criminal offense, or attempts to do so, shall be fined under this title or imprisoned not more than 10 years.[3]

Minors
A person who knowingly transports an individual who has not attained the age of 18 years in interstate or foreign commerce, or in any commonwealth, territory, or possession of the United States, with intent that

Figure 2.1 The Mann Act, or White-Slave Traffic Act, named after Representative James Robert Mann (R-IL) became law on June 25, 1910. It created a federal law against transporting individuals for "prostitution or debauchery, or for any other immoral purpose." It dealt with forced prostitution, harboring immigrant prostitutes, and the transportation across state lines. As of April 1912, the white slave investigations overshadowed the entire balance of the Bureau's (the future Federal Bureau of Investigation (FBI)) work. The Mann Act came at a time when the prostitution debate and the white slave trade were high-profile issues. (Photo courtesy of the Library of Congress.)

the individual engage in prostitution, or in any sexual activity for which any person can be charged with a criminal offense, shall be fined under this title and imprisoned not less than 10 years or life.[4]

The Differences between the Most Current Sex Trafficking Acts Passed by Congress and the Mann Act

The most significant difference between the sex-trafficking laws passed by the Congress between 2000 and 2008 (discussed later in this chapter) and Mann Act violations are that the Mann Act does not require any showing that the transported individual was compelled through improper means to engage in the prohibited sexual activity. In fact, under the Mann Act, it is not even necessary to show that the transported individual engaged in any sexual activity. Rather, it is the act of transporting the individual in interstate or foreign commerce "with the intent" that the individual engage in the prohibited sex act that violates the statute. At the same time, under the Mann Act, physical movement across a state line or international border is required. It also should be noted that the Mann Act does not require that the sexual activity for which the individual is transported be "commercial." So, for example, a person who transports a minor to a different state simply for the purpose of having sex with the minor, i.e., engaging in statutory rape, would be guilty of a Mann Act violation, even though the sexual activity involved no payment or commercial motivation. Lastly, the Mann Act provides an option for plea negotiations where the trafficking case involves adult victims and the evidence of compulsion is not strong, since the law contains no mandatory minimum sentence.

The Mann Act also can be used to prosecute "sex tourism" cases (discussed in Chapter 6), in which the defendant travels to another country for the purpose of engaging in sexual conduct that is illegal in the United States (and also may be illegal in the country where the conduct occurs), such as sex with minors. The Mann Act specifically prohibits persons from traveling from the United States to a foreign country to engage in illegal sexual activity and also prohibits U.S. citizens or permanent residents from traveling *between* foreign countries for this purpose.

Finally, one unique and seemingly underutilized Mann Act provision[5] criminalizes conduct relating to the keeping, harboring, and controlling of illegal aliens for purposes of prostitution or "other immoral purpose."[6] The law requires that anyone who engages in this activity file a statement with the Commissioner of Immigration setting forth each alien's name, where the alien is being kept, and all facts relating to the alien's entry into the United States. The failure to file this report is punishable by up to 10 years' imprisonment.

The Travel Act

The Travel Act federalizes the crime of operating prostitution businesses.[7] It prohibits, in relevant part, the following activities:

Traveling in interstate or foreign commerce or using the mail or
any facility in interstate or foreign commerce, with intent to ...
promote, manage, establish, carry on, or facilitate the promotion,
management, establishment, or carrying on, of any unlawful activity, [including] any business enterprise involving ... prostitution
offenses in violation of the laws of the State in which they are committed or of the United States.[8]

The Travel Act, passed in 1952, is similar to the Mann Act
in that it does not require a showing of compelled prostitution.
It does require a showing of a "business enterprise" that was
involved in prostitution, which has been interpreted to mean "a
continuous course of conduct" as opposed to "isolated, casual,
or sporadic activity."[9] The Travel Act, in contrast to the Mann
Act, also requires the actual carrying on of the prostitution
business as opposed to the mere intent to do so. Like the Mann
Act, there is no statutorily mandated minimum sentence where
adult transportees or victims are involved. The maximum sentence under the Travel Act is only 5 years for each count (unless
death results), as compared to 10 years under the Mann Act.

The Travel Act, however, offers a distinct advantage over
the Mann Act in that it proscribes the use of "any facility
in interstate or foreign commerce," such as a telephone or the
Internet, to carry on the prostitution business.[10] Thus, under
the Travel Act, physical transportation or travel of the person
who performs the prostitution is not required.

Creation of Special Status Visas

Later in this chapter we will be discussing, in detail, the U.S.
Trafficking Victims Protection Act of 2000 and the three additional Trafficking Victims Protection Reauthorization Acts
passed by Congress in 2003, 2005, and 2008. The Acts are col-
lectively intended to protect those individuals who have been
trafficked into the United States and have suffered substantial
physical or mental abuse or have been the victims of certain types
of criminal activities. An important component of the Trafficking
Victims Protection Act of 2000 was the creation of two special status visas. These visas are intended to assist trafficking victims

to stay in the United States as long as certain stipulations are met. Because these special status visas are discussed only briefly later in this chapter, we will, at this time, provide the reader with a more detailed discussion of their specific provisions.

T Nonimmigrant Status Visa

Some of the trafficking victims in the United States are aliens (noncitizens), who are illegally present (i.e., unauthorized/ undocumented aliens). Some of these aliens entered legally, but overstayed their length of legal admittance. Other aliens were smuggled into or illegally entered the United States and then became sex trafficking victims. In addition, some aliens have had their immigration documents confiscated by the traffickers as a form of control. The lack of immigration status may prevent victims from seeking help and may interfere with the ability of the victim to provide testimony during a criminal trial. As such, under U.S. law, there are certain protections from removal (deportation) available to noncitizen victims of trafficking.[11]

The Victims of Trafficking and Violence Protection Act of 2000 (TVPA) created a new nonimmigrant category, known as T status or T-visa, for aliens who are victims of severe forms of Trafficking in Persons (TIP).[12] Aliens who received T status are eligible to remain in the United States for four years and may apply for lawful permanent residence status (LPR) after being continually present in the United States for three years.

To receive T status, the alien also must be admissible to the United States or obtain a waiver of inadmissibility. A waiver of inadmissibility is available for health-related grounds, public charge grounds, or criminal grounds if the activities rendering the alien inadmissible were caused by or were incident to the alien's victimization.[13] Waivers are not automatically granted, and there is no appeal if the inadmissibility waiver is denied. This waiver is especially important for those involved in sexual trafficking because prostitution is one of the grounds of inadmissibility specified in the Immigration and Nationality Act (INA).[14] Additionally, aliens who are present without being admitted or paroled[15] into the United States are inadmissible and would need to obtain a waiver to be eligible for T status. For example, an alien who paid a smuggler to enter the country illegally and then was held in servitude would need to get an inadmissibility waiver to be eligible for T status.

T status is limited to 5,000 principal aliens each fiscal year. Additionally, the spouse, children, or parents of an alien under age 21, in order to avoid extreme hardship, may be given derivative T status, which is not counted against the numerical limit.[16] Individuals who are eligible for T status may be granted work authorization.[17] T status is valid for four years and may be extended if a federal, state, or local law enforcement official, prosecutor, judge, or other authority investigating or prosecuting activity relating to human trafficking certifies that the presence of the alien in the United States is necessary to assist in the investigation or prosecution of TIP.[18]

Under law, aliens who have bona fide T applications[19] are eligible to receive certain public benefits to the same extent as refugees.[20] Aliens who receive derivative T status (i.e., the family members of trafficking victims) are eligible for benefits as well. In addition, regulations require that federal officials provide trafficking victims with specific information regarding their rights and services such as:

- immigration benefits;
- federal and state benefits and services (e.g., certification by the Department of Health and Human Services (HHS) and assistance through HHS's Office of Refugee Resettlement (ORR));
- medical services;
- pro bono and low-cost legal services;
- victim service organizations;
- victim compensation (trafficked aliens are often eligible for compensation from state and federal crime victim programs);[21]
- the right to restitution; and
- the rights of privacy and confidentiality.[22]

Continued Presence

Federal law enforcement officials, who encounter victims of severe forms of TIP and are potential witnesses to that trafficking, may request that the Department of Homeland

Security (DHS) grant the continued presence of the alien in the United States. Historically, the Attorney General has had the discretionary authority to use a variety of statutory and administrative mechanisms to ensure the alien's continued presence.[23] Most of the statutory and administrative mechanisms for continued presence required that the alien depart from the United States once his/her presence for the criminal investigation or prosecution is no longer required. In most cases, victims granted continued presence are eligible for work authorization.[24] Requests for continued presence are handled by the Law Enforcement Parole Branch of DHS's Immigration and Customs Enforcement (ICE) (Figure 2.2).

In some cases, law enforcement prefers giving the alien continued presence rather than T status in order to prevent the appearance, during the prosecution of the traffickers, that the alien's testimony was "bought."[25]

U Nonimmigrant Status

Some victims of trafficking are eligible for U nonimmigrant status. The Violence Against Women Act of 2000, of TVPA, created the U nonimmigrant status, often called the U-visa, for victims of physical or mental abuse.[26,27] To qualify for U status the alien must file a petition and establish:

- He/she suffered substantial physical or mental abuse as a result of having been a victim of certain criminal activities.[28] This refers to one or more of the following or any similar activity in violation of federal or state criminal law: rape, torture, trafficking, incest, domestic violence, sexual assault, abusive sexual contact, prostitution, sexual exploitation, female genital mutilation, being held hostage, peonage, involuntary servitude, slave trade, kidnapping, abduction, unlawful criminal restraint, false imprisonment, blackmail, extortion/manslaughter, murder, felonious assault, witness tampering, obstruction of justice, perjury, or attempt, conspiracy, or solicitation to commit any of the above-mentioned crimes.
- As certified by a law enforcement or immigration official, he/she (or if the alien is a child under age 16, the

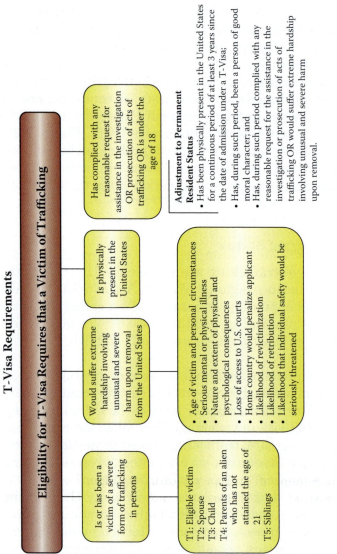

T-Visa Requirements

Eligibility for T-Visa Requires that a Victim of Trafficking

Is or has been a victim of a severe form of trafficking in persons

- T1: Eligible victim
- T2: Spouse
- T3: Child
- T4: Parents of an alien who has not attained the age of 21
- T5: Siblings

Would suffer extreme hardship involving unusual and severe harm upon removal from the United States

- Age of victim and personal circumstances
- Serious mental or physical illness
- Nature and extent of physical and psychological consequences
- Loss of access to U.S. courts
- Home country would penalize applicant
- Likelihood of revictimization
- Likelihood of retribution
- Likelihood that individual safety would be seriously threatened

Is physically present in the United States

Has complied with any reasonable request for assistance in the investigation OR prosecution of acts of trafficking OR is under the age of 18

Adjustment to Permanent Resident Status

- Has been physically present in the United States for a continuous period of at least 3 years since the date of admission under a T-Visa;
- Has, during such period, been a person of good moral character; and
- Has, during such period complied with any reasonable request for the assistance in the investigation or prosecution of acts of trafficking OR would suffer extreme hardship involving unusual and severe harm upon removal.

Figure 2.2 T-visa requirements. (From M. Mattar, *Comprehensive Legal Approaches to Combating Trafficking in Persons: An International and Comparative Perspective, Protection Project,* (Baltimore, MD: Johns Hopkins University, 2006), p. 40. With permission.)

child's parent, guardian, or friend) possesses information about the criminal activity involved.
- He/she has been, is being, or is likely to be helpful in the
investigation and prosecution of the criminal activity
by federal, state, or local law enforcement authorities.
- The criminal activity violated the laws of the United
States or occurred in the United States.

The U category is limited to 10,000 principal aliens per
fiscal year.[29] After three years, those in U status may apply
for LPR status.[30] Unlike aliens with T status, those with U
status are not eligible for assistance through the Office of
Refugee Resettlement or for federal public benefits. Those who
receive U status may be eligible for programs to assist crime
victims through the Department of Justice's Office for Victims
of Crime.

Even when the 10,000 statutory cap has been reached, the
United States Citizenship and Immigration Service (USCIS)
will continue to accept and process new petitions for U status
and will issue a notice of conditional approval to petitioners,
who are found eligible for U status, but are unable to receive U
status because the cap has been reached[31] (Figure 2.3).

Cooperation with Law Enforcement Needed for a U Visa

In addition to establishing that they are victims of a qualify-
ing crime, applicants for U status must show that they have
cooperated with law enforcement in the investigation or prosecution of the crime.[32] This means, according to the statute
creating U status, that they "have been helpful, are being
helpful, or are likely to be helpful" to a federal, state, or local
law enforcement official, prosecutor, or judge.[33]

In contrast to T status, the *only* way for U applicants to
establish that they have cooperated with law enforcement is
by submitting a certificate of cooperation on a form signed by
law enforcement.[34] Note that law enforcement policies about
certifications of cooperation are not uniform throughout the
United States. Not all state or local law enforcement choose to
issue certifications. When agencies do issue U certificates of
cooperation, practices about the timing of certifications vary,

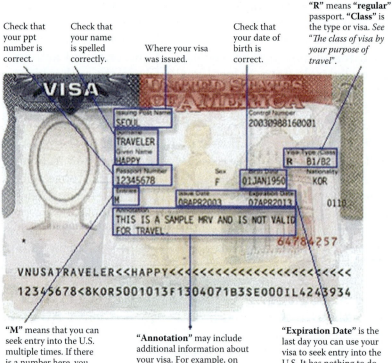

Check that your ppt number is correct.

Check that your name is spelled correctly.

Where your visa was issued.

Check that your date of birth is correct.

"R" means "regular" passport. "Class" is the type or visa. See *"The class of visa by your purpose of travel"*.

"M" means that you can seek entry into the U.S. multiple times. If there is a number here, you may apply for entry that many times.

"Annotation" may include additional information about your visa. For example, on a student visa, it will show your SEVIS number and name of your school.

"Expiration Date" is the last day you can use your visa to seek entry into the U.S. It has nothing to do with how long you may stay in the U.S. See *"What is a Visa?"*

Figure 2.3 The T visa and U visa are recognized by the letter T or U in the upper right side of the card in the box labeled "Type/Class." (From: the U.S. Department of State. Online at: http://travel.state.gov/visa/questions/questions_1253.html)

even within the same municipality. For example, the district attorney's office for one borough in New York City issues U certificates of cooperation at the beginning of an investigation, while the district attorney for another borough delays U certificates until the close of a case. Postponing certification until a case has ended could mean a wait of up to two years before the crime victim can apply for U status.

Authority to issue certificates of cooperation is not limited to police or prosecutors. Under the regulations, any government agent with authority to investigate a crime may issue certificates.[35] Thus, judges as well as agencies with investigative powers, such as child protective services or the Department of Labor, can issue certificates of cooperation.

Trafficking Victims Protection Act 2000

In 2000, the U.S. government enacted the Trafficking Victims Protection Act (TVPA), which makes human trafficking a federal crime, establishes resources to combat human trafficking, and issues measures for the protection of victims, thus squarely targeting human trafficking for federal criminal prosecution.

The key provisions on human trafficking in this law are:[36]

- Directed the Secretary of State to provide an annual report by June 1, listing countries that do and do not comply with minimum standards for the elimination of trafficking, and to provide information on the nature and extent of severe forms of Trafficking in Persons (TIP) in each country and an assessment of the efforts by each government to combat trafficking in the State Department's annual human rights report.
- Called for establishing an Interagency Task Force to Monitor and Combat Trafficking, chaired by the Secretary of State, and authorized the Secretary to establish within the Department of State an Office to Monitor and Combat Trafficking to assist the Task Force.
- Called for measures to enhance economic opportunity for potential victims of trafficking as a method to deter trafficking, to increase public awareness, particularly among potential victims, of the dangers of trafficking, and the protections that are available for victims, and for the government to work with nongovernmental organizations (NGOs) to combat trafficking.
- Provided protection and assistance for victims of severe forms for trafficking while in the United States.
- Amended the federal criminal code to make funds derived from the sale of assets seized from and forfeited by traffickers available for victims assistance programs under this act.

- Amended the Immigration and Nationality Act (INA) to allow the Attorney General to grant nonimmigrant visas (T visas).
- Established minimum standards to combat human trafficking applicable to countries that have a significant trafficking problem. Urged such countries to prohibit severe forms of TIP, to punish such acts, and to make serious and sustained efforts to eliminate such trafficking.
- Provided for assistance to foreign countries for programs and activities designed to meet the minimum international standards for the elimination of trafficking.
- Encouraged the President to compile and publish a list of foreign persons who play a significant role in a severe form of TIP. Also encouraged the President to impose sanctions under the International Emergency Economic Powers Act, including freezing of assets located in the United States.
- Amended the Federal Criminal Code (18 U.S.C.) to double the current maximum penalties for peonage, enticement into slavery, and sale into involuntary servitude from 10 years' to 20 years' imprisonment and to add the possibility of life imprisonment for such violations resulting in death or involving kidnapping, aggravated sexual abuse, or an attempt to kill.
- Called for the United States to withhold nonhumanitarian assistance and instructed the U.S. executive director of each multilateral development bank and the International Monetary Fund to vote against nonhumanitarian assistance to such countries that do not meet minimum standards against trafficking and are not making efforts to meet minimum standards, unless continued assistance is deemed to be in the U.S. national interest (the device used to evaluate compliance by foreign countries is called the Tier System).

The Tier System

Pursuant to the passage of the original 2000 TVPA, the U.S. government created a tier system to be used as a guide in determining which countries would be eligible for certain types of U.S. aid. For example, it is the policy of the U.S. government to deny nonhumanitarian, nontrade-related foreign assistance—including both bilateral and multilateral assistance—to any foreign government that does not comply with the minimum standards for the elimination of trafficking and is not making significant efforts to bring itself into compliance with such standards. Each year the President is required to make a determination on whether to impose such aid restrictions on the Tier 3 countries (discussed later in the chapter) annually identified by the State Department for the subsequent fiscal year. If Tier 3 countries did not receive nonhumanitarian, nontrade-related foreign assistance from the U.S. government in the prior fiscal year, then future U.S. funding for participation of noncompliant country government officials in education and cultural exchange programs may be denied. Pursuant to the TVPA, the President reserves the discretion to waive part or all of the aid and funding restrictions on the basis of national interest reasons.

Elements of the Tier Ranking System

Tier rankings are based upon:

- Enactment of laws prohibiting severe forms of trafficking in persons, as defined by the TVPA, and provision of criminal punishments for trafficking offenses.
- Criminal penalties prescribed for human trafficking offenses with a maximum of at least four years' deprivation of liberty, or a more severe penalty.
- Implementation of human trafficking laws through vigorous prosecution of the prevalent forms of trafficking in the country.
- Proactive victim identification measures with systematic procedures to guide law enforcement and other government-supported frontline responders in the process of victim identification.
- Government funding and partnerships with NGOs to provide victims with access to primary healthcare, counseling, and shelter, allowing them to recount their

trafficking experiences to trained social counselors and law enforcement in an environment of minimal pressure.

- Victim protection efforts that include access to services and shelter without detention and with legal alternatives to removal to countries in which the victim would face retribution or hardship.
- The extent to which a government ensures victims are provided with legal and other assistance and that, consistent with domestic law, proceedings are not prejudicial against victims' rights, dignity, or psychological well being.
- The extent to which a government ensures the safe, humane, and, to the extent possible, voluntary repatriation and reintegration of victims.
- Governmental measures to prevent human trafficking, including efforts to curb practices identified as contributing factors to human trafficking including forced labor, such as employers' confiscation of foreign workers' passports and allowing labor recruiters to charge prospective migrants excessive fees.

Tier rankings and narratives are NOT affected by the following:

- Efforts, however laudable, undertaken exclusively by nongovernmental actors in the country.
- General public awareness events—government-sponsored or otherwise—lacking concrete ties to the prosecution of traffickers, protection of victims, or prevention of trafficking.
- Broad-based development or law enforcement initiatives without a specific human trafficking focus[37] (Figure 2.4).

Tier 1 Countries

Tier 1 countries are made up of those countries deemed by the State Department as having fully complied with the minimum standards for eliminating trafficking[38] (Table 2.1).

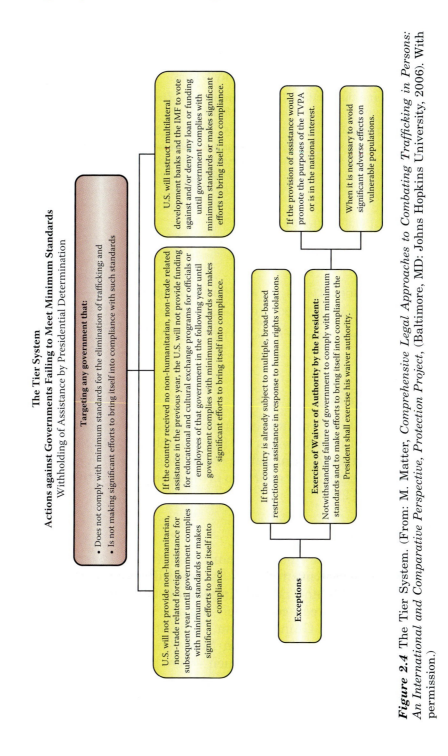

The Tier System
Actions against Governments Failing to Meet Minimum Standards
Withholding of Assistance by Presidential Determination

Targeting any government that:
• Does not comply with minimum standards for the elimination of trafficking; and
• Is not making significant efforts to bring itself into compliance with such standards

U.S. will not provide non-humanitarian, non-trade related foreign assistance for subsequent year until government complies with minimum standards or makes significant efforts to bring itself into compliance.

If the country received no non-humanitarian, non-trade related assistance in the previous year, the U.S. will not provide funding for educational and cultural exchange programs for officials or employees of that government in the following year until government complies with minimum standards or makes significant efforts to bring itself into compliance.

U.S. will instruct multilateral development banks and the IMF to vote against and/or deny any loan or funding until government complies with minimum standards or makes significant efforts to bring itself² into compliance.

Exceptions

If the country is already subject to multiple, broad-based restrictions on assistance in response to human rights violations.

Exercise of Waiver of Authority by the President:
Notwithstanding failure of government to comply with minimum standards and to make efforts to bring itself into compliance the President shall exercise his waiver authority.

If the provision of assistance would promote the purposes of the TVPA or is in the national interest.

When it is necessary to avoid significant adverse effects on vulnerable populations.

Figure 2.4 The Tier System. (From: M. Matter, *Comprehensive Legal Approaches to Combating Trafficking in Persons: An International and Comparative Perspective, Protection Project,* (Baltimore, MD: Johns Hopkins University, 2006). With permission.)

TABLE 2.1
Tier 1 Countries in 2011, by Region

Region	Country Names
East Asia and the Pacific (4 of 26)	Australia, New Zealand, South Korea, and Taiwan
Europe (21 of 46)	Austria, Belgium, Bosnia, Croatia, Denmark, Finland, France, Georgia, Germany, Ireland, Italy, Lithuania, Luxembourg, Netherlands, Norway, Poland, Slovenia, Spain, Sweden, and United Kingdom
Middle East and North Africa (0 of 18)	
South and Central Asia (0 of 12)	
Subsaharan Africa (2 of 43)	Mauritius and Nigeria
Western Hemisphere (3 of 30)	Canada, Colombia, and the United States

Source: U.S. Department of State, 2011 TIP Report.

Tier 2 Countries

Tier 2 countries include countries whose governments the State Department views as not fully complying with the minimum standards for eliminating trafficking but which are seen as making "significant efforts to bring themselves into compliance" (Table 2.2).

Tier 3 Countries

Tier 3 countries include countries whose governments the State Department deems as not fully complying with those standards and not making significant efforts to do so (Table 2.3). Thirteen countries—Algeria, the Central Africa Republic (CAR), Guinea-Bissau, Kuwait, Lebanon, Libya, Mauritania, Micronesia, Papua New Guinea, Saudi Arabia, Sudan, Turkmenistan, and Yemen—were granted *full waivers* from the aid prohibitions. The President determined that continued U.S. support in FY2012 to these 13 countries would be in the U.S. national interest (Table 2.3 and Figure 2.4).

TABLE 2.2
Tier 2 Countries in 2011, by Region

Region	Country Names
East Asia and the Pacific (14 of 29)	Cambodia, Fiji, Hong Kong, Indonesia, Japan, Laos, Macau, Marshall Island, Mongolia, Palau, Philippines, Singapore, Timor-Leste, and Tonga
Europe (17 of 47)	Albania, Armenia, Aruba, Bulgaria, Czech Republic, Greece, Hungary, Iceland, Kosovo, Latvia, Moldova, Montenegro, Romania, Serbia, Switzerland,. Turkey, and the Ukraine
Middle East and North Africa (7 of 18)	Bahrain, Egypt, Israel, Morocco, Oman, and the United Arab Emirates
South and Central Asia (7 of 18)	India, Kazakhstan, Kyrgyz Republic, Nepal, Pakistan, Sri Lanka, and Tajikistan
Subsaharan Africa (21 of 46)	Benin, Botswana, Burkina Faso, Djibouti, Ethiopia, Gabon, Ghana, Kenya, Lesotho, Malawi, Mozambique, Namibia, Rwanda, Senegal, Seychelles, Sierra Leone, South Africa, Swaziland, Togo, Uganda, and Zambia
Western Hemisphere (19 of 32)	Antigua and Barbuda, Argentina, Belize, Bolivia, Brazil, Chile, El Salvador, Guatemala, Guyana, Honduras, Jamaica, Mexico, Nicaragua, Paraguay, Peru, St. Lucia, Suriname, Trinidad and Tobago, and Uruguay

Source: U.S. Department of State, 2011 TIP Report.

TABLE 2.3
Tier 3 Countries in 2011, by Region

Region	Country Names
East Asia and the Pacific (4 of 29)	Burma, Micronesia, North Korea, and Papua New Guinea
Europe (0 of 47)	
Middle East and North Africa (7 of 18)	Algeria, Iran, Kuwait, Lebanon, Libya, Saudi Arabia, and Yemen
South and Central Asia (1 of 12)	Turkmenistan
Subsaharan Africa (9 of 46)	Central African Republic, Democratic Republic of Congo, Equatorial Guinea, Eritrea, Guinea-Bissau, Madagascar, Mauritania, Sudan, and Zimbabwe
Western Hemisphere (2 of 32)	Cuba and Venezuela

Source: U.S. Department of State, 2011 TIP Report.

Trafficking Victims Protection Reauthorization Act of 2003 (TVPRA)

In order to meet the increasing challenges posed by human trafficking, the TVPA 2000 was amended by Congress with the passage of the Trafficking Victims Protection Reauthorization Act of 2003 (TVPRA), which includes new legal resources against trafficking, such as allowing victims to bring civil law suits against traffickers.[39]

This new law authorized substantial increases in funding for antitrafficking programs for 2004 and 2005 (over $100 million for each fiscal year). The law refined and expanded the minimum standards for the elimination of trafficking that governments must meet and placed on such governments the responsibility to provide the information and data by which their compliance with the standards could be judged. The legislation created a "special watch list" of countries that the Secretary of State determined were to get special scrutiny in the coming year. The list was to include countries where (1) the absolute number of victims of severe forms of trafficking is very significant or is significantly increasing, (2) there is failure to provide evidence of increasing efforts to combat severe forms of TIP from the previous year, or (3) the determination that a country is making significant efforts to bring itself into compliance with minimum standards is based on its commitments to take additional steps over the next year. In the case of such countries, not later than February 1 of each year, the Secretary of State is to provide to the appropriate congressional committees an assessment of the progress that the country had made since the last annual report.[40]

Trafficking Victims Protection Reauthorization Act of 2005

As the two previous laws, TVPA 2000 and TVPRA 2003, were operationalized, it became obvious that there were still some shortcomings that needed to be rectified by supplementary legislation. As a result of this, two years after the passage of the TVPRA 2003, another act was passed. The act was the Trafficking Victims Protection Reauthorization Act of 2005. This law gives jurisdiction to U.S. courts over governmental employees who become involved in human trafficking abroad. This amendment also provides new antitrafficking measures, such as developing grant programs directed toward aiding state and local law enforcement antitrafficking initiatives, and expanding assistance programs to aid victims, who are U.S. citizens or resident aliens.[41]

This law also attempted to address the special needs of child victims as well as the plight of Americans trafficked within the United States. It directed relevant U.S. government agencies to develop antitrafficking strategies for post-conflict situations and humanitarian emergencies abroad. It sought to extend U.S. criminal jurisdiction over government personnel and contractors, who are involved in acts of trafficking abroad while doing work for the government. It addressed the problem of peacekeepers and aid workers who are complicit in trafficking.[42]

William Wilberforce Trafficking Victims Protection Reauthorization Act of 2008

The William Wilberforce[43] Trafficking Victims Protection Reauthorization Act of 2008 (TVPRA) authorized appropriations for 2008 through 2011 and establishes a system to monitor and evaluate all assistance under the act (Figure 2.5). The act requires the establishment of an integrated database to be used by U.S. government departments and agencies to collect data for analysis on TIP.[44] The act establishes new provisions to aid domestic trafficking victims, and new measures, such as making it unnecessary for prosecutors to prove the trafficker knew the victim was a minor and requiring them to, instead, demonstrate that the accused had a "reasonable opportunity to observe" the victim. This new law also requires

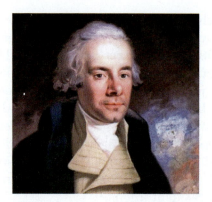

Figure 2.5 William Wilberforce, a 19th century English Member of Parliament. Wilberforce was a deeply religious 19th century social reformer who was very influential in the abolition of the slave trade and eventually slavery itself in the British Empire.

that all types of pimping and pandering be criminalized, and that the President develop a system to monitor federal anti-trafficking programs.[45]

The act increases the technical assistance and other support to help foreign governments inspect locations where forced labor occurs, register vulnerable populations, and provide more protection to foreign migrant workers. The act requires that specific actions be taken against governments of countries that have been on the Tier 2 Watch List for two consecutive years and also requires the U.S. Department of State to translate the TIP Report into the principal languages of as many countries as possible. In addition, among other measures to address the issue of child soldiers, the act prohibits military assistance to foreign governments that recruit and use child soldiers.

Preventing Trafficking to the United States

TVPRA 2008 requires pamphlets on the rights and responsibilities of the employee to be produced and given to employment-based and educational-based nonimmigrants.[46] It also requires consular officers to make sure that certain aliens interviewing for nonimmigrant visas have received, read, and understood the pamphlet. During the interview, the consular officer is also required to discuss the alien's legal rights under U.S. immigration, labor, and employment law.

Measures to Address Trafficking in the United States

The TVPRA 2008 amends the requirements for the T visa, so that an alien would be eligible for a T visa if the alien was unable to comply with requests for assistance in the investigation and prosecution of acts of trafficking due to physical or psychological trauma.[47] The Act also requires, when determining whether the alien meets the extreme hardship requirement for T status, that the Secretary of DHS consider whether the country to which the alien would be removed can adequately address the alien's security and mental and physical health needs. In addition, the act amends the requirements for the T visa so that an alien would be eligible if he/she was present in the United States after being allowed entry to aid in the prosecution of traffickers. The act also broadens the requirements for an alien to receive continued presence in the United States, and makes it easier for families of trafficking victims to be paroled into the United States. In addition, the act amends the law to allow the Secretary of DHS to waive the good moral character requirement for those adjusting from T to LPR status, and allows the Secretary of DHS to provide a "stay of removal" for aliens with pending T applications (with a prima facie case for approval), until the application has been adjudicated. The act also makes aliens with pending applications for T status eligible for public benefits, and makes T visa holders, including derivatives, eligible for public benefits.[48] Furthermore, the act requires the Secretary of Health and Human Services (HHS) to make a prompt determination of eligibility for assistance for child trafficking victims.

TVPRA 2008 has provisions relating to enhancing protections for child victims of trafficking. These provisions include requiring the United States to enter into agreements with contiguous countries regarding the return of unaccompanied minors designed to protect children from severe forms of TIP,[49] and specifying screening procedures for children suspected of being trafficking victims. In addition, the act directs the Secretary of HHS, to the extent possible, to provide legal counsel and appoint child advocates for child trafficking victims and other vulnerable unaccompanied alien children.

Moreover, the act creates new grant programs for U.S. citizen victims of severe forms of trafficking and authorizes appropriations for such programs. The act also requires the Secretary of HHS and the Attorney General, within one year of enactment, to submit a report to Congress identifying any gaps between services provided to U.S. citizens and noncitizen victims of trafficking. It also prohibits DHS from issuing passports to those convicted of sex tourism until the person has completed his/her sentence. Furthermore, the act creates new criminal offenses related to human trafficking, including criminalizing retaliation in foreign labor contracting. The act creates additional jurisdiction in U.S. courts for trafficking offenses occurring in other countries if the alleged offender is present in the United States.

Federal Laws Related to Domestic Minor Sex Trafficking

Following are some of the federal laws that are most commonly used in the prosecution of domestic minor sex trafficking.

U.S. Code—Section 2251: Sexual Exploitation of Children

(a) Any person who employs, uses, persuades, induces, entices, or coerces any minor to engage in, or who has a minor assist any other person to engage in, or who transports any minor in interstate or foreign commerce, or in any Territory or Possession of the United States, with the intent that such minor engage in, any sexually explicit conduct for the purpose of producing any visual depiction of such conduct, shall be punished as provided under subsection (e), if such person knows or has reason to know that such visual depiction will be transported in interstate or foreign commerce or mailed, if that visual depiction was produced using materials that have been mailed, shipped, or transported in interstate or foreign commerce by any means, including by computer, or if such visual depiction has actually been transported in interstate or foreign commerce or mailed.

(b) Any parent, legal guardian, or person having custody or control of a minor who knowingly permits such minor to engage in, or to assist any other person to engage in, sexually explicit conduct for the purpose of producing any visual depiction of such conduct shall be punished as provided under subsection (e) of this section, if such parent, legal guardian, or person knows or has reason to know that such visual depiction will be transported in interstate or foreign commerce or mailed, if that visual depiction was produced using materials that have been mailed, shipped, or transported in interstate or foreign commerce by any means, including by computer, or if such visual depiction has actually been transported in interstate or foreign commerce or mailed.

(c)(1) Any person who, in a circumstance described in paragraph (2), employs, uses, persuades, induces, entices, or coerces any minor to engage in, or who has a minor assist any other person to engage in, any sexually explicit conduct outside of the United States, its territories or possessions, for the purpose of producing any visual depiction of such conduct, shall be punished as provided under subsection (e). (2) The circumstance referred to in paragraph (1) is that—(A) the person intends such visual depiction to be transported to the United States, its territories or possessions, by any means, including by computer or mail; or (B) the person transports such visual depiction to the United States, its territories or possessions, by any means, including by computer or mail.

(d)(1) Any person who, in a circumstance described in paragraph (2), knowingly makes, prints, or publishes, or causes to be made, printed, or published, any notice or advertisement seeking or offering—(A) to receive, exchange, buy, produce, display, distribute, or reproduce, any visual depiction, if the production of such visual depiction involves the use of a minor engaging in sexually explicit conduct and such visual depiction is of such conduct; or (B) participation in any act of sexually explicit conduct by or with any minor for the purpose of producing a visual depiction of such conduct; shall be punished as provided under subsection (e). (2) The circumstance referred to in paragraph (1) is that—(A) such person knows or has reason to know that such notice or advertisement will be transported in interstate or foreign commerce by any means including by computer or mailed; or (B) such notice or advertisement is transported in interstate or foreign commerce by any means including by computer or mailed.

(e) Any individual who violates, or attempts or conspires to violate, this section shall be fined under this title and imprisoned not less than 15 years nor more than 30 years, but if such person has one prior conviction under this chapter, chapter 71, chapter 109A, or chapter 117, or under section 920 of title 10 (article 120 of the Uniform Code of Military Justice), or under the laws of any State relating to the sexual exploitation of children, such person shall be fined under this title and imprisoned for not less than 25 years nor more than 50 years, but if such person has 2 or more prior convictions under this chapter, chapter 71, chapter 109A, or chapter 117, or under section 920 of title 10 (article 120 of the Uniform Code of Military Justice), or under the laws of any State relating to the sexual exploitation of children, such person shall be fined under this title and imprisoned not less than 35 years or life. Any organization that violates, or attempts or conspires to violate, this section shall be fined under this title. Whoever, in the course of an offense under this section, engages in conduct that results in the death of a person, shall be punished by death or imprisoned for any term of years or for life.

U.S. Code—Section 2422: Coercion and Enticement

(a) Whoever knowingly persuades, induces, entices, or coerces any individual to travel in interstate or foreign commerce, or in any Territory or Possession of the United States, to engage in prostitution, or in any sexual activity for which any person can be charged with a criminal offense, or attempts to do so, shall be fined under this title or imprisoned not more than 20 years, or both.

(b) Whoever, using the mail or any facility or means of interstate or foreign commerce, or within the special maritime and territorial jurisdiction of the United States knowingly persuades, induces, entices, or coerces any individual who has not attained the age of 18 years, to engage in prostitution or any sexual activity for which any person can be charged with a criminal offense, or attempts to do so, shall be fined under this title and imprisoned not less than 10 years or for life.

U.S. Code—Section 2423: Transportation of Minors

(a) Transportation With Intent To Engage in Criminal Sexual Activity. A person who knowingly transports an individual who has not attained the age of 18 years in interstate or foreign commerce, or in any commonwealth, territory or possession of the United States, with intent that the individual engage in prostitution, or in any sexual activity for which any person can be charged with a criminal offense, shall be fined under this title and imprisoned not less than 10 years or for life.

(b) Travel With Intent To Engage in Illicit Sexual Conduct. A person who travels in interstate commerce or travels into the United States, or a United States citizen or an alien admitted for permanent residence in the United States who travels in foreign commerce, for the purpose of engaging in any illicit sexual conduct with another person shall be fined under this title or imprisoned not more than 30 years, or both.

(c) Engaging in Illicit Sexual Conduct in Foreign Places. Any United States citizen or alien admitted for permanent residence who travels in foreign commerce, and engages in any illicit sexual conduct with another person shall be fined under this title or imprisoned not more than 30 years, or both.

(d) Ancillary Offenses. Whoever, for the purpose of commercial advantage or private financial gain, arranges, induces, procures, or facilitates the travel of a person knowing that such a person is traveling in interstate commerce or foreign commerce for the purpose of engaging in illicit sexual conduct shall be fined under this title, imprisoned not more than 30 years, or both.

(e) Attempt and Conspiracy. Whoever attempts or conspires to violate subsection (a), (b), (c), or (d) shall be punishable in the same manner as a completed violation of that subsection.

(f) Definition. As used in this section, the term "illicit sexual conduct" means (1) a sexual act (as defined in section 2246) with a person under 18 years of age that would be in violation of chapter 109A if the sexual act occurred in the special maritime and territorial jurisdiction of the United States; or (2) any commercial sex act (as defined in section 1591) with a person under 18 years of age.

(g) Defense. In a prosecution under this section based on illicit sexual conduct as defined in subsection (f)(2), it is a defense, which the defendant must establish by a preponderance of the evidence, that the defendant reasonably believed that the person with whom the defendant engaged in the commercial sex act had attained the age of 18 years.

The Racketeer Influenced and Corrupt Organizations Act (RICO)

Congress enacted RICO in 1970 to "seek the eradication of organized crime."[50,51] Originally formed in response to the increasing problem of organized crime's penetration into lawful business operations,[52] "[a]s finally enacted, RICO authorized the imposition of enhanced criminal penalties and new civil sanctions to provide new legal remedies for all types of organized criminal behavior."[53] This novel combination of criminal and civil penalties was the end result of an opinion by the President's Commission on Law Enforcement and Administration of Justice reporting that antitrust remedies would be effective in dealing with the growing problem of the Mafia.[54] Lower burdens of proof and the possibility of discovery further added to the appeal of civil remedies.[55] Congress, however, decided that a separate statute also was necessary to meet the problem's criminal enforcement and, therefore, it adopted a two-tiered approach; one tier provided civil penalties and the other criminal.[56] Congress passed RICO as part of the Organized Crime Control Act (OCCA) introduced by Senator John L. McClellan as Senate Bill 30 in 1969.[57] OCCA called for sweeping reforms in many areas including grand juries,[58] immunity,[59] contempt,[60] false statements,[61] depositions,[62] and sentencing.[63] Although not originally part of the Act, Congress eventually incorporated RICO into OCCA after substantial congressional debate over its content and witness recommendations concerning its particular provisions.[64] President Nixon signed the bill into law in October 1970.[65]

RICO as a Tool to Combat Sex Trafficking by Organized Crime

Prosecutors have in RICO a statute specifically enacted to fight organized crime.[66] As a result of its liberal construction clause imposed by Congress, RICO has been successfully expanded to prosecute large criminal syndicates involved in narcotics, arms dealing, gambling, prostitution, and sex trafficking.[67] The following case illustrates this.

CASE

In 2010 the Manhattan U.S. Attorney charged 7 members of the Gambino crime family with sex trafficking. The individuals charged were Thomas Orefice, Dominick Difiore, Anthony Manzella, Michael Scotto, David Eisler, Steve Marurro, and Suzanne Porcelli. They are charged with sex trafficking of a minor. From 2008 to 2009, the

Figure 2.6 FBI special agent announcing the arrest of Gambino crime family members. Special Agent in Charge George Venizelos announces the arrest of members of the Gambino organized crime family for racketeering in conjunction with the sex trafficking of minors and children. (Photo courtesy of the FBI/New York.)

defendants operated a prostitution business where young women and girls—including an underage girl who was 15 years old at the time—were exploited and sold for sex. The defendants first recruited various young women and girls—ages 15 through 19—to work as prostitutes. The defendants then advertised the prostitution business on Craigslist and other Web sites. The defendants drove the women to appointments in Manhattan, Brooklyn, New Jersey, and Staten Island to have sex with clients. The defendants also made the women available for sex to gamblers at weekly, high-stakes poker games that Orefice and his crew ran[68] (Figure 2.6).

Harsher Penalties under RICO

A criminal RICO violation allows for a 21-year prison sentence, or more if the underlying offense has a greater penalty.[69,70]

Because a defendant can be charged both with a RICO violation and with conspiracy to violate RICO, the potential for a 40-year sentence exists.[71] Additionally, a defendant can receive consecutive sentences for a RICO violation and a predicate offense, or participants in an enterprise can be convicted of racketeering conspiracy without being convicted of an underlying predicate offense.[72]

Because RICO prohibits racketeering activity that must be continuous, it also enables a prosecutor to bring charges based on predicate acts that might not otherwise be charged because the statute of limitations has run out or the act was the subject of a prior state or federal prosecution.[73] For example, a trafficker, who is part of an enterprise, but is prosecuted and convicted under the TVPA, and who subsequently commits additional racketeering acts within 10 years, could be indicted on RICO charges that include the TVPA conviction as an underlying predicate offense. The same is true if the trafficker was never prosecuted for the underlying offense, which has consequently become time-barred, as long as RICO charges are brought within five years of the commission of at least one predicate act.[74]

Asset Forfeiture and RICO Violations

An additional lure for prosecutors is the portion of the law that requires asset forfeiture of any interest or property gained as a result of a RICO violation.[75] Congress included the criminal forfeiture provision in RICO to "break the economic power of organized crime as well as to punish and deter offenders."[76] The provision mandates the forfeiture of a defendant's entire interest in the enterprise, possibly including the enterprise itself, regardless of whether some parts are engaged in legitimate business.[77] The law also specifies forfeiture of "property or contractual right[s] of any kind affording a source of influence over" the enterprise.[78] In addition to voting rights or management contracts, courts have construed this subsection to include buildings, vehicles, and other instrumentalities used in the racketeering activity[79] and requires a defendant to forfeit all proceeds acquired from a RICO violation, as determined by the court, even if the defendant no longer possesses the funds or uses other funds to meet the forfeiture order.[80]

The Federal Eleventh Circuit Court of Appeals has ruled:[81] "Since RICO forfeiture is a sanction against the individual defendant rather than a judgment against the property itself, 'it follows the defendant as a part of the penalty and thus it does not require that the government trace it, even though the forfeiture is not due until after conviction.'"[82] This prevents the government from having to align forfeited assets with specific criminal activity and ensures that the forfeiture provision covers the entire enterprise.[83] Consequently, although the 2008 TVPRA amendments added forfeiture clauses to several trafficking crimes,[84] the RICO provision is more expansive because all assets and proceeds derived from the enterprise, legitimate or not, are forfeited.[85] If trafficking is conducted in conjunction with other crimes, a RICO conviction and subsequent forfeiture will cripple the entire economic infrastructure of the organization, while singular prosecutions under the TVPA or other statutes might not.

Given the egregious nature of trafficking crimes, and the fact that perpetrators have engaged in a pattern of trafficking activity that by definition must have been continuous, longer prison sentences and financial repercussions are justified. The consequences of a RICO conviction also deter traffickers because, in addition to lengthier incarcerations, the criminal forfeiture provision can irreparably damage the economic infrastructure of a trafficking enterprise.

Money Laundering of Sex-Trafficking Profits

Money laundering entails taking criminal profits and moving them in a prohibited manner.[86,87] Specifically, criminals or persons acting on their behalf, generate proceeds in the form of money or property as a result of committing a crime designated as a specified unlawful activity (SUA).[88] Criminals then move that money, often with the intent to disguise the nature, location, source, ownership, or control of the funds, which is known as "concealment" money laundering.[89] Alternatively, in "promotion" money laundering, they reinvest the money in

Figure 2.7 Money laundering. Billions of dollars are made each year in the sex and narcotics trade, and traffickers are always looking for creative ways to conceal and launder their profits. (From: http://www.justice.gov/dea/ops/money.shtml (accessed December 11, 2012).)

their criminal activities. Either theory suffices for a money laundering charge[90] (Figure 2.7).

Elements Needed to Pursue Money Laundering Charges

The elements needed to prove a basic charge of money laundering under Title 18, Section 1956, U.S. Code are (a) SUA proceeds, (b) knowledge by the perpetrator that the profits resulted from some type of felony, and (c) a financial transaction intended to conceal the proceeds or to promote an SUA.[91]

International Movement of Money

Provided that subjects move the money to or from the United States to promote an SUA, investigators need not prove that the money is dirty. Even clean money sent internationally to promote an SUA will sufficiently support a charge of money laundering.[92] Thus, the only elements requiring proof include

(a) the movement or attempted movement of funds, (b) to or from the United States, and (c) with the intent to promote an SUA.[93]

Reverse Sting Operation

Under the money laundering sting provision, money launderers can be charged as long as they believe they are moving SUA proceeds, even when the profits actually consist of case funds or other government property.[94] This opportunity regularly presents itself when undercover employees or confidential human sources in covert roles get introduced to money launderers. Similarly, an undercover officer or informant can represent himself as seeking a professional money launderer. In either case, law enforcement can engage in a reverse money laundering transaction with these criminals who then can be charged with money laundering. Often, proceeding in this manner also will reveal the network of individuals and bank accounts involved in a professional money laundering network, thus leading to large-scale asset forfeiture.

The elements necessary for a charge of reverse money laundering include (a) transfer or attempted transfer, (b) of funds believed to be SUA profits, and (c) with intent to conceal the proceeds or promote an SUA.[95] The maximum sentence for violating Section 1956 is 20 years' imprisonment.

The Money Spending Statute

In addition to the money laundering violations in Section 1956, a second, often-overlooked money laundering charge exists in Title 18, Section 1957, U.S. Code. Also known as the money spending statute, a 10-year maximum penalty exists for moving SUA proceeds in an amount greater than $10,000 into or through a financial institution. Two important facts about the money spending statute inure to the benefit of the investigator.

First, unlike the money laundering violations in Section 1956, investigators do not need to prove any intent by subjects to promote an SUA or conceal the proceeds thereof. The simple fact of the transaction is all that is required. For this reason, law enforcement may charge Section 1957 along with Section

1956 whenever ample proof supports both. A judge or jury disagreeing with proof of intent to conceal or promote would have to dismiss or acquit on that count of Section 1956, but still could convict on the corresponding Section 1957 charge. Section 1957 is not a lesser-included offense of Section 1956, so a jury can convict on both charges.[96]

Second, the broad definition of what constitutes a financial institution goes well beyond banks and credit unions. It includes most merchants, such as jewelry stores, car and boat dealerships, casinos, travel agencies, pawnbrokers, and many others, through which a criminal ordinarily would spend criminal proceeds.[97]

The elements required to charge a violation of Section 1957 are (a) transfer of SUA proceeds in a transaction over $10,000, (b) involving a financial institution, and (c) knowing that the proceeds are dirty.[98]

Specific Investigative Suggestions for Making an Asset Trace

Investigative subpoenas

- Some banks may notify the account holder of the existence of a state-issued subpoena unless it contains the correct nondisclosure language from the Bank Secrecy Act.
- Coordinate with the U.S. Attorney and State Attorney to ensure the correct language appears on the subpoena.

Public records and commercial public records databases

- These databases can provide leads to vehicles, boats, and land.
- Cross-references between loan and bank accounts to relatives or associates can help reveal when a suspect hides assets in other names.
- Federal legislation requires reporting of certain financial transactions by designated financial institutions and businesses.

- A Suspicious Activity Report (SAR) is required on all cash transactions in excess of $10,000 when the transaction appears to be suspicious. In practice, banks will often file Suspicious Activity Reports (SARs) on amounts less than $10,000 when there appears to be a suspicious pattern of activity by a person or business.
- A Currency Transaction Report (CTR) is required on all cash transactions over $10,000. Casinos are required to file a "Currency Transaction Report (CTR) for Casinos" on cash transactions over $10,000.
- An Internal Revenue Service (IRS) Form 8300 is required on all cash business transactions over $10,000. For example, if a person pays over $10,000 cash for a new car, the dealership has to file this form.
- The Financial Crimes Enforcement Network (FinCEN) records checks by name on CTRs and SARs; and runs wire transfer reports over $10,000.
- The reports include CTRs for casinos, money transmitters, banks, auto dealerships, and other regulated businesses for cash transactions over $10,000.
- The reports include SARs submitted by regulated businesses (banks) when it appears to the bank/business that a person or business is attempting to structure transactions to avoid the reporting threshold or other suspicious cash transactions.
- Proper training in the use of computer software for analysis of information, such as Microsoft® Excel or other spreadsheet software; Microsoft Visio, i2 Analysts Notebook®, or flowchart software.

When tracing assets of a human trafficking operation, investigators are trying to prove the suspect engaged in trafficking for a profit.

- The operation may have legitimate income, such as from contractual payments for leasing housekeeping workers to hotels.
- The company may have excess, unexplained income from exploitation of the workers (excessive debt repayment,

deduction from pay, excessive housing fees, prostitution, and tip confirmation.)

- The asset trace first attempts to identify all legitimate sources of income (loans are included as a source of income), followed by identifying all known expenditures. For our purposes, expenditure includes money placed in savings or checking accounts, loan or credit card payments, down payments, purchases, and utility payments.
- Identify and total all legitimate forms of income (including loans), compare this amount to the amount of the funds the suspect has applied or expended.
- If, for example, the investigation results in the discovery of $1 million of income, and $1.5 million of expenses, then you could conclude that there are either half a million dollars in unidentified legal income, or half a million dollars in illegal income.
- Suspects will usually try to hide the illegal income by making it appear the money came from legitimate sources.
- They may set up shell or front companies with falsified sales contracts and falsify mortgage or property sales transactions to show a larger profit than was actually achieved.
- Credit bureau information that requires a subpoena or court order should be sought.
- Cooperating witness or informant may provide a known bank used by suspects, cell phone numbers, and names of associates in whose names there may be other accounts.
- Mail covers through the United States Postal Service.[99]

Conspiracy as a Separate Charge

Each act of money laundering must be charged as a separate offense.[100] To charge money laundering as a continuing course of conduct, it must be charged as a conspiracy.[101] Additionally, investigators are not required to prove that conspirators knew the precise SUA that generated the laundered proceeds, but only that two or more criminals intended to launder dirty money.[102]

Venue for a money laundering conspiracy includes any district where the agreement to launder money took place or where any act occurred in furtherance of the conspiracy.[103] However, unlike most conspiracies, no overt act is necessary to charge a conspiracy to commit money laundering.[104]

States That Have Sex-Trafficking Laws

As indicated in Figure 2.8, all of the states do have sex-trafficking statutes, but there are significant variations in their coverage and many are still works in progress. It is very important for states, in the early stages of creating, expanding, or modifying their antitrafficking laws, to look to other states' sex-trafficking laws and to federal laws as potential models. It is important that in the modification and creation of antisex-trafficking law that they are consistent with other state and federal laws in scope and penalty so as to prevent migration of sex trafficking from one state to another. This consistency is necessary to prevent the exploitation of any weaknesses or loopholes in the law by sex traffickers.

States with Sex-Trafficking Laws

Alabama	Illinois	Montana	Rhode Island
Alaska	Indiana	Nebraska	South Carolina
Arizona	Iowa	Nevada	South Dakota
Arkansas	Kansas	New Hampshire	Tennessee
California	Kentucky	New Jersey	Texas
Colorado	Louisiana	New Mexico	Utah
Connecticut	Maine	New York	Vermont
Delaware	Maryland	North Carolina	Virginia
District of Columbia	Massachusetts	North Dakota	Washington
Florida	Michigan	Ohio	West Virginia
Georgia	Minnesota	Oklahoma	Wisconsin
Hawaii	Mississippi	Oregon	Wyoming
Idaho	Missouri	Pennsylvania	

Figure 2.8 States with sex-trafficking laws.

The limited number of state statutes set forth herein are provided primarily as examples of what exists today. There are many other states that have their own state statutes on sex trafficking and the reader is urged to examine them also.

The two broad categories of state statutes provided herein deal primarily with:

- the commercial sexual exploitation of children or prostitution of children; and
- the commercial exploitation of both adults and children along the U.S. border.

State Statutes Dealing with the Commercial Exploitation of Children or Prostitution of Children

Following are some state statutes that deal specifically with the commercial sexual exploitation or prostitution of children. A child or minor is defined as someone under the age of 18; none of the statutes requires the elements of force, fraud, or coercion to prove that trafficking has occurred.[105]

Colorado

Colo. Rev. Stat. § 18-6-403(3) (Sexual exploitation of a child) states, "A person commits sexual exploitation of a child if, for any purpose, he or she knowingly: (a) Causes, induces, entices, or permits a child to engage in, or be used for, any explicit sexual conduct for the making of any sexually exploitative material; or ... (d) Causes, induces, entices, or permits a child to engage in, or be used for, any explicit sexual conduct for the purpose of producing a performance." Colo. Rev. Stat. § 18-6-404 (Procurement of a child for sexual exploitation) provides, "Any person who intentionally gives, transports, provides, or makes available, or who offers to give, transport, provide, or make available, to another person a child for the purpose of sexual exploitation of a child commits procurement of a child for sexual exploitation, which is a Class 3 felony." Colo. Rev. Stat. § 18-7-402(1) (Soliciting for child prostitution) makes it a crime when any person "(a) Solicits another for the purpose of prostitution of a child or by a child; (b) Arranges or offers to arrange a meeting of persons for the purpose of prostitution of a child or by a child; or (c) Directs another to a place knowing such direction is for the purpose of prostitution of a child or by a child." Colo. Rev. Stat. § 18-7-403(1) (Pandering of a child) provides, "Any person who does any of the following for money or other thing of value commits pandering of a child: (a) Inducing a child by menacing or criminal intimidation to commit prostitution; or (b) Knowingly arranging or offering to arrange a situation in which a child may practice prostitution." Colo. Rev. Stat. § 18-7-403.5 (Procurement of a child) provides, "Any person who intentionally gives, transports, provides, or makes available, or who offers to give, transport, provide, or make available, to another person a child for the purpose of prostitution of the child commits procurement of a child, which is a Class 3 felony." Colo. Rev. Stat. § 18-7-404(1) (Keeping a place of child prostitution) states, "Any person who has or exercises control over the use of any place which offers seclusion or shelter for the practice of prostitution and who performs any one or more of the following commits keeping a place of child prostitution if he: (a) Knowingly grants or permits the use of such place for the purpose of prostitution of a child or by a child; or (b) Permits the continued use of such place for the purpose of prostitution of a child or by a child after becoming aware of facts or circumstances from which he should reasonably know that the place is being used for purposes of such prostitution." Colo. Rev. Stat. § 18-7-405 (Pimping of a child) makes it a Class 3 felony when a person "knowingly lives on or is supported or maintained in whole or in part by money or other thing of value earned, received, procured, or realized by a child through prostitution. ..." Colo. Rev. Stat. § 18-7-406(1) (Patronizing a prostituted child) provides, "Any person who performs any of the following with a child not his spouse commits patronizing a prostituted child: (a) Engages in an act which is prostitution of a child or by a child, as defined in § 18-7-401(6) or (7); or (b) Enters or remains in a place of prostitution with intent to engage in an act which is prostitution of a child or by a child."

District of Columbia (D.C.)

D.C. Code § 22-1384(a) (Sex trafficking of children) states, "It is unlawful for an individual or a business knowingly to recruit, entice, harbor, transport, provide, obtain, or maintain by any means a person who will be caused as a result to engage in a commercial sex act knowing or in reckless disregard of the fact that the person has not attained the age of 18 years."

Delaware

Del. Code Ann. Tit. 11, § 787 (Trafficking of persons and involuntary servitude) makes sexual servitude of a minor a crime. Del. Code Ann. Tit. 11, § 787(b)(2) provides, "[a] person is guilty of sexual servitude of a minor when the person knowingly: a. Recruits, entices, harbors, transports, provides or obtains by any means, a minor under 18 years of age, knowing that the minor will engage in commercial sexual activity, a sexually explicit performance, or the production of pornography; or b. Causes a minor to engage in commercial sexual activity or a sexually explicit performance."

Illinois

Ill. Comp. Stat. Ann.§ 720 ILCS 5/11-14(d) (Prostitution) refers to Ill. Comp. Stat. Ann. § 720 ILCS 5/10-9 (Trafficking in persons, involuntary servitude, and related offenses) stating, "Notwithstanding the foregoing, if it is determined, after a reasonable detention for investigative purposes, that a person suspected of or charged with a violation of this Section [Prostitution] is a person under the age of 18, that person shall be immune from prosecution for a prostitution offense under this Section, and shall be subject to the temporary protective custody provisions of Sections 2-5 and 2-6 of the Juvenile Court Act of 1987. Pursuant to the provisions of Section 2-6 of the Juvenile Court Act of 1987, a law enforcement officer who takes a person under 18 years of age into custody under this Section shall immediately report an allegation of a violation of Section 10-9 [Trafficking in persons, involuntary servitude, and related offenses] of this Code to the Illinois Department of Children and Family Services State Central Register, which shall commence an initial investigation into child abuse or child neglect within 24 hours pursuant to Section 7.4 of the Abused and Neglected Child Reporting Act."

Louisiana

A separate statute makes sex trafficking of children a crime without regard to use of force, fraud, or coercion when a minor under 18 is used in a commercial sex act.

La. Stat. Ann. § 14:46.3 (Trafficking of children for sexual purposes) states, "A. It shall be unlawful: (1) For any person to knowingly recruit, harbor, transport, provide, sell, purchase, obtain, or maintain the use of a person under the age of eighteen years for the purpose of engaging in commercial sexual activity. (2) For any person to knowingly benefit from activity prohibited by the provisions of this Section. (3) For any parent, legal guardian, or person having custody of a person under the age of eighteen years to knowingly permit or consent to such minor entering into any activity prohibited by the provisions of this Section. (4) For any person to knowingly facilitate any of the activities prohibited by the provisions of this Section by any means, including but not limited to helping, aiding, abetting, or conspiring, regardless of whether a thing of value has been promised to or received by the person. (5) For any person to knowingly advertise any of the activities prohibited by this Section. B. For purposes of this Section, (1) "commercial sexual activity" means any sexual act performed or conducted when anything of value has been given, promised, or received by any person."

Nebraska

Neb. Rev. Stat. § 28-831(2) (Human trafficking; forced labor or services; prohibited acts; penalties) provides, "No person shall knowingly recruit, entice, harbor, transport, provide, or obtain by any means a minor for the purpose of having such minor engage in commercial sexual activity, sexually explicit performance, or the production of pornography, or to cause or attempt to cause a minor to engage in commercial sexual activity, sexually explicit performance, or the production of pornography. ..." A minor is defined as "a person younger than 18 years of age." Neb. Rev. Stat. § 28-830(7). Commercial sexual activity is "any sex act on account of which anything of value is given, promised to, or received by any person." Neb. Rev. Stat. § 28-830(2).

Washington

Wash. Rev. Code § 9.68A.100 (Commercial sexual abuse of a minor) states, "(1) A person is guilty of commercial sexual abuse of a minor if: (a) He or she pays a fee to a minor or a third person as compensation for a minor having engaged in sexual conduct with him or her; (b) He or she pays or agrees to pay a fee to a minor or a third person pursuant to an understanding that in return therefore such minor will engage in sexual conduct with him or her; or (c) He or she solicits, offers, or requests to engage in sexual conduct with a minor in return for a fee. (2) Commercial sexual abuse of a minor is a class B felony punishable under chapter 9A.20 RCW." Wash. Rev. Code § 9.68A.100(4) defines "sexual conduct" as "sexual intercourse or sexual contact." Wash. Rev. Code § 9.68A.101 (Promoting commercial sexual abuse of a minor) makes it a crime to "knowingly advance[] commercial sexual abuse of a minor or profit[] from a minor engaged in sexual conduct" by "caus[ing] or aid[ing] a person to commit or engage in commercial sexual abuse of a minor, procur[ing] or solicit[ing] customers for commercial sexual abuse of a minor, provid[ing] persons or premises for the purposes of engaging in commercial sexual abuse of a minor, operat[ing] or assist[ing] in the operation of a house or enterprise for the purposes of engaging in commercial sexual abuse of a minor, or engage[ing] in any other conduct designed to institute, aid, cause, assist, or facilitate an act or enterprise of commercial sexual abuse of a minor." The provision specifically limits application to situations in which the offender is "acting other than as a minor receiving compensation for personally rendered sexual conduct or as a person engaged in commercial sexual abuse of a minor." Wash.

Rev. Code § 9.68A.103 (Permitting commercial sexual abuse of a minor) states "[a] person is guilty of permitting commercial sexual abuse of a minor if, having possession or control of premises which he or she knows are being used for the purpose of commercial sexual abuse of a minor, he or she fails without lawful excuse to make reasonable effort to halt or abate such use and to make a reasonable effort to notify law enforcement of such use." Wash. Rev. Code § 13.40.219 (Arrest for prostitution or prostitution loitering) within the Juvenile Justice Act states in part that in any juvenile proceeding "related to an arrest for prostitution or prostitution loitering, there is a presumption that the alleged offender meets the criteria for a certification as a victim of a severe form of trafficking in persons as defined in section 7105 of Title 22 of the United States code [the federal Trafficking Victims Protection Act of 2000 (TVPA), as amended], and that the alleged offender is also a victim of commercial sex abuse of a minor."

Wisconsin

Wis. Stat. § 948.051 (Trafficking of a child) states, "(1) Whoever knowingly recruits, entices, provides, obtains, or harbors, or knowingly attempts to recruit, entice, provide, obtain, or harbor, any child for the purpose of commercial sex acts, as defined in s. 940.302 (1) (a), or sexually explicit performance is guilty of a Class C felony. (2) Whoever benefits in any manner from a violation of sub. (1) is guilty of a Class C felony if the person knows that the benefits come from an act described in sub. (1). (3) Any person who incurs an injury or death as a result of a violation of sub. (1) or (2) may bring a civil action against the person who committed the violation. In addition to actual damages, the court may award punitive damages to the injured party, not to exceed treble the amount of actual damages incurred, and reasonable attorney fees." For the purpose of this law, a child is defined as "a person who has not attained the age of 18 years." Wis. Stat. § 948.01(1). Commercial sex acts are "sexual contact for which anything of value is given to, promised, or received, directly or indirectly by any person." Wis. Stat. § 940.302(1)(a).

States along the U.S. Southern Border with State Statues Dealing with the Commercial Exploitation of Both Adults and Children

The following represent a sample of some of the state statutes dealing with the commercial exploitation of adults and prostitution of children that are along the southern U.S. border. These states are major points-of-entry for sex traffickers from Central and South America.[106]

Arizona

In 2005, SB 1372 established the following acts as felonies: sex trafficking of a minor and attempted sex trafficking of a minor, which constitute first degree felonies (from 25 years up to life in prison); sex trafficking and human trafficking for forced labor or services, which constitutes class 2 felonies (five years in prison); and unlawfully obtaining labor or services, which are level 4 felonies (two and a half years in prison).[107] Also, this bill requires the Court to mandate restitution.[108] In 2009, an amendment to SB 1281 was enacted, broadening the definition of human trafficking to include any "sexually explicit performance" resulting from deception, force, or coercion. Knowledge that the victim will engage in prostitution or sexually explicit acts also is classified as an offense under this bill. Furthermore, the bill expands the definition of coercion, and adds a series of activities to the definition of forced labor, such as withholding a person's documents, or intimidating with financial harm or threats.[109]

California

In 2006, AB 22 took effect. This law establishes trafficking in California as a felony crime punishable by a maximum of eight years in state prison. It also makes victim restitution mandatory, enables victims to bring civil action against traffickers, and establishes measures to ensure confidentiality and protect information. In addition, this law directs the Attorney General to give priority to human trafficking over other crimes.[110] In 2006, California also established SB 1569, which enables temporary immediate assistance to victims while they wait to be federally certified as victims of human trafficking (which allows them to receive federal benefits, and which can take up to two years). California was the first state in the country to pass such a law.[111] AB 1278 came into effect in 2008, and makes void any labor contract provision whereby wages are withdrawn to compensate for the movement of a prospective employee into the United States. Also in the same year, California enacted AB 2810 that establishes a series of indicators to identify cases of human trafficking, and requires law enforcement agencies to determine whether victims of other crimes also could be victims of human trafficking at the same time.[112] In 2009, California enacted AB 17 that mandates, among other stipulations, that money or fines from cases of trafficking of minors for sexual purposes be placed in the Victim–Witness Assistance Fund.[113]

New Mexico

In 2008, New Mexico passed SB 71 that makes human trafficking a felony of the third degree (punishable by three years in prison), a second degree felony (punishable by up to nine years in prison), in cases when trafficking victims are under the age of 16, and a first degree felony (punishable by up to 18 years in prison) if the victim is under 13 years of age. This bill also criminalizes knowingly benefiting from human trafficking; establishes that a victim may not be charged as an accessory to the crime of trafficking in persons; mandates victim restitution; and qualifies victims to receive aid and services from the state regardless of their migratory status.[114]

Texas

In 2003, Texas enacted HB 2096, which defines human trafficking and establishes it as a second degree felony (punishable by 2 to 20 years in prison) with the option of becoming a first degree felony (punishable by 5 to 99 years in prison) if the victim is younger than 14 years old, and/or if the trafficked person dies as a result of the trafficking act. This law also directs local enforcement agencies to address and investigate potential cases of human trafficking. In 2007, SB 1288, SB 1287, and HB 1121 were passed by the Texas Legislature with the intent of strengthening the fight against human trafficking and facilitating state-level prosecution. Specifically, SB 1288 requires hotel/motel and similar lodging establishments to display information concerning human trafficking, such as an information and victim assistance toll-free telephone number. SB 1287 requires that holders of licenses to sell alcoholic beverages also post information about the crime of human trafficking along with the national human trafficking hotline number.[115] Among other stipulations, HB 1121 amends the definitions of "forced labor or services" and "traffic" in Texas's Penal Code.[116] In 2009 HB 533 took effect, enabling victims of human trafficking to bring civil action against the perpetrator. The bill also allows victims to sue for damages, court costs, and attorney services.[117] In 2009, Governor Rick Perry signed HB 4009, which establishes the development of a taskforce to enact policies and measures, including issuing reports on the number of human trafficking victims and convictions, transit routes used by traffickers to move their victims, and demand patterns for human trafficking in Texas.[118]

Glossary

Money laundering: This entails taking criminal profits and moving them in a prohibited manner; specifically, criminals or persons acting on their behalf generate proceeds in the form of money or property as a result of committing a crime designated as a specified unlawful activity (SUA).

Racketeer Influenced and Corrupt Organizations Act (RICO): This is the federal law that allows prosecutors to charge a perpetrator with a separate offense if he or she engages in a pattern of racketeering activity consisting of at least two specified illegal acts within a particular time period.

Reverse sting operation: Under the money laundering sting provision, money launderers can be charged as long as they believe they are moving SUA proceeds, even when the profits actually consist of case funds or other government property. Thus, the elements of a charge of reverse money laundering include (a) transfer or attempt to transfer (b) funds believed to be SUA profits, and (c) with intent to conceal the proceeds or promote an SUA.

T visa: This is a visa for aliens who are victims of severe forms of trafficking in persons (TIP).

The Mann Act: Also known as the "White Slave Traffic Act," is one of the oldest U.S. laws relating to sex trafficking prohibitions.

Tier 1 countries: Countries deemed by the U.S. State Department as having fully complied with minimum standards for eliminating trafficking.

Tier 2 countries: Countries whose governments the U.S. State Department views as not fully complying with the minimum standards for eliminating trafficking, but which are seen as making significant efforts to bring themselves into compliance.

Tier 3 countries: Countries whose governments the U.S. State Department deems as not fully complying with those standards for the elimination of trafficking and not making significant efforts to do so.

Trafficking Victims Protection Act 2000: The federal law that made human trafficking a federal crime and established resources to combat human trafficking and issues measures for the protection of victims thus squarely targeting human trafficking for federal criminal prosecution.

Trafficking Victims Protection Reauthorization Act 2003: A law passed by Congress in order to meet the increasing challenges posed by the deficiencies of the TVPA 2000. It included new legal resources against trafficking, such as allowing victims to bring civil law suits against traffickers.

Trafficking in Victims Protection Reauthorization Act 2005: This law gives jurisdiction to U.S. courts over government employees who become involved in human trafficking abroad. The amendment also provides new antitrafficking measures, such as developing grant programs directed toward aiding state and local enforcement of antitrafficking activities and expanding assistance programs to aid victims who are U.S. citizens or resident aliens.

U visa: The Violence Against Women Act of 2000 of TVPA created the U—nonimmigrant status, often called the U visa for victims of physical or mental abuse.

U.S. Code—Section 2251: The federal statute that deals with the sexual exploitation of children.

U.S. Code—Section 2422: The federal statute that deals with coercion and enticement.

U.S. Code—Section 2423: The federal statute that deals with transportation of minors to engage in criminal sexual activity.

William Wilberforce Trafficking Victims Protection Reauthorization Act of 2008: This law authorizes the appropriations for 2008 through 2011 for the TVPA and establishes a system to monitor and evaluate all assistance under the act. The act requires the establishment of an integrated database to be used by U.S. government departments and agencies to collect and analyze data on trafficking in persons.

Review Questions

1. What was the Mann Act also known as when it was passed in 1910?
2. What does the Mann Act prohibit?
3. What did the Travel Act do?
4. How is the Travel Act similar to and also dissimilar to the Mann Act?
5. What kind of public service benefits is a T applicant entitled to?
6. What must an immigrant do to qualify for U status?

7. How can a U applicant establish that he or she has cooperated with law enforcement?
8. What was the purpose of passing the Trafficking Victims Protection Act (TVPA) 2000?
9. What is the Tier System?
10. Why did the Congress pass the Trafficking Victims Protection Reauthorization Act (TVPRA) 2003?
11. Why did the Congress pass the Trafficking Victims Protection Reauthorization Act (TVPRA) 2005?
12. What was established as a result of the passage of the William Wilberforce Trafficking Victims Protection Reauthorization Act of 2008?
13. Who was William Wilberforce?
14. Under the provisions of U.S. Code—Section 2422: Coercion and Enticement, there are certain provisions dealing with the use of the mail or any other facility of interstate or foreign commerce while within the special maritime and jurisdiction of the United States. What are these provisions?
15. What are the minimum and maximum penalties under U.S. Code—Section 2423: Transportation of Minors, for knowingly transporting someone with the intent to engage in sexual activity who has not yet attained the age of 18?
16. Why did Congress enact the Racketeer Influenced and Corrupt Organizations Act (RICO)?
17. Why did Congress include an asset forfeiture provision in the RICO act?
18. What is money laundering?

Endnotes

1. Pamela Chen & Monica Ryan, "Federal Prosecution of Human Traffickers," in *Lawyer's Manual on Human Trafficking: Pursuing Justice for Victims*, eds. Jill Laurie Goodman and Dorchen A. Leidholdt (Supreme Court of the State of New York, Appellate Division, First Department, New York State Judicial Committee on Women in the Courts, 2011), 275–277.

2. *See* 18 U.S.C. §§ 2421 and 2423.
3. 18 U.S.C. § 2421.
4. 18 U.S.C. § 2423.
5. 18 U.S.C. § 2424.
6. 18 U.S.C. § 2424(a).
7. The Travel Act criminalizes travel for the purpose of engaging in other criminal activity, such as acts of violence, gambling, and extortion. *See* 18 U.S.C. § 1952. In addition, as later discussed, the Travel Act also criminalizes the use of certain interstate facilities to commit crimes.
8. 18 U.S.C. § 1952(a)(3) and (b).
9. *United States v. Mukovsky*, 863 F.2d 1319, 1327 (7th Cir. 1988); see *United States v. Bates,* 840 F.2d 858, 863 (11th Cir. 1988) (same*); United States v. Davis*, 666 F.2d 195, 202 n. 10 (5th Cir. Unit B 1982) (same); *United States v. Corbin*, 662 F.2d 1066, 1073 (4th Cir. 1981) (same); *United States v. Cozzetti*, 441 F.2d 344, 348 (9th Cir. 1971) (same). However, the "business enterprise" need not be sophisticated nor prolific. See, e.g., *United States v. Cozzetti*, 441 F.2d at 347–48.
10. *See* 18 U.S.C. § 1952(a).
11. Alison Siskin & Liana Sun Wyler, "Trafficking in Persons: U.S. Policy and Issues for Congress," *CRS Report for Congress* (December 23, 2010), 24–28. Online at: http:// www.fas.org /sgp/ crs/misc/RL34317.pdf/ (accessed June 9, 2010).
12. Section 107 of Division A of P.L. 106-386. "T" refers to the letter denoting the subsection of the Immigration and Nationality Act (INA) that provides the authority for the alien's admission into the United States (i.e., INA §101(a)(15)(T)). Although T nonimmigrant status is often referred to as the T visa, it is not technically a visa if it is given to aliens present in the United States because status is conferred by the Department of Homeland Security (DHS), which does not have the authority to issue visas. Only the Department of State (DOS), through consular offices, may issue visas. Thus, only aliens present outside of the United States can receive T visas, while aliens present in the United States receive T status. For more information on nonimmigrant visa issuance, see CRS Report RL31381, *U.S. Immigration Policy on Temporary Admissions*, by Chad C. Haddal & Ruth Ellen Wasem.
13. INA §212(d)(13).
14. INA §212(a)(2)(D).

15. "Parole" is a term in immigration law, which means that the alien has been granted temporary permission to be in the United States. Parole does not constitute formal admission to the United States and parolees are required to leave when the parole expires or, if eligible, to be admitted in a lawful status.

16. In some cases, immediate family members of trafficking victims may receive a T visa to join the victim in the United States. This may be necessary if the traffickers are threatening the victim's family.

17. From the perspective of trafficking victims' advocates, work authorization is viewed as an important tool in helping the victims become self-sufficient and retake control of their lives.

18. The four-year period of validity for T-visas was codified by The Violence Against Women and Department of Justice Reauthorization Act of 2006 (P.L. 109-162, §821). Prior to P.L. 109-162, the validity period was three years and was specified, not by statute, but by regulation (8 *C.F.R.* 214.11).

19. Bona fide application means an application for T status that, after initial review, has been determined that the application is complete, there is no evidence of fraud, and which presents prima facie evidence of eligibility for T status including admissibility.

20. Refugees are generally eligible for federal, state, and local public benefits. In addition, refugees are eligible for Food Stamps and Supplemental Security Income (SSI) for seven years after entry, and for Medicaid and Temporary Assistance for Needy Families for seven years after entrance and then at state option. From CRS Report RL33809, *Noncitizen Eligibility for Federal Public Assistance: Policy Overview and Trends,* by Ruth Ellen Wasem.

21. Victims also may be repatriated to their home country, if they desire, with assistance from the Department of State, the government of their country of origin, or nongovernmental organizations. The United States Conference of Catholic Bishops et al., *A Guide for Legal Advocates Providing Services to Victims of Human Trafficking,* prepared with a grant from the Department of Health and Human Services, Office of Refugee Resettlement, November 2004, p. Appendix 1–3.

22. 28 C.F.R. § 1100.3–§ 1100.33.

23. 28 C.F.R. Part 1000.35. The mechanisms for continued presence may include parole, voluntary departure, stay of final removal orders, or any other authorized form of continued presence in the United States, including adjustment to an applicable

nonimmigrant status. Some of these authorities were transferred to the Secretary of DHS in the Homeland Security Act of 2002 (P.L. 107-296). Others remain with or are shared by the Attorney General.

24. Viet D. Dinh, Department of Justice. Testimony before the Senate Subcommittee on Near Eastern and South Asian Affairs concerning Monitoring and Combating Trafficking in Persons: How Are We Doing? March 7, 2002.

25. In FY2008, aliens from 31 countries were granted continued presence due to human trafficking. Most victims were from Mexico, the Philippines, and South Korea. In addition, Miami, Newark, Atlanta, San Francisco, and Los Angeles were the cities with the most requests for continued presence. Department of Justice, Attorney General's Annual Report to Congress on U.S. Government Activities to Combat Trafficking in Persons: Fiscal Year 2008, June 2009, p. 33.

26. Siskin & Wyler, "Trafficking in Persons," p. 29.

27. INA 101(a)(15)(U).

28. Certain criminal activity refers to one or more of the following or any similar activity in violation of federal or state criminal law: rape, torture, trafficking, incest, domestic violence, sexual assault, abusive sexual contact, prostitution, sexual exploitation, female genital mutilation, being held hostage, peonage, involuntary servitude, slave trade, kidnapping, abduction, unlawful criminal restraint, false imprisonment, blackmail, extortion, manslaughter/murder, felonious assault, witness tampering, obstruction of justice, perjury, or attempt, conspiracy, or solicitation to commit any of the above-mentioned crimes.

29. INA §214(o)(2). Although the interim final regulations on U status were released in September 2007, prior to that aliens who met the criteria for U status were given immigration benefits similar to U status. In 2005, for example, 287 aliens were given "quasi-U" status. (Unpublished data from DHS.)

30. Department of Homeland Security, "Adjustment of Status to Lawful Permanent Resident for Aliens in T or U Nonimmigrant Status," 73 *Federal Register* 75540-75564, December 12, 2008.

31. U.S. Citizenship and Immigration Services, "Questions and Answers, USCIS Reaches Milestone: 10,000 U Visas Approved in Fiscal Year 2010," press release, July 15, 2010. Online at: http://www.uscis.gov/portal/site/uscis/menuitem.5af9bb95919f3 5e66f614176543f6d1a/?vgnextoid=749a58a734cd9210Vgn VCM1000000 82ca60aRCRD&vgnextchannel=68439c7755cb90 10VgnVCM10000045f3d6a1RCRD.

32. Kathleen Slocum, "Immigration Remedies for Victims of Human Trafficking," in *Lawyer's Manual on Human Trafficking*, eds. Jill Laurie Goodman & Dorchen A. Leidholdt, (Supreme Court of the State of New York, Appellate Division, First Department, New York State Judicial Committee on Women in the Courts, 2011), p. 216. Online at: http://www.nycourts.gov/ip/womeninthecourts/LMHT.pdf (accessed June 9, 2012).

33. INA § 101(a)(15)(U)(i)(III).

34. This must be submitted on USCIS Form I-918 Supplement B. Online at: http://www.uscis.gov.

35. 8 CFR § 214.14.(a)(2).

36. Siskin & Wyler, "Trafficking in Persons," 52–53.

37. Tiers: Placement, Guide, and Penalties for Tier 3 Countries, Trafficking in Persons Report 2011. Online at: http://www.state.gov/j/tip/rls/tiprpt/2011/164222.htm (accessed June 25, 2012).

38. Siskin & Wyler, "Trafficking in Persons," 12–17.

39. Maria Tena, "Modern-Day Slavery in U.S.–Mexican Territory: Human Trafficking at the Border," *Border Brief* (September 30, 2010), p. 4. Online at: http://catcher.sandiego.edu/items/peacestudies/Border_Brief_FINAL_BW_oct4_10.pdf (accessed January 16, 2012).

40. Siskin & Wyler, "Trafficking in Persons," 55.

41. Tena, "Modern-Day Slavery in U.S.–Mexican Territory," p. 4.

42. Siskin & Wyler, "Trafficking in Persons," 55.

43. William Wilberforce was a British politician, philanthropist, and leader of the movement to abolish the trans-Atlantic slave trade in the late 1790s. He also is credited with launching 69 organizations that worked for the betterment of society.

44. Siskin & Wyler, "Trafficking in Persons," 56–58.

45. Northeastern University, *Human Trafficking Data Collection and Reporting Project* (Online Resource Center). Online at: http://www.humantrafficking.neu.edu/ (accessed January 16, 2013).

46. Nonimmigrant visas are commonly referred to by the letter and numeral that denotes their subsection in the Immigration and Nationality Act (INA) §101(a)(15).

47. Siskin & Wyler, "Trafficking in Persons," 57–58.

48. Previously, T visa holders and their derivatives were eligible for public benefits because of a provision in Victims of Trafficking and Violence Protection Act of 2000 (P.L. 106-386) stating for the purpose of benefits that T visa holders are eligible to receive certain public benefits to the same extent as refugees. TVPRA 2008 amends the Personal Responsibility and Work

Opportunity Act (P.L. 104-193, PWORA also known as Welfare Reform) to make T visa holders and their derivatives "qualified aliens" (i.e., eligible for public benefits under PWORA).

49. Unaccompanied minors are aliens, who are in the United States without a parent or guardian.

50. Organized Crime Control Act of 1970, Pub. L. No. 91-452, 84 Stat. 922, 923.

51. Kendal Nichole Smith, "Human Trafficking and RICO: A New Prosecuting Hammer in the War on Modern Day Slavery," *George Mason Law Review* 18 (3) (2011), 776–777.

52. G. Robert Blakey & Brian Gettings, "Racketeer Influenced and Corrupt Organizations (RICO): Basic Concepts—Criminal and Civil Remedies," *Temple Law Quarterly* 53 (1980), 1009, 1014.

53. Ibid., 1013.

54. President's Commission on Law Enforcement & Admin. of Justice, The Challenge of Crime in a Free Society 208 (1967) ("Law enforcement is not the only weapon that governments have to control organized crime. Regulatory activity can have a great effect. ... Government at various levels has not explored the regulatory devices available to thwart the activities of criminal groups, especially in the area of infiltration of legitimate business.").

55. Ibid.

56. Blakey & Gettings, "Racketeer Influenced and Corrupt Organizations (RICO)," 154.

57. 115 *Congressional Record* 769 (1969) (statement of Sen. John McClellan).

58. Ibid., 39,906 (statement of Sen. John McClellan).

59. Ibid.

60. Ibid.

61. Ibid.

62. Ibid., 39,906–07.

63. 115 *Congressional Record* 39,907 (1969) (statement of Sen. John McClellan).

64. Ibid., 6,925, 9,512.

65. 116 *Congressional Record* 37,264 (1970).

66. *See* 153-55 and accompanying text.

67. *See* Part IV.B.

68. U.S. Attorney's Office, Southern District of New York, "Manhattan U.S. Attorney Charges 14 Gambino Crime Family Associates With Racketeering, Murder, Sex Trafficking and Other Crimes," *FBI Press Release*, New York Field Office, April 20, 2010. Online at: http://www.fbi.gov/newyork/press-releases/2010/nyfo042010.htm (accessed August 14, 2012),

69. Kendal Nicole Smith, "Human Trafficking and RICO: A New Prosecutorial Hammer in the War on Modern Day Slavery," *George Mason Law Review* 18 (3) (2011), 785–786.
70. *See* 18 U.S.C. § 1963(a) (2006). The Organized Crime and Racketeering Section will approve a RICO count seeking a sentence beyond 20 years if: (1) the count charges against the defendant a racketeering act for which the penalty includes life imprisonment; (2) the racketeering act charges the necessary facts to trigger the life imprisonment penalty, tracking that portion of the statute that sets forth the factors supporting a penalty of life imprisonment; and (3) the racketeering act cites the appropriate statute or statutes the racketeering act violates. Organized Crime and Racketeering Section, U.S. Dept. of Justice, Criminal RICO: 18 U.S.C. §§ 1961–1968, A Manual for Federal Prosecutors 159 (ed. Frank J. Marine, 5th rev. ed., 2009) [hereinafter *RICO Prosecutor's Manual*]. Online at: http://www.justice.gov/usao/eousa/foia_reading_room/usam/title9/rico.pdf
71. *RICO Prosecutor's Manual*, 260.
72. Ibid. at 177; *see infra* Part V.B.
73. *See, e.g.*, *United States v. Wong*, 40 F.3d 1347, 1367 (2d Cir. 1994). ("Because the limitations period is measured from the point at which the crime is complete, a defendant may be liable under substantive RICO for predicate acts the separate prosecution of which would be barred by the applicable statute of limitations." (citations omitted)); *United States v. Castellano,* 610 F. Supp. 1359, 1413-27 (S.D.N.Y. 1985) (upholding 36 racketeering acts that were either the subject of prior state or federal prosecutions or the subject of a favorable federal ruling).
74. While sex-trafficking and child offenses have no statute of limitations, charges for other trafficking crimes must be brought within 10 years. *See* Charles Doyle, Cong. Research Serv., RL31253 Statutes of Limitations in Federal Criminal Cases: An Overview, app. 19–22 (2007).
75. 18 U.S.C. § 1963(a); *see* Gerard E. Lynch, "RICO: The Crime of Being a Criminal, Parts III & IV, 87," *Columbia Law Review* (1987): 920, 924. ("In some cases, the impetus for the use of RICO in criminal enterprise cases appears to be, as in the white collar and labor cases, its extreme, mandatory and procedurally simple financial penalties.")
76. Blakey & Gettings, "Racketeer Influenced and Corrupt Organizations (RICO)," 1036.

77. *See,* e.g., *United States v. Segal,* 495 F.3d 826, 838 (7th Cir. 2007) (finding that a defendant who owned the entire enterprise was properly required to forfeit the full enterprise, despite the jury's finding that only 60 percent of his interests were "tainted" by racketeering activity); *United States v. Najjar,* 300 F.3d 466, 485-86 (4th Cir. 2002) (upholding order subjecting all of corporation's assets to forfeiture); *United States v. Busher,* 817 F.2d 1409, 1413 (9th Cir. 1987) ("[F]orfeiture is not limited to those assets of a RICO enterprise that are tainted by use in connection with racketeering activity, but rather extends to the convicted person's entire interest in the enterprise."); *see also RICO Prosecutor's Manual,* 189–92.

78. 18 U.S.C. § 1963(a)(2)(D).

79. *See,* e.g., *United States v. West,* 877 F.2d 281, 292 (4th Cir. 1989) (holding that two houses used to store and sell drugs satisfies the requirements of subsection D); *United States v. Zielie,* 734 F.2d 1447, 1458-59 (11th Cir. 1984) (same); *United States v. Rudaj,* No. 04 CR. 1110(DLC), 2006 WL 1876664, at *3-4 (S.D.N.Y. July 5, 2006) (holding that the forfeiture of property used as a meeting place to conduct racketeering activity is proper under subsection D).

80. 18 U.S.C. § 1963(a)(3).

81. 773 F.2d 798 (7th Cir. 1985).

82. Ibid. at 801 (quoting *United States v. Conner,* 752 F.2d 566, 576 (11th Cir. 1985)).

83. *See RICO Prosecutor's Manual,* 196.

84. William Wilberforce Trafficking Victims Protection Reauthorization Act of 2008, Pub. L. No. 110-457, tits. I-III, 122 Stat. 5044, 5045-87 (codified in scattered sections of 6, 8, 18, 22, 28, and 42 U.S.C.); see Part II.B.3.

85. *See RICO Prosecutor's Manual,* 196.

86. Douglas Leff, "Money Laundering and Asset Forfeiture," *FBI Law Enforcement Bulletin* (April 2012): 23–32. (This discussion of money laundering was adapted from this source.)

87. DOJ's Asset Forfeiture and Money Laundering Section (AFMLS) has produced a flip chart, an excellent tool to assist investigators in applying the elements of a money laundering case. Also known as the Money Laundering Flipper, law enforcement officers can obtain it free of charge by calling AFMLS at 202-514-1263; Douglas Leff, "Money Laundering and Asset Forfeiture.

88. Many crimes fall within the definition of an SUA. The entire catalog of these violations is located at 18 U.S.C. §1956(c)(7), which also incorporates other criminal statutes.
89. The movement can be as simple as the handing of money from one party to another. *See* 18 U.S.C §1956(c)(3) for the full definition of "financial transaction," which encompasses most forms of transfer, including physical.
90. 18 U.S.C. §1956(a)(1). Concealment and promotion are the two most common money laundering theories and, therefore, serve as the focus of the article. The less frequently prosecuted theories involve the movement of SUA proceeds to either (a) evade taxes, 18 U.S.C. §1956(a)(1)(A)(ii), or (b) avoid currency reporting requirements, 18 U.S.C. §1956(a)(1)(B)(ii).
91. 18 U.S.C. §1956(a)(1).
92. 18 U.S.C. §1956(a)(2)(A).
93. There also is a provision for charging the international movement of money for concealment, but to prevail on that theory the funds must be SUA proceeds. 18 U.S.C. § 1956(a)(2)(B)(i). Also, moving SUA proceeds to avoid currency reporting requirements may be charged. 18 U.S.C. § 1956(a)(3)(C).
94. Subject to availability, the DOJ Asset Forfeiture Fund may be used to finance reverse money laundering transactions. *See* 28 U.S.C. § 524(c). The Treasury Forfeiture Fund has similar authority. *See* 31 U.S.C. § 9703(a)(2)(B)(i). Investigators should contact their headquarters components to apply for forfeiture funds when needed to carry out a money laundering sting. The author would like to acknowledge DOJ Asset Forfeiture Management Staff Director Candace Olds, Deputy Director Robert Marca, AFMLS Chief Jennifer Shasky, and Business Manager Tim Virtue for their contributions to many FBI money laundering stings over the years, none of which would have been possible without them.
95. 18 U.S.C. § 1956(a)(3). Also, moving SUA proceeds to avoid currency reporting requirements may be charged. 18 U.S.C. §1956(a)(3)(C).
96. *United States v. Huber,* 2002 WL 257851 (D.N.D. 2002); *United States v. Caruso,* 948 F.Supp. 382, 390-91 (D.N.J. 1996).
97. 31 U.S.C. § 5312(a)(2).
98. 18 U.S.C. § 1957(a).
99. *Advanced Investigative Techniques of Human Trafficking Offenses,* Instructors Guide, Unit 2, Lesson 1, Florida Criminal Justice Advanced Course 1166, (Tallahassee, FL: Criminal Justice

Standards and Training Commission, Florida Department of Law Enforcement, 2007), pp. 22–26. (This discussion was adapted from this source.)

100. *United States v. Prescott,* 42 F.3d 1165 (8th Cir. 1994).

101. *United States v. Robertson,* 67 Fed. Appx. 257, 269 (6th Cir. 2003).

102. *United States v. Threadgill*, 172 F.3d 357, 367 (5th Cir. 1999), *cert. denied,* 528 U.S. 871 (1999).

103. *United States v. Angotti*, 105 F.3d 539 (9th Cir. 1997).

104. *United States v. Whitfield*, 543 U.S. 209 (2005), *rehearing denied,* 544 U.S. 913 (2005).

105. Shared Hope International. 2011. *State Report Cards on the Legal Framework of Protection for the Nation's Children.* The Protected Innocence Challenge. Online at: http://www.incasa. org/PDF/2011/HT_Indiana_Full_1Report.pdf (accessed June 8, 2012, p. 27).

106. Tena, "Modern-Day Slavery in U.S.–Mexican Territory."

107. Phillips and Associates Law Firm. *Arizona Felony and Misdemeanor Charges.* Online at: http://www.phillipslaw.com/ arizona-felony-and-misdemeanor-defense-attorneys

108. U.S. Policy Advocacy to Combat Trafficking, Center for Women Policy Studies, 2010.

109. Ibid.

110. California Alliance to Combat Trafficking and Slavery Task Force. (October 2007). *Human Trafficking in California.* Final Report of the California Alliance to Combat Trafficking and Slavery Task Force. Online at: http://www.ohs.ca.gov/pdf/H uman_Traffic king_in_CA-Final_Report-2007.pdf.

111. Ibid.

112. U.S. Policy Advocacy to Combat Trafficking (U.S. PACT), State Laws/Map of the United States, Center for Women Policy Studies, 2010. Online at: http://www.centerwomenpolicy.org/ programs/trafficking/map/

113. Ibid.

114. Ibid.

115. Ibid.

116. Ibid.

117. Ibid.

118. Polaris Project, *What is Human Trafficking.* Online at: http:// www.actioncenter.polarisproject.org (accessed January 16, 2013).

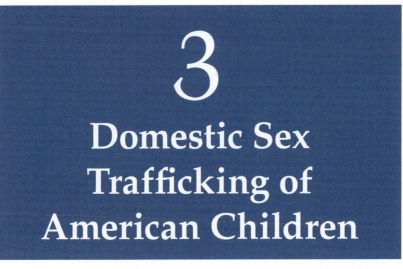

3

Domestic Sex Trafficking of American Children

Children of the Night president Dr. Lois Lee speaks with 17-year-old "Jane" in the cafeteria at Children of the Night in Los Angeles. "Jane" was rescued off the streets of Portland, Oregon, two years ago when she was just 15, at which time she was working as a prostitute. "This place has helped me so much. I was so different when I first got here," "Jane" said. She attends college classes now and wants to be a social worker where she can help people when she graduates. "I just want to help people like Lois has helped me." (Photo courtesy of Garrett Cheen/Special to *The Washington Times*.)

Chapter Objectives

1. Understand the problem of American children being sex trafficked in the United States.
2. Discuss the precipitating factors that contribute to children becoming involved in prostitution.
3. Understand the psychological and emotional difficulties sex-trafficking victims suffer.
4. Discuss why the Stockholm syndrome sometimes occurs and how it can inhibit victim cooperation.
5. Identify the major symptoms of sex-trafficking victims who are suffering from posttraumatic stress disorder (PTSD).
6. Describe the most common physical effects of sex trafficking on victims.
7. Discuss the methods of recruitment, manipulation techniques, and the grooming process of sex-trafficking victims.
8. Understand the relationship between sex trafficking, pornography, drugs, and gangs.
9. Discuss the importance of shelters and services for domestically trafficked minors.

Introduction

The sexual exploitation of children through prostitution is an insidious form of commercialized violence against our most vulnerable citizens, and presents substantial challenges to the criminal justice system, which is charged with the responsibility of holding offenders accountable while also preventing future exploitation.[1]

In this chapter, we will first focus on the sexual exploitation of American children (mostly girls under the age of 18) because, in most cases, they make up the bulk of individual victims who are sexually exploited. This is not to suggest they make up the bulk of the prostitutes in the United States, but they are the ones who are most often sexually exploited and trafficked.

We also will examine the factors in their lives that make these young girls so vulnerable to traffickers, as well as the lifelong consequences to their physical, psychological, and social development. We also will discuss the psychological disorder known as the Stockholm syndrome (trauma bonding), and how it can create problems for rescuers, who often need the cooperation of the victim to move forward with a fully effective prosecution. Lastly, we will discuss the relationship between drug use and prostitution, between gangs and the sex-trafficking trade of minors, and the need for shelters and services for domestically trafficked minors.

Nature and Scope of the Problem

In trying to understand the scope of the problem of youth who engage in prostitution, it is important to recognize that the often hidden population of homeless and runaway youth—from which many prostituted children are drawn—is difficult to study.[2] Data from service providers may reflect only a small segment of homeless youth, and the small sample sizes of some studies cannot be generalized to a larger population.[3] In addition, no reliable estimates of the number of children engaging in prostitution in the United States exist because no one has defined the concept in measurable terms.[4] Nevertheless, while caution regarding some statistics may be warranted, they provide an indication of the extent of the problem which is helpful to having a basic understanding of the current situation.

The Demographics of Sexually Exploited Children

According to one U.S. Department of Health and Human Services report, up to 300,000 prostituted children may be living on the streets in the United States.[5] Many are only 11 or 12 years old, and some are as young as 9.[6] The average age at which they enter prostitution is reported as 14,[7] and the median age of involved youth is 15.5 years.[8] These children come from inner cities, suburbs, and small towns,[9] and there appears to be an increase in recruitment of middle class youth from schools and shopping malls in the suburbs.[10]

The vast majority of youth involved in prostitution are girls,[11] although, some service providers, which give food, shelter, etc., report an increase in the number of boys. Some attribute this reported increase to a greater willingness by the boys to disclose their sexual activities.[12] Larger cities are more likely to have a higher proportion of boys involved in prostitution; however, even service providers in smaller cities report seeing an increase in prostitution activity by boys. These observations by service providers may suggest a migration to smaller urban areas, an increase in visibility due to heightened awareness, or the greater willingness of boys to use the services of these various service providers.[13]

Precipitating Factors Affecting Why Children Become Involved in Prostitution

Children may encounter numerous difficulties in their lives that make them more vulnerable to sexual exploitation through prostitution. Homelessness, poverty, and intolerance of their sexual orientation may all affect children who either are or have been prostituted.[14] General psychological and emotional problems,[15] housing instability,[16] substance abuse, educational and vocational failure,[17] and major problems at home[18] also have been cited as common precipitating factors in the lives of prostituted children.

Various Factors That Leave Youth Vulnerable to Traffickers

The primary factor of vulnerability is the child's age. Preteen or adolescent girls are more susceptible to the calculated advances, deception, and manipulation tactics used by trafficker/pimps—

and no youth is exempt from falling prey to these tactics, which will be discussed in greater detail later in this chapter.

Any child can become a trafficking victim, and domestically trafficked minors are diverse in terms of ethnicity, age, socioeconomic status, sexual orientation, and gender. However, traffickers are particularly able to take advantage of certain life characteristics that leave holes in a child's social and emotional safety net. Youth who come from dysfunctional families in which there is abuse or trauma are particularly vulnerable to a trafficker's/pimp's method of recruitment and control.[19]

Running Away from Home

According to statistics from the National Runaway Switchboard, between 1.6 and 2.8 million children run away from home each year. Traffickers, as well as buyers, strategically prey upon runaway children because of their mental, physical, and financial vulnerability (inability to secure jobs due to their transient nature and age). Traffickers often find their best opportunities to locate unsupervised children at local shopping malls, and, even though many children who do run away from home hitchhike to another location, some also use buses to relocate. Thus, bus stops are places that traffickers target for opportunities to entrap children. It has been determined that one in three runaway children will be approached by traffickers/pimps within 48 hours of being on the street with the purpose of sexually exploiting them.[20]

These children are much more likely to have histories of drug and alcohol abuse or to have contact with the juvenile justice system.[21] Many children, who are prostituted, are socially isolated and unsuccessful in school and with peers, and this often leads them to drop out of school.[22] They also experience more frequent school expulsions and discipline, resulting in lower levels of completed education.[23] Associated problems include parental harassment and fighting,[24] as well as parental drug and alcohol abuse.[25] This dysfunctional family life, combined with an unstructured and unsupervised childhood,[26] characterizes many of the lives of prostituted children and provides greater incentive for them to leave home.

Survival Sex

Among runaway and homeless youth, up to one third report engaging in street prostitution as a form of survival sex in order to achieve the basic necessities of life, such as food, shelter, or money.[27] Among prostitution-involved youth, up to 77% report running away from home at least once.[28] Surprisingly, one study showed that more than half of the interviewed, prostitution-involved youth were living with their parents or families at the time of their most recent experience, and about 30% were living on the streets or in a shelter.[29] Others were staying with friends or in another unspecified arrangement. Other studies, however, show that prostitution-involved youth were less likely to live in a relative's home or shelter. If they were not on the streets, they were more likely to live with unrelated roommates, including other prostituted children or their pimps, who often demanded sexual favors in lieu of rent.[30]

Early Childhood Abuse and Neglect

The homes children run away from are often marked by emotional, physical, or sexual abuse, neglect, and regular violence between the parents. Sexual abuse has a significant impact on the probability that a runaway will become involved with prostitution. Early childhood abuse or neglect is a strong predictor of prostitution for girls, although, it does not seem to have the same impact on boys. Sex abuse appears to indirectly increase the chance of prostitution by increasing the risk of running away—"It is not so much that sexual abuse leads to prostitution as it is that running away leads to prostitution."[31]

While a majority of girls who enter prostitution appear to have suffered prior childhood sexual abuse, not every child who suffers such abuse will become a runaway or prostituted child. However, the sexual exploitation of children, combined with other family tensions or emotional deficiencies, increases the probability that an adolescent runaway will engage in prostitution.

Familial Trafficking

Connected to the issue of physical and sexual abuse is the problem of familial trafficking, such as when a family member trades or rents his/her child for sexual use by another in exchange for money, food, or drugs. Familial trafficking happens at alarming rates in the United States. In fact, the trafficking of children by family members was noted frequently in the assessments done by Shared Hope International, which is one of the best known and best administered nongovernmental organizations (NGOs) providing services to sexually exploited children. Due to a lack of training and understanding of child sex trafficking by state child protection service agencies, professionals often classified the abuse under a different label, such as child sexual abuse. This mislabeling of child sexual abuse instead of child sex trafficking results in the commercial component of the crime being lost. WestCare Nevada, an NGO in Las Vegas, has determined that an estimated 30% of domestically trafficked minors, who receive services at their shelter, were first trafficked by a family member.[32] Staff members at WestCare Nevada are quick to point out, however, that victims rarely disclose family involvement at the beginning of treatment, but typically disclose this much later in the restoration process.[33]

Drug-Addicted Parents

Another common element found among sex-trafficked minors is the existence of a drug-addicted parent. It is not uncommon in these cases for an in-kind commercial exchange to occur with the parent selling sex with their child in exchange for drugs.[34] Having a drug-addicted parent creates several areas of danger—the parents themselves, congregation of other drug-addicted persons with access to the child, faulty parental supervision, and the introduction of drug use to the child. An example of this can be seen in a domestic minor sex-trafficking case that recently took place in Monroe, Louisiana. The mother of a 14-year-old girl sold her child to her crack dealer in order to pay for drugs. Though the mother was arrested and charged with cruelty to a juvenile, the child remained in the custody of the drug dealer (a registered sex offender) who supplied the minor with drugs and continued to sexually abuse her. The drug dealer then prostituted the minor in partnership with another man.[35]

Another example of familial domestic minor sex trafficking emerged in Salt Lake City, Utah, where an 11-year-old was removed from her biological parents' care due to drug use by the parents. Two years after the removal, the child disclosed in therapy that her parents forced her to watch pornography with her brother and then engage in sex acts with him for the entertainment of their parents and their parents' friends. The parents often charged the spectators a fee payable in money or drugs, especially crystal methamphetamine.[36]

Psychological and Emotional Difficulties

Whether caused by problems in the home or some other contributing factor, girls have often experienced psychological and emotional difficulties before they enter prostitution. Many children who are later prostituted are socially isolated and become entangled in a delinquent lifestyle.[37] On the streets, these children seek the emotional attachments that they could not find at home, making them vulnerable to those who would exploit them. In addition, fear of familial rejection or ostracism based on sexual orientation, especially in the case of boys, may increase the likelihood that a teenager will run away, thus increasing the likelihood that the child will engage in prostitution.[38]

Given all of these potential difficulties, it is not surprising that the vast majority of children who enter prostitution have low self-esteem and negative feelings about themselves just prior to doing so.[39] In an attempt to escape circumstances that they consider unbearable, many youth, once on the street, land in situations that may equal or exceed the traumas they experienced in their homes. Also, most victims of sex trafficking will have suffered one or more traumatic events and will have adopted psychological tactics to cope with the effects of these events. To begin to understand these reactions, it is important to first understand a bit about "trauma." According to experts, "The essence of trauma is that it overwhelms the victim's psychological and biological coping mechanisms. This occurs when internal and external resources are inadequate to cope with the external threat."[40] Traumatic experiences suffered by victims of sex trafficking are often complex, multiple, and can occur over a long period of time. For many individuals who are trafficked, abuse or other trauma-inducing events may have started long before the trafficking process.

Studies of trauma in cases of sex trafficking have been conducted, and they offer some guidance and conclusions, especially when they are considered in conjunction with what is generally known about trauma from anecdotal evidence from around the world.

Importance of Understanding Psychological Variations in Sex-Trafficking Victims

No two victims of sex trafficking are the same and the impact it has upon individuals varies. The investigator must not make assumptions about how individuals might or should react to their exploitation. For example, investigator should not expect a victim of sex trafficking to view them as rescuers or saviors. Some might react to them as rescuers, but many may react to the investigators as unwelcome interlocutors, which may further compound what is already a very complex situation. If the victim reacts in a hostile or aggressive way, it may have nothing to do with the investigator personally or the law enforcement organization that is conducting the questioning. Victims may have adopted these tactics and emotions as a psychological mechanism to cope with or to survive their ordeal. It is very likely they would react to anyone else in the same way.

However, it should be kept in mind that not every victim will react to a rescue with hostility. Challenging and direct questioning too early is very likely to alienate and may retraumatize the victim. Challenging the victim's veracity, treating the victim as a suspect, or showing skepticism or signs of disbelief are likely to remind him or her of the defensive position they held during the trafficking ordeal. This will greatly diminish the chance of cooperation, thus this approach should be avoided at all costs. A considered, methodical, and nonjudgmental approach has the best chance of revealing the truth, whatever it may be.

The levels of psychological trauma experienced by some sex-trafficking victims may be so high that they are never going to be able to serve as witnesses in court or even give an account that can be used as the basis of gathering criminal intelligence. Investigators should always be prepared to terminate an interview if necessary and seek immediate psychological assistance for the victim. On the other hand, it also is possible that some individuals, who initially present strong emotional reactions, may become perfectly capable witnesses with time and professional support or counseling.

Mental Health Symptoms

Depression, anxiety, shame, humiliation, shock, denial, disbelief, irritability, recurring nightmares, memories of abuse, difficulties concentrating and sleeping, and feelings of apathy or emotional detachment are all symptoms frequently found among torture victims and victims of other traumatic events, and also are identified as prominent psychological reactions in sex-trafficking victims.[41]

For example, in one study of trafficked women, it was determined, not surprisingly, that the levels of poor mental health they experienced were much higher than that of those in the general female population. However, while in the care of NGOs, victims' symptom levels did decrease, but this decrease happened very slowly and not very often. Even after three months of care, victims' reported depression levels were still at the level of the top 10% of the most depressed women in an average population. Anxiety and hostility levels were not quite as high, but still well above the average. This is likely to inhibit trafficking victims from reengaging in normal daily activities, such as caring for family, employment, or education.[42]

These strong symptoms suggest the need for extremely sensitive and timely approaches to questioning a sex-trafficking victim. As suggested earlier, a victim's expression of hostility

Figure 3.1 Sex-trafficking victims releasing suppressed feelings. Badly traumatized young sex-trafficking victims, who were forced into prostitution before being rescued, are depicted here in a therapy room where they are encouraged to release suppressed feelings by physically acting out. (Photo courtesy of Fr. Shay Cullen, PREDA Foundation, published in D+C.com.)

may be surprising for some investigators, who are more likely to expect victims to appear broken, tearful, and/or fearful. Yet, hostility is a well-documented response to trauma. It will not be uncommon for a victim to be "annoyed or easily irritated," "easily upset," and "irritated by everything," have "temper outbursts."[43] In some forms of therapy of sex trafficking, victims are encouraged to release suppressed feelings by physically acting out in a controlled and safe environment (Figure 3.1).

Dissociation as a Defense Mechanism

Dissociation is defined as an experience where a person may feel disconnected from his/her surroundings. It is a defense mechanism that prostituted women sometimes employ to protect their sense of self from violation and is similar to the dissociation employed by sexually abused children.[44] Norwegian researchers Cecilie Hoigaard and Liv Finstad asked prostituted women, who were interviewed in some detail, about the defense mechanisms they used. They wanted to know: "How do you avoid prostituting yourself when you prostitute yourself?" and considered this to be the "fundamental question for prostitutes around the world."[45] Prostituted women, they explain, have worked out an ingenious, complex system to protect "the real me, the self, the personality from being invaded and destroyed by customers."[46] As they point out, literature on prostitution that has considered these mechanisms reports remarkably similar techniques.[47] The women used different methods to psychologically dissociate themselves when they were engaged in the sex act. They report doing this by thinking about something else, using alcohol, Valium®, or other psychotropic drugs. A young woman, who phoned in and had a conversation with one of the researchers at a New Zealand radio station, while being interviewed about prostitution, explained that a psychiatric nurse employed in her brothel had taught her to form a different personality with a new name to go into and out of at will.[48] Thus, she was able to see the abuse as happening to this other person and not to her. For survivors of childhood sexual abuse and for prostitution survivors, the ability to successfully employ this defense mechanism can reduce the potential for damage to the women's relationships with their bodies and with others.

Hoigaard and Finstad have described in considerable detail the damage done to prostituted women in Oslo in in-depth interviews they conducted with women over a number of years. Their respondents reported destruction of their sex lives. One woman described her experience of seeking a normal sexual relationship while in prostitution but could not. She told the interviewer, "You're a piece of shit, and you make yourself sick. ... I've thrown up during sex, just started throwing up without thinking that it's been awful. It's just happened."[49] Others speak of losing the ability to have an orgasm and having to fake it, and they talk of feeling that they have become hard and cold. One said, "I'm only the genitals that they use."[50] They spoke of the inability to feel anything, not necessarily because of the "violence" they experienced, but because of the numerous "regular, daily tricks."[51]

Posttraumatic Stress Disorder and Sex-Trafficking Victims

Posttraumatic stress disorder (PTSD) is a term that describes a mental health disorder caused, in part, by exposure to one or more traumatic events. This disorder manifests in a number of severe psychological symptoms experienced by those who have been exposed to a life-threatening experience that has had a traumatic effect on them.

PTSD was first formally identified among Vietnam war veterans and more recently among combat veterans having served in Iraq and Afghanistan, but it had been previously detected and labeled with a variety of terms, most often terms associated with warfare, e.g., "shell shock" in soldiers of World War I or "combat fatigue" in World War II.

PTSD is commonly identified in persons in occupations such as the police, first responder emergency care workers, also people who are seriously injured in accidents, and victims of rape, which could certainly include girls and women forced into prostitution, who are raped multiple times every day.

Almost everyone who has a traumatic experience will have feelings of shock, grief, and adjustment; however, not everyone who experiences a traumatic event will develop PTSD, and it should not be confused with the normal response to a disturbing episode.

For sex-trafficking victims, the traumatic events they experience are often repetitive and prolonged—which can sometimes distinguish their reactions from those who have survived a single life-threatening event.

The distinction between PTSD and complex posttraumatic stress disorder is important to investigators because it emphasizes that the reaction to ongoing trauma is actually a physiological reorganizing of the individual's natural responses or instincts that make them hyperprepared to respond to stressful events.

A common characteristic of PTSD is the tendency of symptoms to decline over time in most people, although they can linger and lead to long-term psychiatric conditions in some and may reemerge at stress-filled times.

Symptoms of Posttraumatic Stress Disorder (PTSD)

Studies of sex-trafficking victims have found that they display many PTSD symptoms, the most common of which include:

- Headaches
- Stomach upset
- Nausea
- Weakness and fatigue
- Muscle tension and twitches
- Changes in appetite and sexual functioning
- Sleep impairment, with frequent awakenings and often nightmares
- Intrusive imagery and flashbacks may occur
- Distorted memories
- Anxiety and depression
- Panic attacks
- Unusual and disorienting feelings of helplessness, fearfulness
- Self second-guessing and guilt feelings

The Stockholm Syndrome (Trauma Bonding)

Investigators are sometimes mystified by the unusual reaction of women and children, who they rescue in sex-trafficking operations because, in some cases, the rescued victims not only refuse to cooperate, but appear to be protective of the sex traffickers and/or pimps. In fact, the reaction from the sex-trafficking victim may be a result of her suffering from what is characterized as the "Stockholm syndrome," which is a group of psychological symptoms that occur in some persons in a captive or hostage situation. The term takes its name from a bank robbery that took place in Stockholm, Sweden, in August 1973. The robbers took four employees of the bank (three women and one man) into the vault with them and kept them hostage for 131 hours. After the employees were finally released, they appeared to have formed a paradoxical emotional bond with their captors; they told reporters that they saw the police as their enemy rather than the bank robbers, and that they had positive feelings toward the criminals. The syndrome was first named by Nils Bejerot (1921–1988), a medical professor who specialized in addiction research and served as a psychiatric consultant to the Swedish police during the standoff at the bank. Stockholm syndrome is clinically defined as Survival Identification Syndrome[52] (Figure 3.2).

Figure 3.2 The Stockholm syndrome. A bank robbery in Stockholm, Sweden, in 1973, resulted in a six-day standoff. It was this robbery for which the name Stockholm syndrome was coined. This photo shows one of the robbers, Jan Erik "Janne" Olsson (standing at the right), at a central Stockholm bank with three of the hostages. After six days, the robbers surrendered and the hostages were released. Paradoxically, after the hostages were finally released, they had appeared to form an emotional bond (trauma bonding) with their captors. They told reporters they saw the police, rather than the bank robbers, as their enemy. They had positive feelings toward the robbers. (Photo courtesy of the Stockholm police.)

A Complex Reaction

Stockholm syndrome is considered a complex reaction to a frightening situation, and experts do not agree completely on all of its characteristic features or on the factors that make some people more susceptible than others to developing it. One reason for the disagreement is that it would be unethical to test theories about the syndrome by experimenting on human beings. The data for understanding the syndrome are derived from actual hostage situations since 1973 that differ considerably from one another in terms of location, number of people involved, and time frame. Another source of disagreement concerns the extent to which the syndrome can be used to explain other historical phenomena or more commonplace types of abusive relationships. Many researchers believe that Stockholm syndrome helps to explain certain behaviors of survivors of World War II concentration camps, members of religious cults, battered wives, incest survivors, physically or emotionally abused children, persons taken hostage by criminals or terrorists, and sex-trafficking victims.

Most experts, however, agree that Stockholm syndrome has three central characteristics:

1. The hostages have negative feelings about the police or other authorities.
2. The hostages have positive feelings toward their captor(s).
3. The captors develop positive feelings toward the hostages.

Causes and Symptoms

The Stockholm syndrome does not affect all hostages (or persons in comparable situations). In fact, a Federal Bureau of Investigation (FBI) study of over 1,200 hostage-taking incidents found that 92% of the hostages did *not* develop Stockholm syndrome. FBI researchers then interviewed flight attendants who had been taken hostage during airplane hijackings, and concluded that three factors are necessary for the syndrome to develop:

1. The crisis situation lasts for several days or longer.
2. The hostage takers remain in contact with the hostages; that is, the hostages are not placed in a separate room.
3. The hostage takers show some kindness toward the hostages or at least refrain from harming them.

Hostages abused by captors typically feel anger toward them and do not usually develop the syndrome. In addition, people who often feel helpless in other stressful life situations or are willing to do anything in order to survive seem to be more susceptible to developing Stockholm syndrome if they are taken hostage.

People with Stockholm syndrome report experiencing the same symptoms as those diagnosed with PTSD namely: insomnia, nightmares, general irritability, difficulty concentrating, being easily startled, feelings of unreality or confusion, inability to enjoy previously pleasurable experiences, increased distrust of others, and flashbacks.

Other Psychological Disorders that Sex-Trafficking Victims Can Experience

There are numerous other psychological disorders that sex-trafficking victims can experience besides the ones described so far. These include the following: attachment disorder, attention deficit/hyperactivity disorder (ADHD), conduct disorder, developmental disorder, eating disorders, learning disorders, impulse control disorders, mood disorders, personality disorders, self-harming disorders, sleep disorder, substance abuse disorders, phobias, panic attacks, hyperarousal, hypoarousal, and trauma bonds.[53]

Physical Effects of Sex Trafficking on Victims

Many sex trafficking victims are physically injured by their pimps and customers, with 35% of U.S. females who have been

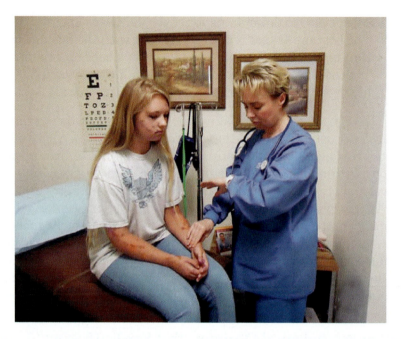

Figure 3.3 Medical services are often needed by sex-trafficking victims. It is important for sex-trafficking victims to be given a medical examination as soon as possible to determine if they have any serious health problems, injuries, are pregnant, or have contracted any sexually transmitted diseases such as HIV/AIDS.

sexually exploited reporting having received broken bones and other serious physical injuries as a result of violence from their pimps and customers.[54] Thus, it is very important for rescuers to get these injuries treated as soon as realistically possible (Figure 3.3). Besides their physical injuries, other potential physical effects include: sexually transmitted diseases, pregnancy, infertility, infections or mutilations, chronic back pain, cardiovascular, or respiratory problems, weak eyes and other eye problems, malnourishment and serious dental problems, infectious diseases like tuberculosis, undetected or untreated diseases, bruises, scars and other signs of physical abuse and torture, substance problems or addictions.

Many victims of sex trafficking have had little sleep due to being forced to have sex with multiple men for long periods of time. Chronic or prolonged sleep loss not only affects an individual's ability to concentrate and think clearly, but also weakens the body's immune system and the ability to endure pain.[55]

Measures to Identify and Protect Sex-Trafficking Victims

There are many measures that can be taken to identify and protect the victims of sex trafficking. They generally fall into five broad categories, discussed in detail in Figure 3.4.

Recruitment and Pimp Control

A trafficker's process of recruitment and control are sophisticated. There is a calculated method to preying on youth, and the traffickers/pimps share tactics with each other, assist one another, and craft their techniques together. Experts and survivors refer to these methods as "brainwashing." One survivor expert noted commonalities between the tactics traffickers use and those utilized by cult leaders.[56]

Traffickers/pimps make it their business to understand the psychology of youth and to practice and hone their tactics of manipulation. The trafficker's goal is to exploit and create vulnerabilities and remove the minor credibility in the eyes of their families, the public, and law enforcement. The trafficker's ultimate goal is profit.

Initial Approach by the Pimp

The pimp's initial approach may be to just gather information about the girl's circumstances. The pimp will befriend her, sweet-talk her, and provide companionship and intimacy.[57] He may try to impress her with promises of money and a comfortable lifestyle. Runaways with problems at home are especially vulnerable to these tactics because all they really want is to belong.[58] The pimp makes the girl feel special and important, lavishing attention on her, buying her clothes and jewelry, and creating a facade of friendship and romance.[59] He may promise to marry her or make a lifetime commitment.[60]

Prevention

S Comprehensive anti-trafficking legislation

S Research

S Warning about the dangers of prostitution

S Micro-credit loans for women and other economic opportunities

S Alleviate social and economic factors that render people vulnerable to trafficking

S Adopt or strengthen legislation to discourage demand

S Improve education to reduce demand

Protection

S Witness protection

S Immigration status

S Civil compensation

S Physical safety/security

Provision

S Shelter

S Medical care

S Job training

S Confidential legal proceedings

S Legal counsel

S Education and training opportunities

S Consider special needs of children

Prosecution

S Law and law enforcement

S Investigation, trial, and conviction

S Forfeiture of assets

S Exchange of information

S Training of law enforcement officials

S Extradition

S Extraterritoriality

Participation

S Public participation

S Role of civil society

S Non-governmental organizations

S Faith-based organizations

S Media

S Academic institutions

S Duty of the ordinary citizen to report

S Codes of conduct adopted by corporations

Figure 3.4 Measures that can be taken to identify and protect victims of sex trafficking. The outlined measures are not exhaustive, but illustrative of the most important measures that must be taken to combat trafficking in persons. (From M. Matter, *Comprehensive Legal Approaches to Combating Trafficking in Persons: An International and Comparative Perspective, Protection Project* (Baltimore, MD: Johns Hopkins University, 2006), p. 15.)

The pimp may then initiate a sexual relationship with the girl, continuing to become the primary person in her life. This pretense of love lulls the girl into thinking theirs is a mutually developing relationship, making her emotionally and psychologically dependent on the pimp as a substitute for the family that abused her or turned her away.[61]

At this point, the pimp may demand that she have sex with someone else, often a "friend" of the pimp, to prove her love for him. Next, she must have sex with a stranger for money.[62] Soon she finds herself prostituted as a condition of her love for him. The young girl, however, continues to think of the pimp as her boyfriend, and this perception of the relationship sustains the control and abuse. After creating this dependency, the pimp begins to dominate, control, and become an integral part of her life[63] (Figure 3.5).

Seasoning Techniques and Tactics of Power and Control

Before a girl has been "turned out," the pimp may "season" her for life as a prostitute with physical and verbal abuse.[64] Seasoning is meant to break her will and separate her from her previous life so that she does not know where to turn for help.[65] He may change her identity and move her around because constant mobility breaks any personal ties she may have developed and ensures new ties are only temporary.[66] The demoralizing and dehumanizing experience of prostitution confirms the child's poor self-image and provides another tool for manipulation by the pimp.[67] Some traffickers and pimps have even resorted to tattooing their victims in order to show that the girls are their personal possession (Figure 3.6).

The pimp may withhold love and affection or use verbal abuse, fear, and violence to control her.[68] By that time, the girl is completely under his control. As one victim explains:

> I was so much in love with him, it really didn't matter as long as he was there. ... When he told me he loved me I believed everything would work out all right. I had been alone for so long and he'd told me I'd be with him for the rest of my life.[69]

The pimp's relationship to the young girl closely parallels the dynamics of a battering relationship.[70] The pimp first

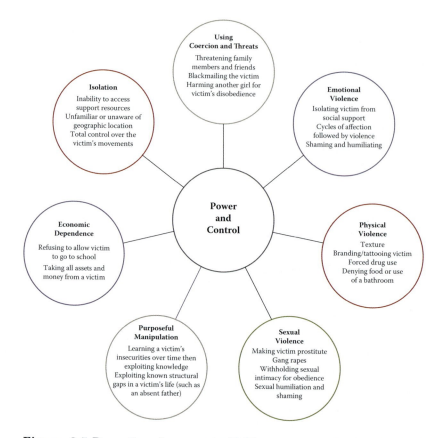

Figure 3.5 Domestic minor sex-trafficking power and control wheel. (From The National Report on Domestic Minor Sex Trafficking: America's Prostituted Children, May 2000, p. 37. Online at http://www.sharedhope. org/Resources/TheNationalReport.aspx

isolates the girl from family and friends and minimizes the exploitative nature of prostitution.[71] He then uses threats and intimidation to control her. Such tactics invariably involve emotional, sexual, and physical abuse. He may beat her up or threaten to leave her.[72] The pimp creates an environment of total emotional deprivation. And, most like a batterer, he uses random acts of violence to establish power.[73]

Physical abuse occurs in over half of pimp–prostitute relationships.[74] When violence is no longer effective in controlling the girl, the pimp may use drugs or threats against her family

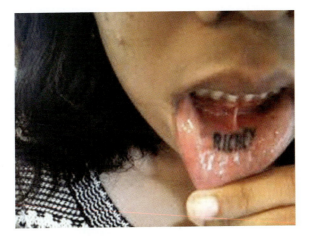

Figure 3.6 A pimp's name is tattooed into the bottom lip of this sex-trafficking victim. In order to show physical possession of the girls who work for them, pimps will occasionally tattoo the girls. In this case, the pimp tattooed his name, "Richey," on the bottom lip of this sex-trafficking victim who was part of his stable of young underage prostitutes. (Photo courtesy of Amita Sharma. Online at: http://www.kpbs.org/photos/galleries/2011/nov/01/child-sex-trafficking-increasing-san-diego/)

or friends.[75] If she becomes pregnant, the pimp uses the baby as leverage to manipulate her.[76]

The prostituted child is expected to turn over all of her earnings to the pimp and is punished if she fails to do so.[77] Because the child becomes financially dependent on the pimp,[78] she must rely on him for all necessities, and this places her even more in his "debt."[79]

Pimps control 80% to 95% of prostitution[80] and pimps can be either men or women.[81] Female pimps are often former prostitutes who recruit younger girls to work for them. An overwhelming majority of prostituted adolescent girls have pimps, but only a minority of juvenile boys do.[82] Boys are significantly more likely to have arranged their own encounters.[83] A young girl also may have a tendency to deny she is controlled by a pimp and may very well consider the pimp to be her boyfriend. Also, once a girl is working for a pimp, her former pimp does not want to lose her as a source of income. If she wants to leave him, her new pimp often requires her to pay a fee ("choosing money") to ensure her safety because he may use a "tracker" or bounty hunter to get her back.[84]

The Recruitment and Grooming Process

Once a trafficker/pimp identifies the physical and/or psychological needs of a child, he seeks to fill them. If the child lacks a loving parental presence, the trafficker/pimp morphs his tactics to become the parent figure. If a youth needs a safe place to sleep, the trafficker/pimp provides housing. In this way, traffickers/pimps work to create a dependency between the minor and themselves. An example of recruitment by providing a physical need was reported by the Dallas Police Department, Child Exploitation/High Risk Victims/Trafficking Unit. A 12-year-old was found stripping in the Dallas strip club, Diamond Cabaret. Police later learned that two traffickers, a man and a woman, had offered the child safe shelter. When the minor accepted the offer, the traffickers took her to the strip club and forced her to dance.[85]

One survivor's story of recruitment in Toledo, Ohio, illustrates how a trafficker uses psychological needs or vulnerabilities to recruit victims. An older, male trafficker "romanced" this child by recognizing that the emotional needs of the child were not being met. He presented himself as a boyfriend in order to gain the minor's affection and dependency. She explained that, for six months, an older man pulled alongside her in his car every morning as she walked to a school for gifted children. He bought the 12-year-old small gifts and told her she was pretty. She finally agreed to a ride to school—and she was trapped.[86]

These grooming and recruitment practices are common to those of other child predators. For example, "traveler" cases investigated by police usually involve an older adult man who targets younger children online. These perpetrators spend time slowly gaining the trust and affection of the youth as well as desensitizing the minor to the idea of sexual activity (e.g., sending the youth increasingly graphic pornography). In the end, the adult sets a meeting with the minor in hopes of engaging in sexual activity. According to police, these "relationships" usually involve the promise of gifts, money, and opportunity, all of which qualify as a commercial exchange under the Trafficking Victims Protection Act (TVPA).[87]

"People who use kids like this are the most brilliant child psychologists on the planet. They know these kids are not credible, they know how to manipulate them into being less credible, they get them addicted to something, anything; then, even if the child does rat them out, no one will believe them."[88]

The Bottom Bitch/Girl

Additionally, traffickers systematically utilize recruitment tactics that distance them from the risk of detection and prosecution by law enforcement. Traffickers use a "bottom bitch/girl," who manages the details of the other girls' exploitation (Figure 3.7). The process of using a "bottom bitch/girl" allows the trafficker/pimp to keep a careful distance from the crime he is committing.[89] Traffickers also maintain a careful distance even from their victims by using street names so the

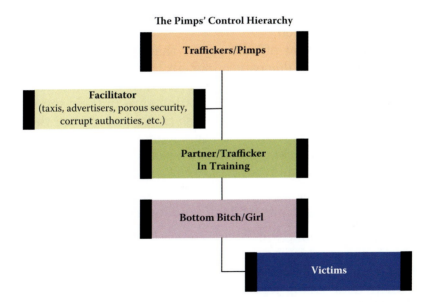

Figure 3.7 Pimps create a control hierarchy that provides as much distance as possible between themselves and the prostitution operation. (From The National Report on Domestic Minor Sex Trafficking: America's Prostituted Children, p. 39. Online at: http://www.sharedhope.org/Resources/TheNationalReport.aspx)

girls never know their real names. A victim's arrest reinforces what the pimp has taught her about distrusting authorities and, due to the pimp's careful secrecy and anonymity, she is both unable and unwilling to provide the level of information law enforcement requires to pursue an investigation. These same tactics exacerbate a potential victim's vulnerable state and protect the trafficker.

Traffickers use and encourage cultural attitudes that view prostituted children not as victims, but as delinquents. This serves to isolate the victim as traffickers tell them that seeking help is a waste of time because no one would believe them because they are "just prostitutes." A study on the demand for sex trafficking found that traffickers often provided drugs to their victims to both sell and take, further marginalizing and criminalizing the minor. The goals of traffickers are three-fold: keep the victim under control, make money, and lower the child's credibility in the eyes of law enforcement and the community, so she is not believed when disclosing information about the exploitation.

Law enforcement officers report that the youth they see victimized through domestic minor sex trafficking are usually exceptionally vulnerable and have low self-esteem. Though traffickers seek out youth with existing gaps in their support network or low self-esteem, they also create and expand these vulnerabilities. There are certain common tactics that traffickers employ in order to break down a child's sense of control, worth, and autonomy.

Use of Pornography as a Means of Control

Forcing performance in pornography is another means by which pimps achieve control over the girls they prostitute. They may take photographs of the nude girl in the context of their relationship and then threaten to send them to the girl's family or school.[90] By learning about the girl's family and friends, the pimp gets her home address and other personal information,[91] then blackmails her. Pimps also use the pornography to control and humiliate the girl and break her resistance.[92] Pornography is often used to normalize the practice of prostitution during the "seasoning" process by weakening the child's resistance.[93]

Pimps also may show pornographic pictures to advertise their girls, while customers often want to take pictures for their later gratification. Customers also may use pornography to describe the sexual act they want and to rationalize their behavior and their demands of the child.[94]

Use of Manipulation

While every tactic used by a trafficker/pimp has some element of manipulation, the subtlety of the manipulation is often overlooked by both the victim and responders to sex trafficking; thus, it is worth examining as a separate and purposeful tactic. Traffickers/pimps utilize manipulation to gain and maintain control over their victims. One example is a trafficker's method of maintaining internal control over his "stable" (the children or adults being prostituted by him). Traffickers commonly use emotional manipulation, such as favoring one girl over the others with frequent changes to the favored position, as a way of preventing collusion for escape or disobedience. This method establishes hierarchy and ensures constant competition with each other for rewards and promotions to the girls who produce the most money and follow the "rules of the game." It also keeps the victims divided and ensures that they remain focused on pleasing the trafficker/pimp rather than creating an escape strategy.

> Nicole, I love you and I love my son, and if I was able to be there, I would never allow for you or him to suffer or be without your needs and wants in life."[95] (Excerpt from a letter to a victim from her convicted trafficker.)

Use of Social Science by Pimps in the Manipulation Process

One self-proclaimed pimp and author of yet another guide on pimping explained how to apply the recognized elements of Maslow's Hierarchy of Needs to the situation of pimping. The author/pimp provides details on how to go about implementing each stage of the Hierarchy of Needs for the manipulation and control of a person in prostitution.[96] Referred to as "the Pyramid," this approach systematically addresses foundational human needs, such as safety, security, love, and belonging. The concept discusses how past sexual abuse, family dysfunction, societal judgment, and systemic failure leave gaps into which traffickers/pimps insert themselves as providers. By offering a false sense of security, respect, and love, a trafficker can establish a trauma bond that will keep the victim vulnerable, completely subject to the trafficker, and the source of profits through her exploitation (Figure 3.8).

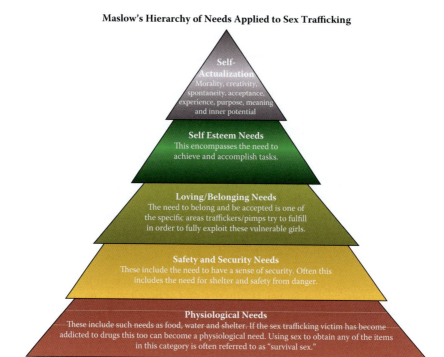

Figure 3.8 Maslow's Hierarchy of Needs applied to sex trafficking. The needs hierarchy is arranged like a pyramid, with lower-order to the higher-order needs. The application of this theory is based on the premise that a person will not be motivated to move up to the next higher needs level in the pyramid until a majority of the prior level's needs are met.

Sex for Drugs

Given the high rate of substance abuse among runaway and homeless youth, the "sex for drugs" phenomenon is not surprising, but the devastation it causes is considerable.

In some cases, the victims have already been drug-addicted when they established a relationship with the pimp. However, in many cases, the pimps provide the girls with drugs so they become addicted. After becoming drug dependent, the girls will willingly exchange sex for drugs and have to look to their pimps for the drugs necessary to feed their habit. At this point, these girls become little more than indentured servants, if not outright slaves, just so they can feed their drug addiction.[97]

Gang Activity in Sex-Trafficking Operations

Inner-city street gangs have learned that, like other illicit activities, the control of prostitution can be very profitable and, therefore, is attractive to criminal networks and gangs (Figure 3.9). This is especially true of the prostitution of young girls as the following news story shows.

In The News

Sold for Sex: The Link Between Street
Gangs and Human Trafficking

by Laura J. Lederer (October 21, 2011)

In April of this year, in Oceanside, California, thirty-eight Crips gang members, their alleged associates, and two hotel owners were arrested for engaging in a sex trafficking enterprise that involved the prostitution of minors and adult females. After raping their victims and threatening to kill them if they tried to escape, the gang members sold the girls online. The girls were trapped in a hotel for twelve hours a day, as men who had purchased their bodies from the gang members had sex with them. Though these commercial

Figure 3.9 MS-13 gang member arrested for sex trafficking. MS-13 is a street gang that originated in El Salvador. It is a violent group that is presently engaged in drug and sex trafficking within the United States. The U.S. Treasury Department has designated it as a transnational criminal organization. This designation allows U.S. officials to target this group more aggressively. (Photo courtesy of the FBI.)

sex acts brought in between $1,000 to $3,000 dollars a day, the young women and children never saw a penny of the money. Their only payment was food, avoiding beatings, and staying alive.

In a similar case this past June, an MS-13 gang member was indicted for trafficking girls at a Super 8 motel just outside of Washington, D.C. At least one of the girls was only fifteen when she was sold. He advertised her as a "high school girl" and "fresh out of the box." A year earlier, in Brooklyn, New York, eight members of the Bloods street gang were also charged with sex trafficking of minors. They solicited customers using online websites. The victims, recruited from local junior high and high schools, were trafficked into prostitution. The traffickers made $500 a day.

The facts from hundreds of criminal cases show a clear link between dangerous street gangs and the scourge of sex trafficking. Over the last decade, the United States has passed numerous laws to address criminal gang activity. Similarly, in 2000, Congress passed the Trafficking Victims Protection Act (TVPA) to curtail trafficking in persons. But the enforcement of each law has developed independently of the others, with little, if any, integration. This is unfortunate and represents a missed opportunity not only to save the victims of a terrible crime, but also to add another prosecution weapon against the dangerous street gangs that endanger our communities and our nation.

With state and national crackdowns on drug trafficking, gangs have turned to sex trafficking for financial gain. Unlike drugs, girls can be used more than once, and it is the girls, not the traffickers, who run the greatest risk of being caught and prosecuted. Case records show that gangs still utilize traditional methods of recruiting, employing the modern equivalent of wining and dining a young girl ("skip parties" and "love showers"), winning her heart and then slowly "seasoning" her for the street by sharing her with other gang members. One young woman described her trafficker's request for a "love donation": sex she had to provide to other men to win her place in the gang.

But women and children also describe being coerced into a life of prostitution after being subjected to severe beatings and gang rapes, and being deprived of food and water. The victims of trafficking are made to feel both afraid of and dependent on the traffickers for their very lives.

New technological advances give gang traffickers the ability to market the services of their victims discreetly. In several high-profile prosecutions of sex trafficking in Seattle, San Diego, and New York, street gangs used online advertisements on websites, such as Craigslist and Backpage to traffic women and girls as young as thirteen. Once arrangements are made over the Internet and by cell phone, the victimization that takes place behind closed doors is the same as in other trafficking cases: women and children are delivered to customers and forced to perform sex acts for money that is paid to and pocketed by their traffickers.

The U.S. government has prosecuted several hundred cases against street gangs, motorcycle gangs, and prison gangs in which commercial sex acts, prostitution, or human trafficking were mentioned; the gang members, however, were charged with drug and weapons trafficking, armed robbery, auto theft, extortion, home invasions, and other felony offenses—not human trafficking. Human trafficking charges are rarely the primary basis for prosecution; though, since late 2010, there have been a few such cases.

One reason that street gangs have not been prosecuted for human trafficking is that too many prosecutors and law enforcement officials assume that human trafficking in America is primarily an international problem. A recent Department of Justice Bureau of Justice Statistics report, however, found that 83% of victims in confirmed sex trafficking incidents are actually U.S. citizens.

The vigorous prosecution of human trafficking can help bring down street gangs that also engage in murder, robbery, and drug trafficking. Before that can happen, however, state and local government officials must learn how to combat the human trafficking that is occurring in their own backyards. The Department of

State's 2011 Trafficking in Persons Report found that less than 10% of state and local law enforcement agencies have any kind of protocol or policy on human trafficking. While great strides have been made in addressing international human trafficking and local street gang activity, little has been done to link the two.

Source: Public Discourse: The Witherspoon Institute. Online at: http://www.thepublicdiscourse.com/2011/10/4034 (accessed July 18, 2012).

How to Combat Street Gangs Involved in Sex Trafficking

In order to combat street gang involvement in sex trafficking more effectively, new approaches must be undertaken:

1. State and local governments must add sex trafficking to the list of suspect activities for criminal gangs.
2. Gang and sex-trafficking task forces must coordinate and plan joint prosecutions.
3. Gang investigations should include specific tactics for actively spotting sex trafficking.
4. Gangs involved in sex trafficking should be charged under the TVPA or state trafficking-in-persons laws in addition to other criminal charges.
5. Communities should develop specialized outreach, education, and training programs to address gang-related trafficking.
6. Asset forfeiture laws should be utilized more extensively in gang-related sex-trafficking cases.
7. New and creative approaches to prosecution (such as using the child soldiers provision in the TVPA) should be explored and established.

Street gangs are increasingly turning to sex trafficking as a way to generate the funds that are necessary for their existence and operations. Little is known about the dynamics involved in this trafficking, and additional research on the methods of recruiting, transporting, harboring, marketing, buying, and selling involved in gang-related sex trafficking is important.

Street gangs engage in sex trafficking because the risk is low, and the profit is high. New laws must target gang-related sex trafficking. In addition, diligent law enforcement tactics that help identify street gangs involved in sex trafficking must be developed. Federal and local law enforcement authorities should encourage collaboration between the current efforts to address sex trafficking and prosecute street gangs. Finally, education about street gangs and sex trafficking that is tailored for parents, teachers, and community leaders is critical to strengthening community resistance to sex trafficking and other criminal gang activities.[98]

Shelters and Services for Domestically Trafficked Minors

The importance of the availability of shelters and services for domestically trafficked minors cannot be over emphasized. However, there are certain problems that regularly occur with such shelters that both law enforcement officers and shelter personnel must be aware of. For example, trauma bonds, pimp control, threats against family members or the victim, and stigma, cause the majority of domestically trafficked minors to flee nonprotective shelters. Another common issue is traffickers/pimps actually going to shelters, or the neighborhoods where the shelters are located, in order to retraffic or recruit their victims.[99]

With so few appropriate shelters available for victims of domestic minor sex trafficking, victims are often arrested and placed in detention facilities for their protection—though this is not done for domestic violence victims, rape victims, or other child sexual abuse victims. While this is sometimes viewed as the only option available to arresting officers, it is a practice that pulls the victim deeper into the juvenile justice system, revictimizes, and hinders access to services. Furthermore, the arrest and detainment of the victim confirms the identity that has been assigned to her by the pimp/trafficker and reinforces the belief that she is not worthy of rescue or justice as a victim of a violent crime.

Lack of Protective Shelters

In 9 out of 10 assessments conducted by Shared Hope International, it was determined that there was a lack of protective shelters for child sex trafficking victims. Only five residential facilities specific to this population exist across the country. These include the Girls Educational and Mentoring Services (GEMS) Transition to Independent Living (TIL) in New York City, Standing Against Global Exploitation (SAGE) Safe House in San Francisco, Children of the Night in Los Angeles, Angela's House in Atlanta, and the Letot Center in Dallas. The term *protective shelter* refers to a facility with the ability to separate a victim from a trafficker/pimp and provide the victim a restorative home to stabilize, heal, and move toward independence. How the protective nature of a restorative home manifests can depend on the individual shelter. Some ways that protective shelters have manifested are through:

- Distance: Isolate the shelter from major transportation centers and common trafficking/pimping areas.
- Staff Secure: A large ratio of staff to minors can help keep a minor from being retrafficked and hinder running away.
- Formal Security: Security systems, such as outdoor and indoor cameras, can go a long way to providing security. Highly secure facilities that are restorative in nature also can assist in hindering both outsiders obtaining entry and youth running away.

Protective shelter can be either a mandatory or voluntary placement depending on the situation. Many social service professionals argue against mandatory, secured facilities for domestic minor sex-trafficking victims, as this can exacerbate a victim's reluctance to trust authorities and is compared by the victim to the control previously exerted by the trafficker.[100] On the other hand, protective shelters that utilize distance and staff security, as well as camera systems, have reported success. For example, the Letot Center in Dallas, Texas, is a staff-secure facility and reports that in one year, just three youth ran away out of the 350 youth placed at the facility.[101]

There Is a Lack of Specialized Services Geared toward the Unique Needs of Domestic Minor Sex-Trafficking Victims

Shared Hope International found a profound lack of specialized services in all 10 research sites. For instance, in the Baton Rouge/New Orleans assessment, it was found that though child protective services reported 35 allegations of domestic minor sex trafficking from 19 parishes from July 2006 to the time of the assessment in April 2008, there were no services or protocols specifically in place for the victims.[102]

The pervasive misunderstanding of the crime of domestic minor sex trafficking has several consequences leading to the failure of specialized services for the victims. First, victims of domestic minor sex trafficking are often categorized and then treated as victims of some other type of child sexual abuse. While recognition of existing familial child sexual abuse is necessary in addressing and treating root causes, as the exploitation shifts to sex trafficking, the diagnosis and treatment must shift as well. Second, victims of domestic minor sex trafficking are often labeled "child prostitutes." This label places blame and assumes a choice by the child victim, failing to take into account the effect of pimp control dynamics and trauma bonds. Without considering these critical elements of control over the child victim, treatment is nearly impossible for the victim. It is imperative that service providers know about the unique needs of victims of child sex trafficking in designing intake procedures, making diagnoses, and planning and monitoring treatment to better serve this population of victims. Though several agencies in the 10 locations were found to have designed a program for youth at-risk or victimized through sex trafficking, these agencies were operating mostly alone in their communities and were rare. This is a problem encountered across the country resulting in child victims of sex trafficking not receiving needed services.

The issue of a lack of specialized services is compounded by domestic, minor sex trafficking victims being adjudicated in the juvenile justice system. Juvenile detention staff stated they felt juvenile detention was an inappropriate placement for victims, and they felt unequipped to handle the complex trauma and needs of a domestically trafficked minor. This pervasive issue is a major concern for law enforcement, prosecutors, social service agencies, and other first responders across the country. Without specialized services, the child victim cannot be stabilized, which hinders investigations, prosecutions, and restoration. While domestic minor sex trafficking is a form of sexual abuse, it is complex with unique dynamics that must be taken into account. When these aspects are not addressed, services are ineffective or fail.

Child Protective Services (CPS) Interactions with Domestic Minor Sex-Trafficking Victims

Domestically trafficked minors have experienced both abuse and neglect; however, most CPS workers state that unless the perpetrator is a family member or "caregiver," their mandate does not allow them to become involved. There are several problems with this often-cited complication:

1. Even when the trafficker is not a family member, minors are often vulnerable to victimization due to parental neglect.
2. Though the definition of "caregiver" varies from state to state, traffickers have taken control and care over the child for extended periods of time through the pimp control dynamic. Many state definitions would allow for a trafficker to be defined as a caregiver if child protective services chose to address it.
3. Taking into account the vast number of domestic minor sex trafficking victims that have histories of familial abuse, these children either have already had contact with child protective services or should have but did not.

In addition, CPS agencies reported large caseloads and limited resources resulting in a highly structured prioritization process of the complaints received for investigation and action. Several CPS staff reported that youth over 15 years of age are deemed to be sufficiently capable of calling for help if abuse occurs again; this in spite of the mandate to protect all children under 18 and in spite of abuse having been reported already. This de facto emancipation of minors is detrimental for victims of domestic minor sex trafficking, many of whom fall within this unprotected range of 15 to 18 years of age. Assessments in many locations found that CPS workers often choose to narrowly interpret their mandate resulting in significant confusion over whose responsibility it is to provide protection, shelter, and services to domestically trafficked minors. With different entities unequivocally stating that it is "not their responsibility," these child victims are left without the safety net CPS is intended to provide.

Intake Categories Misidentify Domestic Minor Sex Trafficking

The majority of CPS caseworkers interviewed for the assessments were not familiar with sex-trafficking terminology or laws; however, they were keenly aware of the situation of one type of domestic minor sex trafficking (DMST), primarily: familial prostitution. The misidentification of a child sex trafficking victim exploited through familial prostitution is a reflection of the lack of training on child sex trafficking and the failure of the intake process to include identifiers of domestic minor sex trafficking. CPS agencies in each state have their own protocols and management; the intake process varies, but most procedures dictate that allegations are categorized broadly with specifics of the abuse recorded separately in a narrative section. For example, a hotline call reporting a family member selling sex with their child to a landlord typically would be identified in the report as "sexual abuse." This general categorization prevents statistics to be calculated for disaggregated types of abuse, such as familial prostitution, because the narrative section would not populate the statistics. As a result, information on the prevalence of commercial sexual exploitation of children in the CPS cases was obtained through interviews. In spite of these gaps, nearly every CPS caseworker interviewed for the assessments was able to recall at least one, if not multiple cases, which had indicators for domestic minor sex trafficking.

Adolescents Are Lower Priority

Child protective services across the United States have taken a tiered approach to addressing child sexual abuse and neglect cases due to being severely underresourced and understaffed. Though each state is different, CPS caseworkers stated that adolescents were routinely regarded as low priority. This is often because adolescents are assumed to have a greater ability to protect themselves. The self-protection assumption is faulty when a youth is faced with a systematic, violent, and organized criminal entity.

Contributing to this lack of prioritization is a lack of screening mechanisms that also plagues law enforcement and social service agencies. When community members report a potential case of child abuse or neglect to the state hotline, the calls are screened on the basis of the CPS mandate determining whether there is an imminent harm to the minor. Traffickers are rarely defined as a caregiver, and adolescents are frequently categorized as low risk; therefore, cases of domestic minor sex trafficking are screened out before ever reaching a caseworker. Furthermore, when a case is referred for investigation, it is often under the generalized rubric of "sexual abuse," and data is not collected that could inform investigators on the scope and nature of DMST occurring in a community.

There are, however, some promising practices emerging. For instance, child protective services in Boston implemented the GIFT Network in 2008, which specifically provides services, shelter, and specialized foster care for domestic minor sex-trafficking victims. A progressive step forward, the GIFT Network is available for 50 victims, aged 12 to 17, who are currently in the Massachusetts CPS system.[103] In addition, Louisiana and Florida also recently changed their intake documents to allow caseworkers to select commercial sexual exploitation or prostitution underneath the category of sexual abuse.

This will enhance the states' abilities to track and understand domestic minor sex trafficking within their communities.

Glossary

Attachment disorder: The condition in which individuals have difficulty forming lasting relationships. They often show nearly a complete lack of ability to be genuinely affectionate with others. They typically fail to develop a conscience and do not learn to trust.

Attention deficit/hyperactivity disorder (ADHD): A chronic condition that affects millions of children and often persists into adulthood. ADHD includes some combination of problems, such as difficulty sustaining attention, hyperactivity, and impulsive behavior.

Bottom bitch/girl: The prostitute who gains a pimp's/ trafficker's trust and who manages the details of the other girls' exploitation.

Conduct disorder: A repetitive and persistent pattern of behavior in which the basic rights of others or major age-appropriate norms are violated.

Hyperarousal: A state of increased psychological and physiological tension marked by such effects as reduced pain tolerance, anxiety, exaggerated startle responses, insomnia, fatigue, and accentuation of personality traits.

Hypoarousal: A state of decreased psychological and physiological tension marked by a numbness and avoidance, which represent self-protective efforts by the brain to keep overwhelming feelings under control.

Impulse control: Psychological disorders characterized by the repeated inability to refrain from performing a particular action that is harmful either to oneself or others.

Learning disorder: A group of disorders characterized by academic functioning that is substantially below the level expected on the basis of the patient's age, intelligence, and education.

Maslow's Hierarchy of Needs: A theory that systematically addresses foundational human needs, such as physiological, safety/security, loving/belonging, self-esteem, and self-actualizing.

Mood disorder: Mental disorders characterized by disturbances of mood, manifested as one or more episodes of mania, hypomania, depression, or some combination of the two main subcategories being *bipolar disorders* and *depressive disorders*.

Personality disorder: A category of mental disorders characterized by enduring, inflexible, and maladaptive personality traits that deviate markedly from cultural expectations and either generate subjective distress or significantly impair functioning.

Protective shelters: Facilities that can be either mandatory or voluntary, depending upon the situation involving the domestically sex-trafficked minor.

PTSD (Posttraumatic Stress Disorder): Is a term that describes a mental health disorder caused, in part, by exposure to one or more traumatic events.

"Seasoning": A term used to describe a combination of physical and verbal abuse meant to break a girl's will and separate her from her previous life so she does not know where to turn for help.

Self-harming disorder: Self-injury is the act of deliberately harming your own body, such as cutting or burning yourself. It is not meant as a suicide attempt. Rather, self-injury is an unhealthy way to cope with an emotional pain, intense anger, and frustration.

Sleep disorder: Chronic disorders involving sleep, either primary (dyssomnias, parasomnias) or secondary to factors including a general medical condition, mental disorder, or substance use.

"Stable": A term used by pimps/sex traffickers for the children or adults under their control who are being prostituted by them.

Stockholm syndrome: This syndrome refers to a group of psychological symptoms that occur in some persons in a captive or hostage situation. It also is known as Survival Identification Syndrome. Victims develop negative feelings toward police and positive feelings toward their captors.

Substance abuse disorder: Any of the mental disorders associated with excessive use of or exposure to psychoactive substances including abuse of drugs, medications, and toxins. The group is divided into *substance use ds* and *substance induced ds.*

Survival identification syndrome: Another name for the Stockholm syndrome.

The Pyramid: Another name for Maslow's Hierarchy of Needs.

Trauma bonds: The development of strong emotional ties formed between two persons, with one person intermittently harassing, beating, threatening, abusing, or intimidating the other.

Review Questions

1. What are some of the major precipitating factors as to why children become involved in prostitution?
2. Why are children at greater risk for sex trafficking if their parents are drug addicts?
3. How does the dissociation defense mechanism work?
4. What are the most common symptoms for posttraumatic stress disorder (PTSD)?
5. What are the circumstances under which the Stockholm syndrome is most likely to manifest itself?
6. What were the circumstances under which the term the Stockholm syndrome was created?
7. FBI researchers have concluded there are three factors necessary for the Stockholm syndrome to develop. What are they?
8. What are the most common health and physical effects of sex trafficking on victims?
9. In what ways does the pimp's relationship to the girl he is trying to cultivate into prostitution closely parallel the dynamics of a battering relationship?
10. What is the role of the "bottom bitch/girl" in the pimp-control hierarchy?
11. How is pornography used to control prostituted girls?

12. How did one self-proclaimed author/pimp explain how to apply each stage of Maslow's Hierarchy of Needs to sex trafficking?
13. What is it that causes the majority of domestically trafficked minors to flee nonprotective shelters?
14. Why are adolescents considered a lower priority by many child protective service agencies in the United States?

Endnotes

1. *Draft Declaration and Agenda for Action*, World Congress Against Commercial Sexual Exploitation of Children at 2, Stockholm, Sweden (August 27–31, 1996) [hereinafter *Draft Declaration*].
2. Beth E. Molnar, et al., "Suicidal Behavior and Sexual/Physical Abuse Among Street Youth," *Child Abuse Neglect* 22 (3) (1998): 213–214; Maggie O'Neill, "Prostitute Women Now," in *Rethinking Prostitution: Purchasing Sex in the 1990s,* eds. Graham Scambler & Annette Scambler, (London: Routledge, 1997), p. 19; Debra Whitcomb & Julie Eastin, *Joining Forces Against Child Sexual Exploitation: Models for a Multijurisdictional Team Approach* (United States: Office of Juvenile Justice and Delinquency Prevention, 1998).
3. *See* Debra Whitcomb, Edward De Vos, & Barbara E. Smith, *Program to Increase Understanding of Child Sexual Exploitation, Final Report* at 3 (Washington, D.C.: Education Development Center, Inc., and ABA Center on Children and the Law, 1998). (Since much of the literature is "based on the same (or related) research efforts by the same (or collaborating) authors, the actual research base is even smaller. Many of these studies lack scientific rigor and are based on extremely small sample sizes.").
4. Ibid.
5. *Report of the Special Rapporteur on the Sale of Children, Child Prostitution and Child Pornography*, United Nations Economic and Social Council, Commission on Human Rights, 52d Sess., Agenda Item 20, ¶ 35, U.N. Doc. E/CN.4/1996/100 (1996) [hereinafter *Report of the Special Rapporteur*].
6. In one study of 200 prostitutes in San Francisco, about 60% were 16 and younger, many were 10, 11, and 12 years old. Mimi H. Silbert & Ayala M. Pines, "Entrance into Prostitution,"

Youth Society 13 (4) (1982): 471, 473. A more recent sample of 83 sexually exploited youth interviewed in shelters in Dallas, Pittsburgh, and San Diego showed a majority (62%) between the ages of 14 and 17, and 12% between 10 and 13. Twenty-six percent were older than 18. Whitcomb et al., *Program to Increase Understanding of Child Sexual Exploitation,* 66.

7. Whitcomb & Eastin, *Joining Forces Against Child Sexual Exploitation,* 36 (citing *Community Consultation on Prostitution in British Columbia, Overview of Results* (March 1996)); Mimi H. Silbert & Ayala M. Pines, "Occupational Hazards of Street Prostitutes," *Criminal Justice and Behavior* 8 (1981): 397.

8. *Program to Increase Understanding of Child Sexual Exploitation, Assessment Report, Volume II* (Education Development Center, Inc., and ABA Center on Children and the Law, 1994) [hereinafter *Assessment Report*].

9. Byron Fassett & Bill Walsh, "Juvenile Prostitution: An Overlooked Form of Child Sexual Abuse," *The APSAC Advisor* 7 (1) (1994): 9–10 (American Professional Society on the Abuse of Children, 1994).

10. Whitcomb & Eastin, *Joining Forces Against Child Sexual Exploitation,* 36 (citing *Community Consultation on Prostitution in British Columbia, Overview of Results* (March 1996)).

11. Whitcomb et al., *Program to Increase Understanding of Child Sexual Exploitation,* 65 (76% of exploited youth interviewed in shelters were girls).

12. *Assessment Report.* Some service providers also mentioned an increase in the number of homeless boys, which they sometimes linked to cutbacks in other community services.

13. *Assessment Report.*

14. David Barrett & Wilma Beckett, "Child Prostitution: Reaching out to Children Who Sell Sex to Survive," *British Journal of Nursing* 5 (18) (October 12, 1996): 1120–1125, note 18.

15. Silbert & Pines, "Occupational Hazards of Street Prostitutes," 485.

16. Alex H. Kral, et al., "Prevalence of Sexual Risk Behavior and Substance Use Among Runaway and Homeless Adolescents in San Francisco, Denver, and New York City," *International Journal of STD and AIDS* (1997): 109.

17. Kathryn V. Wurzbacher, et al., "Effects of Alternative Street School on Youth Involved in Prostitution," *Journal of Adolescent Health* 12 (1991): 549–554.

18. Silbert & Pines, "Occupational Hazards of Street Prostitutes," 490.

19. Linda A. Smith, Samantha Healy Vardaman, & Melissa A. Snow, *The National Report on Domestic Minor Sex Trafficking: America's Prostituted Children*, Shared Hope International, May 2009. Online at: http://www.sharedhope.org/Resources/ The National Report (accessed July 9, 2012).

20. Kacie L. Macdonald, "Human Trafficking: A Service Provider's Guide to Recognizing and Assisting Victims of Modern Day Slavery. Paper presented at North American Association of Christians in Social Work (NACSW), Indianapolis, IN, October 2009). Online at: http://www.nacsw.org (accessed January 17, 2013).

21. Magnus J. Seng, "Child Sexual Abuse and Adolescent Prostitution: A Comparative Analysis," *Adolescence* 24 (1989): 665, 671.

22. Wurzbacher, et al., "Effects of Alternative Street School on Youth Involved in Prostitution," 549. *See also* Whitcomb, et al., *Program to Increase Understanding of Child Sexual Exploitation,* 21 (of sexually exploited youth interviewed in a Dallas shelter, 81% had been truants, 34% had been suspended or expelled, and 12% were drop-outs).

23. Augustine Brannigan & Erin Gibbs Van Brunschot, "Youth Prostitution and Child Sexual Trauma," *International Journal of Law and Psychiatry* 20 (3) (1997): 337–354.

24. Silbert & Pines, "Occupational Hazards of Street Prostitutes," 490.

25. Brannigan & Gibbs van Brunschot, "Youth Prostitution and Child Sexual Trauma," 350.

26. Wurzbacher, et al., "Effects of Alternative Street School on Youth Involved in Prostitution," 549.

27. Among girls, 14% reported exchanging sex for money; 11% for drugs or alcohol; and 10% for food, shelter, or clothing. Among boys, 23% reported exchanging sex for money; 7% for drugs or alcohol; and 10% for food, shelter, or clothing. Kral, et al., "Prevalence of Sexual Risk Behavior and Substance Use Among Runaway and Homeless Adolescents in San Francisco, Denver and New York City," 113. Various studies have found that 22% of boys and 7% of girls on New York City streets had engaged in prostitution at some time, while 26 to 28% of boys and 26 to 31% of girls in Los Angeles did so. Mary Jane Rotheram-Borus, et al., "Sexual Abuse History and Associated Multiple Risk Behavior in Adolescent Runaways," *American Journal of Orthopsych* 66 (1996): 390–391. Although less than 1% of minority nonhomeless youth at a medical clinic in a New York City public high

school reported using sex to obtain money or drugs, 13% of homeless youth in Chicago had recently engaged in prostitution. Prostitution also was reported by 54% of street youth in Toronto, 26.4% of a sample of runaways in Los Angeles, and 19% of runaway and homeless youth in Houston. T. P. Johnson, et al., "Self-Reported Risk Factors for AIDS Among Homeless Youth," *AIDS Education and Prevention* 8 (4) (August 1996): 308, 318 (citing numerous studies). *See also* Gary L. Yates, et al., "A Risk Profile Comparison of Runaway and Non-Runaway Youth," *American Journal of Public Health* 78 (1988): 820–821.

28. Seng, "Child Sexual Abuse and Adolescent Prostitution," 671.

29. Whitcomb, et al., *Program to Increase Understanding of Child Sexual Exploitation,* 74.

30. Gary L. Yates, et al., "A Risk Profile Comparison of Homeless Youth Involved in Prostitution and Homeless Youth Not Involved," *Journal of Adolescent Health* 12 (1991): 545, 547.

31. Seng, "Child Sexual Abuse and Adolescent Prostitution," p. 673.

32. M. Alexis Kennedy & Nicole Joey Pucci, *Domestic Minor Sex Trafficking Assessment Report—Las Vegas, Nevada* (Springfield, VA: Shared Hope International, August 2007), 106.

33. Ibid.

34. Kelli Stevens, et al., *Domestic Minor Sex Trafficking Assessment Report—Fort Worth, Texas* (Springfield, VA: Shared Hope International, July 2008): 35.

35. Jennifer Bayhi-Gennaro, *Domestic Minor Sex Trafficking Assessment Report—Baton Rouge / New Orleans, Area Assessment* (Springfield, VA: Shared Hope International, April 2008), 13, citing E. Fitch, "Grand Jury Indicts Murder Suspect." *The News-Star.* June 14, 2006.

36. Nicole Hay, *Domestic Minor Sex Trafficking Assessment Report— Dallas, Texas* (Springfield, VA: Shared Hope International, 2008), 11.

37. Silbert & Pines, "Occupational Hazards of Street Prostitutes," 481. After leaving school and before getting into prostitution, the vast majority of young women in the study reported being either isolated, with no friends (40%), or deeply involved with friends exhibiting deviant behavior (80%).

38. M. A. Morey & L. S. Friedman, "Health Care Needs of Homeless Adolescents," *Current Opinion in Pediatrics* 5 (4) (1993): 395–399. Self-identified homosexual or bisexual homeless teenagers are five times more likely to engage in survival sex than heterosexual homeless youth.

39. Silbert & Pines, "Occupational Hazards of Street Prostitutes," 485.
40. Jose Saporta & Bessel A. van der Kolk, "Psychobiological Consequences of Trauma," in *Torture and Its Consequences,* ed. Metin Basoglu (Cambridge: Cambridge University Press, 1992).
41. Linda A. Smith, Samantha Healy Vardaman, & Melissa A. Snow, *The National Report on Domestic Minor Sex Trafficking* (Springfield, VA: Shared Hope International, 2009).
42. Ibid.
43. Ibid.
44. Judith L. Herman, *Trauma and Recovery: From Domestic Abuse to Political Terror* (London: Pandora, 1994).
45. Cecilie Hoigaard & Liv Finstad, *Backstreet: Prostitution, Money and Love* (Cambridge: Polity Press, 1992), 64.
46. Ibid.
47. Claude Jaget, ed., *Prostitutes, Our Life* (Bristol, U.K.: Falling Wall Press, 1980); Eileen McLeod, *Women Working: Prostitution Now* (London: Croom Helm, 1982).
48. Sheila Jeffreys, "Globalizing Sexual Exploitation: Sex Tourism and the Traffic in Women," *Leisure Studies* 18 (3) (1999): 179–196.
49. Hoigaard & Finstad, *Backstreet*, 192.
50. Ibid., 112.
51. Ibid.
52. Definition of Stockholm syndrome. Online at: http://medical-dictionary.thefreedictionary.com (accessed June 7, 2012).
53. For further information regarding these various psychological disorders, see the *Diagnostic and Statistical Manual of Mental Disorders DSM-IV-TR,* 4th Ed. (Washington, D.C.: American Psychiatric Publishing, 2000).
54. Virginia Tenias De-Lopez, *Domestic Teen Sex Trafficking,* (slide presentation), Rutgers University, School of Social Work, 2010.
55. Ibid.
56. Remarks by K. Childs. Shared Hope International National Training Conference on the Sex Trafficking of America's Youth. (Transcript on file with authors.)
57. Evelina Giobbe, "Juvenile Prostitution: Profile of Recruitment," in *Chile Trauma I: Issues and Research,* ed. Ann Wolbert Burgess (New York: Garland Publishing, Inc., 1992), 118.
58. O'Neill, "Prostitute Women Now," 14.
59. Children of the Night, *Training Manual* 11 (February 1993). www.childrenofthenight.org
60. Fassett & Walsh, "Juvenile Prostitution: An Overlooked Form of Child Sexual Abuse," 30.

61. *Assessment Report*, 162; Kathleen Barry, *The Prostitution of Sexuality* (New York: New York University Press 1995), 208.

62. Barry, "Juvenile Prostitution: An Overlooked Form of Child Sexual Abuse," 106.

63. Jean Faugier & Mary Sargeant, "Boyfriends, 'Pimps' and Clients," in *Rethinking Prostitution: Purchasing Sex in the 1990s*, eds. Graham Scambler & Annette Scambler (London: Routledge, 1997), 123.

64. Neal K. Katyal, "Men Who Own Women: A Thirteenth Amendment Critique of Forced Prostitution," *Yale Law Journal* 103 (1993): 791, 793.

65. Barry, "Juvenile Prostitution: An Overlooked Form of Child Sexual Abuse," 208.

66. Annette U. Rickel & Marie C. Hendren, "Aberrant Sexual Experiences," in *Adolescent Sexuality*, eds. Thomas Gullotta, Gerald Adams, & Raymond Montemayor (Newbury Park, CA: Sage Publications 1993).

67. Ibid., 153.

68. Fassett & Walsh, "Juvenile Prostitution: An Overlooked Form of Child Sexual Abuse," 30.

69. Barry, "Juvenile Prostitution: An Overlooked Form of Child Sexual Abuse," 200.

70. Evelina Giobbe, "An Analysis of Individual, Institutional and Cultural Pimping," *Michigan Journal of Gender and Law* 1 (1) (1993): 33, 46. Others have also come to this conclusion: "By listening to survivors describe the tactics of control that kept them trapped in the sex industry and comparing this to our knowledge about battering, we've come to recognize that prostitution is violence against women." Holly B. Fechner, "Three Stories of Prostitution in the West: Prostitutes' Groups, Law and Feminist 'Truth,'" *Columbia Journal of Gender and Law* 4 (1994): 26, 36–37 (citing WHISPER Progress Report 1985–1989 at 1 (WHISPER, Minneapolis, MN)). WHISPER endorses abolition of all laws that penalize women and children in prostitution and seeks enhanced penalties for pimps and customers as well as increased enforcement of existing laws; Ibid.

71. Giobbe, "An Analysis of Individual, Institutional and Cultural Pimping," 47.

72. Ibid., 48.

73. Ibid., 50.

74. Minouche Kandel, "Whores in Court: Judicial Processing of Prostitutes in the Boston Municipal Court in 1990," *Yale Journal of Law and Feminism* 4 (1992): 329. The Council for

Prostitution Alternatives found that 53% of prostitutes they interviewed were "horribly" beaten by pimps an average of 58 times per year. Barry, "Juvenile Prostitution: An Overlooked Form of Child Sexual Abuse," 202.

75. Fassett & Walsh, "Juvenile Prostitution: An Overlooked Form of Child Sexual Abuse," 30; Giobbe, "An Analysis of Individual, Institutional and Cultural Pimping," 48.

76. Fassett & Walsh, "Juvenile Prostitution: An Overlooked Form of Child Sexual Abuse," 30.

77. *See* expert testimony presented in *State v. Simon*, 831 P.2d 139 (Wash. 1992).

78. Ibid.

79. *Pierce v. United States*, 146 F.2d 84 (5th Cir. 1944); *People v. Kent*, 96 Cal. App. 3d 130 (1979) (prostitute beaten for not bringing in enough money).

80. Barry, "Juvenile Prostitution: An Overlooked Form of Child Sexual Abuse," 198.

81. *See* Whitcomb, et al., *Program to Increase Understanding of Child Sexual Exploitation*, 79.

82. *Assessment Report*, 158. In an older study, over three quarters of juveniles involved in prostitution reported they had a pimp. Silbert & Pines, *Occupational Hazards of Street Prostitutes, Criminal Justice and Behavior*, 498. Another study of prostituted juveniles found that only 10% had never worked for a pimp, compared to 28% of adults. Kandel, "Whores in Court," 347 (citing Dorothy H. Bracey, *"Baby-Pros:" Preliminary Profiles of Juvenile Prostitutes* 37 (1979)).

83. Whitcomb, et al., *Program to Increase Understanding of Child Sexual Exploitation*, 92.

84. Giobbe, "An Analysis of Individual, Institutional and Cultural Pimping," 48.

85. Hay, *Domestic Minor Sex Trafficking Assessment Report—Dallas, Texas*, 9, citing T. Eiserer, "Club where girl, 12, stripped will keep license," *Dallas Morning News*, March 27, 2008. Online at: http://www.dallasnews.com/sharedcontent/dws/news/localnews/crime/stories/DN-clubs_27met.ART.West. Edition1.1589397.html (accessed April 5, 2008).

86. Personal interview, "Tonya," December 13, 2008.

87. TVPA, 22 USC 7101 §103(3).

88. Reid, *Domestic Minor Sex Trafficking Assessment Report—Clearwater, Florida*, p. 68, quoting assessment interviewee from Hillsborough Kids, Inc., Clearwater, FL.

89. Remarks by C. Johnson. Shared Hope International National Training Conference on the Sex Trafficking of America's Youth. (Transcript on file with authors.)

90. Ibid. *See also* Giobbe, "An Analysis of Individual, Institutional and Cultural Pimping," 124.

91. Margaret A. Baldwin, "Pornography and the Traffic in Women: Brief on Behalf of Trudee Able-Peterson, et al. Amici Curiae in Support of Defendant and Intervener-Defendants, Village Books v. City of Bellingham," 1 *Yale Journal of Law and Feminism* 1 (1989): 111, 130.

92. Ibid., 128. *See also* Rickel & Hendren, "Aberrant Sexual Experiences," 151.

93. Baldwin, "Pornography and the Traffic in Women," 140.

94. Ibid., 132. Runaways who "come under the control of pornographers and pimps become susceptible to subsequent physical and sexual victimization by pimps and customers." Cathy S. Widom & Joseph B. Kuhns, "Childhood Victimization and Subsequent Risk for Promiscuity, Prostitution and Teenage Pregnancy: A Prospective Study," *American Journal of Public Health* 86 (11) (1996):1607–1612.

95. *Prostituted Children in the United States: Identifying and Responding to America's Trafficked Youth*, Seg. 3. Prod. Shared Hope International and Onanon Productions. DVD. Washington, D.C.: Shared Hope International, 2008.

96. R. J. Martin, "How to be a Pimp Using Maslow's Hierarchy of Human Needs to Make the Most Money," *Associated Content* (October 26, 2006). Online at: www.associatedcontent.com/article/75184/how_to_be_a_pimp_using_maslows_hierarchy.html?cat=7 (accessed January 20, 2009).

97. Giobbe, "An Analysis of Individual, Institutional and Cultural Pimping," 43. Another commentator analyzes forced prostitution as slavery under the 13th Amendment's prohibition against slavery and involuntary servitude, advocating that government officials act unconstitutionally under the 13th Amendment if they fail to enforce laws against pimps. Katyal, "Men Who Own Women."

98. Public Discourse: Ethics, Law and the Common Good, Online at: http://www.thepublicdiscourse.com/2011/10/4034 (accessed July 18, 2012).

99. Smith et al., *The National Report on Domestic Minor Sex Trafficking,* 67–68, 72–73.

100. Heather J. Clawson & Lisa Goldblatt Grace, "Finding a Path to Recovery: Residential Facilities for Minor Victims of Domestic Sex Trafficking," Study of HHS Programs Serving Human Trafficking Victims (prepared for the Office of the Assistant Secretary for Planning and Evaluation (ASPE), U.S. Department of Health and Human Services by Caliber: September 2007). Online at: http://aspe.hhs.gov/hsp/07/HumanTrafficking/ResFac/ib.htm (accessed April 30, 2009).

101. Remarks by Cathy Brock. Shared Hope International National Training Conference on the Sex Trafficking of America's Youth (Dallas, Texas: September 15–16, 2008). (Transcript on file with authors.)

102. Bayhi-Gennaro, *Domestic Minor Sex Trafficking Assessment Report—Baton Rouge / New Orleans, Louisiana*, pg. 133.

103. Remarks by Katie Carlson, Director GIFT Network, Boston, MA. Shared Hope International National Training Conference on the Sex Trafficking of America's Youth (Dallas, Texas: September 15–16, 2008). (Transcript on file with authors.)

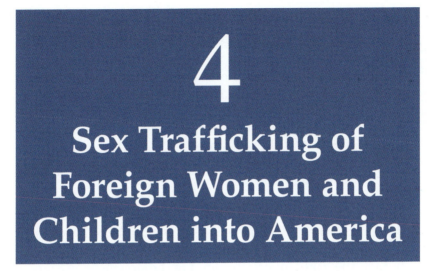

4

Sex Trafficking of Foreign Women and Children into America

Two tearful women from Eastern Europe who were forced into prostitution comfort each other after being rescued by law enforcement officers. (Photo courtesy of Philippe Lopez/AFP.)

Chapter Objectives

1. Discuss the four stages of the sex trafficking of international women into the United States.
2. Understand the ways in which foreign women are sex trafficked, transported, delivered, marketed, and exploited in the United States.
3. Describe the role coyotes play in the smuggling and sex-trafficking process.
4. Understand the role of organized crime in sex trafficking.
5. Identify those locations where sex-trafficked women are most likely to be found.
6. List the right questions for law enforcement officers to ask in order to properly analyze the sex-trafficking problem.
7. Explain what investigators can do to maximize the acquisition of information in the interviewing process of foreign women.
8. Discuss the strategies that are most effective in combating the international sex trafficking of women and children.
9. Describe how to best educate the public about sex trafficking.
10. Understand why it is so useful for law enforcement officers to work with immigration officials.
11. Be aware of the services both governmental organizations and nongovernmental organizations (NGOs) may be able to provide to sex trafficking survivors.

Introduction

In the previous chapter, we focused primarily on the ways in which American children are sex trafficked in the United States. In this chapter, we will focus primarily on women and children who are trafficked into the United States from foreign countries and then forced into prostitution. We will examine the ways in which they were recruited and transported into this country, the methods used for marketing them once they arrive, as well as the role of organized crime in the sexual exploitation of these women and children.

Also included in this chapter is a list of suggested questions that will assist investigators in locating, identifying, helping, and interviewing foreign victims who have been trafficked into the United States as well as the importance of local law enforcement establishing a working relationship with immigration officials. Lastly, we will discuss the important role that can be played by governmental as well as nongovernmental organizations in assisting sex-trafficking survivors.

Stages of International Sex Trafficking

There are essentially four stages of the trafficking of international women into the United States namely: recruitment, transportation, delivery/marketing, and exploitation.[1]

Recruitment

Recruiters, traffickers, and pimps who engage in trafficking foreign women for the purpose of sexual exploitation have developed common methods of recruitment. One method is through advertisements in newspapers offering lucrative job opportunities in foreign countries for low skilled jobs, such as waitresses and nannies. Some advertisements promise good salaries to young, attractive women who will work as nannies, models, actresses, dancers, and hostesses. Women, especially from Eastern European countries, are recruited through social events and auditions, such as photo sessions. The process is usually complex, with detailed deception calculated to reassure the women that the employment opportunity is genuine.[2] It is estimated that 20% of trafficked women are recruited through media advertisements.

Another method of recruitment is through "marriage agencies," sometimes called mail-order-bride agencies or international introduction services. According to the International

Organization for Migration, all mail-order bride agencies with women from the republics of the former Soviet Union (discussed later in this chapter) are under the control of organized crime networks.[3] Many of these agencies operate on the Internet.[4] Recruiters use "marriage agencies" as a way to contact women who are eager to travel or emigrate. This route into the sex industry can take several forms. The recruiters may be traffickers or work directly with traffickers. The woman may meet with a man who promises marriage at a later date. The man may use the woman himself for a short period of time, then coerce her into making pornography and later sell her to the sex traffickers in the sex industry, or he may directly deliver the woman to a brothel. There are, however, strict U.S. laws intended to regulate the marriage broker industry (Figure 4.1).

Some traffickers use the woman's legal documents and tourist visas to legally enter the destination countries. The women may be put on a circuit by pimps in which they are moved from country to country on legal tourist visas or entertainers' visas. Other times, the woman is given false documents. In this case, the woman is even more vulnerable after she arrives in the destination country because she is there illegally.

Transportation

The main means of trafficking women from Eastern Europe and Asia into the United States is by air.[5] Most often, these women are trafficked according to a previously planned route, often using the services of a tourist agency that may or may not be linked to trafficking. Trafficked women may be transported across borders with or without legitimate documentation. The use of forged or stolen passports and visas and the use of tourist visas are common.[6] Again, the interplay between smuggling and trafficking is evident at this stage of the process.

In some locations, especially those states along the U.S.– Mexican border (Arizona, Texas, New Mexico, and California) where the borders are porous or stretch across inhospitable or isolated territory, smugglers and traffickers, also known as coyotes, or *polleros*, may offer safe passage across established or known routes. Smuggling along these routes is accomplished

U.S. International Marriage Broker Regulation Act of 2005

Definition of an International Marriage Broker	Responsibility of International Marriage Brokers
An international marriage broker is a legal entity that charges fees for providing dating, matrimonial matchmaking services, or social referrals between a U.S. citizen, or aliens lawfully admitted to the U.S. as permanent residents, and foreign national clients by providing personal contact information or otherwise facilitating communication between individuals. [*Sec.*833e(4)(A)]	International marriage brokers are prohibited from marketing, providing contact information, photographs or general information about children under the age of 18. [*Sec.*833(*d*)(1)] Each international marriage broker shall search the National Sex Offender Public Registry. [*Sec.*833(*d*)(2)(A)(*i*)] Each international marriage broker shall collect background information about the U.S. client; to whom the personal contact information of a foreign national client would be prohibited. [*Sec.*833(*d*)(2)(*ii*)] International marriage brokers shall collect a certification signed by the U.S. client attesting: • Any civil protection order or restraining order issued against the U.S. client; • Any federal, State, or local arrest or conviction for homicide, murder, manslaughter, assault, battery, rape, domestic violence, torture, child abuse or neglect, incest, sexual exploitation, trafficking, peonage, holding hostages, involuntary servitude, slave trade, kidnapping, stalking, prostitution, procuring, and receiving proceeds of prostitution; • Marital history of the U.S. client • All states and countries in which the U.S. client has resided since he was 18. [*Sec.*833(*d*)(2)(*B*)] An international marriage broker shall not provide any U.S. client or representative with the personal contact information of any foreign national client unless and until the international marriage broker has collected the required information. [*Sec.*833(*d*)(3)(A)]
Individual Responsibility	
The Secretary of State shall develop an information pamphlet, which shall include a warning concerning the potential use of K non-immigrant visas by U.S. citizens who have committed domestic violence, sexual assault, child abuse, or other crimes. [*Sec.*833(*a*)(2)]	
Government Responsibility	
A person who knowingly discloses, uses, or causes any information obtained by an international marriage broker to be used for any purposes other than the disclosures required under this paragraph shall be punished by a fine and imprisonment for up to a year." [*Sec.*833(*d*)(3)(c)]	

Figure 4.1 U.S. International Marriage Broker Regulation Act of 2005. (From M. Mattar, *Comprehensive Legal Approaches to Combating Trafficking in Persons: An International and Comparative Perspective*, p. 53. Online at: http://www.protectio nproject.org/wp-con tent/uploads/2010/ 09/PP_Chartbook_English.pdf)

either on foot or by loading a multitude of immigrants into vehicles, such as trucks or vans, and then surreptitiously crossing the border into the United States. However, women and children who are transported to the United States from Mexico by traffickers face not only the risks inherent in being trafficked, but also the serious risks of the journey.[7] Each year, between 400 and 500 people are known to die while attempting to cross the border between Mexico and the United States. The U.S. Department of Homeland Security reported that 417 people died trying to cross the U.S.–Mexico border in 2009, the most recent year for which statistics are available.[8] The numbers are probably higher. These are only the cases discovered or reported in the United States; the numbers of those who die while still in Mexico are not known. Also not known is the number of victims who have been swallowed up by the deserts and unforgiving conditions of the American Southwest, never to be discovered.[9]

Young girls often unwittingly become trafficking victims when they are singled out by their smugglers during the journey north. They are told they can travel at no cost if they will agree to work later to pay off their debts. These smugglers/traffickers deceive and dupe the girls through false promises of jobs and other economic opportunities waiting for them in the United States. During their journeys, the girls are shown favoritism, and even given clothes, makeup, and gifts. Upon arriving at their destinations, however, they are informed that they owe a debt to their smugglers and they will have to pay it off by working in the sex industry. In the United States, these girls are often held in slavery-like conditions and forced into prostitution. They are terrorized emotionally, forced to take drugs, moved frequently, locked up, raped, beaten, deprived of sleep, and starved. The smugglers knew from the start that exploitation would be the cost of the "travel now, pay later" deal (Figure 4.2).

Of course, not everyone who is illegally smuggled across the border by paid guides is being trafficked. Trafficking specifically targets the victim as an object of criminal exploitation. The purpose from the beginning of the trafficking enterprise is to profit from the exploitation of the victim. Smuggling can quickly become trafficking, however, as many people who agree

Figure 4.2 Migrants and a female coyote. This female "coyote" and migrants are gathering in the Mexican town of Sásabe, in the state of Sonora. They have been divided into groups and are preparing to illegally cross the border from Mexico into the United States. Women are often involved in sex-trafficking operations because it is easier for another woman to deceive young naïve women. (Photo courtesy of Claudia Núñez/ *La Opinión*.)

to pay for assistance entering the United States are then forced to provide additional funds, labor, or services to the smugglers when they cross the border.[10]

Some victims of trafficking even possess the necessary documents to enter the United States legally. These women and children typically rely upon traffickers for transportation and sponsorship, only to discover that there is a price for these services. Other victims are kidnapped, sold, and forced to come to the United States, as the following two cases illustrate:

Case 1

In September, 2006, Immigration and Customs Enforcement Special Agent Greg W. Swearngin received information that underage girls from Mexico were being forced to work in several Mexican brothels in the Memphis, Tennessee, area. On October 13, 2006, search warrants were executed on seven locations there. Investigators took 27 individuals into custody on a variety of criminal and immigration charges. Information obtained from the search warrants revealed that Juan Mendez and Christiana Perfecto of Nashville, Tennessee, were supplying underage girls to brothels located throughout the southeastern United States.

Using the information from the search warrants, the prosecution team was able to locate and rescue a 14-year-old minor, "S.C." Through S.C., the prosecution team learned that Juan Mendez would send his girlfriend, Christiana Perfecto, to a rural village in Oaxaca, Mexico, to recruit young girls to come to the United States to work in a Nashville restaurant and to attend American schools. Once the girls arrived, they were threatened, beaten, raped, and then forced to work in brothels in several different states. While these girls agreed to be smuggled into the United States, they were in no way prepared for what awaited them.[11]

Case 2

Maria (not her real name) was 16 years old when she was lured into a border gang by a young man on the streets of the deadly Mexican border town of Ciudad Juarez. Maria came from a poor family, with six brothers and sisters. The attention paid to her by a young man with money and promise of work in the United States, overcame the warnings of others to stay away from the man, whom many believed to be associated with a local cartel. Maria found herself staying in a house on the outskirts of Juarez, with a number of other young women and children. She was introduced to drug use, often against her will. The day came when Maria was asked to have sex with other men to make money for the young man who had brought her into the house. When she refused, Maria was raped by the man and four others.

Any pretense of affection disappeared as Maria was expected to service as many as 30 men a day in a small bedroom with a mattress on the floor and little else. Maria later recounted stories of abuse and beatings for trying to run away or refusing the orders of her handlers. She witnessed other girls undergo the same abuses, some being made examples while the remaining girls were forced to watch.

Before she was 17, Maria was smuggled across the border to El Paso, Texas, and later Phoenix, Arizona. There she worked out of an apartment, again as a prostitute, her money now going to a middle-aged woman who oversaw at least a half dozen girls and women, servicing dozens of men each day. Maria was ultimately caught up in a sweep of undocumented immigrants and returned to Mexico. There is no indication that she tried to tell immigration officials of her circumstances.

Upon return to Mexico, Maria was forced back into the only means of survival she knew. She was involved in prostitution, often servicing *Norteños* or northerners who would travel from the United States to the brothels and massage parlors of Juarez for her services. Maria told human rights officials in Mexico that she witnessed young children, some less than 12-years-old, moved through the houses where she worked. By the age of 19, Maria had disappeared. She has not been seen by her family since. They fear that hers may be one of the more than 250 bodies of young women discarded each year in vacant lots and fields around Ciudad Juarez.[12]

Delivery/Marketing

Both before and after a woman has reached the United States, the availability for her sexual services can be marketed through standard outlets, such as advertising in personal columns, but by far the most effective marketing is via Internet chat rooms, bulletin boards, and the many Web sites that offer matchmaking services for men and women.[13] Where a prior arrangement has been reached to traffic a woman for prostitution, she is handed over to her intended employer upon arrival at her destination. In cases where there is no delivery to a specific person or organization, the woman is technically not trafficked, but smuggled. In this case, if she is young, without family, and without the ability to speak English, she may end up in the sex trade, and her trafficked status will be difficult to determine by local police.

If she is forced to become a prostitute, she may be confined within particular ethnic communities where men seek to purchase sex from women or young girls of their own ethnicity. This serves to further isolate trafficked women from the broader community.[14] Recent research suggests that there is considerable sex trafficking of women between various U.S. cities. The frequent movement of women serves three purposes:

- It makes detection more difficult and removes the incentive for local investigative agencies to become involved.
- It provides a variety of women for customers.
- It inhibits women from establishing ties to their communities.[15]

Exploitation

Trafficked women are extremely vulnerable for three reasons. First, as illegal aliens, many women do not know they have rights and, therefore, are fearful of seeking assistance from police or other service agencies. Second, women and their families are often in debt to the traffickers. This debt is characterized as a debt bondage and occurs when a person provides a loan to another who uses his or her labor or services to repay the debt. When the value of the work, as reasonably assessed, does not apply toward the liquidation of the debt, the situation becomes a debt bondage.[16] Third, should a woman's situation, such as working in the sex trade, become known back home, her family's honor may be damaged. As a result, those who "employ" trafficked women have enormous control over them. In effect, conditions of employment become conditions of slavery.[17] However, the definition of exploitation is difficult because trafficked persons—and even legal immigrants—often consent to exploitation in the hope that they can improve their circumstances by doing so.[18] This creates a serious problem for local police because victims may refuse to cooperate and may even resist attempts to improve their circumstances.

Factors Contributing to the Exploitation of Trafficked Women

Understanding the factors that contribute to sex-trafficking problems can help frame local analysis, identify effective remedial measures, recognize key intervention points, and select appropriate responses.

The Market for Commercial Sex

Supply

The international proliferation of trafficking has created a supply of trafficked women that is so large that it drives the market. Countries that make no attempt to control sex trafficking[19] use the trade as a means of importing foreign currency, espe-cially U.S. dollars and Euros. This is achieved both by encour-aging sex tourism in the originating country and by tacitly approving the exportation of women to wealthy countries.[20] Globalization, along with dramatic shifts in the politics and economies of some countries, has facilitated the movement of women for the sex trade from one country to another. This is especially true for women from four Eastern European countries that were part of the former Soviet Union: Ukraine, Russia, Belarus, and Latvia. In 1991, the Soviet Union col-lapsed politically and economically, thus resulting in many countries that had been part of the former Soviet Union becom-ing independent states. As independent states emerged from the former Soviet Union, they lacked organized efficient regu-latory agencies to hinder the growth and activities of crime networks.[21] When the state system was no longer able to pay the salaries of many employees, they joined the criminal net-works.[22] For example, in Ukraine, people who were no longer able to support themselves with one salary or weren't being paid for long periods of time, sought additional work. The only jobs available were in the newly emerging privatized or crimi-nal businesses. The result was the criminalization of the econ-omy in general and expansion of organized criminal networks.

Transnational trafficking of women became a new type of crime in the republics of the former Soviet Union. This activity first started during perestroika in 1986,[23] which was a pro-gram of economic, political, and social restructuring that also resulted, in part, on the restrictions on international travel being eased. It also opened borders for travel, migration, and privatized trade, all of which facilitated the operations of crim-inal networks. Sex industries in receiving countries created demand for women that transnational crime networks (from the newly independent states) organized to fill with relatively low risk and high profit for the networks. Trafficking exists to meet the demand for women, who are then used in broth-els, massage parlors, bars, and stretches of streets and high-ways, where women are sold to men in prostitution. Ukraine, especially, has become a major source of young women for the international sex markets, including the United States.[24]

Demand

Some argue that trafficking for the sex trade is simply a response to a natural need, that is, men will be men. Others argue that this is a misconception, and rather than men's sexual needs being such that prostitution must exist to fulfill them, the truth is that men's sexual appetites respond to the opportunities offered them by the purveyors of prostitution.[25] In other words, it is the market—the trafficking in women—that creates the demand, not the customers. If there is a plentiful supply of vulnerable women and girls, a profitable business plan follows: Offer the services of young women that cater to any customer preference at a competitive price and pay the women little or nothing.[26]

Organized Crime and Sex Trafficking

In the case of sex trafficking, organized crime can be grouped into three broad classifications: First, large-scale mafia-like networks, such as the Russian and Albanian syndicates that control about 60% of prostitution in Western Europe. These networks also traffic in drugs,[27] but have increasingly turned to trafficking in women because the profit margins are higher. Highly organized from the recruitment to the exploitation stages, these groups are well connected financially and politically, and are typically cruel and brutal in doing business. Second is the medium-scale networks that specialize in trafficking women from a particular recruitment country to a particular destination country. These networks usually arrange transportation and also own their own brothels in the destination country. Third, informal "family" networks of individuals who have come together to reap the financial benefits usually have legitimate jobs in other fields and operate trafficking businesses on the side. The Cadena sex-trafficking case is one of the more notorious ones that fall into this category.[28]

Case 3

This case involved the trafficking of approximately 25 to 40 Mexican women who were forced into prostitution in the state of Florida. All the women were from Vera Cruz, had previously lived alongside members of the Cadena family, and, in some cases, had known them for many years.

The victims' contact with the traffickers began with seemingly casual approaches, with the recruiting most often done in the victims' hometowns by a well-dressed Mexican woman. None of the victims reported previous exploitation in Mexico; their vulnerability appears to have been heightened by their inability to comprehend the kind of exploitation they would eventually suffer. In at least two instances, relatives were complicit in the recruiting: one woman was trafficked by her cousins, and another by the daughter of her stepfather. The traffickers typically offered the young women six-month contracts in Florida working in the Cadena family's restaurants or serving as nannies in the home of the Cadena brothers. Such jobs proved illusory. Charging their victims approximately $2,000 in smuggling fees, the traffickers ultimately coerced the victims into sexual servitude as a means of supposedly acquitting this debt. Guarded constantly by armed pimps upon their arrival in Florida, the women suffered repeated beatings, rapes, and threats against the lives of their families in Mexico.

The women were confined together in trailers that functioned as brothels in migrant farm worker communities throughout Florida. Their periods of captivity ranged from several months to a year, during which time their traffickers forced them to have sex with 25 to 30 men per day. Holding them in groups of four to five, they generally worked 12 hours per day, 6 days a week, and the women were rotated under armed guard every 15 days or so among brothels, to give customers "fresh faces" and to keep the women disoriented and unable to make any deep connections with customers or local residents. Customers were given business cards with the address of the Fort Pierce brothel and a hand-drawn map and it was estimated the family made $2.4 million in two years from the ring. All of the women were eventually rescued by law enforcement in a raid and four members of the Cadena family were arrested[29] (Figure 4.3).

Understanding and Assessing the Local Problem

Carefully analyzing the local problem will help in designing an effective response strategy. The most difficult problems to be faced in any community will be the clandestine nature of the exploitation of trafficked women, which is made possible by the isolation and separation of trafficked women from the

Figure 4.3 The Cadena family. (Left to right) Rafael Alberto Cadena and Carmen Cadena. These individuals were two of the four people found to be responsible for deceiving and trafficking 25 to 40 Mexican women into coming to the United States and forcing them into prostitution in which they had sex with 25 to 30 men per day while working in brothels servicing migrant farm workers. (Photo courtesy of Florida Department of Law Enforcement, Tallahassee, FL.)

local community. Although trafficked women are hidden from public view, there is one point of weakness, which is that sex traffickers must break the isolation they maintain in order for their trafficked women to service their customers. In fact, prostitutes are often hidden in plain view; their presence is usually well known in a local community. However, the public may not recognize or know that they are also trafficked women.

Attractive Features of Certain Locations

The following are some features that make certain locations more attractive for sex trafficking than others:

- Communities that tolerate red light districts, strip clubs, and late night bars and clubs. Where domestic prostitutes are plentiful, internationally trafficked women can blend in without drawing much attention.
- Areas around military bases where there is a constant supply of men willing to purchase sexual services, frequently from foreign women.[30]
- Old warehouse and manufacturing districts where sweatshops can flourish out of sight of local communities.

- Isolated rural areas where trafficked women may be employed as seasonal farm laborers or be used to provide sexual services to male seasonal laborers as in the Cadena case.
- Locations close to poorly patrolled border entry points or in immigrant communities that are neglected by local government.
- Areas with large immigrant or foreign-born populations that may frequent establishments set up in culturally familiar styles.

Locating Trafficked Women

Illegal immigrants are not necessarily trafficked, and trafficking victims are not always illegal immigrants. Thus, although brothels are commonly placed in migrant areas, the police should not assume that they will always find trafficked women in those areas. In fact, traffickers may keep victims away from areas where their languages are spoken, even while catering to customers who speak those languages. The first contact with trafficked women will most likely be by members of the local law enforcement agency's vice squad. However, unless vice squad officers have been trained to identify sex-trafficking victims, they may believe that they are women who have voluntarily entered into prostitution to make money.[31]

Indications of Sex-Trafficking Venues

Indicators of a venue where sex trafficking may be found include:

- Buildings with heavy on-premises security, such as barred windows, barbed wire fences, especially those with the barbed wire facing inward indicating that it is intended to keep people in rather than to keep people out, locked doors, including interior bedroom doors that have exterior locks to keep women imprisoned at night, and electronic surveillance (Figure 4.4).
- Buildings in which women both live and work.
- Brothels that advertise only in foreign language newspapers or that restrict services to members only.

Locks on the Outside of a Bedroom Door

Figure 4.4 Locks on the outside of a bedroom door. This is the door to a bedroom where the sex-trafficking victim was forced to have sex with "johns." At night, the door was padlocked to keep her imprisoned. (Photo courtesy of the Florida Department of Law Enforcement, Tallahassee, FL.)

- Advertisements for escorts or other sexual services.
- Internet Web sites and chat rooms with a strong sexual orientation.

Other possible sources of information to verify sex trafficking:

- Hospital emergency rooms and health and abortion clinics
- Ethnic healthcare providers
- Immigrant support groups
- HIV/AIDS community groups
- Money wire transfer receipts
- Phone records, especially to overseas locations (Figure 4.5)
- Legal or fraudulent identification, immigration documents
- Weapons

Items at the scene that can be used to verify or strongly suggest a sex-trafficking operation:

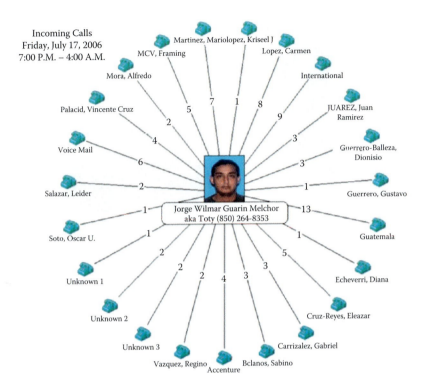

Figure 4.5 Phone records can be invaluable in proving a sex-trafficking conspiracy is occurring. For example, as used in the arrest and prosecution of Jorge Wilmar Guarin Melchor, who was a member of a Colombian ring of high school friends who trafficked both drugs and women. He is a pimp who operated the Tallahassee "franchise" of the sex-trafficking network. They drove the women to motels and trailer parks to have sex with johns. (From the Florida Department of Law Enforcement, Tallahassee, FL.)

- Personal lubricants
- Alcohol and paper towels
- Overcrowded and inadequate living and working conditions[32]
- Travel photographs
- Business cards (Figure 4.6)
- Handwritten maps to the brothel
- Locations with large numbers of transient males, such as military bases, sports venues, conventions, and tourist attractions
- Nail salons, bars, and strip clubs serving as fronts for sex-trafficking operations (Figure 4.7)

Figure 4.6 A business card used in a sex-trafficking operation. This business card was distributed to Mexican–American stores in the United States by a Colombian sex trafficker. The pimp placed his name and phone number on the back of the card. In this operation, the women would be delivered to the locations where men had requested they be delivered for the purpose of prostitution. (From the Florida Department of Law Enforcement, Tallahassee, FL.)

Figure 4.7 Federal authorities bust sex-trafficking strip club. Federal agents escort Anthony Vecchione, a reputed member of the Gambino organized crime family, from Federal Plaza on Tuesday, April 20, 2010, in New York. (Photo by AP/Jin Lee. With permission.)

If there are no visible signs of the sex trade in an area, the investigators should look into the informal networks that exist in all localities. Word of mouth, whether from a bartender or a taxi driver, is a typical way of finding out about the underground sex trade. The purveyors of sex must advertise their services. If customers can learn about these services, so can the police.

Indications of Women Being Sex Trafficked

The following are indications that a women is possibly being sex trafficked:[33]

- Women who are too frightened to speak, especially to police or other officials, including healthcare and social workers
- The presence of very young prostitutes in brothels and massage parlors
- Workers who look sickly or who display signs of physical abuse
- Prostitutes who cannot speak English
- Women who are unable or unwilling to explain how they came into the United States or what they did before gaining entry
- Women who are closely supervised when taken to a doctor or hospital
- Women who are denied clothing other than those provided by a brothel
- Prostitutes whose legal representation is supplied by their trafficker, often as a means of controlling their testimony
- Women who appear fearful of collaboration between traffickers and police
- Women who do not know how their travel documents were obtained or where they are
- Women who paid a fee to obtain travel documents or make travel arrangements

An Interview Protocol That Will Facilitate the Obtaining of Valuable Information from Sex-Trafficking Victims

Over the years, experienced sex-trafficking investigators have gained valuable experience in identifying those protocols that result in the most successful interviews. The following list has a series of suggestions that less-experienced sex-trafficking investigators may find useful.

- Be aware that traffickers might not be easy to distinguish from victims.
- Educate yourself on trauma, its impact and effects on the sex trafficking victim and consider collaborating with a trauma specialist to assist with the interviews.
- Adopt a compassionate and nonjudgmental manner.
- If possible, conduct interviews with victims/witnesses while in plain clothes and keep attire informal.
- Do not display weapons or badges during the interview process.
- When an interpreter is needed, select one that is in no way connected to the traffickers. While a good interpreter is essential, the interviewer must use the vocabulary the victim understands. Briefing and debriefing an interpreter can ensure that the victim will understand the language used in the interview. An interpreter trained in sex-trafficking issues also can help eliminate confusion regarding language nuances, such as differences in dialect and other culturally sensitive issues.
- Do not ask: "Are you a trafficking victim?"
- Allow the interviewees to describe what happened to their counterparts before focusing on their own suffering; it is often easier for them to initially talk about what happened to other people.
- Only persons absolutely essential to the interview should be present.

- Provide victims the opportunity to tell their story; it may help for them to be able to do so.[34] Investigators should avoid repeatedly interviewing the victim because the process can be physically and psychologically exhausting and may result in retraumatizing the victim who will be reliving her experience every time she has to talk about it.
- Do not use interrogation methods. Investigators must remember that this is an *interview*.
- It is best to use a conversational approach rather than a rapid series of questions in order to obtain preliminary information.
- Open-ended questions will elicit more information from victims than those answerable with a yes or no response.[35]
- It can be very helpful to have trusted victim service providers conduct a parallel interview because they can assist in reducing the victim's fear of law enforcement personnel. They will not be gathering the facts of the crime, but instead will be assessing practical needs of the victim.
- Be sure the victim has some control in the situation (breaks, water, seating placement).
- Allow the victim to set the length and pace of the interview.
- Do not make promises you may not be able to keep.
- Do not videotape or audiotape the initial conversations. It is quite likely that the victim will still be in shock and somewhat traumatized by her first encounter with American law enforcement. As a matter of fact, she might even be under the influence of drugs and or alcohol during the initial interview. This is not the kind of interview prosecutors want to have recorded and then be required to show to a jury. It tends to exacerbate the problem of inconsistencies should the victim later change her testimony when she is sober and/or has developed a level of trust with the investigator.

Interviewing the Sex-Trafficking Victim

Sex-trafficking victims often provide the valuable information and testimony that becomes evidence in the future prosecution of a case. The victim will have to be depended upon in order to show the existence of coercion or threats. In evidence-based investigations, investigators may handle the case as if the victim will not testify, but in sex-trafficking investigations, the victim has a much greater role.[36] However, in order to maximize the possibility of cooperation from the victim, it is absolutely essential that she feel safe at all times.

It is important that the initial interview be held in a location that makes the victim feel comfortable. Unfortunately, many police buildings do not have the kinds of facilities that lend themselves to creating a comfortable and nonthreatening atmosphere for victims. Therefore, it is absolutely essential that, if efforts are going to be made to find an alternative location, a formal relationship already be established with those organizations willing to provide a facility. Examples of these include churches, safe houses, hotels, or domestic violence shelters.

Key Questions to Ask the Victim of Sex Trafficking

Background Questions

- Where were you born?
- With whom do you live now?
- How many people live with you?
- How many beds are in your room?
- How much do you pay for rent?
- Are you able to contact your family?
- Are you able to have a private conversation with your family?
- Do you go to church?
- Where do you go to church?
- Did anyone tell you what to say?

Immigration Questions

Avoid using the term *immigration* when talking with the victim. Obtain any identification and immigration documents later in the interview, in a low-key manner, without making the victim feel as though you are investigating her as opposed to the traffickers.

- How did you come to the United States?
- When did you come to the United States?
- Why did you come to the United States?
- What is your date of birth?
- What are the names of your parents?

Physical Abuse Questions

- Did someone threaten you with harm if you tried to leave?
- Did you ever witness any threats against other people if they tried to leave?
- Has someone threatened your family?
- Has another person told you that someone threatened your family?
- Did someone physically abuse you?
- Did you ever witness abuse against another person?
- What type of physical abuse did you witness?
- Were there any objects or weapons located where you were staying?
- Did you tell someone outside of the situation that someone is abusing you (police reports, domestic violence reports, hospital records, social service records)?
- Did you receive medical care?
- If you did receive medical care, who provided it?

Safety/Coercion Questions

The investigator should first make it clear to the victim that he/she is interested in the safety of the victim and her family.

- Has anyone threatened your family?
- Did someone harm you physically?
- Did someone deprive you of food, water, sleep, medical care, or any other necessities?
- Has anyone ever forced you to take medications?

Freedom of Movement Questions

- Do you buy clothes or food on your own?
- Can you come and go by yourself or does someone have to go with you to the store?
- Is your freedom of movement restricted?
- Do you live and work in the same place?
- What are the conditions under which you are alone?
- Are there instances of physical restriction through locks, chains, etc.?
- Are there locks on the doors? If so, who has the key?
- How is movement in public places handled (car, van, bus, subway)?
- Who supervises your movement in public places?
- How is the purchase of private goods and services handled (medicines, prescriptions)?
- What forms of media or telecommunication do you have access to (television, radio, newspapers magazines, telephone, the Internet)?
- Where do you go shopping? Do you go by yourself or with friends?

Psychological Coercion Questions

Be aware of the fact that traffickers do not have to be physically abusive with victims to control them. For example, some questions to determine if psychological coercion was ever used against the victim include:

- Are you afraid of someone?
- Why are you afraid of them?
- What would you like to see happen to the people who hurt you (jail, deportation)?
- How do you feel about the police? Why?[37]

Specific Responses to the Exploitation of Trafficked Women

There are three approaches to reducing or preventing the exploitation of trafficked women:

- Enforcing laws directed against exploiters, traffickers, and men who purchase sex
- Reducing demand for commercial sex and cheap labor
- Changing the environment so that it is inhospitable to traffickers and exploiters

Adopting an Unambiguous Enforcement Policy

Enforcement attitudes to the sex trade are currently in flux. At the international level, some countries, such as Sweden argue that trafficked prostitutes are victims rather than offenders, and that the purchasers of sex should be punished, and not the sex workers. This view was first translated into law in Sweden in 1998, and has increasingly become the policy of the U.S. Department of State and the Department of Defense. It is too early to tell whether this approach will be translated into policy or law at the local levels of criminal justice, or whether it will contribute to the reduction of trafficking in women for the sex trade, as claimed by some early Swedish research.[38] Whatever policy a department adopts, it should be clear and unambiguous, leaving no room for ambivalent enforcement, such as occasional sweeps and raids. The success of any policy also depends upon training officers to understand the diverse ethnic and cultural issues outlined in the preparatory responses above, and the clarity with which the policy of enforcement is applied in that setting.

Working with Immigration Officials

Developing a close working relationship with immigration officials is essential to the successful investigation and prosecution of sex-trafficking cases because the victim is always the key witness. It also will help in identifying trafficked women and in establishing their immigrant or refugee status.

Unfortunately, there is a long history of conflict between local police and federal immigration officials in many parts of the United States in part because even though local police have the legal and constitutional responsibility to enforce federal immigration laws, they may be concerned that enforcing immigration laws will damage their acceptance in local immigrant communities.[39] Because the situation of trafficked women is complicated by their ambiguous status as both illegal aliens and crime victims, extensive policies and procedures must be worked out between local and federal officials, especially in terms of establishing the status of one who has suffered a "severe form of sex trafficking" as defined by the Trafficking Victims Protection Act (TVPA). Without cooperation on both sides, a trafficking victim could be deported or detained for immigration-related crimes, thus resulting in the loss of valuable eyewitness testimony needed to prosecute traffickers.

When potential traffickers are encountered, their immigration status often can be verified if they have been issued an Alien Number (also known as an "A number"). ICE (Immigration and Customs Enforcement) maintains a 24/7 hotline (866-347-2423) for U.S. law enforcement officers that can be called to determine if a trafficker is already in the ICE system. If a trafficker is not legal, he or she can often be held on immigration charges (smuggling, transporting, or harboring illegal aliens) while a human trafficking investigation continues.

The Role of Governmental Organizations in Assisting Sex-Trafficking Victims

There are a number of governmental organizations that are available to assist sex-trafficking victims. They are described below.

U.S. Department of Health and Human Services (HHS)

HHS leads the Rescue and Restore Victims of Human Trafficking public awareness campaign, funds organizations to conduct outreach to foreign and U.S. citizens, funds comprehensive case management and support services for foreign victims in the United States, and certifies foreign victims of a severe form of sex trafficking to be eligible to receive federal benefits and services to the same extent as refugees. A range of programs also assists youth at risk of trafficking, including the Runaway and Homeless Youth Program. HHS also funds the National Human Trafficking Resource Center that provides a nationwide 24/7 hotline at 888-373-7888.

U.S. Department of Education (ED)

ED's Office of Safe and Drug-Free Schools uses the Web, listserves, and training awareness to prevent sex trafficking of children and to increase victim identification of trafficked children in schools. Trafficking often involves school-aged children—particularly those not living in their homes—who are vulnerable to coerced labor exploitation, domestic servitude, or commercial sexual exploitation. Traffickers target minor victims through telephone chat lines, social networking Web sites, as well as confronting them on the streets, in malls, and by using girls to recruit other girls at school and in after-school programs. The Office of Safe and Drug-Free Schools develops and disseminates materials about preventing human trafficking, such as "Human Trafficking of Children in the United States: A Fact Sheet for Schools" and the Readiness and Emergency Management for Schools Web site. Online at: http://rems.ed.gov/index.php?page=resources_Additional&section=1i&section=1i1.

U.S. Department of Homeland Security (DHS)

DHS consists of more than 20 component agencies and offices, including both law enforcement entities and the nation's immigration services. In 2010, DHS launched the Blue Campaign, a first-of-its-kind campaign to coordinate and enhance the Department's effects to combat human trafficking. The Blue Campaign, which include 17 DHS components, such as U.S. Immigration and Customs Enforcement, U.S. Citizenship and Immigration Services, U.S. Customs and

Border Protection, the U.S. Coast Guard, and the Federal Law Enforcement Training Center, harnesses and leverages the varied authorities and resources of the Department to deter human trafficking by increasing awareness, protecting victims, and contributing to a robust criminal justice response.

As the largest investigative agency within DHS, U.S. Immigration and Customs Enforcement Homeland Security Investigations (HSI) conducts domestic and international investigations of human trafficking, child sex tourism, and focuses investigative resources on investigating U.S. citizens and lawful permanent residents that travel abroad to engage in illicit sexual activity with minors. Worldwide, HSI conducts law enforcement training and public awareness campaigns, such as Hidden in Plain Sight, as part of its outreach efforts. HSI also provides trafficking victims with short-term immigration relief, manages the HSI Victim Assistance Program, and operates a 24-hour hotline to report potential trafficking activity at 866-DHS-2-ICE (866-347-2423).

U.S. Citizenship and Immigration Services (USCIS) grants immigration relief to sex-trafficking victims, while also conducting training for nongovernmental organizations (NGOs) and law enforcement. USCIS officers are trained to identify potential trafficking victims and to notify law enforcement personnel upon encountering such individuals.

U.S. Customs and Border Protection (CBP) conducts public campaigns, such as No Te Engañes, to raise awareness among potential victims and vulnerable communities. CPB also screens unaccompanied alien children to identify human trafficking victims.

The U.S. Coast Guard routinely conducts maritime operations independently and with other federal law enforcement agencies and international partners to combat illegal migration, including human trafficking.

The Federal Law Enforcement Training Center provides human trafficking training to federal, state, local, campus, and tribal law enforcement officers throughout the United States.

Additionally, human trafficking training is delivered at several of the International Law Enforcement Academies including the academy in Gaborone, Botswana, which is managed by the Federal Law Enforcement Training Center. DHS is the chair of the Human Smuggling and Trafficking Center steering group in coordination with the U.S. Department of Justice and Department of State. The Center provides a mechanism to bring together federal agency representatives from the policy, law enforcement, intelligence, and diplomatic areas to work together on a full time basis to achieve increased effectiveness, and to convert intelligence into effective law enforcement and other action. For more information, please visit the DHS Blue Campaign Web page (www.dhs.gov/blue-campaign/blue-campaign) or the DHS Blue Campaign Facebook page.

U.S. Agency for International Development (USAID)

USAID funds international programs that prevent trafficking, protect and assist victims, and support prosecutions through training for police and criminal justice personnel. USAID reinforces successful antitrafficking initiatives by funding programs that support economic development, child protection, women's empowerment, good governance, education, health, and human rights. USAID supports individual country assessments of the scope and nature of trafficking and the efforts of government, civil society, and international organization to combat it.

The Role of Nongovernmental Organizations (NGOs) in Assisting Sex-Trafficking Victims

An NGO is an institution or organization, commonly nonprofit in nature and fully independent from the government, which is organized to focus on addressing a particular common interest. NGOs can provide a variety of services and functions that may include bringing citizen concerns to governments, advocating or monitoring policies, encouraging political participation through distribution of information, and participating in a direct service

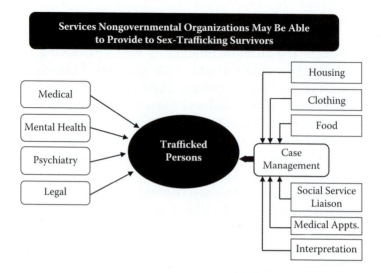

Figure 4.8 Services nongovernmental organizations may be able to provide to sex-trafficking survivors. (From Florrie Burke, Renee Huffman, and Ayuda Kavitha Sreeharsha, *National Conference on Human Trafficking, The TVPRA Decade: Progress and Promise,* U.S. Department of Justice, May 3–5, 2010, p. 30.)

provider role. They also can provide analysis and expertise, provide warning mechanisms, and help to monitor and implement laws and agreements, both internationally and domestically.

The NGOs' main goal, as it relates to sex trafficking, is to provide services in order to address various needs of sex-trafficking survivors (Figure 4.8). Safe housing is essential, from safe emergency housing to transitional housing with supportive services to permanent affordable housing. Medical assessment and follow-up care, including HIV testing, as well as appropriate mental health assessment and follow-up care are also of crucial importance. Some victims also might need programs to address dependence on alcohol and drugs. Safety planning is another necessity and may be particularly complex if the victim's trafficker is part of an organized crime network or otherwise well-connected in the community, or if the victim is traumatically bonded with the trafficker. Safety planning also can be complex because the victim's family members may be vulnerable as well. These include family members who face physical dangers from the traffickers who are determined to retaliate against them if a sex-trafficking victim makes a decision to cooperate with the police in the prosecutorial process.

Various NGOs help victims of sex trafficking to navigate the legal system. When traffickers are prosecuted, victims may require assistance interacting with the criminal justice system, which could include local or state police officers, FBI agents, representatives from immigration services, or local, state, or federal prosecutors. Some victims may defend themselves, therefore, coordination and advocacy with their criminal defense attorney is essential. Sex trafficking victims who are undocumented in the United States will need referrals to immigration lawyers who have experience with the specific remedies available to victims of sex trafficking. (This was discussed in greater detail in Chapter 2.)

The lawyers should be able to provide the victims with answers to the following questions:

- What will happen during the prosecution of the criminal case?
- What can they expect at each stage of the process?
- Who will be involved?
- What are the victim's rights (e.g., state and federal victim–witness and human trafficking laws)?
- What type of legal services can they expect?[40]

Locating an Appropriate NGO

There are a variety of NGOs in many communities, but not all are in a position to assist with rescued sex-trafficking victims and others may not service that type of clientele. For example, some NGOs that have an interest in human trafficking may want to concentrate their efforts on providing services to those individuals rescued during labor exploitation violations, such as those involving migrant workers, factory workers, and so forth. Therefore, it is essential for a law enforcement agency that is looking to establish a working relationship with an NGO to do so with one that has a goal and philosophy that is consistent with the agency's position and that provides for the needs of women who have been sex trafficked and rescued. (See the Appendix at the back of the book which identifies numerous nongovernmental organizations and U.S. government agencies available to assist sex trafficking victims.)

There also are important questions that need to be addressed by law enforcement agencies attempting to develop a policy on referrals with NGOs. These include answers to the following questions:

1. Will the agency respond to emergencies?
2. Will the agency respond to multiple survivors, and if so, how many will they be able to accommodate?
3. How much prior notice does the agency need before a rescue attempt is going to be made?
4. Will the agency respond to those sex-trafficking victims, who are legally considered to be children?
5. What resources does the agency have to provide housing shelter, food, medical care, legal advice, interpreters, security, etc.?
6. Does the NGO currently have a protocol for the intake of new clients?[41]

It is absolutely essential that all of the above questions be answered before victims are rescued. In most traditional law enforcement operations, law enforcement officers do not normally deal with multiple victims. However, in sex-trafficking cases, it is possible that as many as 15 to 20 victims may be rescued. Many of these victims may be children who are similar to the adults, in that they are from different cultures, who very likely speak little or no English. Therefore, specific attention has to be paid to creating both a strategic and tactical framework for dealing with all the issues in response to the six questions listed above.

Preraid Communications with the NGO

If a rescue operation is anticipated and the investigator knows that there is a good likelihood that sex-trafficking victims will be rescued, it is absolutely essential that contact be made with these organizations ahead of time so that they can be prepared to accept these sex-trafficking victims once they are rescued.

In addition, law enforcement officers should advise personnel at the facility of the anticipated number of women who may be rescued so they will be in a better position to provide for their needs, such as food, beds, medical care, etc.

Glossary

Brothel: A house or other structure where men pay to have sexual intercourse with prostitutes.

Coyote: Someone who specializes in human smuggling.

Debt bondage: When a person provides a loan to another who uses his or her labor or services to repay the debt; when the value of the work, as reasonably assessed, is not applied toward the liquidation of the debt.

Massage parlor: An establishment that provides massage treatments, or one offering sexual services in addition to or in lieu of a massage.

Marriage agencies: Agencies that are sometimes used as fronts for deceiving and tricking women who are coming to the United States for a marriage, when, in fact, they are being brought here for the purposes of being prostitutes in the sex trade.

Nongovernmental organization: An NGO is an institutional organization commonly nonprofit in nature and fully independent of the government, which is organized to focus on addressing a particular common interest.

Organized crime: A widespread group of professional criminals who rely on illegal activities as a way of life and whose activities are coordinated and controlled through some form of centralized syndicate.

Pimp: A person, usually a man, who solicits customers for a prostitute or a brothel, in return for a share of the money that is generated, usually the lion's share.

Pollero: Another name used for a coyote.

Prostitution: The practice or occupation of engaging in sex with someone for payment.

Sex industry: The commercial enterprises related to sale or purchase of sex-related services, ranging from individual "workers" in prostitution to the pornographic end of the entertainment industry.

Sex trade: Exploitation for the purpose of forced prostitution.

Trafficked women: Women who have been specifically tricked or deceived into coming to the United States, thinking that they were engaging in one kind of work, but who were then forced into prostitution.

Review Questions

1. What are the four stages of the trafficking of women into the United States?
2. What is a coyote or *pollero*?
3. What caused the dramatic increase in the sex trafficking of women from Russia, Ukraine, Belarus, and Latvia?
4. In the case of sex trafficking, organized crime can be grouped into three classifications. What are they?
5. What are the indications of women possibly being involved in sex trafficking?
6. What was recommended, as it relates to the officer's attire, when conducting an interview with a trafficking victim?
7. What type of facilities were recommended for conducting the preliminary interview of sex-trafficking victims?
8. Why should there be an unambiguous enforcement policy when it comes to prostitution enforcement?
9. Why is it necessary for local and state police officers to develop a close working relationship with immigration officials?
10. What governmental agencies are available to assist sex-trafficking victims?
11. What role can nongovernmental organizations play in assisting sex-trafficking victims?

Endnotes

1. Graeme R. Newman, *The Exploitation of Trafficked Women* (Washington, D.C.: U.S. Department of Justice, Office of Community Oriented Policing Services, February 2006), 10–51. Much of this discussion was adapted with minor modifications from this source.

2. MiraMed Institute, "Who is trafficking CIS women?" *Preliminary Survey Report on Sexual Trafficking in the CIS* (Moscow: MiraMed Institute, June 1999).

3. International Organization for Migration, *Information Campaign Against Trafficking in Women from Ukraine-Research Report* (Geneva, Switzerland: International Organization for Migration, July 1998).

4. Donna M. Hughes, "Sex Tours via the Internet." *Agenda: A Journal about Women and Gender* 28 (1996): 71–76.

5. J. Raymond & D. Hughes, *Sex Trafficking of Women in the United States: International and Domestic Trends* (North Amherst, MA: Coalition Against Trafficking in Women, 2001). Online at: http://action.web.ca/ home/catw/attach/sex_traff_us.pdf.

6. One study found that over 50% of trafficked women entered the Unites States with tourist visas and overstayed their visas. Raymond and Hughes, *Sex Trafficking of Women in the United States.*

7. Jim Walters & Patricia H. Davis, "Human Trafficking, Sex Tourism, and Child Exploitation on the Southern Border," *Journal of Applied Research on Children: Informing Policy for Children at Risk* 2 (1) (Article 6), (2011), 3–8.

8. S. Gamboa, "Migrant Border Deaths Reach 417 in 2009," *Associated Press*. May 6, 2010. Online at: http://www.msnbc.msn.com/id/37004712/ns/us_news-life (accessed January 15, 2011).

9. M. Jiminez, "Humanitarian Crisis: Migrant Deaths at the U.S.–Mexico Border," ACLU of San Diego & Imperial Counties/*Comisión Nacional de los Derechos Humanos*, October 2009. Online at: http://www.aclu.org/immigrants-rights/humanitarian-crisis--migrantdeaths-us-mexico-border (accessed January 15, 2009).

10. Office of the Attorney General of Texas, "Texas Human Trafficking Prevention Task Force Report to the Texas Legislature. (January 2011). Online at: https://www.oag.state.tx.us/oagnews/release.php?id=3202 (accessed January 15, 2011).

11. U.S. Department of Justice, United States Attorney's Office, Western District of Tennessee. USAO Press Release. October 27, 2010. Online at: http://www.justice.gov/usao/tnw/press_releases/ 2010/2010OCT27A. GAwards.html (accessed January 15, 2011).

12. Walters & Davis, "Human Trafficking, Sex Tourism, and Child Exploitation on the Southern Border," 8.

13. D. Hughes, *The Impact of the Use of New Communications and Information Technologies on Trafficking in Human Beings for Sexual Exploitation: A Study of the Users*. (Strasbourg, France: Council of Europe, Committee for Equality between Women and Men, 2001).

14. E. Parrado, C. Flippen, & C. McQuiston, "Use of Commercial Sex Workers Among Hispanic Migrants in North Carolina: Implications for the Spread of HIV," *Perspectives on Sexual and Reproductive Health* 36 (2004), 150–156.

15. United Nations Economic and Social Commission for Asia and the Pacific (UNESCAP), *Combating Human Trafficking in Asia: A Resource Guide to International and Regional Legal Instruments, Political Commitments and Recommended Practices* (Bangkok, Thailand: UNESCAP, 2003). Online at: http://www.unescap.org/publications/detail.asp?id=841

16. When a person provides a loan to another who uses his or her labor or services to repay the debt; when the value of the work, as reasonably assessed, is not applied toward the liquidation of the debt.

17. In the pre-Civil War South, replacing a slave cost the modern equivalent of $40,000. Slaves in the 21st century can be purchased for as little as $90. For example, a family in Thailand was reported to have sold a daughter into the sex trade in order to buy a television set (Florida State University, Tallahassee, Center for the Advancement of Human Rights, 2003), 14.

18. United Nations Economic and Social Commission for Asia and the Pacific (UNESCAP). *Combating Human Trafficking in Asia: A Resource Guide to International and Regional Legal Instruments, Political Commitments and Recommended Practices* (Bangkok, Thailand: UNESCAP, 2003) Online at: www.unescap.org/publications/detail.asp?id=841

19. The TVPA established a set of standards for countries to combat trafficking. Countries are rated annually according to these standards and allocated to one of three tiers: (1) full compliance, (2) some compliance, and (3) no compliance or no effort to comply. As of 2005, all countries are required by U.S. law

to collect and publish prosecution and conviction statistics on human trafficking. Countries making no effort to combat trafficking are subject to various U.S. sanctions (Washington, D.C.: U.S. Department of State, 2004, 2005).

20. U.S. Department of State, *Trafficking in Persons Report* (Washington, D.C.: U.S. Department of State, 2004). Online at: http://www.state.gov/g/tip/rls/tiprpt/2004/

21. Donna Hughes, "The 'Natasha' Trade: Transnational Sex Trafficking," *National Institute of Justice Journal* (246) (January 2001).

22. Todd S. Fogelsong & Peter H. Solomon, *Crime, Criminal Justice and Criminology in Post-Soviet Ukraine—A Report* (Washington D.C.: National Institute of Justice, August 30, 1999).

23. *Perestroika*—From modest beginnings at the 27th Party Congress in 1986, perestroika, Mikhail Gorbachev's program of economic, political, and social restructuring, became the unintended catalyst for dismantling what had taken nearly three quarters of a century to erect: the Marxist–Leninist–Stalinist totalitarian state.

24. Chris Bird, "100,000 Ukrainians Slaves of West's Sex Industry," *Reuters*, July 6, 1998.

25. This is the rationale that underlies the Swedish legislation outlawing the purchase of sexual services. As its advocate says: "It is the market that is the driving force. Demand is defined by the services produced, not vice versa, which contradicts certain popular traditional market theories." (Sven-Axel Mansson, interviewed by Maria Jacobson, 2002.)

26. There is some evidence of a growing demand by purchasers of sex for foreign women of various ethnic backgrounds. There is considerable evidence that men's sexual expectations are driven by ethnic stereotypes and myths, Donna Hughes, *Best Practices to Address the Demand Side of Sex Trafficking* (Washington, D.C.: U.S. Department of State, 2004).

27. Drug use is common in prostitution, serving as another weapon to keep trafficked women dependent on their pimps or managers and isolated from the outside world. Raymond & Hughes, *Sex Trafficking of Women in the United States*.

28. Terry Coonan, "Human Trafficking: Victims' Voices in Florida," in *International Sex Trafficking of Women and Children,* ed. Leonard Territo and George Kirkham (Flushing, NY: Looseleaf Law Publications, 2010), 19–20.

29. Ibid., 16–21.

30. Military bases are magnets for trafficked women. For example, as a result of the presence of 16,000 U.N. soldiers in Cambodia between February 1992 and September 1993, the number of prostitutes in Phnom Penh reportedly increased from 6,000 to 20,000. G. Ekberg, "The Swedish Law That Prohibits the Purchase of Sexual Services," *Violence Against Women* 10 (10), 1197. October 2004. This pattern is repeated around military bases within the United States. Raymond and Hughes, *Sex Trafficking of Women in the United States.*

31. Donna Hughes, *Hiding in Plain Sight: A Practical Guide to Identify Victims of Trafficking in the U.S. With Particular Emphasis on Victims of Sexual Trafficking as Defined by the Trafficking Victims Protection Act 2000* (Providence: University of Rhode Island, 2003). Online at: http://www.uri.edu/artsci/wms/hughes/hiding_in_plain_sight.pdf

32. *Advanced Investigative Techniques of Human Trafficking Offenses*, May 10, 2007, Instructor Guide, Florida Criminal Justice Advanced Course 1166, Criminal Justice Standards and Training Commission, Florida Department of Law Enforcement, Unit 2, Lesson 1, pp. 10–15.

33. B. Venkatraman, "Guide to Detecting, Investigating, and Punishing Modern-Day Slavery," *Police Chief* 70 (12) (2003), 34–43.

34. International Association of Chiefs of Police, *The Crime of Human Trafficking: A Law Enforcement Guide to Identification*, 11. Online at: http://www.vaw.umn.edu/documents/completehtguide /completehtguide.pdf

35. U.S. Office of Justice, *Anti-Human Trafficking Task Force Strategy and Operations e-Guide,* 68. Online at: http://www.ovcttac.gov/TaskForceGuide

36. *Advanced Investigative Techniques of Human Trafficking Offenses*, Florida Criminal Justice Advanced Course 1166, Instructor's Guide, Unit 2, Lesson 4, pp. 5–6. May 10, 2007.

37. Ibid., 12–17.

38. M. Jacobsen, "Why do Men Buy Sex? An interview with Sven-Axel Mansson." *Journal of the Nordic Institute for Women's Studies and Gender Research* 1 (2002), 22–15.

39. J. Edwards, *Officers Need Backup: The Role of State and Local Police in Immigration Law Enforcement. Backgrounder* (Washington, D.C.: Center for Immigration Studies, 2003). Online at: http:// www.cis.org/articles/2003/back703.html

40. Florrie Burke, Renee Huffman, & Ayuda Kavitha Sreeharsha, *National Conference on Human Trafficking, The TVPA Decade: Progress and Promise* (Washington, D.C.: U.S. Department of Justice, May 3-5, 2010), 9.
41. Ibid., 21.

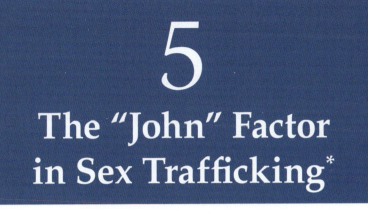

5
The "John" Factor
in Sex Trafficking[*]

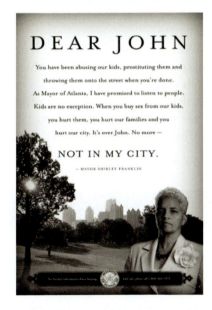

DEAR JOHN

You have been abusing our kids, prostituting them and
throwing them onto the street when you're done.
As Mayor of Atlanta, I have promised to listen to people.
Kids are no exception. When you buy sex from our kids,
you hurt them, you hurt our families and you
hurt our city. It's over John. No more —

NOT IN MY CITY.

— MAYOR SHIRLEY FRANKLIN

This is the main print media message for the Atlanta, Georgia, Dear John
Public Education Awareness Program. It warns men about not trying to
prostitute Atlanta's children or try to buy sex from prostituted children in
Atlanta. (From the City Newsbytes: The Official e-newsletter for the city of
Atlanta. Online at: http://174.37.215.145/media/cityne wsbytes_121807.aspx)

---

[*] This chapter was adapted from Michael Shively, Kristina Kliorys, Kristin
Wheeler, & Dana Hunt, *A National Overview of Prostitution and Sex Trafficking
Demand Reduction Efforts,* Final Report, April 30, 2012, prepared for the National
Institute of Justice by Abt Associates Inc., Document number 238796 (Cambridge,
MA: Abt Associates Inc.).

Chapter Objectives

1. Discuss demand reduction as a primary prevention to the solicitation of prostitution.
2. Describe the most common public education and awareness programs intended to eliminate the commercial sex trade.
3. Explain how reverse stings and sting operations work.
4. Discuss how the Internet is used in the transactions of commercialized sex and how the police can use it to track down sexual predators.
5. Understanding how surveillance cameras are used in some communities as a deterrence to keep men from soliciting prostitutes.
6. Discuss how vehicle seizure and driver's license suspension programs work and what the pros and cons are about such programs.
7. Explain why shame can be such an effective deterrent to men who are inclined to solicit prostitutes.
8. Understand the rationale for the creation of "john schools."

Introduction

Thus far in this book, we have focused on many dimensions of sex trafficking in the United States, including detailed discussions of both victims and the traffickers. However, in this chapter, we will focus primarily on the role of the customers (the johns) of commercialized prostitution because without them the profits generated in sex trafficking would not exist. We will discuss demand reduction as a primary approach to prevention, public education awareness programs specifically addressing demand for commercial sex, and the police tactic known as "stings" or "reverse stings," and other tactics employed to reduce demand, such as vehicle seizure and driver's license suspensions and the use of shame. Lastly, we will discuss "john schools," which are intended to both educate and treat men arrested for soliciting illegal commercial sex.

Demand Reduction Is Primary Prevention

Primary prevention refers to stopping events before they occur or ensuring that people do not become afflicted by crime (or disease), rather than treating its symptoms. Secondary prevention refers to early detection in an effort to minimize harm, while tertiary prevention addresses recovery from fully realized afflictions.[1]

The total elimination of commercial sex markets is unrealistic as a short-term goal, but there is no reason to assume that markets cannot be significantly reduced if the root causes are addressed, thereby resulting in fewer victims—that is the hallmark of primary prevention.

To correctly be considered preventive, it must be demonstrated that the approach reduces the prevalence and/or incidence of sex trafficking or exploitation. Approaches that simply displace crime from one street to the next, from the streets to indoors, from one town to another, or from one set of victims to another, may be considered effective by people at the original locations, but not by the new hosts of sexual exploitation or by the new set of victims. Similarly, programs that help survivors recover from being enslaved or exploited, or punish those who profit from selling sex, cannot be considered prevention programs unless they reduce the size of the overall markets (although we again stress that efforts to help survivors and prosecute traffickers are critically important to restore lives and seek justice, and should be strengthened and expanded).

The only methods empirically demonstrated to substantially reduce the size of commercial sex markets are those featuring a focus on (or included as a component) combating demand. There is a lack of evidence showing that attacking pimps and traffickers or rescuing survivors affects the markets substantially, and reductions in commercial sex markets should not be expected as long as demand is strong.

From an examination of the logic and causal mechanisms of any market, and the history of efforts to suppress illicit markets, one should not expect secondary or tertiary prevention efforts to have a substantial impact because they address the symptoms more than the cause. Applying these lessons to sex trafficking, one could expect that if every survivor were rescued and every pimp and trafficker were arrested tomorrow, others would quickly emerge or be trafficked to take their place. When demand is strong and the trade lucrative, as in the illicit drug trade, new supplies will be found if current ones are interrupted, and new people will step into the role of traffickers as long as there are profits to be made.

The men who buy sex are often viewed as too inept to obtain sex conventionally, and thus are vulnerable to the enticement of prostituted women. Others view them as driven by the inherently flawed nature of males, who are predisposed by evolution to obtain sex by whatever means necessary, and who are enabled by patriarchal systems, misogynistic cultures, and the commodification of sex. In these portrayals, the individual buyers of sex are rarely viewed as the chief cause of all commercial sex and most sexual slavery. Frequently, police will raid brothels or conduct street operations and arrest persons engaged in selling sex, and occasionally arrest a pimp, but they simply let the "customers" go without any intervention, or after receiving less serious sanctions than the victims or pimps. The weight of the evidence shows that there is less interest in pursuing the buyers of sex than there is in helping survivors or prosecuting pimps and traffickers, although demand has been identified as a primary driver of commercial sex and trafficking markets.

Public Education and Awareness Programs

For the purpose of gathering information about public education and awareness programs addressing demand for commercial sex, we have defined the terms broadly. We have counted as an awareness program any broadly targeted attempt to focus attention on the role of the buyers of sex in contributing to problems associated with prostitution and/or sex trafficking.

In some communities, such efforts involve posting signs or billboards informing johns about police activity or penalties for buying sex. For example, Rochester, New York, put up billboards reading, ***"Dear John, you're not welcome in our community."*** In Cleveland, there was a neighborhood-initiated campaign targeting johns in which residents took turns carrying signs in troubled neighborhoods stating, ***"Dear Johns, your plate number is being recorded. Yours truly, the neighbors."*** This kind of approach is designed to deter buyers, and to send a general message to the public about police action to address the problem and, as noted below, not to educate the public about demand to any real depth.

Another approach is to aim awareness efforts at the general public rather than to actual or potential johns. This usually involves placing signs or posters for the public to see, or brief presentations about demand at meetings of community groups. We have considered an education program to be a more intensive and sustained effort to convey a larger amount of information. An example would be a curriculum developed to teach high school students or employees of a company about how buying sex drives prostitution and sex trafficking, and the negative consequences.

While most experts agree that public education and awareness are critical to combating prostitution and sex trafficking, there are relatively few examples of programs designed specifically to address demand for commercial sex, when compared to the number of programs addressing supply and distribution. The primary means of raising awareness and providing education include:

- Posters
- Billboards
- Brief presentations at community meetings
- Interviews appearing in print and electronic media
- Education programs, involving a curriculum and a sustained presentation to target audiences that convey substantial amounts of information

The best-known and most ambitious public awareness campaign focused on demand is the "Dear John" campaign implemented in the greater Atlanta, Georgia, area, and discussed in detail below. Most other communities have engaged in less extensive campaigns, and have used simpler methods. For example, in San Antonio, Texas, a neighborhood-initiated campaign involved residents taking photos of johns in cars, recording license plate numbers, and sending the photos and information to police.

Atlanta's "Dear John" Public Awareness Program

This program involves a series of professionally produced public service announcements and print media images that were circulated via the Internet, television, in print media, and signs posted in public areas (such as buses) in Atlanta.

The "Dear John" campaign was initiated by the mayor's office of the City of Atlanta and was designed to provide a platform to raise public awareness on the issue of commercial sexual exploitation (of children, in particular, but also more broadly). The objective was to generate public and political pressure to spur state and local agencies (as well as nongovernmental organizations (NGOs), such as faith-based organizations and nonprofits) into concrete action against prostitution and sex trafficking. The substantive focus of the campaign was on the buyers of sex and reducing demand.

Education and Awareness Program
in Chicago and Cook County

Over the past several years, the area that has had the highest level of activity focused on combating demand for commercial sex is, arguably, the Cook County and Chicago areas of Illinois. An "umbrella" organization or coalition called End Demand Illinois (EDI) is comprised of over a dozen partner organizations that have launched a wide range of initiatives targeting demand. Some of these organizations had been in focus initiatives that were in place before EDI existed, and some of the activity has been through collective action organized or facilitated by EDI.

EDI has engaged in a number of education and awareness activities in the past few years. For example, a collaboration of the Chicago Alliance Against Sexual Exploitation

(CAASE), the Women of Power Alumni Association (WoPAA), the Polaris Project, the Voices and Faces Project (Voices), and the Schiller DuCanto and Fleck Family Law Center of DePaul University College of Law (Schiller), and the Illinois Coalition Against Sexual Assault, launched a new Web site and coordinated events in the fall of 2009. For example, an EDI volunteer, Katie Feifer (also affiliated with the Voices and Faces Project of San Francisco-based research group KGF Insights), conducted 31 interviews with a group of Illinois residents to gather feedback about statistics, beliefs, and slogan statements, and the philosophy and messaging employed by EDI's public education efforts. The conclusions and recommendations from the study served as the basis of campaign outreach materials. At the same time, Larissa Malarek, a volunteer documentarian, conducted 23 on-camera interviews with policymakers, law enforcement officials, service providers, and survivors throughout the state concerning prostitution, sex trafficking, and demand in Illinois. These interviews were conducted to form the basis of the production of short documentary vignettes used for EDI public education initiatives. An initial clip of the documentary was released at EDI's launch event in September of 2009.

U.S. Military Program to Combat Sexual Exploitation and Trafficking

There is a long history of the military contributing to prostitution and sex trafficking.[2] Relatively recently, the U.S. Department of Defense (DoD) has taken substantial action designed to reduce or eliminate the historic contributions (such as government agencies, large corporations, or others) of military personnel to prostitution and sex trafficking. Their approach is multifaceted and features a focus on combating demand for commercial sex.

Over the past decade, the DoD has taken substantial action designed to reduce or eliminate the historic exacerbations of prostitution and sex trafficking that is due to the actions of military personnel. Their approach is multifaceted, and features a focus on combating demand for commercial sex. (While the scope of the military level of control over personnel is atypical of most organizations, the objectives and basic steps they have taken can prove instructive to other large organizations or agencies.)

Thus, the uniform code of military justice and policies have been strengthened, clarifying the language and imposing substantial penalties on any military personnel (including civilian staff and contractors) engaging in commercial sex. The Law Enforcement Policy and Support Office of the DoD has established the Trafficking in Persons Program, which has developed a series of training modules for military staff. A key component of their effort is training about commercial sexual exploitation and human trafficking, with a key message in the training materials addressing demand.

The training contains definitions and several messages about the nature of human trafficking, and includes a focus on an antidemand messages, such as: "Don't assist the perpetrators: You aid and encourage trafficking in persons without engaging in it directly by:

- Hiring prostitutes
- Attending nightclubs or strip clubs
- Patronizing businesses that are heavily guarded
- Not reporting cases of suspected trafficking
- Patronizing establishments that use forced labor

Military personnel are informed of the Uniform Code of Military Justice (UCMJ) "Military Personnel Legal Prohibition on Prostitution." DoD contractors are also subject to the Defense Federal Acquisition Regulation (DFAR) TIP (trafficking in persons) rule. Contractors have a trafficking clause in their employment contracts that stipulates they are responsible for following UCMJ prohibitions on buying sex, and that this responsibility applies to any and all subcontractors of a given company working for the DoD.

Reverse Stings

The most commonly used tactic to address demand for commercial sex is usually referred to as the "reverse sting." These

Figure 5.1 Female police officers posing as prostitutes. A car is shown slowing down to take a closer look at two female police officers posing as prostitutes in southern California during a major prostitution reverse sting operation. (Photo courtesy of David McNew/Getty Images,)

police special operations feature one or more female police officers serving as a decoy (or decoys) by posing as prostitutes to await being approached by those attempting to purchase sex[3] (Figure 5.1).

The term *reverse sting* is an artifact of the historic gender inequity in the enforcement of prostitution. Until relatively recently, the vast majority of police attention devoted to prostitution was focused on arresting providers of commercial sex. The most common police tactic to combat commercial sex has been using plainclothes male officers to elicit offers of commercial sex from prostitutes. These operations were known as *stings*. Beginning in the 1960s, but not becoming widespread until well into the late 1980s, were operations focusing on buyers rather than providers of commercial sex. To distinguish those operations from the more traditional stings, the term *reverse stings* evolved into common usage, and implies that those operations are something other than the typical or default tactic.

The term is somewhat controversial, particularly for advocates of approaches in which the majority of police attention is focused on buyers rather than sellers of sex. It has been proposed by many that the movement to eradicate sexual exploitation should promote the use of the term *sting* to apply to operations aimed at johns, and not to arrest providers of commercial sex at all.

Street-Level Reverse Stings

In descriptions gathered from interviews with police and reviews of the literature,[4] the following were found to be typical. Areas of the city known to be active for street prostitution are selected, and a tactical plan is either discussed or written and submitted for a supervisor's approval. Usually, five or more officers are used in a street reverse sting. In addition to the female officer, there are usually several additional undercover male police officers in supporting roles. The operations often consist of one or two male plainclothes officers on foot, posing as pedestrians, at least one unmarked car carrying plainclothes officers, and at least one police patrol car with officers that may be in uniform. There are usually other officers who support the operations by processing arrestees and their vehicles. In some cases, police use a van serving as a mobile booking or screening station, and, in other instances, processing occurs in nearby police stations or substations. In the latter circumstance, the operations require more onsite officers so that there is less "down time" between arrests. At least two officers are usually required to transport each arrestee away from the site of the arrest: at least one escorting the arrestee and the other driving the arrestee's vehicle (when applicable). In our research, we found that at least five police officers are usually deployed for each decoy used in a reverse sting.

A supervising sergeant is usually in charge of the reverse stings. Decoys are escorted to drop-off locations near where the operations will occur. An unmarked police van serving as a mobile screening or booking station is usually parked nearby, but out of sight of the street operation. In some locations, police stations or substations are nearby, so a mobile unit is not necessary. The female decoy officer usually has a hidden recording device and a cell phone (the first to collect evidence, the latter for safety, in case she is abducted). Some police departments videotape the reverse stings surreptitiously from an unmarked police car.

The decoy always tries to remain in visual contact with the other officers. When potential "clients" speak with the decoy, the supporting officers track her until she makes a pre-arranged signal indicating a "good case," which is when the man has made an offer of money in exchange for sex and has committed an "act in furtherance" of that offer. An act in furtherance is any overt behavior that can be construed reasonably as progress toward consummating the act of prostitution being negotiated by the john and female police officer. Such acts, in addition to the verbal exchange, complete the legal requirements for making an arrest. Acts in furtherance can include reaching for a wallet, pointing to money on a car seat, driving around the block to the area where the sex act was arranged to take place, or opening a car door so that the decoy can enter.

When the signal for a "good case" is given, the officers on foot or in unmarked cars converge and make the arrest. At this point, the decoy officer enters the police car as quickly as possible and leaves the scene, while the man is arrested and driven to a point where he will be processed. Sometimes he is driven in his own car by a plainclothes officer, and other times he is driven in a police car while another officer drives the offender's car. Arrestees who are on foot are driven to the van or police station in a patrol car.

The license plate number of the car and the man's driver's license number and other identifiers are radioed or sent via computer to a dispatcher, and the determination is made whether to issue a citation and notice to appear in court, or to book the arrestee and take him into custody. If they have identification and no outstanding warrants, they are usually issued a citation and allowed to leave. If these conditions do not apply or if there are concurrent offenses (e.g., possession of drugs or illegal weapons), the johns can be taken into custody.

Reverse stings are the entry point for most kinds of interventions developed to focus on male buyers of illegal commercial sex. In order for john schools, community service programs, geographic exclusion zones, and several other tactics to be applied, johns must first be arrested. The means by which the vast majority of johns are arrested is through reverse stings, which have been established as the primary way to produce the evidence necessary to satisfy criminal justice requirements.

After the decision to cite or arrest is made, offenders in jurisdictions with criminal justice diversion programs for johns are issued a citation and informed of their responsibility to call the prosecutor's office for processing (either a city attorney's office when johns are cited for violating municipal ordinances or the district attorney's office when johns are arrested for committing a penal code violation).

While officers are processing the arrestee, the decoy officer usually remains in an unmarked car writing notes for her report and (if applicable) checking to ensure that the quality of the tape of the transaction is acceptable. She then removes and marks the tape and inserts a blank tape in the recorder. She stays out of sight of the arrestee and away from the location where the arrest was made, until it is time to reset the operation. When reverse stings use multiple decoys, it is possible to keep the street operations going continuously. If one or two of the decoys have made a good case and the men are being processed, there can still be one or more decoys active, provided that there are enough support officers for a safe operation.

Police Units, Agencies, and Multijurisdictional Task Forces Conducting Reverse Stings

A range of law enforcement agencies, and units and departments within agencies, are trained and deployed to conduct reverse stings. Some of the departments or units focus on crimes on the lower end of the crime seriousness scale (measured by the felony/misdemeanor distinction), such as nuisance abatement or neighborhood safety units. Others focus on felonies and higher-end crimes, such as multijurisdictional drug task forces that focus on organized crime, felony-level drug trafficking, and violent crime. Others fall in between, including regular patrol units. Many police departments' vice units, even in large cities, are relatively small (e.g., seven officers for San Francisco) and others have severely downsized or eliminated their vice units, so other divisions or units (such as nuisance abatement or special investigations units) fill the void.

In addition to cross-unit collaboration within departments, there are cross-agency and cross-jurisdictional collaborations.

A wide array of state, local, and federal agencies, and multijurisdictional task forces collaborate on reverse stings. Among the configurations of law enforcement collaboration that conduct reverse stings are:

- Cross-unit collaborations within a police agency (e.g., patrol and community nuisance abatement); federal agencies, particularly Immigration and Customs Enforcement (ICE)
- Multijurisdictional task forces
- Multiple municipal police departments
- Municipal police departments and county sheriff's departments
- State agencies that focus on alcohol enforcement
- State police agencies
- State probation/parole agencies

The most common type of organizational collaboration scenario is for one city or county law enforcement agency (a city police department or a county sheriff's department) to conduct an operation within their jurisdiction. However, it also is common to see multiagency collaborations within cities or counties, as well as multijurisdictional teams. There are roads and areas in which street prostitution becomes institutionalized, and these areas sometimes cross jurisdictions. Reverse stings can involve many different kinds of units within an agency, and can involve partnerships among agencies and across all levels of government (city, county, state, and federal) (Figure 5.2).

Variations and Innovations in Reverse Stings

A number of variations on basic models have been developed to meet particular challenges or to take advantage of opportunities. Several examples are described in more detail below:

- *Replacing prostituted women with police decoys.* In street operations, police may go to "strips," "strolls," or "tracks" arrest women engaged in prostitution, and replace them with police decoys. A similar concept is

Figure 5.2 Trenton, New Jersey, police arresting a john. A Trenton police officer is seen here arresting an individual for solicitation of prostitution from an undercover female officer posing as a prostitute. (Photo courtesy of Beverly Schafer/for *The Times*.)

sometimes used to arrest the customers of brothels. Brothel raids typically focus on investigating whether prostitution occurs and then, if the necessary evidence is gathered, to arresting the women selling sex and the brothel's pimps or traffickers. Usually, the johns are either ignored entirely, or those that are present during the raid or "take-down" may be arrested, but no further effort is expended in attempting to arrest additional customers beyond those that happened to be present. However, in some communities police have taken advantage of the opportunity to identify and arrest additional customers. In storefront brothels, such as nail salons or massage businesses, the staff and survivors are removed and replaced with police officers who continue to make appointments and arrest johns until the news circulates that the brothel is controlled by undercover police.

- *Borrowing decoys from other police departments.* Many police departments, particularly smaller ones, have had trouble staffing reverse stings due to a shortage of women police officers willing to serve as decoys, or because the decoys become too well-known to potential buyers to be effective. A solution to this problem used by some police agencies is to borrow staff from other departments.

The Use of the Internet

The Internet has been used with increasing frequency to transact commercial sex. Ads are posted on Web sites devoted to commercial sex (eroticreview.com, worldsexguide.com, myredbook.com) or on Web sites serving as a venue for a broader spectrum of transactions, such as BackPage.com, Yellow Pages, Craigslist.com, and periodicals, such as the *Phoenix New Times* or *SF Weekly*. It is widely observed that the solicitation of commercial sex throughout the United States has shifted from the streets to online. For example, in San Francisco, the average yield of arrests per street-level reverse sting fell by half between 2004 and 2007,[5] and the police department's vice unit personnel believed that much of the declining yield was because of the rise of online solicitation, particularly the use of Craigslist through 2009, and Backpage since then. Other factors cited in the decline in street prostitution are the effectiveness of the city's john school program, and the persistence of police in conducting hundreds of reverse stings over the years. Craigslist has eliminated its adult or "erotic services" section that had been a central source of transacting commercial sex (although it is still used for commercial sex through posing as massage or other services),[6] but it has been largely replaced by Backpage.com since 2010.

Online Reverse Stings

Many police departments throughout the United States have used online ads for commercial sex to their advantage. Approximately one third of all police departments that conduct street-level reverse stings also have implemented Web-based reverse stings. Online reverse stings are easy for police to initiate. The typical procedure is to post a decoy ad, and when potential johns respond with a phone call or an email, the officers pose as prostituted persons or pimps and arrange for a meeting, usually at a hotel that has been prepared for a reverse sting. At the hotel, a female officer poses as a prostituted person, and once the john is face-to-face with the officer, the operation is essentially the same as that used in conventional reverse stings.

Variation on the Basic Web-Based Reverse Sting Model

In Web-based reverse stings, the basic model involves police posting a bogus advertisement on Web sites used to transact prostitution, and placing a female police decoy and support team in a hotel room or apartment for appointments with johns. This requires substantial planning, such as obtaining a phone for police to use that is not detectable as a police phone, and constructing a realistic ad. It can pose challenges in acquiring hotel or apartment space, due to the expense of renting and getting hotel or apartment management to cooperate with a police operation that may disrupt their business. A variation on the basic model that is designed to solve some of these challenges begins with police searching real Web ads for prostitution, rather than placing their own "decoy" ads. Police respond to the real ads with undercover male officers posing as johns. They remove the woman or girl involved in prostitution or who is being trafficked, and install a police decoy, who continues making appointments with johns on the survivor's phone. Typically, a support team is stationed in an adjoining room.

Surveillance Cameras

While cameras are very widely used for general surveillance purposes, and the growth in their use began decades ago, their use specifically to target men who are (or may be) buying sex has not been widely adopted. Some applications are covert,

Figure 5.3 Use of surveillance cameras to control prostitution. Vallejo, California, uses 22 cameras to control prostitution. City council approved expanding the cameras from 6 to 22 because of the success of these cameras in controlling prostitution. (AP photo. With permission.)

with hidden cameras used to produce visual evidence that can be used by police and prosecutors (Figure 5.3). Other uses are overt and designed for deterrence rather than punishment. Following are examples of some cities that use surveillance cameras to control prostitution:

- Tacoma, Washington: Conspicuous surveillance cameras are placed in active prostitution areas with signs saying, "Smile johns, you're on camera." A YouTube channel, called StopCrimeOnTacomaAve posts videos of apparent prostitution and drug deals.
- Rochester, New York: Surveillance cameras are covertly placed in prostitution areas.
- Durham, North Carolina: Thirteen wireless cameras focus on "hot spots" of crime, including prostitution.

Vehicle Seizures

Most state criminal codes allow for the seizure of vehicles used in the commission of crimes. Often this is interpreted as the use of vehicles in felonies, such as kidnapping, drug smuggling, etc., but over 100 communities have seized autos used while soliciting prostitution, a misdemeanor or ordinance violation in nearly all cities and counties in the United States. In the majority of communities that seize the autos of men attempting to purchase sex, the vehicles are retrievable after paying an impound fee of $400 or less.

Court Challenges

Auto seizures have been successfully challenged in courts. The basic issues generally are whether the auto seizure constitutes a penalty that exceeds the maximum allowed for misdemeanors, and, in other instances, local ordinances may conflict with state law. For example, on July 26, 2007, the California State Supreme Court overturned the city of Stockton's ordinance, causing the practice to be suspended throughout the state while ordinances were being reviewed or revised. Seizures resumed in several California cities in 2008 (e.g., Riverside, Sacramento). Similarly, a Miami ordinance that was passed by the city council in 1997 was declared unconstitutional in response to a 1999 case, and that decision was upheld on appeal. Washington, D.C., had a seizure program that was declared unconstitutional and suspended in 2003 and later resumed after revision.

Forfeiture Programs

A few communities have instituted forfeiture programs in which cars used by men to solicit sex with prostituted persons could be forfeited, sold at auction, and the proceeds retained by law enforcement to fund their efforts. For example, the Easton, Pennsylvania, city council passed an ordinance in 2008 allowing for forfeiture of vehicles within one year of arrest, allowing time for due process. However, the first set of men arrested in reverse stings who had their autos seized filed suit, challenging the forfeitures as excessive punishment since the penalty of the local ordinance exceeded misdemeanor penalty standards for prostitution violations. Within two months of the ordinance's passage and the first set of arrests to which it was applied, all of the autos in Easton were returned and forfeitures suspended pending the outcome of the lawsuit. In Genesee County, Michigan, johns have been required to forfeit vehicles and can buy them back for $900 after a first arrest, $1,800 for a second, and $2,700 for a third arrest. If they don't pay, the vehicle is sold at auction. The following news story provides an example of a successful vehicle confiscation program conducted in Memphis, Tennessee.

In The News

Soliciting Prostitutes Can Cost Car Used During a Crime, Cars of Customers Will Be Seized, Says Gibbons

By Jody Callahan
April 23, 2008

If you're caught with a prostitute, local authorities plan to seize your car.

That was the message conveyed at a press conference Tuesday afternoon, where officials with the Memphis Police and the District Attorney General's Office announced the arrests of 64 people in a three-day prostitution sting.

As a result of those arrests, authorities will attempt to seize 42 cars: 39 from those charged with soliciting prostitutes, as well as one from a suspect facing drug charges and two because the owners had revoked driver's licenses.

Shelby County Dist. Atty. Gen. Bill Gibbons paces near a line of vehicles at the West Tennessee Drug Task Force Impound Lot that were seized during a three-day prostitution sting operation Tuesday afternoon (Figure 5.4).

"They were used in the commission of a crime. Under state law, they are subject to seizure," Dist. Atty. Gen. Bill Gibbons said, when asked if the seizures seemed excessive. "I think it's a good law. But if you think it's too stringent, talk to your legislators."

Added Memphis Police Director Larry Godwin: "I'd say seize every dad gum vehicle and send a message."

Those whose cars were seized will be able to seek a court hearing, authorities said.

Figure 5.4 Cars confiscated from johns. Shelby County Tennessee District Attorney General Bill Gibbons paces near a line of vehicles confiscated from johns who were attempting to solicit sex from undercover female police officers. These vehicles are being stored in the police impound lot. (Photo by Jim Weber/*The Commercial Appeal*. With permission.)

Memphis isn't the only city in the country to try this type of enforcement, as it has become a somewhat frequent effort to stem prostitution.

A local spokesman for the American Civil Liberties Union said they would investigate, if asked.

"If we receive complaints of citizens who are affected by this, we'll go through our process of analyzing it and see if there's a violation of the state or federal constitution, and take action," spokesman Bruce Kramer said.

The operation ran from Thursday through Sunday and targeted two locations on Lamar, one near Pearson and the other at Clearpool Circle.

A total of 55 people are facing class A misdemeanor charges of patronizing prostitution, since police said their arrests took place within 1.5 miles of schools.

Also, four more people were charged with promoting prostitution, a felony, while two more were hit with felony drug charges.

Of those arrested, two—Devon Hamilton and Edward Rogers—were Memphis Light, Gas and Water Division employees who were on-duty in an MLGW truck. The truck wasn't confiscated when they were charged with soliciting a prostitute.

"We at MLGW are disappointed in this alleged incident involving two employees. ... We take seriously any actions that adversely affect the reputations of MLGW, its employees and our service to the community," said MLGW President Jerry Collins in a statement, adding that the utility would also investigate.

One man, according to police, solicited a prostitute while his 7-year-old daughter was in the car. She'd received a bike for her birthday that day, Godwin said. The bike wasn't confiscated, he added. (From: http://www.commercialappeal.com/news/2008/apr/23/solicitations-can-cost-car/ (accessed June 4, 2012).

Driver's License Suspension

Of the tactics identified to combat demand, driver's license suspension is the least frequently used. The first identified use of license suspensions was in Tampa, Florida, in 1985. Few cities have followed this example.

The concept and execution of license suspensions are simple. There must be an ordinance or a statute in place to support the suspensions for misdemeanor offenses, and, if so, judges or magistrates can choose to mete out this punishment for arrested johns. Suspensions are not long, among the small number of cases we could identify. For example, in Casselberry, Florida, the suspension can last up to one year, although it is rare for the maximum suspension to be imposed.

The objections to license suspensions are similar to those of shaming (also discussed below) and auto seizure. Given that many johns are married, in relationships, and employed, some punishments can have a negative impact on significant others and families. For example, a license suspension can pose hardships for children who rely on a father for transportation, and the father may be the only family member with a driver's license.

Shaming

Shaming is a simple tactic for combating demand: The identities of men arrested for soliciting commercial sex are publicized, typically through police press releases that are carried by local media outlets or on police Web sites.

For many police departments, revealing arrestees' identities proceeds from the intent to deliver a punishment, which will serve as a specific deterrent. It also pursues general deterrence—sending a message to potential johns that their identities will be revealed if they are apprehended for soliciting sex. For some police departments, publicizing identities does not appear to be programmatic or to specifically target demand for illicit commercial sex. It is instead a matter of routine, whereby identities of adult arrestees across all offense categories are revealed. For example, the identities of arrestees sometimes appears in local news "crime logs" or "police blotters," with johns' identities revealed alongside those of burglars, vandals, and drunk drivers. However, the lack of a specific intent of reducing demand for commercial sex does not directly affect its potential for effectiveness as a deterrent.

The most common method of disseminating identities is through news outlets—both online and in print. Other methods include police Web sites[7] (e.g., Alton, IL; El Cajon, CA; Metro Nashville, TN Police Department) (Figure 5.5); billboards

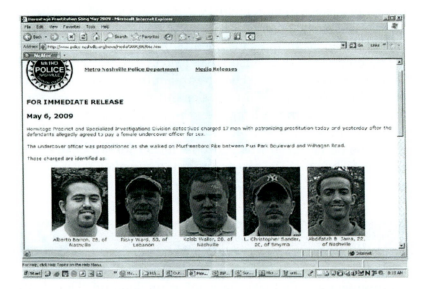

Figure 5.5 Men arrested by the Metro Nashville, Tennessee, Police Department for allegedly agreeing to pay a female undercover police officer for sex.

(e.g., Rochester, NY; Minneapolis, MN); community Web sites (e.g., "Trick the Johns" in Chattanooga, TN, "JohnTV" in Oklahoma City, OK); and public access television (e.g., New York City). Variations on shaming tactics include an effort in Baltimore County, Maryland, in which police inform residents of court dates for prostitution-related cases, encouraging them to appear at hearings and trials. The tactic is intended not only to shame offenders by bringing residents to witness the men being accused in court, but also to encourage judges and prosecutors to follow through with charges and impose fair penalties. The Costa Mesa, Arizona, Police Department uses a press release that publicizes the identities of arrested johns (Figure 5.6).

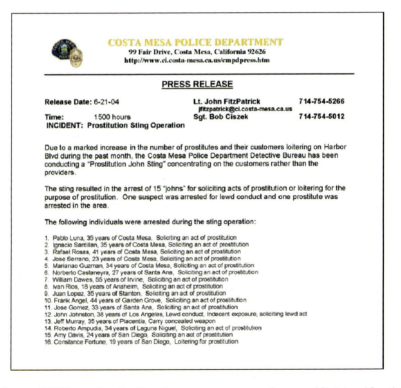

Figure 5.6 Example of police department press release publicizing identities of arrested johns.

"Dear John" Letters

Another variation of shaming is to send letters to the homes of alleged buyers of commercial sex, or to the homes of registered owners of vehicles. These letters are often described as "Dear Johns." This tactic has been employed in at least 40 U.S. communities and involves sending letters to the homes of known or suspected buyers of commercial sex. The intention is to make it more difficult for johns to engage in sexual exploitation anonymously or, at least, unbeknownst to spouses or partners. People who were interviewed for the national assessment cite as the primary reasons for using this tactic: (a) to alert partners of buyers of commercial sex so that they can protect themselves from contracting infectious disease, given the higher probability that johns may be carriers, and (b) to bring pressure to bear from whomever lives with sex buyers to discourage them from that activity.

Variants of This Approach

There are two main variants of this approach. The first is sending letters to the registered owners of cars seen "cruising" known prostitution strips for the apparent purpose of soliciting sex from prostituted persons. This tactic requires that police acquire the license plate number of the car that is being used in a way consistent with soliciting commercial sex. An example of suspicious behavior would be when a car circles a block repeatedly and then stops so the driver can talk with women who appear to be engaged in street prostitution and/or are familiar to police due to prior prostitution arrests. Police sometimes also observe people known to have been prostituted repeatedly entering cars that pull up to the curb and returning minutes later.

While the purpose of this interaction is apparent on a commonsense level, in most jurisdictions there would be insufficient evidence to arrest the john for soliciting commercial sex, because some jurisdictions will record the license number of the vehicle and later find the address of a registered owner and send him a letter. Sometimes the observation is made not by the police, but instead by members of the community, who observed this kind of activity and record the license plate numbers and make a report to police departments. For example, police in Minneapolis, Minnesota, and Des Moines, Iowa, have asked residents to record license plate numbers and descriptions of johns, and to forward the information to police so they can send letters to the alleged offenders. Some police departments have forms for recording the information, which asked members of the community to record the location of the event; the time, make, model and color of the vehicle; and, most importantly, the plate number. Once police have been given this information, they can follow the same procedure as if they had made the observations themselves.

The letters typically strive to make it clear that police do not assume that the registered owner of the vehicle was necessarily driving the car when the suspicious behavior was observed. The letter does not constitute being charged with a crime. Some of the letters explicitly address the fact that the suspicious behavior may have occurred while someone other than the registered owner was driving. The tone may even be friendly, suggesting that the registered owner's vehicle is being used improperly, and that they should take care not to allow others to use their vehicle for such purposes.

Another application of "Dear John" letters is sending letters to the homes of arrestees. Such letters do not say that suspicious behavior occurred, but, instead, that an arrest of the addressee was made for prostitution. A sample letter used by the Escambia County, Florida, Sheriff's Office is shown in Figure 5.7.

The use of "Dear John" letters has not been evaluated, so it is not known whether the approach is effective in deterring sex buyers. These letters also can raise objections similar to those in response to newspaper or Web site shaming. It can be argued they violate due process protections if they are assumed to be punishments and are applied to people prior to conviction. The letters we have encountered are carefully crafted to avoid these due process concerns, but the objections could be valid if the letters are not properly constructed.

DAVID MORGAN

John Doe
276 Main Street
Pensacola, FL 32509

Vehicle: 1990 Toyota
Location of arrest: Arlington Ave & W Street
Date and Time of arrest: 2:15 am 7/1/09

Dear John,

The vehicle registered in your name was involved in an arrest for violation(s) of Florida's laws prohibiting prostitution. Attached is a copy of the Florida Statute for your review. The individual arrested from your vehicle is _____. As vehicle owner, you should be aware of the Florida Contraband Forfeiture Act wherein motor vehicles can be seized if they are used in violation of this act. The Escambia County Sheriff's Office is notifying you so that you can consider these factors in deciding whether to allow others to drive your automobiles.

It is important for you to realize that the above named person and his/her significant other may have been exposed to a Sexually Transmitted Disease (STD). Certain STDs, like HIV, are incurable and may not be noticeable for a long time. It is possible to be exposed to an STD even if your partner was with a prostitute only once. Getting tested is important to your health and may impact your future ability to have children. Confidential STD testing is available through your private doctor or the Escambia County Health Department (850-595-6532). Fees may be involved.

It is a common myth that prostitution is a "victimless crime" or that it is "an act between two consenting adults." Prostitution is a crime which is linked to drugs (use and sale), acts of violence toward prostitutes and their customers and in the worst cases, human trafficking in juveniles for the sex trade. In addition to STD's, other viruses can spread through intimate contact with random individuals whom you may not know. Hepatitis, HIC and HPV can all be unknowingly transmitted and can lead to serious, and fatal, illness.

Prostitution, soliciting for prostitution and the other activities described in the attached statute (F.S.S. 796.07) will not be tolerated in Escambia County. If you think you may have been exposed to any communicable diseases after reading the contents of this letter, please contact your health care provider or the Escambia County Health Department for evaluation before having intimate contact with other people to help prevent the spreading of serious conditions.

Sincerely,

David Morgan
Sheriff, Escambia County

ESCAMBIA COUNTY SHERIFF'S OFFICE
Telephone (850) 436-9512 • www.escambiaso.com • P.O. Box 18770 • Pensacola, Florida 32523

***Figure* 5.7** "Dear John" letter used by the Escambia County, Florida, Sheriff's Office.

Arguments for and against Shaming

There are compelling arguments both for and against shaming. Proponents argue that it is a powerful deterrent, perhaps more important than arrest and legal sanctions. Surveys and anecdotal evidence lend support to this argument,[8] as does a body of criminology literature on the effects of extralegal sanctions on deterrence.[9] For example, when asked to name tactics that would deter men from buying sex, having identities publicly circulated was listed most frequently. In the Durschlag and Goswami study,[8] 87% of the men listed "photo and or name in local paper" in response to the question" "What would deter you from buying sex?" This was the most frequently cited potential consequence, followed by "jail time" and "photo and/or name on billboard" (both at 82%), "photo and/or name on the Internet" (82%), and "a letter sent to family saying you were arrested for soliciting a woman in prostitution" (79%). Four of the five consequences that men most frequently cite as deterrents involve others finding out that they have had sex with prostituted persons. While men's perceptions of what may deter them in hypothetical situations does not necessarily correspond to what actually deters men in real situations, the results are provocative and provide an empirically based reason to suspect that shaming might be effective.

Opponents of shaming contend that its deterrence is unproven, that it violates due process rights since identities are typically publicized upon arrest and prior to adjudication, and that it negatively affects families of arrestees. Some cities that are strongly committed to combating demand (e.g., San Francisco) do not pursue shaming specifically because of the impact it may have on those associated with alleged offenders, such as the children, spouses, and other friends and family members.

John Schools

"John school" is a generic term that is used to describe a wide range of programs that involve an education or treatment component. A useful working definition for john school is: *An education or treatment program for men arrested for soliciting illegal commercial sex.* To that basic definition, one could add, that in order for an education program to be considered a john school, it must cover a range of topics designed to persuade or deter men from buying sex. That criterion would separate john schools from other kinds of court-ordered or diversion programs that focus only on health education. There are several education programs in the United States that involve education for arrested johns that we would not consider to be a john school. For example, at least 10 communities in the United States have a health education session (usually focused on HIV) for prostitution arrestees—including johns—but some may not consider it to be a john school program, because the model's basic intention is to help men avoid infection and not necessarily to convince men to avoid commercial sex because of the harm it causes. The state of Virginia requires health education for anyone convicted of a prostitution offense; we would not define that as a john school for the male sex buyers who must attend.

The following news story discusses a john school, which was intended to accomplish a number of objectives including deterring men from being arrested for solicitation of prostitution, understanding the impact on young girls who are prostituted, and the potential for contracting a sexually transmitted disease (Figure 5.8).

In The News

School for Johns

Arrested for Soliciting Sex, Men Wind up in a Brooklyn Classroom

By Aina Hunter Tuesday
May 3, 2005

"When I was in the lifestyle, I didn't care anything about all you," begins Rosetta Menifee, a blonde woman in her late forties wearing glasses and a suit. Talking to a class of 50 men at the Brooklyn John School, she looks like a social worker, but she sounds like Lil' Kim.

"I wanna ask you," she says to the men, most of whom appear to be in their late thirties, "how many of you would take advantage of a physically retarded person, you know, like deformed? Well then, why would you take advantage of someone who is emotionally

Figure 5.8 Men being educated in a John School in Brooklyn, New York. These men, who have been arrested for solicitation of prostitution are attending a john school. The unit of instruction they are being exposed to deals with the dangers associated with contracting venereal diseases and the photo specifically depicts a sexually transmitted disease in the mouth of a prostitute. Part of the reason for this discussion is to dispel the myth some men might have that sexually transmitted diseases cannot be contracted through oral sex. (From http://www.villagevoice.com/2005-05-03/news/school-for-johns/; accessed June 4, 2012)

retarded? Because that's what prostitutes are. We were victimized as children. We are empty shells."

Introducing herself as a community educator and former prostitute, Menifee apologizes for not giving a shit about giving her customers HIV or herpes, much less the hepatitis C and B she picked up along the way. She says it was impossible to care about them when she didn't care about herself. Cops didn't help, she says, when they busted her with johns and told the guys to "get the hell out of here." They put cuffs on her and laughed at her, called her "bitch," called her a disease-ridden crackhead.

In Brooklyn, first-time offenders arrested for alleged solicitation of prostitution have the option of attending "Project Respect," the Brooklyn John School, instead of going to trial. Unique in New York City, Brooklyn's John School is similar to programs in Washington, D.C.; West Palm Beach, Florida; Pittsburgh; and Buffalo. San Francisco operates the oldest and largest such program, focusing not only on johns, but also on helping sex workers.

The choice is stark in Brooklyn: Show up for the class, pay the $250 tuition, stay out of trouble for six months, and charges are dismissed. Or go to court and risk up to 90 days in jail. But most men, perhaps telling their wives and girlfriends they have traffic school, show up at the district attorney's office on Jay Street to get scared straight for five hours.

In the lobby, they get name tags that read, in clear black letters: "Sex Crimes." In class, they hear from people like Menifee, and from a clinician from the Fort Greene Health Center, who shows the men slides of swollen, dripping, oozing, diseased sex organs—male and female.

"This man had oral sex performed on him," the clinician says brightly. "She had herpes in her throat."

The men also hear from Detective Marcella Makebish of the Brooklyn Special Victims Unit. A former decoy prostitute, Makebish, with her big hair and deep tan (and a purple blouse that allows for a generous display of cleavage) is all about audience participation.

"I know many of you have issues with law enforcement," she says coyly. The room erupts into yelps and guffaws. "How many of you think it was entrapment?"

"Damn right!" comes a shout.

"Yes, in my case it was," begins a man with a heavy accent.

"Bullshit!" spits an old man. "It was bullshit!"

Cops providing security pace the aisle nervously. "Keep it down," one of them barks. "You need to keep it down. If you think you're innocent, you can take it to court!"

The D.A.'s office says that since the launch of the John School in 2002 only two participants have been rearrested in Brooklyn. But not everyone thinks john schools—whatever the stats say—are a good investment. Juhu Thukral, director of the Sex Workers Project at the Urban Justice Center, says that johns who get caught just turn to escort services or Internet hookups. "John schools are part of an effort to address the demand side of the industry, but it's really just a revolving door," she says.

On the supply side, the grim truth is that younger and younger girls are getting into the life. The National Center for Missing and Exploited Children still reports the average age of entry as 14, but advocates say that number has dropped as low as 12, particularly in the poorest neighborhoods, like East New York and other sections of Brooklyn, Queens, and the Bronx. Up to 30 percent of street prostitutes are under the age of 18, according to some experts.

Younger pimps are also more common. Some experts in the field theorize that, because of harsh mandatory sentences for drug trafficking, young men find it less risky to pimp than to sell drugs.

New York's pimp network is well entrenched. Sex workers say that everyone knows everyone, and if you turn on your pimp, his friends might kill you. As for police catching a pimp without a prostitute's cooperation, it's nearly impossible. An undercover cop would have to convince a streetwise pimp that she's a sex worker who wants his protection. Then he'd ask her to prove it. "The protocol is, usually the pimp has sex with the girl first. An officer couldn't do that, of course," says Legal Aid veteran Kate Mullen, who counsels sexually exploited children. Only a few times in her career, she says, has she seen the pimps of the girls he defends go to jail.

Menifee, who now works in HIV prevention, says the relationships pimps develop with their workers parallel the most extreme cases of domestic abuse. "Why are they hard to catch?" she says incredulously. "Those women love their man. That's all the love they know. They're not going to testify against this man because it's the game they're in. They are living a whole different reality."

Besides, it would be dumb for a sex worker to rat out the only person who can bail her out of jail, which is why Menifee, like many New York activists, favors a conservative brand of decriminalization—not legalization, she's quick to emphasize, but a reduction in the severity of the offense, so that women who she says are "emotionally retarded" enough to sell their bodies would no longer be threatened with jail time. If they did not need protection from vice cops, pimps would have less of a chokehold on them.

"You want to get rid of pimps? Decriminalize," says Robyn Few, an activist from the Sex Workers Outreach Project (SWOP) in Berkeley. She calls john schools and similar scared-straight programs for prostitutes "shame based" and misdirected. Decriminalization is no panacea, she says, because young girls will still get tricked into the life. But at least they would be able to seek help without fear of being locked up.

The way, Few sees it, prostitution is already legal—but only for the middlemen. Operators of massage parlors, escort services, and topless bars are just pimps who pay taxes and get a wink and a nod from police. "Everyone in America knows what goes on in there," says Few, "and when they open a Yellow Pages and flip to (the escort section) they know what those places are." The employees of these de facto brothels have little recourse when they're ripped off or assaulted.

The Bay Area has an active decriminalization movement, says Thukral, of New York's Sex Workers Project. New Yorkers, on the other hand, have been slow to agitate for radical change. That could be due in part, she says, to Giuliani's "quality of life" campaigns in the '90s that made sex workers feel even more targeted by law enforcement and thus more wary of organizing. This could be slowly changing; a few organizations, like Prostitutes of New York, have come out in support of decriminalization, and a new industry magazine called *Spread* (written for and by sex workers) is being circulated.

Still, the Urban Justice Center has not taken an official position. Thukral says local energies are for now concentrated on other issues. "Most sex workers we talk with," she says, "express a need for services like ESL and other education. Then there's the problem of not being able to make living wages in traditional low-skill fields. Law enforcement should put money into helping prostitutes find a way out, not into arresting johns."

"I'm not calling you guys child molesters, but these are just kids, guys," a young assistant district attorney tells the John School class. "We don't have a program for [molesters]—our program for that is jail. You guys have to realize, what if she were your daughter and a guy like you approached her?"

The Brooklyn D.A. does have an intervention program for young prostitutes called "Saving Teens at Risk," which has received mixed reviews. A more established program for minors, the nonprofit Girls Educational and Mentoring Services, is based in Manhattan and has produced a video that's used in the John School.

In the video, African American teens—faces blurred to protect their identities—tell stories of being lured from their homes by pimps who acted like boyfriends. In soft, childish voices, the girls describe being punched, kicked, and stranded outside in the dark after failing to meet their quotas for the night. They talk about their shame and terror and, most of all, how much they hate the johns.

"Y'all know you're wrong," one whispers. "I was only 13. Come on, you knew I wasn't 20. I should've been home with my family." (From: http://www.villagevoice.com/2005-05-03/news/school-for-johns/ (accessed June 4, 2012).

A wide variety of programs are often grouped together and labeled john schools. Among the key dimensions of variability include:

- **Number of sessions:** Most john schools are single sessions, but they can range up to 10 sessions spaced a week apart.
- **Diversion versus sentencing option:** About two thirds of john schools in the United States are structured as criminal justice diversion programs, and the remainder are structured as conditions of a sentence. In the former, charges are usually dismissed upon completing the education program; in the latter, they must complete the john school to satisfy the conditions of their sentence, but doing so does not result in their charges being dismissed.
- **Fees or fines:** The average fee or fine for john schools in the United States is roughly $400, and the range is from $0 to $1,500.

- **Curricula:** the common denominators of most john schools are that they discuss health and legal consequences for johns if they were to continue engaging in commercial sex, and the negative impact of prostitution on prostituted women and girls and communities. With a common foundation, there is a wide range of topics covered by at least one john school. For example, the Indianapolis "Red Zone" program features a community impact panel, and then has the men spend three hours doing community service by picking up trash on the streets with high levels of prostitution activity. Other curriculum components include discussions of healthy relationships, anger management, sexual addiction, pimping and pandering, human trafficking, and johns' vulnerability to criminal victimization while engaged in commercial sex.

Generic John School Logic Model

Like any program, john schools are grounded in a set of goals. To pursue these goals, programs use resources that support activities intended to produce targeted results—from those results that are immediate and specific to those that are broader and longer-term outcomes. A logic model is a useful device for illustrating the linkages from program goals to the resources committed to the program to activities to outputs (the direct representation of activities) to program outcomes (the manifestation of the change that activities are seeking to accomplish), and, finally, to impacts (the indications that the program's broader goals have been realized). The generic john school logic model is presented in Figure 5.9.

The ultimate program goal is to decrease the demand for prostitution and, hence, reduce the amount of human trafficking and sexual exploitation that occurs. Program goals are pursued by committing resources (inputs) that support program activities (in john schools, the primary program activity is the educational intervention for arrestees). The measurable indicators of these activities are the program "outputs." The activities are designed to lead to the aforementioned outcomes of knowledge and attitude change: increased awareness of the

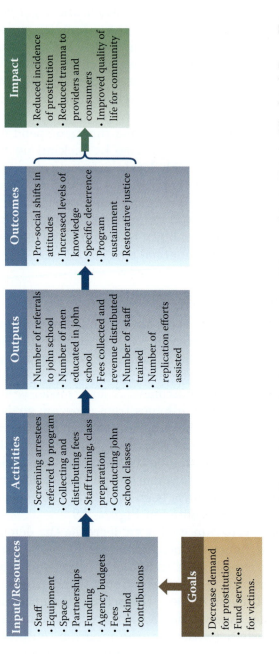

Figure 5.9 Generic john school logic model. (From: Michael Shively, Kristina Kliorys, Kristin Wheeler, & Dana Hunt, *A National Overview of Prostitution and Sex Trafficking Demand Reduction Efforts*, Final Report, April 30, 2012, prepared for the National Institute of Justice by Abt Associates Inc., document number 238796 (Cambridge, MA: Abt Associates Inc.), 63.

legal and health risks of engaging in prostitution, and awareness of the negative impact of the behavior on prostitutes, communities, and others. These outcomes are intended to reduce the likelihood that men will continue to solicit prostitution (i.e., the program impact).

Targeting the Educational Intervention

John school directors typically assume that there are several key attitudes and beliefs that cause or allow men to solicit sex, and that the programs reach at least some of the men by countering erroneous beliefs and filling gaps in their knowledge. The programs target some or all of the following:

1. The belief that the risk of arrest and legal sanction is low.
2. Denial or ignorance of the risk of contracting STDs or HIV through purchased sex.
3. Ignorance of the risk of being robbed or assaulted by prostitutes or pimps.
4. Denial or ignorance of the negative impact prostitution has on the neighborhoods in which it occurs.
5. Ignorance of the links between street prostitution and larger, organized systems of sex trafficking.
6. Denial or ignorance of what motivates them to solicit prostituted women or girls (e.g., addictions, compulsions, unmet social or sexual needs).
7. Denial or ignorance of the negative impact of prostitution on "providers."
8. Denial or ignorance of the fact that money is the only reason prostituted persons have sex with them.
9. The mistaken belief that the women they hire care about them, and that they are in some kind of relationship with them.
10. Denial or ignorance of the anger, revulsion, or indifference that many prostituted women have while they are having sex with johns.
11. Ignorance about how to have the healthy relationships that could replace their reliance upon commercial sex.

Men who solicit sex would be correct in assuming that there is a low risk of arrest and legal sanction. On this point, john schools do not seek to confirm this perception, but instead try to elevate the perceived risk from whatever level exists prior to taking the class. Since many of the men in john schools are first-time arrestees, they may be ignorant of the sanctions they may face if arrested a second time, and the program was designed to provide them with this information. On most of the other points, the program managers usually assume that the men are ignorant or in denial about the risks and negative impact of prostitution, and the program curriculum was designed to provide them with factual information and "break down their denial systems."[10]

A precondition for a sustainable john school program is a sufficient flow of eligible participants. This requires a proactive approach on the part of law enforcement to conduct operations designed to arrest men for soliciting. Several john school programs have been suspended or discontinued due to an insufficient flow of participants (e.g., Buffalo, Tampa). This flow is determined primarily by whether police have and will commit the resources needed to conduct reverse sting operations. Programs whose fees are used only to support john school classes can survive with very small numbers (as few as 10 to 20 per year, enough for one class per year), but programs that rely upon the fee revenue to sustain programs for women and girls involved in commercial sex must have a reliable and substantial volume of program participants. A serious, current challenge for all john schools is cutbacks in police budgets that have resulted in reducing the frequency of reverse stings.

John School Curriculum Items

John schools curricula vary, as one would expect. The First Offender Prostitution Program (FOPP) curriculum has been represented elsewhere and represents a "baseline" for john school topics covered. To address the informational needs of offenders, the FOPP established a curriculum that was designed to be delivered in one 8-hour day. The outline below captures most of what the program has addressed since its inception. The current curriculum is divided into six main sections, which are outlined briefly here:

1. ***Prostitution Law and Street Facts***, focusing on the legal consequences of subsequent offenses and addressing johns' vulnerability to being robbed or assaulted while involved in prostitution.
2. ***Health Education***, describing the elevated risk of HIV and STD (sexually transmitted disease) infection associated with prostitution, and stressing that many STDs are asymptomatic and/or difficult to detect and have long-term negative impacts on health.
3. ***Effect of Prostitution on Prostitutes***, focusing on numerous negative consequences for women serving as prostitutes, such as vulnerability to rape and assault, health problems, drug addiction, and various forms of exploitation.
4. ***Dynamics of Pimping, Recruiting, and Trafficking***, featuring discussions of how pimps and traffickers recruit, control, and exploit women and girls for profit, and the links between local street prostitution and larger systems of human trafficking.
5. ***Effect of Prostitution on the Community***, describing the drug use, violence, health hazards, and other adverse consequences that co-occur with street prostitution.
6. ***Sexual Addiction,*** focusing on how involvement in commercial sex may be driven by sexual addiction, and where help for this condition can be sought.

Although not listed as a core component of the FOPP curriculum, many of the classes contain a section on *policing prostitution*. The discussions focus on police surveillance of all types of commercial sex (street, brothels, escort services, massage parlors, storefronts, and Web-based) and are intended to provide participants with the impression that they will stand a great chance of rearrest if they continue involvement in any type of commercial sex.

Other john schools have been found to have longer programs with more items covered in their curricula, and others shorter with fewer items. For example, the Sexual Exploitation Education Program (SEEP) that operated in Portland, Oregon, from 1995 to 1997 was a 3-day, 15-hour intervention. Other programs are delivered in a multiple-session counseling format. The most involved of these is the program in Salt Lake City operated by Umoja Training; an outline of their curriculum is provided below.

Week 1: Male Socialization
Purpose: To gain understanding of the male socialization process and its impact on male–female relationships.
Week 2: Female Socialization
Purpose: To identify differences between male and female socialization, understand how female socialization affects female relationship behavior, and gain insight into personal treatment of women.
Week 3: Sexual Messages
Purpose: To gain perspective about how familial relations, upbringing, religion, peers, and the media impact our sexual relationships and behavior.
Week 4: Prostitute Panel
Purpose 1: To dispel myths about why women prostitute and educate about prostitution's impact on women.
Purpose 2: To encourage class participants to evaluate their sexual treatment of women and to recognize and respect their sexual partner's limits.
Weeks 5 and 6: Communication
Purpose: To make class participants aware of the relational impacts of different communication styles and to introduce new interpersonal skills.
Week 7: Anger
Purpose: To help class participants identify the way they express anger and the relational impact of their anger style, and increase awareness of alternative anger management choices.
Week 8: Healthy Intimate Relationships
Purpose: To differentiate between healthy and unhealthy interpersonal and sexual relationships.
Week 9: HIV and Sexually Transmitted Infection Prevention
Purpose: To decrease the spread of HIV and other sexually transmitted infections between prostitutes, johns, and their partners.

Week 10: Personal Power
Purpose: To encourage class participants to make healthier decisions about their lives.

Other programs are shorter and simpler. For example, the john school portion of the Indianapolis "Red Zone" program covers community impact and health consequences, although other topics will arise in the mediated discussion format. The Norfolk john school program is delivered in one to two hours, and the new video john school produced by the Cook County Sheriff's Office covers the basic elements, but in just 14 minutes. An expanded set of information on john school curricula will be provided on the Web site at http://www.courtinnovation.org/research/prostitution-indianapolis. The relative impact of the various program models is not known, as most program models have not been evaluated for their impact on reoffending.

Glossary

Act of Furtherance: This is any overt behavior that can be construed reasonably as progress toward consummating the act of prostitution being negotiated by a john with a female undercover police officer.

Cruising: This involves an individual driving in an area where prostitutes are available with the purpose of soliciting sex from them.

Dear John letters: This involves sending letters to alert the partners of buyers of commercial sex so they can protect themselves from contracting infectious disease, also to bring pressure to bear from whoever lives with sex buyers to discourage them from that activity in the future.

End Demand Illinois (EDI): An umbrella organization, in Chicago and Cook County, which is comprised of over a dozen organizations. They have launched a wide range of initiatives targeting demand for prostitution.

John: A term used to describe men who are soliciting prostitutes for sex.

John schools: A generic term that is used to describe a wide range of programs that involve education or treatment for men arrested for soliciting illegal commercial sex.

Primary prevention: This refers to stopping events before they occur or ensuring that people do not become afflicted by crime or disease rather than treating its symptoms.

Reverse sting: The police special operations feature one or more women officers serving as a decoy posing as a prostitute to await being approached by those men attempting to purchase sex.

Secondary prevention: This refers to early detection in an effort to minimize harm.

Shaming: This is a process where the identities of men arrested for soliciting commercial sex are publicized typically through police press releases that are carried by local media outlets or on police Web sites.

Sting: A police operation in which a male police officer dressed in plain clothes and in a civilian vehicle approaches prostitutes and attempts to negotiate a purchase price for sex. If the woman agrees to the officer's overture, she is then arrested.

Strips/Strolls: These are locations where prostitutes tend to congregate and walk making themselves conspicuously available to potential johns.

Tertiary prevention: This addresses recovery from fully realized afflictions.

Vehicle seizures: A tactic used to permanently confiscate vehicles owned by men who are soliciting prostitutes.

Review Questions

1. What does the term *primary prevention* refer to as it relates to men soliciting prostitutes?
2. How are men who buy sex often viewed?

3. What are the primary means of raising awareness and educating the public as it relates to awareness and prevention programs?
4. What is a "reverse sting"?
5. What are examples of the various configurations law enforcement employs in their collaboration with other agencies involved in reverse sting operations?
6. How can surveillance cameras be used to deal with men who are soliciting prostitution?
7. What are the basic issues raised in challenging the seizure of automobiles of men who have been arrested for soliciting prostitutes?
8. What objections were raised to driver's license suspensions?
9. What is "shaming"?
10. What are "Dear John" letters?
11. What are the arguments for and against shaming as a prevention and deterrent for men soliciting commercial sex?
12. What is a "john school"?
13. What are the six main sections in the curriculum for john schools?

Endnotes

1. Michael Shively, Kristina Kliorys, Kristin Wheeler, & Dana Hunt, *A National Overview of Prostitution and Sex Trafficking Demand Reduction Efforts,* Final Report, April 30, 2012, prepared for the National Institute of Justice by Abt Associates Inc., Document number 238796 (Cambridge, MA: Abt Associates Inc.).
2. Kathryn Bolkovac, *The Whistleblower* (New York: Palgrave MacMillan, 2010); V. Malarek, *The Johns: Sex for Sale and the Men Who Buy It* (New York: Arcade Publishing, 2009).
3. M. Dodge, D. Starr-Gimeno, & T. Williams, "Puttin' on the Sting: Women Police Officers' Perspectives on Reverse Prostitution Assignments," *International Journal of Police Science and*

Management 7 (2) (2005), 71–85; L. Jetmore, "The Oldest Profession: Investigating Street-level Prostitution," *Law Officer Magazine* 4 (10) (2008).

4. Jetmore, "The Oldest Profession"; G. R. Newman, *Sting Operations,* U.S. Department of Justice, Office of Community Oriented Policing Services: Problem-Oriented Guides for Police Response Guides Series, #6, (2007); T. W. Nolan, "Commentary: Galateas in Blue: Women Police as Decoy Sex Workers," *Criminal Justice Ethics,* 20 (2) (2001), 63–67; G. G. Scott, "Winning the Prostitution Clean-Up Campaign: Teamwork, Routine, and Danger," in *Field Study on the Vice/Prostitution Unit in Oakland*, presented to the Citizen's Police Academy Alumni Association. Behavior Research Associates, 1999; R. Spruill, *Undercover Operation: Deputy Poses as Prostitute* (IndependentMail.com: Anderson County, SC, 2009). Online at: http://www.independentmail.com/news/2009/sep/26/undercover-operation-deputy-posesprostitute/

5. M. Shively, et al., *Final Report on the Evaluation of the First Offender Prostitution Program* (U.S. Department of Justice, Office of Justice Programs, National Institute of Justice, 2008).

6. Sex ads on Craig's List. Online at: http://www.upi.com/Top_News/US/2010/09/06/Sex-ads-still-appearing-on-Craigslist/UPI-49661283790775/; http://www.salon.com/life/broadsheet/2010/09/06/craigslist/

7. Police Web sites. Online at: http://www.jonesboropolice.com/jpd_news.php?item=69

8. R. Durchslag & S. Goswami, *Deconstructing the Demand for Prostitution: Preliminary Insights from Interviews with Chicago Men Who Purchase Sex* (Chicago Alliance Against Sexual Exploitation, 2008); M. Farley, "Theory Versus Reality: Commentary on Four Articles About Trafficking for Prostitution," *Women's Studies International Forum* 32 (4) (2009), 311–315.

9. G. Vold, B. Thomas, & J. Snipes, *Theoretical Criminology* (New York: Oxford University Press, 1998); Franklin Zimring & Gordon Hawkins, *Deterrence: The Legal Threat in Crime Control* (Chicago: The University of Chicago Press, 1973).

10. N. Hotaling, Interview. Standing Against Global Exploitation, San Francisco, CA. January 27, 2006.

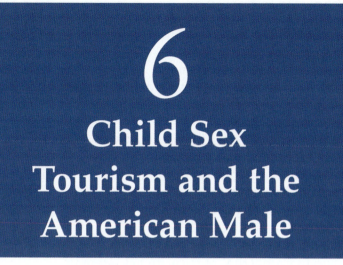

6

Child Sex Tourism and the American Male

An elderly "child sex tourist" is seen here with a young girl at the beach. These men are aware that in many developing countries law enforcement is lax and even if they are apprehended there is a good possibility they will be able to bribe their way out of the situation. (Photo courtesy of Kay Chernush/U.S. Department of State, 2005.)

Chapter Objectives

1. Define child sex tourism.
2. Be familiar with U.S. laws prohibiting child sex tourism.
3. Discuss the demographic profile of the American child sex tourist.
4. Understand the differences between situational and preferential child molesters.
5. Explain how children in foreign countries are located by child sex tourists.
6. Discuss the extreme and long-lasting damage done to victims of child sex tourism.
7. Understand the underlying reasons for child sex tourism in Cambodia, Mexico, and Guatemala.
8. Discuss the elements of the policy recommendations made to develop a comprehensive child recovery program in Mexico.
9. Describe the enforcement efforts by the ICE (Immigration and Customs Enforcement) Cyber Crimes Center as it relates to the investigation of child sex tourism by Americans.
10. Discuss why it has become easier to prevent American men from engaging in child sex tourism.

Introduction

In this chapter, we will first be discussing how child sex tourism is defined and the penalty for American men who engage in this practice. We are then going to examine the profile of the American child sex tourist, how they go about finding local children in foreign countries, and the extreme and lasting damage done to the victims by them. We will focus primarily on three countries, which are among the major destinations for American child sex tourists, namely Cambodia, Mexico, and Guatemala. The selection of these three countries is in no way meant to suggest that they are the only ones that face this problem, and, in fact, there are many more countries that also are destinations for child sex tourism. However, these three countries provide good examples of why certain countries are so attractive to the child sex tourists. With very few exceptions, the underlying reasons, discussed within the context of each of these three countries, apply to almost every other developing country where child sex tourism is a problem. Lastly, we will discuss the role of the United States Immigration and Customs Enforcement (ICE) Cyber Crimes Center in child sex tourism and what can be done to decrease child sex tourism by American men.

Child Sex Tourism Defined

Child sex tourism is defined as traveling to a foreign country to engage in sexual activity with a child younger than 18 years of age, and it is a crime for a U.S. citizen or permanent resident to travel abroad for this purpose. Even if the American citizen or permanent resident overseas is on an ordinary trip, not intending to engage in sex with minors, but at some point during the trip does engage in sex with a minor, they are still subject to prosecution. American men, who are among some of the world's biggest offenders, are subject to prosecution under U.S. laws,[1] even when they committed the crime on foreign soil. The penalty for conviction for such a crime is a fine or imprisonment of no more than 30 years or both (Figure 6.1).

Profile of the Child Sex Tourist

American child sex tourists are typically Caucasian males aged 40 or older and may be broadly categorized as either situational or preferential child sex tourists. A situational child sex tourist abuses children by way of experimentation or through the anonymity and impunity afforded by being a tourist. He does not have an exclusive sexual inclination for children and often is an indiscriminate sex tourist who is presented with

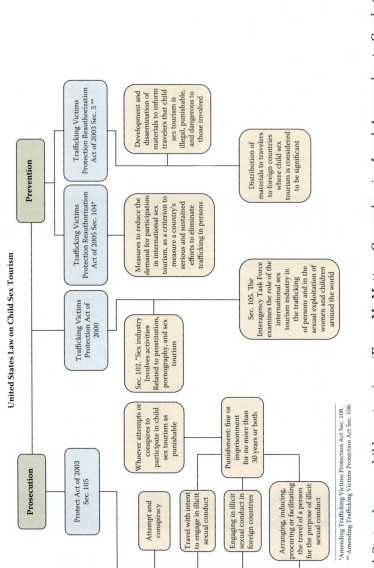

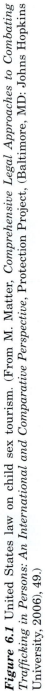

United States Law on Child Sex Tourism

Figure 6.1 United States law on child sex tourism. (From M. Matter, *Comprehensive Legal Approaches to Combating Trafficking in Persons: An International and Comparative Perspective*, Protection Project, (Baltimore, MD: Johns Hopkins University, 2006), 49.)

the opportunity to interact sexually with a person under the age of 18 and takes it. A preferential child sex tourist, on the other hand, is a true pedophile and his sexual fantasies and erotic imagery focus on children. He will actively search for pubescent and adolescent children for sexual contact.[2]

Child sex tourists also are aware that, in many cases, law enforcement in the developing countries they travel to is lax, and, even if they are apprehended, there is a good possibility they will be able to bribe their way out of the situation.

How the Children Are Located by Sex Tourists

Upon entering these foreign countries, these men often obtain information about brothels that offer children for sex or other available children from local taxi drivers, hotel concierges, restaurant wait staff, or newspaper advertisements. Child sex tourists also solicit children independently in foreign destinations at beaches or on the street, particularly if the sex tourist is seeking boys. Some predators also contact foreign children through the Internet and arrange to meet them on the trip. Child sex tourists also gain information about local children through Internet chat rooms, message boards, and online forums. These Internet forums provide locations of child brothels, prices, accounts of child sexual abuse by other sex tourists, and sites for trading child pornography.[3]

Extreme and Long-Lasting Damage to Victims

The children abused by sex tourists suffer not only sexual abuse, but also physical abuse and lasting health problems. Child sex tourists are often violent in abusing children because they believe their victims will not report the offenses. Children sold in brothels often suffer from illnesses, exhaustion, malnourishment, infections, physical injuries, and sexually transmitted diseases. Living conditions are poor and medical treatment is rarely available to them. Children who fail to earn enough income generally are subject to severe punishment, such as beatings and starvation.[4]

Misperception about HIV/AIDS Infection among Young Prostitutes

There is a mistaken belief on the part of these men that younger prostitutes are less likely to carry the HIV/AIDS virus than older ones and, because of this misperception, there is a growing incidence of HIV/AIDS around the world directly related to the exploitation of these children. Because many of the customers seek younger and younger girls almost 50% of prostituted children have HIV/AIDS. Sex with young girls is particularly dangerous because their young, sensitive tissue tears easily, thus exposing their system to the HIV/AIDS virus and other sexually transmitted diseases (Figure 6.2).

Figure 6.2 Extreme and long-lasting damage to young victims. Sex with girls as small and as young as the ones depicted in this photo is particularly dangerous because their young sensitive tissue tears easily thus exposing their system to the HIV/AIDs virus and other sexually transmitted diseases. (Photo: www.Globalgiving.org)

Creating Child Pornography

Child sex tourists are increasingly creating child pornography by recording their acts of child sexual abuse to bring home as souvenirs. After returning home, child sex tourists may share or sell their images and videos with other child predators. Images of the child's abuse are permanently memorialized and impossible to remove from circulation once they enter the Internet stream. Some child sex tourists also write graphic online accounts of their experiences and share information on how to find and abuse children in foreign locations. These accounts may entice other predators to engage in child sex tourism.[5]

Child Sex Tourism in Cambodia

It is estimated that there are 800,000 prostitutes in Cambodia and one third of these are children. Not surprisingly, there is no single explanation for why this occurs, but rather a combination of underlying reasons including economic, social, and corruption.[6]

Economic Reasons

It is important to understand that sex tourism is big business, which generates billions of dollars for many types of individuals including, traffickers, pimps, tourism promoters, owners of brothels, and owners of hotels and bars.

Social Reasons

There are social reasons that are common to many developing countries, previously referred to as third-world countries. To begin with, it is important to understand that, especially in a country like Cambodia, sex trafficking of children begins at

Figure 6.3 Families partner in child sex trade. This man sold his 13-year-old daughter into prostitution for the equivalency of $114 (her younger sister appears to her father's right). After the sale was made, his wife, the mother of the sold girl, seated on the porch, (center rear) chastised him for not asking the trafficker for more money. She felt if they had pushed the trafficker they could have gotten the equivalent of $228 for their daughter. At the conclusion of the sale when the trafficker had left with their daughter, she angrily told her husband, "He robbed us." (Photo courtesy of Andrew Perrin.)

a very early age, some as young as five to seven years of age. Most of these children come from rural areas and are born to impoverished families that are no longer able to support themselves on subsistence farming. In most of the areas where the children come from, there is little in educational opportunities, which means that the cycle of underemployment and poverty is impossible for them to escape. When families are approached by individuals interested in purchasing their young daughters, in most cases, they are told their daughters will be going into legal work and as a result will be able to send money back to help the family support itself. Also, in Cambodia there is a cultural acceptance of child prostitution as a fact of life and, once the children leave, it is unlikely they will ever see their parents again (Figure 6.3).

The parents who sell their children very likely have little or no concept of the psychological and physical trauma their children will likely go through after being forced into a life of prostitution.

Corruption as a Major Problem

One researcher, Dr. Robert Taylor, a highly respected scholar, actually went to Cambodia and studied the problem of child sex tourism in that country and was able to obtain much information that supports the allegations that the Cambodian police were a major part of the problem.[7] He learned that brothels often pay monthly allotments to the police for protection and, in some cases, the brothels are actually owned by government, military, or police officials. It is important to note that corruption of the police and other government officials is an endemic problem in almost all developing countries.

Where Do Most of These Children in Cambodia Come From?

Dr. Taylor also learned that almost all the children involved in prostitution in Cambodia came from areas of extreme poverty, which is typical of most developing countries where child sex tourism occurs. The migration pattern tends to be from poor rural areas to cities and children who were interviewed indicated, for the most part, they were not kidnapped, not forced into prostitution, and willingly participated for the money. Some of the children even commented that it was better than starving to death. Very few used or sold drugs. In some brothels, children as young as six to eight years of age were found.

Recently, MSNBC *Dateline* went undercover with a human rights group to expose child sex tourism in Cambodia. The following is an adapted narrative from that TV episode titled "Children For Sale: Dateline goes undercover with a human rights group to expose sex trafficking in Cambodia."[8] This episode was narrated by Chris Hansen.

Case

Svay Pak is a rundown village on the outskirts of Phnom Penh. After a 20-minute drive, the *Dateline* investigators found themselves on a dirt road dotted with cafes and gated storefronts. It took just a second for a pimp to approach them.

Everyone in Svay Pak assumed that they were tourists there for sex with children. As soon as the team sat down at one of the cafes, they were greeted by a young hustler named Po. He was only 15, but characterized already as being "a real operator." He told the investigators he had grown up in the village and even introduced them to his mother, who knew exactly what he did and was taking a cut of the money he brings in.

Po advised the team he could get them girls as young as they want. He requested they follow him through some alleys into a ramshackled house. When they arrived there, the investigators found girls, some so young they could have been in kindergarten, all for sale. We think we've already seen it all, but who could be prepared for this? They reported that throughout the village, we see the same scene at one brothel after another. All seemed to know a little English. When the team members were talking to the children about sex, they used simple child-like terms, such as "yum-yum" meaning oral sex. "Boom-boom" meaning intercourse.

Two of the girls they met, who were 9 and 10, advised that the yum yum would cost $30 for one and $60 for two girls. The pimp who was there advised the investigators that, if two girls were not enough, they could find three.

When the team left and returned to their car, they had commented that none of them had ever seen anything like this in their lives; this included a 20-year police veteran who was part of the investigative team.

They concluded that if they wanted any results, what they needed was the blessing of a senior Cambodian government official. They knew that getting their attention requires help from someone with real clout. Thus, they contacted the U.S. Ambassador in Cambodia who agreed to assist them in getting official help, which they did.

A plan was set up to conduct a raid one week later with the assistance of the Cambodians. It involved tricking the pimps into bringing the girls to a supposed sex party at a house outside the village. There it would be easier for the police to arrest the pimps and rescue the children.

To get the pimps on board, one of the investigators posed as a sex tour guide and advised the pimp that his clients were reluctant to come into the village; they considered it dangerous and wanted the pimps to deliver the children to a predesignated hotel.

One of the pimps became suspicious and asked one of the investigators if he had a hidden camera. The investigator denied it. The pimp wanted him to prove that he was really a sex tourist and wanted him to have sex with a five-year-old girl. When the investigator refused, the pimp became suspicious and angry told him if he returned again he would kill him.

Eventually pimps were found who were willing to let some of their girls leave the village for the supposed "sex party." The pimps, however, said they wanted to come along to keep an eye on the girls, which played right into the plan, because when they did deliver the girls they would be rescued and the pimps would be arrested.

These would not be the first arrests in Svay Pak. The Cambodian police have set up a unit to deal with sex trafficking. But they've never been involved in anything like this. This time, 60 officers were assigned to the raid.

But the big question is: Can they all be trusted? There were no guarantees that the cops were not on the payroll of the pimps. As a matter of fact, one of the investigators had met one of the police officers earlier in the investigation in Svay Pak who thought he was a sex tour operator and said that for $150 he could make sure neither Robert nor his clients would be arrested.

One hundred fifty dollars—that's the equivalent of five month's pay for the average Cambodian police officer, which pretty well concluded that, if a corrupt police officer, like the one who wanted to be bribed, knew about that raid, they would alert the pimps and the whole operation would never come to pass.

The operation began with a ride on a bus, which also is supposed to be used to rescue the girls from Svay Pak. The bus waits on the outskirts of the village. A half a dozen motor bike drivers took the investigative team and the camera people to go get the girls. The drivers stopped by a pathway that leads to the brothel, where the girls are supposed to be waiting, but there were no signs of the children. After much discussion with the pimps, two children (sisters) are brought into the waiting area. The investigators have seen these girls twice. The first time, when they were brand new to Svay Pak and had not yet been sold for sex. But only a few weeks later, the girls apparently had lost their innocence. They'd been forced to perform oral sex. One acknowledging she had had oral sex five times since then and, one, twice.

At first, everything seemed on track, but then suddenly the pimps change their minds and wouldn't let the girls leave the brothel. Investigators suspected the operation had been compromised and believed that somehow they found out about the investigation. Interestingly, even though the pimps were suspicious, they did not want the "sex tourists" to go away, but, in fact, invited them to have their sex party right there at the brothel. There was not much choice on the part of the investigators except to play along. A phone call was made to alert the police who were standing by. The raid was conducted and by the end of the day a dozen suspected pimps and madams were in custody, and 37 girls rescued, many under the age of 10. As the children were loaded into the van, they were in shock and in tears and didn't seem to understand that they were about to be taken to a safe place.

Interestingly, the Cambodian police officer who had offered to guarantee safe protection of the *Dateline* team for $150 was at the scene dressed in plain clothes. He was pointed out by a member of the investigative team to the uniformed officers at the scene and was arrested.

Child Sex Tourism in Mexico

The Mexican border is a major center for child sex tourism. Thousands of preferential child sex tourists and situational child sex tourists from the United States and other western countries cross into Mexico daily looking for cheap sex with underage prostitutes.[9]

According to the U.S. Department of Justice, "Some perpetrators rationalize their sexual encounters with children with the idea that they are helping the children to financially better themselves and their families. Paying a child for his or her sexual services allows a tourist to rationalize guilt by convincing himself he is helping the child and the child's family to escape economic hardship. Others try to justify their behavior by reasoning that children in foreign countries are less "sexually inhibited," and through the belief that their country does not have the same social taboos against having sex with children. Still other perpetrators are drawn toward child sex, while abroad, because they enjoy the anonymity that comes with being in a foreign land."[10]

An estimated 16,000 children are currently involved in prostitution, pornography, and sex tourism in Mexico.[11] Child prostitutes live in constant fear. They live in fear of sadistic acts by clients, fear of being beaten by pimps who control their lives, and fear of being apprehended by the police.

It has been determined that Mexican children who are sex trafficked often suffer long-lasting psychological damage including depression, low self-esteem, and feelings of hopelessness. As a result, the suicide rate among Mexican children who are trafficked is triple the national average. In addition, the Mexican children face some of the same problems as the children in Cambodia, namely, possible pregnancy, complications of childbirth, violence, sexually transmitted diseases (including HIV-AIDS), but, unlike the children in Cambodia, they also are often addicted to alcohol and drugs.

In Mexico, children are increasingly falling into the hands of the child prostitution and pornography networks that are associated with the crime cartels, which in the past have concentrated their criminal activities primarily on the drug trade. However, as noted in earlier chapters, one of the key differences between the drug trade and the sex trade is that people can be "used" over and over again, while a drug can only be consumed once. As a result, it is in the best economic interest of the cartels to keep those in captivity under their complete control, sometimes for years. If a girl becomes pregnant or sick, or is arrested, or dies, the traffickers will quickly discard her and replace her with another girl.

It is ironic that the violence related to drug trafficking on the border is increasingly cutting into the profits of the cartels' border sex tourism and pornography enterprises. Mexican officials have recently reported a dramatic decrease in sex tourists on the border as a result of the drug war between rival cartels in the area. Although border violence has impacted operations, the cartels are not deterred, and they continue to smuggle girls into the United States.[12]

Most investigators and service providers agree that, just as in Cambodia, both economic and social factors push children into prostitution in Mexico. Mexico and other Latin American countries, with thriving child sex tourism industries, are ones that suffer from widespread poverty resulting from turbulent politics and unstable economies. Poverty also often correlates with illiteracy, limited employment opportunities, and bleak financial circumstances for families. Children in these families become targets for traffickers in search of young children. They are lured away from broken homes by "recruiters," who promise them jobs in a city and then force them into prostitution.

Sadly, just as in Cambodia, some Mexican families prostitute their children or sell their children into the sex trade. Although street and orphaned children are particularly vulnerable to trafficking into the sex industry, a large percentage of children in Mexico, who have been trafficked, continue living with their families and engage in commercial sex activity in order to contribute to household income.

Ironically, there are cases in which the abusers are sometimes seen as saviors by the residents of these impoverished communities. This was the case of Thomas Frank, an American man accused of sexually abusing up to 79 Mexican boys. Yet,

Figure 6.4 The poster boy for child sex tourism in Mexico. Thomas White was returned to Mexico in July, 2005, where he was charged with federal and state charges of rape, child sex abuse, child prostitution, and providing drugs to minors. He was subsequently convicted and sentenced to 7½ years in prison. (AP photo. With permission.)

after having financed the installation of potable water in the community, he was seen as the rescuer of the disadvantaged town and many residents believed that he had done more good than harm to their community (Figure 6.4).

In The News

Thomas Frank White Convicted of Raping Teenage Boy

Lorena Moguel—Associated Press

PUERTO VALLARTA—A U.S. businessman was convicted of raping a teenage boy and sentenced to more than 7 years in jail in Mexico.

Thomas Frank White, of San Francisco, who has spent the last four years jailed in Thailand and Mexico on allegations of having sex with minors, was sentenced to 7 years and 7.5 months in prison, Judge Laila Adriana Cholula said Tuesday.

White's lawyer in Mexico could not be reached for comment, but court officials expect the case will be appealed to the Jalisco State Supreme Court.

A friend said White, being held in a prison outside the Pacific coast resort of Puerto Vallarta, was shaken by Monday's verdict and planned to replace his legal team.

"He is a little bit shocked," Pat Kelly, who visits White daily in his cell, told the *San Francisco Chronicle*.

White, who founded the brokerage firm Thomas White & Co. in 1978, was arrested in Thailand in 2003 at the behest of Mexican officials and later extradited. At the time, he owned homes in Puerto Vallarta, San Francisco, and Thailand.

In August, White agreed to pay $7 million to settle two civil suits filed by American and Mexican youths who claimed they were molested by the financier. That settlement was approved by a federal judge in San Francisco, but was later appealed.

International child advocates say White's case is just one example of how Americans are traveling overseas to have sex with minors.

But Kelly said White is being singled out without proof.

"There was a lot of political pressure in this case," Kelly said. "Thomas White is the poster child for sex tourism in Mexico—a lot of people are invested in his guilt."

White became a familiar face starting in the early 1990s in Puerto Vallarta, where he owned a hotel. He was known as a philanthropist and model citizen who rubbed shoulders with city officials and high society.

But allegations of abuse later surfaced, scuttling his plans to build a $4 million center for street kids. (From: Associated Press. With permission.)

Combined American/Mexican Enforcement Actions

Local legislators, nonprofit organizations, and surviving families of abduction victims have advocated for serious improvements in the ability of Mexican officials to protect victims of abductions, trafficking, and exploitation. U.S. officials complain about the complexities of investigating cases, which originate in Mexico or in which victims from the United States are taken into Mexico. Confusing laws, jurisdictional issues, and communications barriers are daunting hurdles for their efforts to protect children on the border.[13]

Mexican officials also face their own problems in protecting children, including a lack of resources and severe internal security issues. These have made it difficult for them to intake, respond to, or investigate child exploitation cases with the same degree of attention that they receive in the United States.

Southern Border Initiative (SBI)

A project called the Southern Border Initiative (SBI) has been created to assist in developing solutions for these problems. This initiative has been inspired, in part, because of the success of the AMBER Alert initiative in the United States. The AMBER Alert has generated considerable interest in Mexico, and a number of Mexican state and federal agencies are beginning to develop similar child recovery models in their respective regions.[14]

In an effort to develop a comprehensive strategy for addressing issues related to cross-border abductions, exploitation, and trafficking, officials from Mexico have been meeting with officials from the United States and SBI for the past five years. These efforts are taking place despite the personal risk to Mexican officials who face competing demands of state security and the struggle with drug cartels in their states. Since its inception, the SBI has seen strong support in Mexican border states. The states of Tamaulipas and Baja California have adopted statewide child recovery programs, while regional programs modeled on the AMBER Alert program are already in place in Monterrey in the state of Nuevo Leon, and Ciudad Juarez in Chihuahua.

Recently, representatives of six Mexican states, the Mexican federal government, and municipal agencies met with officials from U.S. state, local, and federal agencies to develop strategies for implementation of cross-border training programs for officials from both countries.

The goal of this cross-border training project is to enable both U.S. and Mexican personnel to develop a greater understanding of the issues surrounding cross-border abductions and sex trafficking on the border, while also increasing cooperation, joint response, and investigative capabilities. Through the efforts of the U.S. Department of Justice Office of Justice Programs, a number of promising initiatives, such as joint training, open communications, and capacity building in Mexico have been put into place, which are designed to protect children and help communities on both sides of the border.

The meeting with Mexican federal officials held in Mexico City was designed to move the program to the next level—to combine the grassroots efforts of the states and region with the support and oversight of the federal government. This meeting, which was hosted by the U.S. Department of Justice Resident Legal Advisor to Mexico, was unique in that U.S. experts in child abduction and exploitation from SBI began the process of partnering with their Mexican federal counterparts to design procedures and programs to aid in the recovery of abducted, endangered, and missing children on both sides of the border.

The challenge of this ongoing, bilateral effort is to work together in developing a comprehensive child recovery strategy, which will ultimately eliminate the border as an obstacle to protecting children.

Policy Recommendations

1. Develop and provide training and awareness programs directed at law enforcement and other services providers (fire, EMS, social services, school systems, etc.) and recognition of and response to trafficking.
2. Conduct training for local law enforcement, prosecutors, and judges on model programs for interdiction, investigations, prosecution, and prevention.
3. Develop programs targeting juveniles at high risk for victimization and exploitation, with the goal being to intervene, redirect, and support runaway, throwaway, and exploited children who are at risk of trafficking, or who are being exploited.
4. Develop public service programs to reach out to victims of trafficking, and educating the victim on his/her rights and protections, with the aim of increasing the number of self-referrals and rescues.
5. Create collaborative programs on the southern border to build the capabilities of U.S. and Mexican officials to combat trafficking, sex tourism, and exploitation.

6. Create teams of researchers, journalists, social service groups, advocacy groups, and law enforcement to
develop "on-the-ground" and "real time" information
relating to strategies employed by traffickers, numbers
of victims being trafficked, and to develop a comprehensive understanding of sex trafficking as it is inter-
related to labor trafficking, drug trafficking, and other
organized criminal enterprises.[15]

Child Sex Tourism in Guatemala

The increased level of international awareness about the prevalence of child sex tourism in Southeast Asia has increasingly
forced the illicit industry to shift to Central American countries, most notably Guatemala.[16] Like many other developing
countries in which child sex tourism is a problem, there are factors that make Guatemala attractive, these include: socioeconomic disparities, gender perceptions, and governance issues.

Socioeconomic Disparities

Guatemala's current economic situation is defined by high
levels of poverty, and the pressure to increase revenues from
services rather than agricultural production. This, in turn,
has produced a haven for the child sex tourism industry.
According to a recent report by the United Kingdom Foreign
and Commonwealth Office, Guatemala has the world's third
most unequal wealth distribution, as measured by its Gini
coefficient (a measure of statistical dispersion).[17] Although no
child should be forced, directly or indirectly, to enter the vicious
cycle of sexual exploitation for commercial means, the reality of this dilemma is embedded in an economic framework of
high demand for child sex tourism and the readily accessible
supply of economically marginalized Guatemalan children.

Gender Perceptions

In all economic, social, and political levels of the Guatemalan
society, gender perceptions are entrenched in the ideology of

machismo, which views females as sexual objects and has contributed to the societal tolerance to exploitation of vulnerable minors, especially girls. Men are encouraged to have sex before marriage while women are encouraged to remain virgins until marriage, thus creating the demand for prostitution. Another factor is the misleading perception that masculinity is measured by the numbers of virgins with whom men have sex.[18]

Machismo and other cultural beliefs deeply rooted in the idea that men are superior to women negatively affect the self-esteem of young girls. Even more alarming are the findings of a study conducted by Casa Alianza (an international not-for-profit NGO [nongovernmental organization] and Latin American branch of Covenant House) activists, who infiltrated the dangerous child prostitution network in Central America. They found that many of the female minors spoke of their exploiters in positive terms.[19] Moreover, Guatemalan families make daughters take significant responsibility for their economic well being. Based on these cultural practices that perpetuate gender discrimination and inequality, sex tourists often believe that it is culturally acceptable to have sex with minors in developing countries such as Guatemala.[20]

Governance Issues

The Guatemalan government's failure to truly recognize that the problem exists is characterized by the lack of adequate legislation to protect child exploitation. Also, persistent corruption among law enforcement officers is a key factor contributing to the present situation. Due to the illegal nature of this industry, estimates of the total number of victims are very difficult to establish. By using this limitation as a pretext, the Guatemalan government fails to acknowledge that the child sex exploitation industry constitutes an alarming problem. The current policies dealing with children's issues are inadequate, outdated, and paternalistic. For instance, the 1969 Children's Code in Guatemala allows judges to incarcerate children for their own protection.[21,22] It is not surprising that most victims choose not to report abusers because they are afraid of the police.

A central problem stems from the government's inability to stop corruption among law enforcement. It is common for child sex tourists (who may be arrested) to pay police officers a *mordida* (bribe), a small amount of money that allows them to go home with no criminal record. Corruption also affects other branches of the government that are needed to protect children from exploitation. Several years ago, the Discipline Unit of the Guatemalan Supreme Court investigated 503 cases of wrongdoing, which resulted in 14 judges being sanctioned, 32 being suspended, and 4 being sanctioned with the recommendation to be removed.[23] The persistent problem of corruption in the judicial system results in ineffective prosecution of child exploiters, especially child traffickers.

Even honest law enforcement officials are part of the problem. They fail to be effective due to lack of proper training and adequate knowledge of the legislation on how to deal, not only with child sex tourists, pimps, and traffickers, but also the victims.

United States ICE Cyber Crime Center and Child Sex Tourism Unit

The ICE Cyber Crimes Center is actively involved in investigating the sexual exploitation of children overseas by American men. It also supports child sex tourism investigations through assistance provided by its Computer Forensics program. Its Computer Forensics agents have assisted in the examination of numerous computers seized in conjunction with child sex tourism investigations. Child sex tourism cases are among the most difficult cases to investigate. The child victims are frequently from very poor families in rural areas of underdeveloped countries. Often, ICE agents must travel for days to reach the site of the crime and then identify the victims. Investigators must then face the difficult obstacle of bringing the children back to the United States to testify against the perpetrator. Prior to the trial, many children and their families simply disappear back to rural villages, some "paid off," often by wealthy

Figure 6.5 This Texas man was arrested by ICE agents for having had sex with an underage girl in Mexico. (Photo courtesy of ICE.gov.)

defendants. However, despite obstacles, many American child sex tourists are arrested and, in fact, prosecution has become easier. Since the enactment of the Prosecutorial Remedies and Other Tools to the Exploitation of Children Today (PROTECT) Act of 2003, ICE has conducted over 495 investigations of U.S. citizens traveling abroad for the purpose of sexually exploiting children. This has resulted in more than 65 convictions. As a result of this new law, prosecutors are no longer required, as they were in the past, to prove that the offender traveled to a foreign country with the intent of having sex with a minor. Prosecutors only need to show that the offender, in fact, traveled to a foreign country and engaged in sexual conduct with a minor[24] (Figure 6.5).

In The News

EL PASO, Texas—U.S. Immigration and Customs Enforcement (ICE) special agents on Wednesday arrested a San Elizario, Texas, man who allegedly traveled to Mexico to have sex with a teenage girl in Ciudad Juarez, Chihuahua, Mexico.

A federal grand jury indicted Gustavo Solis-Martinez, 35, on July 16 [2008] for traveling out of the country with the intent to engage in illicit sexual conduct with a minor, a federal offense that falls under the PROTECT Act. The Act authorizes fines and/or imprisonment of up to 30 years for U.S. citizens or residents who engage in illicit sexual conduct abroad, commonly known as "sex tourism."

"Sex tourism is a felony offense that ICE investigates aggressively with the help of our international law enforcement partners," said Roberto G. Medina, special agent in charge of the ICE Office of Investigations in El Paso. "This case exemplifies our international resolve to ensure that those who prey on children do not go unpunished."

Solis-Martinez remains in federal custody at the El Paso County Detention Facility after going before a U.S. federal magistrate judge for an initial appearance July 24.

In a separate ICE investigation, a federal judge this past April sentenced John Dickens Armstrong, 51, to more than nine years in prison after he pleaded guilty to engaging in sexual activity with teenage girls in Ciudad Juarez, Mexico. ICE special agents obtained an arrest warrant for Armstrong last year after learning that Ciudad Juarez police officers arrested him for engaging in sexual conduct with underage girls.

Immigration and Customs Enforcement, News Release, "ICE arrests west Texas man who traveled to Mexico to have sex with minor." July 25, 2008, El Paso, TX. (From: http://www.ice.gov/news/releases/0807/080725elpaso.htm (accessed June 12, 2012.)

Decreasing Child Sex Tourism by American Men

In order to diminish child sex tourism by American men, an awareness campaign should be created that focuses, in part, on the travel industry and the need for the industry to warn American tourists of the harsh penalties they face should they engage in this practice. Travel agents also must be aware of the penalties for assisting men who wish to engage in this practice. For example, under U.S. law, travel agents who "knowingly arrange, induce, procure, or facilitate for profit the travel of a person when they know the person is traveling for the purposes of engaging in elicit sexual conduct with minors" can be prosecuted. As part of this campaign, brochures discussing this issue should be given to tourists at tourist agencies and main ports of entry, and billboards should be strategically

Figure 6.6 Warning posters for English-speaking tourists. A poster in Cambodia encourages people to advise the authorities when they see what they believe to be a child sex tourist with a young child. (From: "Ads for good: Billboard strategies in cross-cultural social service advertising campaigns," by Lynne Ciochetto. Online at: http://www.eyemagazine.com/blog/post/ads-for-good. Photo courtesy of Lynne Ciochetto, Cambodia, 2006.)

placed in tourist locations (Figure 6.6). Also, the creation of a hotline where the general public anonymously can report suspected cases of child sex exploitation should be a priority.

Glossary

1969 Guatemalan Children's Code: A code that allows judges to incarcerate children for their own protection.

AMBER Alert: A voluntary partnership between law enforcement agencies, broadcasters, transportation agencies, and the wireless industry to activate an urgent bulletin in the most serious child abduction cases. The goal of an AMBER Alert is to instantly galvanize the entire community to assist in the search for and the safe recovery of the child.

Boom-boom: A simple, child-like term used in Cambodia meaning sexual intercourse.

Child sex tourism: Defined as traveling to a foreign country with the intent to engage in sexual activity with a child younger than the age of 18.

ICE Cyber Crimes Center: The U.S. federal law enforcement agency actively involved in the investigation of the sexual exploitation of children overseas by Americans.

Human Rights Curriculum: The curriculum recommended to be incorporated into the Guatemalan educational system for both primary and secondary education, with gender discrimination being a priority at the secondary level.

Machismo: An ideology that views females as sexual objects and has contributed to the societal tolerance to exploitation of vulnerable minors, especially girls.

Southern Border Initiative (SBI): A program created to assist in developing solutions for child sex tourism problems along the U.S.–Mexican border.

Svay Pak: A rundown village on the outskirts of Phnom Penh, Cambodia, which is one of the most notorious cities in the country for child sex tourism.

Yum-yum: A simple, child-like term used in Cambodia meaning oral sex.

Review Questions

1. How is child sex tourism defined?
2. What is the penalty if an American is convicted of child sex tourism?
3. What is the difference between the situational child molester and the preferential child molester?
4. Why are young children who are forced to have sex with adult males so much more vulnerable to being infected with the HIV/AIDS virus than fully mature adults?
5. How do some child sex tourists rationalize their sexual encounters with children?
6. What was the goal of the cross-border training project for U.S. and Mexican law enforcement personnel?

7. What has caused child sex tourism to be redirected from Southeast Asia to Central American countries, most notably Guatemala?
8. What are the elements of the ideology of "machismo"?
9. What is the relationship between the ICE Cyber Crime Center and the investigation of child sex tourism by Americans?
10. What can be done to decrease child sex tourism by American men?

Endnotes

1. See U.S.C. § 2423(c) for a more detailed discussion of this law.
2. *The National Strategy for Child Exploitation Prevention and Interdiction*, A Report to Congress (U.S. Department of Justice, August 2010) 36. Online at: http://www.projectsafechildhood. gov/docs/natstrategyreport.pdf (accessed June 20, 2012).
3. Ibid.
4. Ibid.
5. Ibid., p. 37.
6. Much of the information provided herein regarding child sex trafficking in Cambodia was provided by Dr. Robert W. Taylor, Department of Criminal Justices, University of Texas at Dallas in 2007. His university was awarded a $1 million grant by the U.S. State Department to train the entire Cambodian National Police force on the topics of sex trafficking investigation, prosecution, and prevention. The major sources of information were provided by government officials in Thailand and Cambodia, Law Enforcement and Justice officials from Australia, Japan, and the United States. Interviews with nongovernmental agencies (NGOs) working with children and adult prostitutes, children and adults actively involved in the sex trade, and children rescued during police raids.
7. Taylor's study of sex trafficking in Cambodia.
8. Chris Hansen, "Children For Sale: Dateline Goes Undercover With a Human Rights Group to Expose Sex Trafficking in Cambodia," MSNBC, (online report). Online at: http://www. msnbc.msn.com/id/4038249 (accessed June 12, 2012).

9. Jim Walters & Patricia H. Davis, "Human Trafficking, Sex Tourism, and Child Exploitation on the Southern Border," *Journal of Applied Research on Children: Informing Policy for Children at Risk* 2 (1) (2011), 9–11.

10. U.S. Department of Justice Child Exploitation and Obscenity Section. Child Sexual Trafficking. Online at: http://www.justice.gov/criminal/ceos/sextour.html (accessed January 15, 2011).

11. E. Azola, "Boy and Girl Victims of Sexual Exploitation in Mexico," UNICEF-DIF. June 2000. Online at: http://www.gvnet.com/childprostitution/Mexico.htm (accessed January 15, 2011).

12. U.S. Senate Foreign Relations Committee—Near Eastern and South Asian Affairs Subcommittee Hearings on International Trafficking of Women and Children. April 4, 2000. Online at: http://www.paho.org/english/hdp/hdw/traffickingPaper.pdf (accessed January 15, 2011).

13. Walters & Davis, "Human Trafficking, Sex Tourism, and Child Exploitation on the Southern Border," p. 11.

14. The AMBER Alert program is a voluntary partnership between law enforcement agencies, state transportation officials, and radio, television, and Internet broadcasters to activate an urgent news bulletin in child abduction cases. Broadcasters use the Emergency Alert System, formerly known as the Emergency Broadcast System, to air a description of the missing child, the suspected abductor, and any vehicles involved in the abduction. The program was first introduced after the kidnap and murder of nine-year-old Amber Hagerman of the Dallas–Fort Worth area and is now established in all 50 states.

15. Walters & Davis, "Human Trafficking, Sex Tourism, and Child Exploitation on the Southern Border," 11–12.

16. Glenda L. Giron, "Underexposed Child Sex Tourism Industry in Guatemala," in *International Sex Trafficking of Women and Children,* ed. L. Territo & G. Kirkham (Flushing, NY: LooseLeaf Law Publications, 2010), 445–455.

17. U.K. Foreign and Commonwealth Office, "Country Profiles: Guatemala," 2004. Online at: http://www.fco.gov.uk/servlet/Front?pagename=OpenMarket/Xcelerate/ShowPage&c=Page&cid=1007029394365&a=KCountryProfile&aid=1020262398293 (accessed January 23, 2013).

18. Giron, "Underexposed Child Sex Tourism Industry in Guatemala," 448–449.

19. Casa Alianza, "Central America: Activists Infiltrate Child Sex Rings," International Movement Against All Forms of Discrimination and Racism, April 5, 2002. Online at: http://www.imadr.org/project/guatemala/news3.html
20. U.K. Foreign and Commonwealth Office.
21. S. Wallenberg, U.S. Servas, "Sex Tourism." Online at: http://www.usservas.org /un_summer_2002.htm
22. Giron, "Underexposed Child Sex Tourism Industry in Guatemala," p. 449.
23. Department of State, Bureau of Democracy, Human Rights, and Labor, "Guatemala: Country Reports on Human Rights Practices," 2003. Online at: http://www.state.gov/g/drl/rls/hrrpt/2002/18333.htm (accessed January 23, 2013).
24. The National Strategy for Child Exploitation Prevention and Interdiction, pp. 37–38.

7

Interrogation of Sex-Trafficking Suspects

A multiple-image recording system installed at the Lawrence, Kansas, Police Department's Investigation and Training Center, which can be used to record both audio and video interrogations of sex-trafficking suspects. Detective M. T. Brown is shown in the Monitoring and Equipment Room. (From: www2.ljworld.com. Photo courtesy of Mike Yoder.)

Chapter Objectives

1. Explain the differences between interviews and interrogations.
2. Discuss the objectives of an interrogation.
3. Understand the essential qualities needed by an investigator to be a good interrogator.
4. Describe how an interrogation room should be set up in order to be most effective in obtaining a voluntary confession.
5. Discuss the advantages of using electronic recordings for interrogations.
6. Understand the legal limitations related to the use of admissions and confessions at trial.
7. Explain the impact of the *Miranda v. Arizona* ruling of the U.S. Supreme Court and other past and current landmark U.S. Supreme Court cases as they relate to the admissibility of confessions and admissions.
8. Discuss the kinds of behaviors that indicate deception.

Introduction

Interviewing, as opposed to interrogation, is primarily a non-accusatory process and is intended for the purpose of gathering information. Interrogation, on the other hand, is an investigative process intended to match acquired information to a particular suspect in order to secure a confession. It also is accusatory and more confrontational in tone and is intended to verify or disprove information obtained from a particular suspect.

In this chapter, we will discuss those aspects of interrogation in sex-trafficking cases, which are essential for investigators to fully understand in order to maximize their effectiveness. This will include the objectives of the interrogation process, and what is hoped to be accomplished; the essential qualities an investigator must have in order to be effective in conducting an interrogation in sex-trafficking cases; creating the right environment that will be conducive to obtaining a voluntary confession; the value of using electronic recordings of the interrogation process, as well as a comparison of the types of confession documents in descending order of believability to juries; the most important U.S. Supreme Court cases that affect the admissibility of confessions and admissions; and, lastly, those behaviors, on the part of a suspect, that would suggest he or she is attempting to be deceptive.

Objectives of Interrogation

There are four commonly recognized objectives in the interrogation process. These include:

1. Obtaining valuable facts
2. Eliminating the innocent
3. Obtaining a confession that can lead to valuable physical evidence, as well as the identification of other suspects and accomplices
4. Results in a successful prosecution of the guilty

As the investigator moves from the preliminary task of gathering valuable facts to the concluding task of obtaining a confession, the difficulty of acquiring information increases. That difficulty, however, is rewarded by an increase in the value of the information. Figure 7.1 illustrates these relationships. In attempting to obtain a confession from a suspect, the investigator also gains information about the facts and circumstances surrounding the commission of an offense. In seeking such information, the investigator must be concerned with asking the basic questions that apply to all aspects of the investigative process namely: Who? What? Where? When? How? and Why?[1]

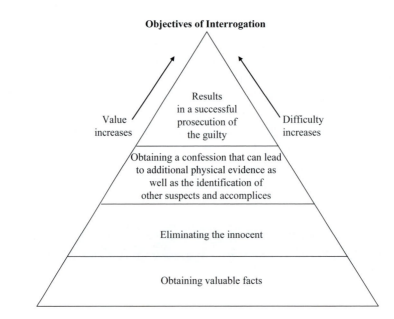

Objectives of Interrogation

Results in a successful prosecution of the guilty

Obtaining a confession that can lead to additional physical evidence as well as the identification of other suspects and accomplices

Eliminating the innocent

Obtaining valuable facts

Value increases

Difficulty increases

Figure 7.1 Objectives of interrogation.

Essential Qualities Needed by the Sex-Trafficking Investigator in the Interrogation Process

In order to be an effective interrogator, it is absolutely essential that the investigator be knowledgeable in all aspects of sex-trafficking investigations, especially about their state statutes and federal statutes dealing with sex trafficking offenses. The investigator also must be totally familiar with the major cultural aspects of those victims and suspects, especially foreign nationals who he or she is likely to encounter in sex-trafficking investigations. Persuasiveness and perseverance are also essential to success. The investigator must make himself/herself easy to talk to. By the appropriate use of vocal inflection, modulation, and emphasis, even the Miranda warnings (discussed later in this chapter) can be presented to a suspect in a manner that does not cause the suspect to immediately assume a defensive posture. The words can be spoken without creating an adversarial atmosphere. The investigator must have a flexible personality and be able to convey empathy, sympathy, anger, fear, and joy at appropriate times, but must always remain objective. The investigator must keep an open mind and be receptive to all information, regardless of its nature. This is especially true in sex-trafficking cases where the acts of abuse by suspects toward the victims may be particularly despicable and cruel.

During an interrogation, the investigator must carefully evaluate each development while studiously avoiding the pitfall of underestimating the capabilities of the subject being interrogated. Screaming or shouting, belittling the subject or the information provided, sneering, and other such unplanned and uncontrolled reactions most often adversely affect the interrogation. The investigator must at all times maintain control of the interrogation without being openly domineering, by being a good active listener, by being serious and patient, and, most importantly, by being persistent and persuasive.[2] An ability to categorize the psychological and emotional traits being manifested by the suspect helps the investigator react in a manner that increases the possibility of conducting a successful interrogation, because it is the job of the investigator to make it easy for a suspect to confess even to the commission of the most despicable crimes. However, it is equally important for investigators to remember that part of their task also is to eliminate those individuals who are innocent of the crime of which they are accused.

The Interrogation Room

Furnishings

The traditional interrogation room should be sparsely furnished, usually with only two chairs. The chair the suspect is sitting in should have straight legs. However, the investigator should consider using a chair with rollers so that he or she can easily move into closer proximity to the suspect, if this is a tactic he/she chooses to employ. There should be no physical barriers, such as tables or desks, between the investigator and the suspect. From the officer's standpoint, such barriers may create an unwanted feeling of psychological well being on the part of the suspect. If there is a table or desk in the room, it should be moved out of the way, or the chair should be moved. This arrangement permits the investigator to eliminate any physical or psychological barriers between him/her and the person being interrogated.[3] Also, the walls should be kept blank so the suspect is not distracted.

Proximity

Proximity in an interrogation also can be important. Research has shown that the comfort zone for white American middle-class males is approximately 27 inches. A distance closer than that seems to result in some discomfort.[4] There, however, are considerable differences in both the comfort zones and body language of various ethnic groups, and investigators must make it a point to know as much as possible about the unique psychological, social, and cultural characteristics of the individuals they are most likely to encounter both in interviews as well as interrogations. For example, a comfortable social distance for conversations in some cultures may be as little as 15 inches. Thus, what would appear to be an uncomfortable distance for a white American middle-class male would not necessarily be a distance that would make individuals from some other cultures uncomfortable. There are other important cultural differences as well. For example, in Middle Eastern countries it is considered highly disrespectful for individuals sitting and engaged in conversations to show the soles of their shoes. There is no way that an American investigator would know this or many other aspects of a different culture, unless:

- they were from the same culture;
- they had been personally exposed to it through previous contact with the culture;
- they were individually informed by people familiar within the culture; or
- they had been formally trained to understand these important cultural differences.

There are additional and important cultural differences that will be discussed in greater detail later in this chapter.

The Use of Two-Way Mirrors in the Interrogation Room

The two-way mirror, although still a useful tool for allowing others to observe the interrogation and useful for officer safety, is widely known, especially to experienced criminals, and may cause some subjects to refuse to cooperate in the interrogation. If a two-way mirror is to be used, it should be small and unobtrusive. As a standard practice, the interrogation room should be equipped with a video or audio system that includes a recording device, unless prohibited by state law. (The use of electronic recording in the interrogation process will be discussed later in this chapter.)

Although the traditional interrogation room is designed to ensure control and domination over the interrogation process because of its privacy, security, and aura of authority, it may not impress the habitual or experienced offender who understands the rules and standards of conduct of the classical interrogation process. If the offender is skilled and intelligent, he/she may not only be able to cope with the psychological influences such a setting is designed to foster, but perhaps also can become the dominant force, or at least be on the same psychological level as the investigator. When this occurs, the skills of the investigator become even more important. This is especially true for those sex traffickers who may have come to the United States from developing countries where they have previously been exposed to police officers who are often corrupt and routinely use brutal interrogation tactics in order to extract information and confessions.

Assessing the Suspect

Prior to the start of the interrogation, the investigator should try to obtain as much personal background information on the suspect as possible. This information should include aliases and the names of other sex-trafficking suspects or individuals who may have been involved with the suspect. If a suspect is not

Figure 7.2 Preparing for an interrogation. Prior to starting an interrogation, the investigator should review all statements of rescued victims or witnesses, including all available file information pertaining to the suspect.

a U.S. citizen, determine his/her nationality and immigration status as well as their level of English competency, date and place of birth, education, marital status, employment history, financial history, prior offenses, past and present physical and mental health, any drug or alcohol abuse or addiction, and relationship, if any, to the victim or crime(s) scene (Figure 7.2).

Documenting Interrogations

Documenting an interrogation consists of three main phases: note-taking, recording, and obtaining written statements. All three phases are geared to accomplishing two basic functions: first, retaining information for the benefit of the investigator and the continued investigation, and, second, securing a written statement or confession from the accused for later use as evidence in court.

The Use of Electronic Recordings for Interrogations

Electronic recording of an interrogation is the best means of documentation. Audio, video, or a combination of both may be used, but case law and local requirements should be checked prior to being utilized.

At present, 238 law enforcement agencies in 38 states record custodial interviews of suspects in felony investigations. These agencies are located in every area of the United States and are quite diverse in size and individual practices. Following are some of the elements addressed in their respective policies as they relate to the use of electronic recordings for interrogation:[5]

- *Mandatory or discretionary*: Most departments leave the recording decision to the discretion of the investigator in charge, although recordings are customarily made by the investigators in cases covered by discretionary policies.
- *When to begin recordings*: Most departments use either audio and/or video recording devices to record interrogations of persons under arrest in a police facility starting from the point when the *Miranda* warnings (discussed later in this chapter) are given until the interrogation has ended, with no intentional breaks or omissions in the recordings.
- *Crimes under investigation*: Most departments record only in "major" or "serious" felony investigations, such as sex trafficking, homicide, sexual assault, armed robbery, other crimes against persons, and those involving weapons.
- *Equipment*: Some departments use a single camera focused on the suspect, while others use multiple cameras from different angles.[6]
- *Suspect's knowledge*: Federal law enforcement officers do not have to notify a suspect that the interrogation is being recorded. However, state eavesdropping laws govern whether suspects must be told they are being recorded. "One-party consent" laws allow the police to record without informing the suspects. "Two-party consent" laws require the police to obtain the suspects' consent. Most state laws permit police to record surreptitiously although sophisticated suspects and repeat offenders may be aware without being told. Most

departments inform suspects that the session will be recorded and/or place the recording equipment in plain view although most of them are not required by state law to do so. Almost all investigators turn the recording devices off if the suspect declines to talk while being recorded.

Benefits of Recording Interrogations

Electronic recording of interrogations has proved to be an efficient and powerful tool for both investigators and prosecutors. Audio is good, but video is better. Both methods create a permanent record of exactly what occurred. Recordings prevent disputes about the investigator's conduct, the treatment of suspects, and the voluntariness of statements they made. Investigators are not called on to paraphrase statements or try later to describe suspects' words, actions, and attitudes. Instead, viewers and listeners see and/or hear precisely what was said and done, including whether suspects were forthcoming or evasive, changed their versions of events, and appeared sincere and innocent or deceitful and guilty. An electronic record is law enforcement's version of instant replay.

Experience also shows that recordings dramatically reduce the number of defense motions to suppress statements and confessions. The record is there for defense lawyers to see and evaluate; if the investigators conduct themselves properly during the questioning, there is no basis to challenge their conduct or exclude the defendants' responses from evidence. Investigators are spared from defending themselves against allegations of coercion, trickery, and perjury during hostile cross-examinations.

The use of recording devices, even when known to the suspect, does not impede investigators from obtaining confessions and admissions from guilty suspects. When suspects decline to talk if recorded, the investigators simply turn the recorder off and proceed with taking hand-written notes.

Recordings permit investigators to focus on the suspect rather than taking copious notes of the interrogation. When investigators later review the recordings, they often can observe inconsistencies and evasive conduct that they overlooked while the interrogation was in progress.

Electronic recording forces investigators to better prepare for conducting interrogations. It has additional benefits as well. This includes:

- clarifying whether an investigator missed something that requires further questioning
- giving prosecutors a better understanding of cases, thereby fostering better charging decisions, plea-bargaining options, and case preparation
- minimizing challenges by defense attorneys about the accuracy of the electronic recordings and the completeness of written confessions
- reducing doubts about the voluntariness of confessions
- jogging the investigators' memories when they are testifying

In addition, electronic video recordings can be reviewed and used as training aids for less experienced investigators who are attempting to develop their own interrogation skills[7] (Figure 7.3).

Figure 7.3 The use of electronic video recordings of interrogations as a training device. By viewing the interrogation techniques employed by highly experienced and successful investigators, less experienced investigator can begin to develop and enhance their own interrogation skills, thus becoming more effective in the interrogation process. (Photo courtesy of the FBI.)

The Written Statement

After the use of electronic recordings, the next best form is a signed statement written in the first person by the suspect in his or her handwriting. Sometimes, however, it is not possible to convince a suspect to prepare such a statement, or perhaps the suspect is illiterate and cannot write.

There are other forms in which statements may be admitted into evidence. Table 7.1 shows them in descending order of the believability to juries.

The form and content of a written statement should include a heading, which incorporates the data identifying the circumstances under which the statement was taken, the body of the statement, and a verification. The statement should open with an indication of the time and place where it was taken, and an identification of the person giving the statement that includes his/her name, address, and age. The heading also must include a definite statement to the effect that the subject is giving the statement freely and voluntarily after having been appropriately advised of his/her constitutional rights.

The body of the statement, which acknowledges the subject's involvement in the crime under investigation, should, if possible, be phrased in the first person, allowing the suspect to include his/her own ideas in a free-flowing manner. However, if this is not possible or practical, then the question-and-answer format is permissible. The terminology used should include the words, grammar, idioms, and style of the person making the statement. The body of the statement should be arranged so that its content follows the chronological order of the subject's involvement in the case under investigation.

At the end, the statement should indicate that the suspect has read the statement or has had it read to him/her, that its contents and implications are understood, and that the suspect attests to its accuracy.

Other suggestions for the investigator to keep in mind include:

- Each page of the statement should be numbered consecutively with an indication that it is page no. ___ of ___ pages. This is done so that, if the pages get separated, they can later be easily restored to the correct order.

TABLE 7.1
Comparison of Types of Confession Documentation
(in Descending Order of Believability to Juries)

Type	Advantages	Disadvantages
1. Electronic video or audio recording	• May be required by legislative or judicial directive • Shows all, including fairness, procedures, and treatment • Easy to do • Can be relatively inexpensive	• May face legal constraints
2. Audio recording	• Can hear conversations • Can infer fairness	• Some words or descriptions may be meaningless without pictorial support • Necessitates identifying people and things involved
3. Statement written and signed in suspect's own handwriting	• Can be identified as coming directly from suspect	• Cannot see the demeanor or hear voice inflections • The suspect may not agree to the procedure
4. Typed statement signed by suspect	• The signature indicates knowledge of and agreement with the contents of the statement	• Less convincing than the methods described above
5. Typed unsigned statement acknowledged by suspect	• Contents of confession or admission are present • Acknowledgment helps show voluntariness	• Reduced believability of voluntariness and accuracy of contents
6. Testimony of someone who heard confession or admission given	• Contents admissible	• Carries little weight with juries

Source: Charles R. Swanson, et al. *Criminal Investigation*, 11th ed. (New York: McGraw-Hill, 2012), p. 135. With permission.

- The investigator should ensure that each page is initialed by the subject. If the subject is unwilling to sign, the statement should be acknowledged by him/her. If the subject cannot write, another identifying mark may be used.
- On occasion, an investigator may encounter someone who says, "I'll tell you what I've done, but I'm not writing anything, and I'm not signing anything." In such circumstances, the investigator can explain that the suspect confessed, and the investigator or some other person, who heard the confession can go into court and testify about it. By preparing or signing a statement, the suspect protects himself/herself against the investigator's testifying to something more damaging by changing the story in court (another good reason for electronic recording.)
- If the suspect cannot read, the statement must be read to him/her, and the investigator must ensure the suspect understands its contents before being allowed to attest to its accuracy.
- All errors in the statement should be corrected on the final copy and initialed by the suspect. The investigator may accommodate the suspect by allowing small errors if this will help obtain the suspect's initials on each page of the statement.
- The investigator should make sure the suspect understands all the words used in the statement. If some words are confusing, their meanings should be explained to the suspect and the suspect should be required to explain them back in front of witnesses in order to confirm this understanding.
- During the process of drafting and attesting to a statement derived through interrogation, there should be at least one additional witness, who can testify to the authenticity of the statement and the circumstances under which it was obtained. After the suspect signs the statement in ink, the witnesses should sign their names, addresses, and positions.[8]

Admissibility of Confessions and Admissions

Before 1936, the only test for the validity and admissibility of a confession or admission was its voluntariness. However, the determination as to whether it was given voluntarily by the suspect was subject to very loose interpretation. There were no rules restricting the method by which law enforcement obtained "voluntary" statements. Physical violence, psychological coercion, empty promises, and meaningless guarantees of rewards were not considered objectionable procedures; however, this all changed in 1936 in the case of *Brown v. Mississippi*.

The Free-and-Voluntary Rule

The first notable incidence of U.S. Supreme Court intervention into interrogation practices came about in *Brown v. Mississippi*.[9] In this 1936 case, the Supreme Court held that under no circumstances could a confession be considered freely and voluntarily given when it was obtained as a result of physical brutality and violence inflicted by law enforcement officials on the accused. The reaction to this decision by law enforcement was not unexpected. Many threw up their hands and claimed they could no longer function effectively because "handcuffs had been put on the police." However, as was true with many other decisions placing procedural restrictions on law enforcement agencies, the police found they were able to compensate by conducting thorough criminal investigations.

Subsequent to the *Brown* decision, the Supreme Court, in a succession of cases, has continued to reinforce its position that any kind of coercion, whether physical or psychological, would be grounds for making a confession inadmissible as being in violation of the **free-and-voluntary rule**. This includes such conduct as threatening bodily harm to the suspect or members of the suspect's family,[10] using psychological coercion,[11] engaging in trickery or deceit, or holding a suspect incommunicado.

Investigators also are cautioned about making promises to the suspect that cannot be kept. All these practices were condemned in *Miranda v. Arizona* (discussed in much greater detail later in this chapter).[12] Despite the appearance that Miranda has eliminated all coercive techniques previously used in interrogations, this is not actually the case. What Miranda seeks is to abolish techniques that would prompt untrue incriminatory statements by a suspect. Thus, unlike physical coercion, psychological coercion, threats, duress, and some promises, the use of trickery, fraud, falsehood, and similar techniques are not absolutely forbidden. If such methods are not likely to cause an individual to make self-incriminating statements or to admit to falsehoods in order to avoid threatened harm, confessions or admissions so obtained are admissible.[13]

The Delay-in-Arraignment Rule

In 1943, the U.S. Supreme Court delivered another decision concerning the admissibility of confessions. Even though the free-and-voluntary rule was in effect in both the federal and state courts, another series of statutes seemed to have gone unheeded. Every state and the federal government had legal provisions requiring that, after an arrest, a person must be taken before a committing magistrate "without unnecessary delay." Before 1943, if there was an unnecessary delay in producing the accused before a committing magistrate, the delay was merely one of a number of factors the courts were required to take into consideration in determining whether the confession was freely and voluntarily given. However, this all changed in the case of *McNabb v. United States.*

The facts of *McNabb v. United States*[14] reveal that McNabb and several members of his family were involved in bootlegging. They were arrested after the murder of federal officers who were investigating their operation in Tennessee. McNabb was held incommunicado for several days before he was taken before a committing magistrate. He subsequently confessed, and the confession was admitted into evidence at his trial. He was convicted, but on appeal to the Supreme Court, the conviction was reversed. The Court held that the failure of federal officers to take the prisoner before a committing officer without necessary delay automatically rendered his confession inadmissible. The significance of this case is that, for the first time, the Court indicated that failure to comply with this procedural requirement would render a confession inadmissible regardless of whether it was obtained freely and voluntarily. Thus, instead of examining the facts of the case to determine the voluntariness of the confession, the Court ruled, as a matter of law, that the procedural violation also rendered the confession inadmissible. The holding in the *McNabb* case was emphatically reaffirmed in 1957 by the Supreme Court in *Mallory v. United States.*[15]

As the mandate of the Supreme Court in the *McNabb* and *Mallory* cases applied only to federal prosecutions, the states were free to interpret their own statutes on unnecessary delay as they saw fit. Few chose to follow the *McNabb–Mallory* **delay-in-arraignment rule**. The majority have continued to require that there must be a connection between the failure of law enforcement to produce the accused before a committing magistrate without unnecessary delay and the securing of a confession.

Preinterrogation Legal Requirements

Preinterrogation legal requirements became of critical concern during the 1960s. As a result, the Supreme Court handed down a landmark decision that dramatically affected the conditions under which interrogations take place. The issue revolved around the Fifth Amendment protection against self-incrimination and the Sixth Amendment guarantee of the right to counsel, both as made applicable to the states through the due process clause of the Fourteenth Amendment.

Miranda v. Arizona

In **Miranda v. Arizona,**[16] the Supreme Court, in a five-to-four decision, spelled out the requirements and procedures to be followed by officers when conducting an in-custody interrogation of a suspect. The facts of this case are:

In March 1963, Ernest Miranda was arrested for kidnapping and rape. After being identified by the victim, he was questioned by police for several hours and signed a confession that included a statement indicating that the confession was given voluntarily. The confession was admitted into evidence over the objections of Miranda's defense counsel, and the jury found him guilty. The Supreme Court of Arizona affirmed the conviction and held that Miranda's constitutional rights had not been violated in obtaining the conviction because following the ruling from *Escobedo v. Illinois*[17] the year before, in which Escobedo's confession was ruled to have been improperly admitted because he asked to see his lawyer, but was denied that right, Miranda had not specifically requested counsel. The U.S. Supreme Court, in reversing the decision, attempted to clarify its intent in the *Escobedo* case by spelling out specific guidelines to be followed by police before they interrogate persons in custody and attempt to use their statements as evidence. In clarifying the requirements of *Escobedo*, the Court felt compelled to include the Fifth Amendment requirements against self-incrimination in the decision. The guidelines require that after a person is taken into custody for an offense and before any questioning by law enforcement officers, if there is any intent to use a suspect's statements in court, the person must first be advised of certain rights (Figure 7.4 and Figure 7.5).[18]

Warning-Rights Card in English and Spanish

The Explanation of The Admonition and Use or Waiver of Your Rights	La Explicacion Del Aviso Y EL Uso O No De Tus Derechos
1) You have the right to remain silent — you do not have to talk.	1) Tienes el derecho de quedar en silencio — no tienes que hablar.
2) What you say can be used, and shall be used against you in a court of law.	2) Lo que digas se puede usar y se usará en contra de ti en la corte de ley.
3) You have the right to talk with an attorney before you talk to us, and you have the right to have the attorney present during the time we are talking to you.	3) Tienes el derecho de hablar con un abogado antes de hablar con nosotros, y tienes el derecho de tener el abodado presente durante el tiempo que nosotros estamos hablando contigo.
4) If you do not have the funds to employ an attorney, one shall be appointed to represent you free of charge.	4) Si no tienes el dinero para emplear un abodado, uno sere fijado para que te represente, sin pagar.
5) Do you understand these rights as I have explained them to you, yes or no?	5) ¿Comprendes estos derechos como te los expliqué, si o no?
6) Do you want to talk to us about your case now, yes or no?	6) ¿Quieres hablar con nosotros de tu caso ahora, si o no?
7) Do you want an attorney present during the time we are talking to you, yes or no?	7) ¿Quieres un abodado presente durante el tiempo que estamos hablando contigo, si o no?

Figure 7.4 Warning rights card in English and Spanish.

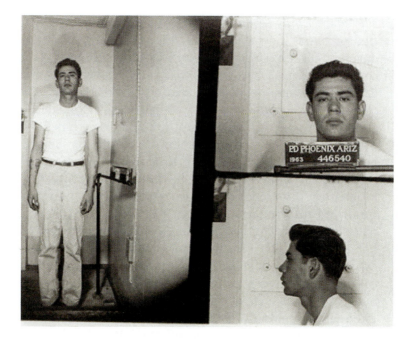

Figure 7.5 The case involving the conviction of Ernest Miranda for kidnapping and rape was a landmark case and in 1966 the U.S. Supreme Court spelled out specific guidelines to be followed by police when they interrogate a person in custody and attempt to use the statements obtained from them as evidence. In 1976, Ernest Miranda, who was then 34 years of age, was stabbed to death in a bar fight over a $3 poker debt. (Photo courtesy of the Phoenix, Arizona, Police Department.)

Suspect's Response: Waiver and Alternatives

It is common practice for the investigator to ask the suspect if he or she understands the rights as they have been explained. If the answer is yes, then the investigator may ask if the suspect wants to talk with the investigator. At this point, four alternatives are open to the suspect:

1. *The suspect may choose to remain silent,* not wanting even to respond to the investigator's questions. The courts have held that choosing to remain silent does not imply consent to be interrogated and no questions should be asked.

2. *The suspect may request counsel.* At that point, the investigator must not undertake any questioning of the suspect, for anything said will not be admissible in court. In *Edwards v. Arizona* in 1981, the Supreme Court held that no police-initiated interrogation may lawfully take place once the suspect has invoked the right to counsel unless, and until, an attorney has been provided or unless the defendant voluntarily begins to talk with the officers.[19] In **Minnick v. Mississippi** in 1990, the Supreme Court held that once counsel is requested, interrogation must cease; officials may not reinitiate interrogation without counsel being present, whether or not the accused has consulted with his or her attorney. The requirement that counsel be made available to the accused refers not to the opportunity to consult with a lawyer outside the interrogation room but to the right to have the attorney present during custodial interrogation. This rule is necessary to remove suspects from the coercive pressure of officials who may try to persuade them to waive their rights. The rule also provides a clear and unequivocal guideline to the law enforcement profession.[20]

The *Edwards* and *Minnick* lines of cases remained constant until the Supreme Court ruled in **Maryland v. Shatzer** in 2010. The facts involved an attempt by a detective to question Shatzer in 2003 about allegations that he had sexually abused his son. At the time Shatzer was in prison on an unrelated offense. Shatzer invoked his *Miranda* rights to have counsel present during the interrogation. The detective terminated the interview, and the case was subsequently closed. Shatzer was returned to the general population. Another detective reopened the investigation three years later and attempted to interrogate Shatzer, who was still in prison. Shatzer waived his *Miranda* rights this time and, in 2006, made some inculpatory statements that were admitted at his trial for sexually abusing his son. Shatzer was convicted. After several appeals, which held the trial court was wrong to admit Shatzer's incriminating statements since he had previously asked for an attorney, the appeals courts held there was no exception once the request for an attorney had been made in accordance with the *Edwards* decision, since Shatzer was still being held in custody. The Supreme Court, however, agreed with the trial court, allowing the statements to be used against Shatzer. The Court reasoned that because Shatzer experienced a break in *Miranda* custody, lasting more than two weeks between the first and second attempts at interrogation, *Edwards* did not require suppression of his 2006 statements. The Court said that even though Shatzer was still in prison during the time between the 2003 and 2006 interrogations, he was in the general population, where he could have spoken with a lawyer during the three-year break and was no longer in a police-dominated atmosphere on the sexual abuse case. Even though he was still in prison, Shatzer resumed his "normal life."[21,22]

3. *The suspect may waive his or her rights and agree to talk with law enforcement without the benefit of counsel.* The waiver of rights is a sensitive topic for law enforcement because it is the responsibility of law enforcement and the prosecutor to prove in court the waiver was validly obtained. A valid waiver must be voluntarily, knowingly, and intelligently given by the suspect. The burden is on the prosecution to prove that the suspect was properly advised of his or her rights, that those rights were understood, and that the suspect voluntarily, knowingly, and intelligently waived those rights before the court will allow the introduction of any incriminating testimony in the form of a confession. The waiver cannot be presumed or inferred. It must be successfully proved by the prosecution. Therefore, it is preferable for the investigator who secures a waiver of rights from a suspect to attempt to get the waiver in writing with sufficient witnesses to substantiate its voluntariness. Figure 7.6 is a sample rights waiver form. Most law enforcement agencies also attempt to get individuals in custody to sign a rights waiver form as one more

Rights Waiver Form

<u>YOUR RIGHTS</u>

Date _____
Time _____

<u>WARNING</u>

Before we ask you any questions, you must understand your rights.
You have the right to remain silent.
Anything you say can and will be used against you in court.

You have the right to talk to a lawyer for advice before we ask you any question and to have him with you during questioning.

If you cannot afford a lawyer, one will be appointed for you.
Geauga County has a Public Defender. Before answering any questions, you have a right to talk with the Public Defender.

If you decide to answer questions now, without a lawyer present, you will still have the right to stop answering at any time. You also have the right to stop answering at any time until you talk to a lawyer.

Do you understand these rights? _____

Signed: _____

Witnesses:

_____
_____

<u>WAIVER OF RIGHTS</u>

I have read this statement of my rights and I understand what my rights are. I am willing to make a statement and answer questions. I do not want a lawyer at this time. I understand and know what I am doing. No promises or threats have been made to me and no pressure or coercion of any kind has been used against me.

Signed: _____

Witnesses:

_____
_____

Date: _____
Time: _____

Figure 7.6 Rights waiver form. (From Geauga County, Ohio, Sheriff's Department.)

step to show a good faith effort to comply with the requirements of the *Miranda* ruling.

However, a suspect who has waived his or her rights is free to withdraw that waiver at any time. If this occurs during questioning, the investigator is under a legal obligation to cease the interrogation at that point and either comply with the suspect's request for representation or simply cease the interrogation if the suspect refuses to talk.

4. *The suspect may indicate a desire not to talk with the investigators.* At this point, law enforcement has no choice other than to refrain from attempting to interrogate the suspect concerning the events of the crime for which he/she has been arrested. In this event, the case must be based on independent evidence, which may or may not be sufficient to warrant prosecution. The U.S. Supreme Court's emphatic position on terminating interrogation once a suspect has invoked the right to remain silent was announced in 1975 in the case of *Michigan v. Mosley.*[23]

Because the responsibility is on the prosecution, supported by evidence provided by the investigators, to substantiate the voluntariness of the waiver and the propriety of the warnings given to the suspect, many law enforcement agencies provide printed cards with the exact wording of the required warnings. They further recommend or require that when warnings are given they be read verbatim from the printed card. In this manner, the officer, when testifying in court, can positively state the exact words used in advising the suspect of his/her constitutional rights. Such a procedure avoids any confrontation with the defense as to the exact wording and contents of the *Miranda* requirements. But in 1989, in *Duckworth v. Eagen*, the Supreme Court held that it was not necessary that the warnings be given in the exact form described in the *Miranda* decision, provided the warnings as a whole fully informed the suspect of his or her rights.[24] This position was reaffirmed in a 2010 case, *Florida v. Powell.*[25]

A person being subjected to **in-custody interrogation** often chooses not to answer any questions posed by law enforcement—or at least not until an attorney is present. When counsel is made available to the suspect before or during interrogation, it is almost universal practice for the attorney to advise the client not to say anything to the police. Therefore, the effect of the *Miranda* decision has been to reduce significantly the number of valid interrogations by law enforcement agencies in this country today. For the most part, however, confessions obtained in compliance with prescribed rules are of better quality and are more likely to be admissible in court.

It must be impressed on investigators that the failure to properly advise a suspect of the rights required by *Miranda* does not invalidate an otherwise valid arrest, nor does it necessarily mean a case cannot be successfully prosecuted. Even in light of the line of court decisions indicating that *Miranda* warnings may not be required in all interrogation situations, good practice or departmental policy may require that all suspects in custody be advised of their rights.

In-Custody Interrogation

For investigators to understand the proper application of the *Miranda* requirements, it is essential they understand the meaning of in-custody interrogation. The *Miranda* case involved simultaneous custody and interrogation. Subsequent police actions revealed that all cases were not so nicely defined, and the meanings of "in custody" and "interrogation" required clarification. Although it may be difficult to separate the custody from the interrogation in certain factual situations, the two concepts must be considered separately.

Custody

Custody occurs when a person is deprived of his/her freedom in any significant way or is not free to leave the presence of law enforcement. Analyses of case decisions show there is not yet a universally accepted definition of custody. Rather, case-by-case analysis is used to determine the applicability of the *Miranda* requirements discussed earlier in this chapter.

Miranda and Misdemeanors

The question of whether *Miranda* applies to misdemeanor arrests was the subject of controversy for many years. In 1984, the Supreme Court settled this issue. The Court ruled in *Berkemer v. McCarty* that *Miranda* applies to the interrogation of an arrested person regardless of whether the offense is a felony or a misdemeanor. The justices found that to make a distinction would cause confusion because many times it is not certain whether the person taken into custody is to be charged with a felony or a misdemeanor.[26]

Interrogation as Defined by the U.S. Supreme Court

For legal purposes, interrogation includes any express questioning or any verbal or nonverbal behavior by a law enforcement officer that is designed to elicit an incriminating statement or response from the suspect of a crime. For many years following the *Miranda* ruling, there was considerable confusion over what constituted questioning or interrogation. For example, in a 1977 case, the U.S. Supreme Court found that an impermissible interrogation occurred when an investigator delivered what has been called the "Christian burial speech" to a man suspected of murdering a young girl. While the suspect was being transported between cities, the investigator told the suspect to think about how the weather was turning cold and snow was likely. He pointed out how difficult it would be to find the body later. The investigator went on to say that the girl's parents were entitled to have a Christian burial for the little girl, who had been taken from them on Christmas Eve and murdered. Subsequent to this little speech, the suspect led the investigators to the spot where he had disposed of the body. The Supreme Court held this to be an interrogation within the scope of *Miranda*, even though direct questions had not been asked of the suspect.[27]

The Supreme Court faced the question of what constitutes interrogation for the first time in the 1980 case of *Rhode Island v. Innis*. In that instance a robbery suspect was arrested after the victim had identified him from photographs. The prisoner was advised several times of his constitutional rights and was being transported by three officers who had been specifically ordered not to question the suspect. During the trip, two of the officers were having a conversation about the case, and one commented how terrible it would be if some unsuspecting child found the missing shotgun (used in the robbery) and got hurt. The conversation was not directed at the suspect, nor did the officers expect a response from the suspect. However, the suspect interrupted the conversation and, after again being advised of his rights, led the officers to the shotgun. The Supreme Court stated the rule regarding interrogation as follows:

> We conclude that *Miranda* safeguards come into play whenever a person in custody is subjected to either express questioning or its functional equivalent. That is to say, the term "interrogation" under *Miranda* refers not only to express questioning, but also to any words or actions on the part of the police (other than those normally attendant to arrest and custody) that the police should know are reasonably likely to elicit an incriminating response from the suspect. The latter portion of this definition focuses primarily upon the perceptions of the suspect, rather than the intent of the police. This focus reflects the fact that the *Miranda* safeguards were designed to vest a suspect in custody with an added measure of protection against coercive police practices, without regard to objective proof of the underlying intent of the police.[28]

As a general rule, *Miranda* warnings need not precede routine booking questions that are asked in order to obtain personal history data necessary to complete the booking process. As long as the questions are for that purpose and not a pretext to obtain incriminating information, *Miranda* warnings need not be given.[29]

Most Recent U.S. Supreme Court Decision on the Right to Remain Silent

On June 1, 2010, the U.S. Supreme Court's decision in the case of ***Berghuis v. Thompkins*** was decided and shines new light on issues surrounding both the invocation and waiver of the *Miranda* right to remain silent.[30,31]

In *Berghuis*, Van Chester Thompkins was arrested in Ohio for a shooting that occurred approximately one year earlier in Southfield, Michigan. While in custody, Thompkins was questioned by two detectives in a police interview room. At the beginning of the interrogation, the detectives presented Thompkins with a general set of *Miranda* warnings.[32]

To make sure Thompkins could understand English, one of the detectives asked Thompkins to read a portion of the warnings out loud, which he did. Thereafter, the detective read the rest of the warnings to Thompkins and asked him to sign the form, indicating that he understood his rights. Thompkins refused to sign the form, and the officers began interrogating Thompkins. "At no point during the interrogation did Thompkins say he wanted to remain silent, did not want to talk to the police, or wanted an attorney."[33]

With the exception of some minor verbal responses and limited eye contact, Thompkins remained silent for most of the three-hour interview. Approximately 2 hours and 45 minutes into the interrogation, one of the detectives asked Thompkins if he believed in God. Thompkins said he did. The detective then followed up by asking Thompkins if he prayed to God. Thompkins said, "Yes." The detective then asked, "Do you pray to God to forgive you for shooting that boy down? To which, Thompkins answered, "Yes." Thompkins refused to make a written statement, and the interrogation ended.[34]

Court Proceedings

Thompkins filed a motion to suppress the statements he made during the interrogation and claimed his Fifth Amendment right to remain silent had been violated. The trial court denied the motion, and Thompkins' admission was used against him at trial. Thompkins was convicted of first-degree murder and sentenced to life in prison without parole.

Thompkins appealed.[35] The Michigan Court of Appeals rejected the *Miranda* claim, and the Michigan Supreme Court denied review. Thereafter, Thompkins filed a petition for a writ of habeas corpus in the U.S. District Court for the Eastern District of Michigan that was likewise denied. The U.S. Court of Appeals for the Sixth Circuit reversed the district court ruling in favor of Thompkins.[36] However, for the reasons set forth herein, the Supreme Court reversed the judgment of the Sixth Circuit Court of Appeals and found no *Miranda* violations.

Right to Remain Silent: Invocation

In filing his motion to suppress the statements he made during the interrogation, Thompkins first argued he had invoked his right to remain silent by not saying anything for the first

2 hours and 45 minutes of the interrogation. If, in fact, he had invoked his right to remain silent, it is undisputed the officers would have been obligated to stop questioning.[37] However, Justice Kennedy, in writing the majority opinion, explained that Thompkins' mere silence in the face of questioning was not a clear and unambiguous invocation of his right to remain silent.[38] The Court noted that, unlike its earlier ruling in *Davis v. United States* regarding the invocation of the *Miranda* right to counsel, it never had defined whether an invocation of the right to remain silent must be unambiguous. In *Davis*, the defendant initially waived his *Miranda* rights and was interrogated for 90 minutes before saying, "Maybe I should talk to a lawyer." The Court held that if a subject is unclear, ambiguous, or equivocal in requesting a lawyer, officers can ignore the reference and proceed with the interrogation.[39]

In *Berghuis*, the Court acknowledged "there is no principled reason to adopt different standards for determining when an accused has invoked the *Miranda* right to remain silent and the *Miranda* right to counsel at issue in *Davis* ... both protect the privilege against compulsory self-incrimination ... by requiring an interrogation to cease when either right is invoked." Moreover, the Court explained there are no practical reasons for requiring that an invocation of the right to silence be clear and unambiguous. Namely, "an unambiguous invocation of *Miranda* rights results in an objective inquiry that "avoid[s] difficulties of proof and ... provide[s] guidance to officers on how to proceed in the face of ambiguity."[40] Accordingly, *Berghuis* does for the invocation of the right to silence what *Davis* did for the invocation of the right to counsel—it mandates that an invocation of either *Miranda* right must be clear and unambiguous to be effective.

Right to Remain Silent: Waiver

Thompkins next argued that absent an invocation of his right to silence, his statements still should be suppressed because he never adequately waived his right to silence. Two portions of the original *Miranda* decision seem to tilt the scale in Thompkins' favor on this issue. First, the *Miranda* Court said, "a valid waiver will not be presumed simply from the silence of the accused after warnings are given or simply from the fact that a confession was, in fact, eventually obtained."[41] Additionally, "a heavy burden rests on the government to demonstrate that the defendant knowingly and intelligently waived his privilege against self-incrimination. ..."[42]

However, the Supreme Court has clarified its position with respect to the waiver since the *Miranda* decision. The impact has been to keep *Miranda* focused on the right to refrain from speaking and to consult an attorney. As the Court in *Berghuis* noted: "The main purpose of *Miranda* is to ensure that an accused is advised of and understands the right to remain silent and the right to counsel. ...[43] Thus, if anything, our subsequent cases have reduced the impact of the *Miranda* rule on legitimate law enforcement while reaffirming the decision's core ruling that unwarned statements may not be used as evidence in the prosecution's case in chief."[44]

Detection of Deception

It can be safely assumed that at some stage of the sex-trafficking investigation some victims, witnesses, and suspects will lie. As part of the arsenal of skills the sex-trafficking investigator should have in the interrogation process is a basic understanding of those kinds of behaviors that would tend to suggest deception. However, identifying deceit is so difficult that repeated studies begun in the 1980s show that most people (including judges, attorneys, clinicians, police officers, FBI agents, politicians, teachers, mothers, fathers, and spouses) are no better than chance (50.50) when it comes to detecting deception.[45,46] It is disturbing but true. Most people, including professionals, do no better than a coin toss at correctly perceiving dishonesty. Even those who are truly gifted at detecting deception (probably less than 1% of the general population) are seldom right more than 60% of the time. Consider the countless jurors who must determine honesty or dishonesty, guilt or innocence, based on what they think are deceptive behaviors. Unfortunately, those behaviors most often mistaken for dishonesty are primarily manifestations of stress, not deception.[47]

There is simply no single behavior that is indicative of deception—not one.[48]

This does not mean that we should abandon our efforts to study deception and observe for behaviors that, in context, are suggestive of it. But a realistic goal is to be able to read nonverbal behaviors with clarity and reliability.

Signs of Discomfort in an Interaction

We all show signs of discomfort when we do not like what is happening to us, when we do not like what we are seeing or hearing, or when we are compelled to talk about things we would prefer to keep hidden because they are both painful and shameful. We display discomfort first in our physiology, due to arousal of the limbic brain.[49] Our heart rate quickens, we perspire more, and we breathe faster. Beyond the physiological responses, which are autonomic (automatic) and require no thinking on our part, our bodies manifest discomfort nonverbally. We tend to move our bodies in an attempt to block or distance ourselves from the source of our discomfort. We rearrange ourselves, jiggle our feet, fidget, twist at the hips, or drum our fingers when we are scared, nervous, or significantly uncomfortable.[50] We have all noticed such discomfort behaviors in others—whether at a job interview or being questioned about a serious matter. These actions do not automatically indicate deception, but do indicate a person is uncomfortable in the current situation for any number of reasons.

When attempting to observe discomfort as a potential indicator of deception, especially during the interview of a suspect, the best setting, as discussed earlier, is one that has no objects (such as tables or desks) between the person being observed and the investigator. Movements of the lower limbs can be particularly revealing. Thus, if a person is behind a desk or table, the investigator should move it because such an obstacle will block the vast majority (nearly 80%) of the body surfaces that need to be observed. In fact, the investigator should watch for the deceptive individual using obstacles or objects to form a physical barrier between the investigator and himself or herself. The use of objects is a sign that an individual wants distance, separation, and partial concealment because the subject is being less open, which goes hand in hand with being uncomfortable or even deceitful.

When it comes to questioning someone, more nonverbal clues can be obtained from standing rather than sitting. Lots of behaviors cannot be observed to the same degree while sitting.

Other clear signs of discomfort seen in people during a difficult or troubling interview include rubbing their forehead; covering their throat; difficulty swallowing; clearing the throat, coughing, covering or twisting the mouth; biting or licking lips; yawning and sighs; itching and rubbing the nose, mustache, or beard; tugging at their ears or covering their ears; pulling, twirling, or grooming their hair; flushing of the skin or extremely pale; squeezing their face; rubbing their neck; or stroking the back of their head with their hand. People may show their displeasure with the process by rolling their eyes in disrespect, picking lint off themselves (preening), or talking down to the person asking the questions—giving short answers, becoming resistant, hostile, or sarcastic, or even displaying microgestures with indecent connotations such as giving the finger.[51]

When making false statements, liars will rarely touch or engage in other physical contact with the investigator. Because touching is more often performed by the truthful person for emphasis, this distancing helps to alleviate the level of anxiety a dishonest person is feeling. Any diminution of touching observed in a person engaged in conversation, especially while hearing or answering critical questions, is more likely than not indicative of deception.[52]

When observing a person's face for signs of comfort or discomfort, investigators should look for subtle behaviors, such as a grimace or a look of contempt.[53] Also, the person's face should be observed to see if his/her mouth is quivering. This is a clear indication of nervousness and discomfort. Any facial expression that lasts too long or lingers is not normal, whether a smile, a frown, or a surprised look. Such contrived behavior during an interview is intended to influence the investigator's opinion and lacks authenticity. Often when people are caught doing something wrong or lying, they will hold a smile for an unusual period of time. Rather than being an indication of comfort, this type of false smile is actually an indication of discomfort.

On occasion, when we do not like what we are hearing, whether a question or an answer, we will often close our eyes as if to block it. The various forms of eye-blocking mechanisms are analogous to folding one's hands tightly across the chest or turning away from those with whom we disagree. These blocking displays are performed subconsciously and occur often, especially during a formal interview, and are usually related to a specific topic. Eyelid flutter is also observed at times when a particular subject causes distress.[54]

All of these eye manifestations are powerful clues as to how information is registering, or what questions are problematic for the recipient. However, they are not necessarily direct indicators of deceit. Little or no eye contact is *not* indicative of deception.[55] As a matter of fact, habitual liars actually engage in greater eye contact than most individuals, and will lock eyes with the person they are communicating with. Research clearly shows that psychopaths, con men, and habitual liars will actually increase eye contact, and it is consciously employed by these individuals because they are aware it is so commonly (but erroneously) believed by many that looking someone straight in the eye is a sign of truthfulness.

However, as suggested earlier in this chapter, it is important to understand that there are not only cultural differences in the comfort zones related to physical proximity, but also in making eye contact during conversations. For example, individuals belonging to many groups, such as African Americans, Latin Americans, and people from the Middle East, are often taught to look down or away when being questioned by individuals in a position of authority. This is considered to be a gesture of respect and deference.[56] Thus, failure to understand these unique cultural features could lead an investigator to erroneously conclude that the person is being deceptive.

Indications of nervousness do not necessarily mean deception. A person's voice may crack or may seem inconsistent when being deceptive; swallowing becomes difficult as the throat becomes dry from stress and they begin to swallow hard. These can be evidenced by a sudden bob or jump of the Adam's apple and may be accompanied by the clearing or repeated clearing of the throat—all indicative of discomfort. These behaviors are indicators of distress, not guarantees of deception. For example, many honest people who testify in court display these behaviors simply because they are nervous and not because they are lying. Even after years of testifying, many law enforcement officers still acknowledge they still get nervous on the witness stand. Thus, it is important to remember that signs of tension and stress need to be deciphered within the context in which they are occurring.

Glossary

Body language: The specific physiological reactions that occur when someone may be under stress and useful in detecting deception.

Custody: This occurs when a person is deprived of his/her freedom in any significant way or is not free to leave the presence of law enforcement.

Delay in Arraignment Rule: In the case of *McNabb v. the United States,* the U.S. Supreme Court ruled the failure of federal officers to take a prisoner before a committing officer without necessary delay automatically renders his confession inadmissible.

Electronic recordings: This is an audio, video, or combination of both that may be used to record the interrogation process.

Free and Voluntary Rule: The Supreme Court ruled in *Brown v. Mississippi* in 1936 that under no circumstances could a confession be considered free and voluntarily given when it was obtained as a result of physical brutality and violence inflicted by law enforcement officials on the accused.

Interrogation: For legal purposes, the U.S. Supreme Court has ruled that interrogations will include any expressed questioning or any verbal or nonverbal behavior by law enforcement officers that is designed to elicit an incriminating statement or response from the suspect of a crime.

Interview: A process that is primarily nonaccusatory and intended to get information.

Miranda v. Arizona: The case in which the U.S. Supreme Court spelled out guidelines to be followed by police before they interrogate persons in custody and attempt to use their statements as evidence.

Review Questions

1. What are the differences between interviews and interrogations?
2. What are the four commonly recognized objectives in the interrogation process?
3. What are the essential qualities needed by the sex-trafficking investigator in the interrogation process?
4. What should an interrogation room look like?
5. What information should an investigator try to obtain before interrogating a suspect?
6. What are the benefits of electronic recording of interrogations for both law enforcement officers and prosecutors?
7. What was the first notable incident of U.S. Supreme Court intervention into interrogation practices and what was the impact of the ruling?
8. What was the significance of the *McNabb v. U.S.* ruling by the U.S. Supreme Court?
9. What requirements are imposed on law enforcement personnel regarding the warning they must give to a person in custody under the provisions of *Miranda v. Arizona*?
10. What are the facts and the significance of the U.S. Supreme Court case involving *Maryland v. Shatzer* in 2010?
11. How has interrogation been defined by the U.S. Supreme Court?
12. In which cultures are people sometimes discouraged from making eye contact with those they are engaged in conversation with and why is this so?

Endnotes

1. Charles R. Swanson, Neil C. Chamelin, Leonard Territo, & Robert W. Taylor, *Criminal Investigation*, 11th ed. (New York: McGraw-Hill, 2012), 123–144.
2. Ibid., 81–84; Charles L. Yeshke, *The Art of Investigative Interviewing* (Boston: Butterworth-Heinemann, 1977), 56–68.
3. John E. Hess, *Interviewing and Interrogation for Law Enforcement* (Cincinnati: Anderson, 1997), 84.
4. William Hart, "The Subtle Art of Persuasion," *Police Magazine*, January 1981, 10.
5. Thomas P. Sullivan, "Police Experiences with Recording Custodial Interrogations," *Northwestern University School of Law* 1 (Summer 2004): 4.
6. See the discussion of camera angles in G. Daniel Lassiter, et al., "Criminal Confessions on Videotape: Does Camera Perspective Bias Their Perceived Veracity?" *Current Research in Social Psychology* 7 (1) (2001). Online at: at http:// www.uiowa. deu/~grpproc/criop/crisp.y.1.htm
7. Sullivan, "Police Experiences with Recording Custodial Interrogation," 5–10.
8. See Timothy T. Burke, "Documenting and Reporting a Confession: A Guide for Law Enforcement," *FBI Law Enforcement Bulletin* 70 (2) (Feb. 2001): 17–21.
9. 297 U.S. 278 (1936).
10. *Payne v. Arkansas*, 560 U.S. (1958).
11. *Miranda v. Arizona*, 436 U.S. (1966).
12. Ibid.
13. Robert L. Donigan, et al., *The Evidence Handbook* (Chicago: Traffic Institute of Northwestern University, 1975), 44–48. See also *Frazier v. Cupp*, 394 U.S. 731 (1969); *Oregon v. Mathiason*, 429 U.S. 492 (1977).
14. 318 U.S. 332 (1943).
15. 354 U.S. 449 (1957).
16. *Miranda v. Arizona*, 384 U.S. 436 (1966).
17. *Escobedo v. Illinois*, 378 U.S. 478 (1964).
18. 384 U.S. 436 (1966).
19. 451 U.S. 477, 101 S.Ct. 1880 (1981).

20. 498 U.S. 146 (1990).
21. See Kenneth A. Myer, "Miranda Update: Fifth Amendment Protection and Breaking Custody," *FBI Law Enforcement Bulletin* 79 (5) (May 2010), 26–32, for a more detailed discussion of this case.
22. 559 U.S. __. 130 S.Ct. 1213 (2010).
23. 423 U.S. 96, 96 S.Ct. 321 (1975).
24. 492 U.S. 195, 109 S.Ct. 2875 (1989).
25. 130 S. Ct. 1195, 175 L.Ed.2d 1009 (2010).
26. 82 L. Ed. 317 (1984).
27. 430 U.S. 387 (1977).
28. 446 U.S. 291, 100 S.Ct. 1682 (1980).
29. *United States v. Clark*, 982 F.2d 965, at 968 (6th Cir. 1993).
30. Jonathan L. Rudd, "You have to Speak Up to Remain Silent: The Supreme Court Revisits the *Miranda* Right to Silence," *FBI Law Enforcement Bulletin* (September 2010), 25–31.
31. *Berghuis v. Thompkins,* 560 U.S. __ (2010).
32. Ibid. "Notification of Constitutional Rights and Statement (1) You have the right to remain silent. (2) Anything you say can and will be used against you in a court of law. (3) You have a right to talk to a lawyer before answering any questions. (4) If you cannot afford to hire a lawyer, one will be appointed to represent you before any questioning, if you wish one. (5) You have a right to decide at any time before or during questioning to use your right to remain silent and your right to talk with a lawyer while you are being questioned."
33. Ibid.
34. Ibid.
35. Thompkins also filed a motion for a new trial claiming ineffective assistance in counsel. This motion was likewise denied and followed the appeal regarding alleged *Miranda* violations to the U.S. Supreme Court.
36. The Sixth Circuit Court also ruled in favor of Thompkins on the effective-assistance-of-counsel claims.
37. *Miranda* at 446. In *Michigan v. Mosley*, 423 U.S. 96 (1995), the Court explained that when a subject invokes his right to silence, all questioning must cease. However, the Court further held that the invocation of the right to remain silent does not mean that police never may resume questioning. Indeed, in *Mosley*, the Court held that the police had scrupulously honored the suspect's Fifth Amendment rights when a different officer questioned the suspect in a different location about a different crime

after two hours had elapsed since the subject invoked his right to remain silent. (Note: This differs from an invocation of the right to counsel, wherein officers would not be allowed to reinitiate contact after merely the passage of time. See *Edwards v. Arizona*, 451 U.S. 477 (1981) and *Maryland v. Shatzer,* 559 U.S. ___ (2010).

38. Justice Kennedy delivered the 5–4 opinion of the Court in which Chief Justice Roberts and Justices Scalia, Thomas, and Alito joined. Justice Sotomayor filed a dissenting opinion, in which Justices Stevens, Ginsberg, and Breyer joined.

39. *Davis v. United States,* 512 U.S. 452 (1994).

40. *Berghius v. Thompkins.*

41. *Miranda*, at 475.

42. Ibid.

43. *Davis v. United States*, at 460; *Moran v. Burbine*, 475 U.S. 412, at 427 (1986).

44. *Dickerson v. United States*, 530 U.S. 428 428 (2000), 443–444.

45. Joe Navarro, with Marin Karlins, *What Every Body Is Saying* (New York: HarperCollins, 2008), 213–218.

46. C. V. Ford, *Lies!, Lies!!, Lies!!! The Psychology of Deceit* (Washington, D.C.: American Psychiatric Press, Inc., 1996), 217. P. Ekman, *Telling Lies: Clues to Deceit in the Marketplace, Politics, and Marriage* (New York: W.W. Norton & Co., 1991), 162.

47. P. Ekman & M. O'Sullivan, "Who Can Catch a Liar?" *American Psychologist* 46 (1991), 913–920.

48. Ekman, *Telling Lies*, 187–188.

49. In the study of nonverbal communications, the limbic brain is where the action is. Because it is the part of the brain that reacts to the world around us reflexively and instantaneously, in real time and without thought. For that reason, it gives off a *true* response to information coming in from the environment (D. G. Myers, *Exploring Psychology,* 2nd ed. (New York: Worth Publishers, 1993), 35–39). Because it is uniquely responsible for our survival, the limbic brain does not take breaks. It is always "on." The limbic brain is also our emotional center. It is from there that signals go out to various other parts of the brain, which in turn orchestrate our behaviors as they relate to emotions or our survival (J. LeDoux, *The Emotional Brain: The Mysterious Underpinnings of Emotional Life* (New York: Touchstone, 1996), 104–137). These behaviors can be observed and decoded as they manifest physically in our feet, torso, arms, hands, and faces. Since these reactions occur without thought,

unlike words, they are genuine. Thus, the limbic brain is considered the "honest brain" when we think of nonverbal communication (D. Goleman, *Emotional Intelligence* (New York: Bantam Books, 1995), 13–29).

50. G. de Becker, *The Gift of Fear* (New York: Dell Publishing, 1997), 133.

51. Ekman, *Telling Lies*, 101–133.

52. D. J. Lieberman, *Never Be Lied to Again* (New York: St. Martin's Press, 1998), 24.

53. Ekman, *Telling Lies*, 158–169.

54. J. Navarro and J. R. Schafer, "Detecting Deception," *FBI Law Enforcement Bulletin* (July, 2001), 9–13.

55. A. Virj, *Detecting Lies and Deceit* (Chichester, U.K.: John Wiley & Sons, Ltd., 2003), 38–39.

56. R. R. Johnston, "Race and Police Reliance on Suspicious Non-Verbal Cues," *Policing: An International Journal of Police Strategies & Management* 20 (2) (2007), 280–281.

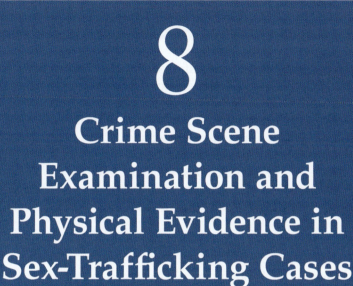

8

Crime Scene Examination and Physical Evidence in Sex-Trafficking Cases

The scientific analysis of recovered physical evidence at the sex-trafficking crime scene can be of invaluable assistance in the prosecutorial process. (Photo courtesy Dr. Jalika Rivera Waugh, Department of Criminal Justice, Saint Leo University, Florida.)

Chapter Objectives

1. Determine what types of observations and actions are necessary to take upon entering the crime scene.
2. Explain what a crime scene is.
3. Discuss the role of forensic science and its application in sex-trafficking investigations.
4. Describe the types of physical evidence most commonly found in sex-trafficking investigations.
5. Outline the basic actions required to process, discover, and recover physical evidence at sex-trafficking crime scenes.
6. Understand what databases are and how the Combined DNA Index System (CODIS) is used.
7. Discuss the importance of retrieving information technology (IT) and communications equipment at the scenes of sex-trafficking cases.
8. Understand the importance of protecting and controlling access to the crime scene.
9. Discuss why it is so important to have an experienced sex-trafficking investigator at the crime scene.
10. Be familiar with the steps to be taken in the examination of sex-trafficking victims in order to obtain important physical evidence.
11. Explain what steps need to be followed in obtaining a search warrant in order to recover DNA evidence.
12. Discuss the steps to be followed in order to systematically examine a sex-trafficking suspect for physical evidence.

Introduction

Forensic science is defined in its broadest definition as the application of science to law. The use of a multitude of forensic science tools in processing a sex-trafficking crime scene is essential to the recovery of all available physical evidence. It can be used to identify specific suspects for traditional court evidence, as an investigative tool to guide the police investigation, and to gather intelligence to help detect trends and patterns for other components of a sex-trafficking operation. However, even though forensic science should always be seen as an important tool in an overall investigation, it is not the sole investigative tool. It is very important to remember that even the best physical evidence can be easily discredited if not properly secured, processed, collected, packaged, transported, and stored in an appropriate way.

In this chapter, we will focus on the initial observations to be taken upon entering the crime scene and the main types of physical evidence likely to be present in sex-trafficking cases, namely, biological materials, fingerprints, documents, and communication technologies. We will examine specific features that are unique to sex-trafficking crime scenes and how best to preserve and protect evidence found at the scene. This also will include how to go about obtaining important physical evidence from both sex-trafficking victims and sex-trafficking suspects and the importance of cooperation between the investigator and forensic personnel at the crime scene. Lastly, we will examine the elements necessary to obtain a search warrant in a quest to retrieve DNA evidence and how transport vehicles or vehicles where sexual liaisons occur may be sources of important physical evidence in sex-trafficking cases.

The Initial Observations and Actions to Be Taken upon Entering the Crime Scene

All too often a sex-trafficking crime scene may not be completely identified as such upon initial observation. For example, a vice unit or street crimes unit serving a search warrant for narcotics may uncover a sex-trafficking operation, but, because they are focusing on the narcotics aspect of the operation and have not been trained to recognize a sex-trafficking crime scene, they may fail to recognize it as such. This also could apply to uniformed patrol officers who are responding to a location for a totally unrelated call, such as a disturbance. If these officers have not been trained to recognize a sex-trafficking operation, then they will not approach the crime scene with the idea of preserving physical evidence for that purpose or gathering intelligence that could be relevant to future investigations.

Crime Scene Examination

A crime scene is any physical scene that contains fragile records of past activities and can be locations (indoor or open air), vehicles, and persons, which involves both victims and suspects. Crime scene examination is guided by the fundamental principle of forensic science that every contact leaves a trace. This includes any contact of a person with a person, person with a vehicle or location, vehicle with a location, and so forth. In general, all activities leave some traces and, in sex-trafficking cases, this includes both physical evidence as well as evidence found on and in electronic equipment at the crime scene.[1]

Types of Potential Physical Evidence at Sex-Trafficking Crime Scenes

Biological Materials

Biological materials include such items as blood, semen, skin cells, tissues, organs, muscle, bone, teeth, hair, saliva, fingernails, and urine. Preliminary tests on these materials can reveal the presence of drugs and the type of body fluid. Another value of the body fluids is the possible identification of the victim or suspects' deoxyribonucleic acid (DNA).

Deoxyribonucleic Acid (DNA) Analysis

Advances in technology have resulted in DNA testing becoming an established part of criminal justice procedure. Previous questions about the validity and reliability of forensic DNA test methods have been addressed, but, for the most part, validity and reliability have been established. As a result, the admissibility of DNA test results in the courtroom has become routine.

All 50 states, plus the District of Columbia, now require that offenders convicted of certain crimes submit DNA samples. Most states require that all felons submit DNA samples for future use in DNA databases[2] (discussed later in this chapter). In recent years, DNA evidence has become the "gold standard" of forensic testing, and is an invaluable tool for the criminal justice system.[3]

DNA consists of molecules that carry the body's genetic information and establish each person as separate and distinct and can be obtained from a variety of sources, such as blood, tissue, spermatozoa, bone marrow, hair roots, saliva, skin cells, urine, feces, and a host of other biological specimens, all of which may be found at crime scenes. DNA has been recovered from fingerprints, cigarette butts, drinking cups, hatbands, and other articles of clothing.

DNA is generally found in cells that have a nucleus, but some biological cells do not have nuclei, such as those forming fingernails, hair shafts, and teeth. What these cells do have is a more primitive form of genetic coding called **mitochondrial DNA (mtDNA)**, which are organelles that are found in the body of the cell. When a sperm and an egg join at conception, the new individual gets half of his or her nuclear genetic information from each parent. Conversely, mitochondrial DNA is inherited only from the mother. At conception, all of the new person's mitochondria come from the mother. Since mitochondrial DNA is passed directly through maternal relatives, it serves as a perfect identity marker for those relatives.[4] The mitochondrial DNA sequencing technique was originally developed by anthropologists to help trace human ancestors.

Identifying and Collecting DNA at a Crime Scene

DNA evidence may be found and collected from virtually everywhere at a crime scene, and only a few cells are sufficient to obtain useful DNA information. DNA does more than just identity the source of the sample, it can place a specific person at a crime scene, refute a claim of not having had sex with someone, disprove a claimed alibi, and put a weapon in a suspect's hand. Consequently, it is important that investigators know how DNA evidence can be used to link a suspect, but it is equally important to know how DNA evidence can be used to exonerate those who are innocent of a crime.[5]

Protecting against Contamination

Because samples of DNA are easily contaminated, extreme care should be taken while collecting samples. The following precautions are offered to maintain the integrity of the sample for future analysis:

- Gloves should always be worn and changed often.
- Touching any area where it is believed DNA may exist should be avoided.
- The standard recommendation for collecting biological evidence is not to remove the stain from an object but rather to collect the object with the stain, provided that the stain can be adequately protected from contamination. If the entire object cannot be collected, then the next best way to gather such evidence is to remove the stain by cutting it out (e.g., from a piece of carpet or clothing).
- When it is not possible or practical to collect a stain by cutting the object, the two preferred methods of collection are (a) to use a dampened cotton swab (with distilled water) to collect the stain or (b) to use a clean instrument, such as a razor blade to scrape the stain into a clean pharmaceutical fold.[6]
- If the samples are damp or wet, they should be allowed to air dry before being packaged. If it is not possible for them to be air dried, they should be dried in a laboratory using a drying hood. However, it is important the table below the drying hood be clean from contamination.
- Plastic bags should not be used for collection and storage because they are air tight and this lack of air will likely result in the rapid decomposition or overall degradation of items that contain any body fluid, especially blood. Thus, such items should be stored in clean

paper evidence bags and sealed with evidence security tape (not stapled), which is designed to tear if someone attempts to open it.

- Disposable instruments should be used. However, if nondisposable instruments are going to be used, they should be thoroughly cleaned before and after each sample is handled. The method of cleaning may vary. In some cases it may be done with alcohol and, in other cases, it may be done with hydrogen peroxide. The protocol for cleaning instruments may vary with different crime labs. Thus, the approved method will be dictated by their protocol.
- Enough of the sample should be used to optimize the chance of getting a viable result, but consideration must be given to leaving a sufficient amount of the sample so that a second test can be conducted by the defense.
- Physical and face barrier protections should be used whenever possible, and sneezing or coughing over evidence also should be avoided.
- Crime scene personnel should avoid touching their face, nose, and mouth when handling evidence.
- Biological evidence should be placed in a freezer for long-term storage.[7]

Databases and Combined DNA Index System (CODIS)

As already indicated, all U.S. jurisdictions have legislation requiring the collection of DNA evidence of convicted offenders. However, in some jurisdictions, DNA can be collected only from offenders convicted of sex-related crimes and criminal homicides. In others, legislation has been expanded to allow for the collection of DNA specimens from all convicted offenders. This development has dramatically increased the workload of laboratories that are processing the material to establish the databases.

In addition to individual jurisdiction databases, there is a national investigation support database developed by the FBI, called the Combined DNA Index System (CODIS). CODIS is used in the national, state, and local index system networks to link DNA typing results from unresolved crimes with cases in multiple jurisdictions or persons convicted of offenses specified in the data banking laws passed by the jurisdictions. By alerting investigators to similarities among unsolved crimes, CODIS can aid in apprehending perpetrators who commit a series of crimes. As of April 2012, the database contained over 10.6 million offender profiles. This number includes convicted offenders, arrestees, detainees, and legal profiles.[8]

Today, DNA analysis is used for a variety of forensic purposes, from identifying the remains of victims of mass disasters (such as destruction of the twin towers at the World Trade Center on 9/11 and Hurricane Katrina) to tracing a person's ancestry. Each state collects a DNA sample and fingerprints from serious offenders, such as persons convicted of rape and criminal homicide, but a few states have extended this practice to all arrestees, not just those successfully prosecuted for violent crimes. California, Florida, Louisiana, Texas, and Virginia are the five states with such legislative provision, and there are others focusing more on child predators and offenders associated with crimes against children.[9]

Fingerprints

Several different parts of the body, such as palms, fingers, toes, and the soles of the feet, have friction ridges on the skin that can form distinct and identifiable prints. All such prints are collected, preserved, and identified using similar methods. However, it may not be immediately apparent which part of a body made the print; as used here, "fingerprint" includes all prints made by friction ridges. Basically, a **fingerprint** is a replica of the friction ridges that touched the surface on which the print was found. These ridges' characteristics also are called **minutiae**[10] (Figure 8.1).

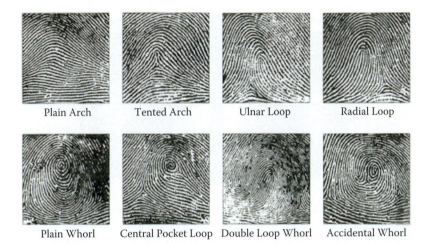

Plain Arch   Tented Arch   Ulnar Loop   Radial Loop

Plain Whorl   Central Pocket Loop   Double Loop Whorl   Accidental Whorl

Figure 8.1 Fingerprint patterns. Fingerprints are initially classified into one of the major classifications shown here. About 65% of the population has loops, roughly 30% have whorls, and the remaining 5% have arches.

With just a few exceptions—persons with birth defects or amputees—everyone has fingerprints. This universal characteristic is a prime factor in establishing a standard of identification. Because a print of one finger has never been known to duplicate exactly another fingerprint (even from the same person or an identical twin[11]), it is possible to identify an individual with just one impression. The relative ease with which a set of inked fingerprints can be taken as a means of identification is a further reason for using this standard. This unfaltering pattern is a permanent record of the individual throughout life.

Latent Fingerprints

Latent prints refer to the three categories of prints that can be found at the scene of the crime or on items of investigative interest, such as prints found on a computer in a brothel or those found in a transport vehicle. They also refer specifically to latent/invisible prints. Ordinarily, the context in which the term *latent fingerprints* is used helps in understanding which meaning is intended.

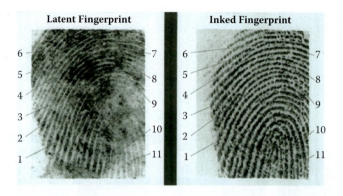

Figure 8.2 Courtroom fingerprint display. This side-by-side display was prepared for use at a criminal trial and was used to show the jury that there were 11 points of similarity between the latent fingerprint found at the crime scene (on the left) and the inked fingerprint taken from the suspect (on the right) obtained at the time he was booked into the county jail.

- **Latent/invisible prints** are unseen or hidden. When a crime scene is processed for latent fingerprints, they are made visible by "developing" them. The four most common methods of developing them are (a) use of traditional powders, (b) use of fluorescent powders, (c) application of chemicals, and (d) cyanoacrylate or superglue fuming. However, the most common method of developing latent/invisible prints is through the use of traditional powder.[12] Latent prints are associated with the small amounts of body perspiration and oil that are normally found on the friction ridges and are created when the friction ridges deposit these materials on a surface (Figure 8.2).
- **Plastic prints** are three-dimensional; they are molded, indented, or impressed into some pliable surface. They are created when fingers touch material, such as a painted surface that is still "tacky," oil films, explosives, edible fats, putty, dust, caulking, and similar surfaces.
- **Patent/contaminated/visible prints** result after fingers, contaminated with foreign matter, such as soot, oils, face powder, ink, and some types of safe insulation, touch a clean surface. The most common type of contaminated print results when a finger is pressed

into a thin layer of dust before touching a smooth surface. Fingerprints that result from blood contamination are sometimes less distinct than those that result from other types of contamination. Patent prints are readily visible to the eye.

Conditions Affecting the Quality of Latent Fingerprints

The quality of latent fingerprints is affected by a number of conditions, including:

- *The surface on which the print is deposited:* The type of surface on which latent prints are left affects their durability and the type of process used to develop them. There are three broad categories of surface:[13]
  - Nonporous surfaces, which are not absorbent. These surfaces often appear polished and repel moisture. Examples include mirrors, glass, smooth ceramics, plastic, and painted wood. Prints on these types of surfaces are more susceptible to damage because they are on the outermost surface. Undisturbed, they might last for years.
  - Porous surfaces, which are absorbent, such as documents and cardboard. Prints on documents, for example, may be durable and fairly stable over a period of years or they can quickly fade or deteriorate beyond the point of being useful if they are subject to high humidity or if they become wet.
  - Semiporous surfaces, which do not fit easily into the previous categories because they both resist and absorb fingerprints, which may or may not soak into the surface. Semiporous examples include glossy cardboard, magazine covers, and some types of cellophane. The durability of prints on these surfaces is variable. Textured surfaces, such as the "pebbled" effect of some computer monitors, are both nonporous and porous because the pebbled effect creates an inconsistent contact between the friction ridge skin and the surface, producing a

discontinuous appearance when developed and a lack of fine detail.

- *The nature of the material contaminating the finger-print:* Patent fingerprints resulting from contamination by soot, safe insulation, and face powder are quickly destroyed; those made with blood, ink, or oil can last longer periods of time under favorable conditions.[14]
- Any physical or occupational defects of the person making the print.
- *How the object on which the prints appear was handled:* The distance between friction ridges is very small, and if the finger moves even slightly, that ridge detail can be lost.
- *The amount of the contamination:* When the finger leaving the print is very contaminated, both the ridge surfaces and their "valleys" get filled up, resulting in a smeared appearance with little value as evidence.

Locating Latent Fingerprints

Proper latent print processing begins with wearing latex, nitrile, or other suitable gloves.[15] Latent prints are such valuable evidence that extraordinary efforts should be made to recover them. The investigator must adopt a positive attitude about this, regardless of apparent problems or past failures.

It is imperative that the investigator thoroughly search all surface areas in and around the crime scene that might retain prints. Shining a flashlight at an oblique angle to the surface being examined is often helpful in this search. The fact that an individual may have worn gloves in no way lessens the need for a complete search. On occasion, gloves themselves leave impressions as individualized as fingerprints. Moreover, although unusual, it may be possible to develop a latent finger-print on the inside of a glove recovered from a crime scene.[16] Particular attention should be paid to less obvious places, such as the undersides of toilet seats, toilet handles, table-tops, and dresser drawers; the surfaces of dinner plates and filing cabinets; the back of rear view mirrors; the trunk lids of automobiles; travel documents; and condom cases. Frequently handled objects, such as doorknobs and telephones, ordinarily do not yield good prints. But, because they are likely to have been touched, they should always be processed.

Documents as Evidence in Sex-Trafficking Cases

The illegal reproduction of identity and travel documents for foreign nationals is important evidence in sex-trafficking cases. Documents can be counterfeited (reproduced as original) or forged (altered originals by adding, removing, or substituting relevant information). Other documents for the transportation and recruitment may exist as well. The documents may contain direct evidence, e.g., some records about a victim being bought or sold. They also are likely to have other physical evidence on them, such as fingerprints and traces of DNA.

The detection of false documents is crucial and, in some circumstances, may show evidence of the device used in its creation, such as marks from printing machines and typewriters.

Handwriting analysis, either of a large amount of text or a signature, will assist in identifying the author of a document/note.[17] For example, in one case, a single scrap of paper was recovered on the bedroom dresser of a sex-trafficking suspect. The only writing on the paper was a local address. The investigator went to the address on the paper and learned that it was occupied by the mother of the rescued sex-trafficking victim. This information corroborated the victim's testimony that the trafficker knew where her mother lived and had threatened to harm her mother if she cooperated with the police.

Examination of Documents

Sex trafficking is a commercial process and, as in any type of business, records must be kept. These records are frequently very valuable for investigators. Forensic investigations present a number of opportunities to determine the authenticity of a document or the author of a handwritten document or note. It is important to remember that documentary evidence should always be handled with gloves, and anything that appears to be a record should be seized no matter how informal that record may look.[18] Examples of significant documents that may be found in sex-trafficking investigations include:

- Accounts of money taken in brothels or other illegitimate businesses
- Bank statements and details of informal transactions, such as use of the hawala-type system, which is an informal channel for transferring funds from one location to another through nontraditional service providers[19]
- Utility bills, such as gas, electricity, or phone bills
- Records of rent paid, details from landlords about rental payment arrangements
- Tickets, boarding cards, and other travel documents
- Records of bills paid for advertising
- Credit card details of customers
- Documents providing "menus" of "sexual services" and costs that are available
- Photographs of employees
- Records of cash receipts, or how many "clients" have visited a particular woman

Fibers and Micro Traces

Fibers from clothes and other material can be transferred on contact. For example, a person lying on a bed when clothed will transfer fibers from his/her clothing to bedding and vice versa. Transfer of fibers between clothing and seats in cars and other vehicles also has proved useful in some sex-trafficking investigations. Other micro traces, such as paint, glass, soil, seeds, fragments of metal can be transferred and recovered as well. Also, fibers and micro traces may remain where they were deposited for a considerable period of time. Washing, exposure to the environment, and further contact with other materials are examples of how this type of evidence may be lost.[20]

Recovery and Preservation of Information Technology (IT) and Electronic Communications Equipment

Information technology and electronic communications equipment often contains valuable evidence, such as stored emails, details of financial transactions, and records of contacts. Equipment also is likely to have other physical traces on it, such as fingerprints or biological material, which can then link individuals to those pieces of equipment.

Properly Handling Information Technology (IT)

The ideal would be to have a forensic IT expert respond to the crime scene or speak to one before the scene is visited. If neither option is possible, the below listed steps should be taken to preserve and protect any electronic equipment that may be found at the scene. However, a note of caution is in order. A search of electronic devices without permission from the owner or without a search warrant could result in any evidence obtained from the device being deemed inadmissible in court. Thus, consent to search or a search warrant should be obtained before attempting to access data on any IT equipment.

Steps to Follow to Preserve and Protect Electronic Equipment

- Video or photograph the equipment exactly as found.
- No one should be allowed to touch any IT or communications equipment, including the investigator.
- The equipment should not be turned off because shutting down some types of equipment may damage the information on it. This should be done by experts, but where one is not available, the equipment should be kept turned on as long as realistically possible. However, if it has to be moved, it is best to unplug it rather than to turn it off.
- Before disconnecting the equipment, consideration should be given to marking the wires connecting the equipment with labels or pens.

- Photographs or labels on connections allow the equipment to be reconnected later by experts for forensic examination.
- Fingerprints and other contact evidence is likely to be found on equipment that could help link suspects to the equipment; when seizing equipment, it should be done in a way that will not disturb the contact evidence. It also should be stored in an appropriate way.
- Wherever possible, do not just seize the hard drive, but also all of the equipment. This includes printers, blank paper, and other items that can be forensically compared later with other material recovered in the investigation.
- A log should be kept of everyone who enters the crime scene including uniformed officers as well as investigators, crime scene personnel, etc. This may become an issue when it comes time to examine custody and contamination issues at trial.[21]
- Retrieve all records of calls made, numbers held, photographs and videos, etc., on phones, both mobile and fixed line.
- Similar records from fax machines, pagers, and phones that record messages (where these have a tape, the tape should be seized) should be retrieved.
- Retrieve emails, bank details, advertising material, accounts held on computers, including desktop, laptops, and small personal devices.
- Diaries and similar items, such as personal organizers, filofax, Personal Digital Assistants (PDAs), Blackberries, and notebooks should be seized.

Organization of the Work at the Scene of Crime

There should be a coordinated approach in processing a crime scene. The roles and responsibilities of those managing and attending a scene should be defined and documented, but an initial crime scene evaluation is required before it can be determined what approach is to be followed. Someone with the necessary specialized expertise should be appointed to have overall control of the scene and someone should be appointed with the specific responsibility to manage the recording and storage of exhibits. Also, it is advisable to be certain there is communication between those managing the investigation and those making the scene examination.[22]

Protection of the Crime Scene

Scene protection starts when an incident is first discovered (arrival of the first responder) and ends only when the entire examination process is completed. An initial decision should be made on how large an area needs to be protected. The scene should be protected from unnecessary activities that may irrevocably compromise the evidence, and access to the scene by the public and law enforcement, staff, and others should be controlled. The basic rule to be followed is that if a person does not need to be there, they should not be there. This can be controlled, in part, by placing physical barriers to prevent access. This will include the use of crime scene tape or fencing, assuming they are available. Protective clothing should be worn by those at the crime scene to prevent contamination, and staff who have been to one scene or dealt with a suspect or victim should not go to another scene. This precaution will prevent cross contamination of scenes. Lastly, those entering and departing the crime scene should leave by a marked pathway to avoid unnecessary cross contamination.[23]

Recording Scenes

The importance of thoroughly photographing and videotaping a crime scene cannot be over emphasized. Photographing the crime scene will help tell the story to the jury. For example, photographs of hallways, doors, and highlighting the only door that is padlocked from the outside and is the bedroom belonging to the victim is extremely important. Showing what the victim has and does not have can explain a system of control or

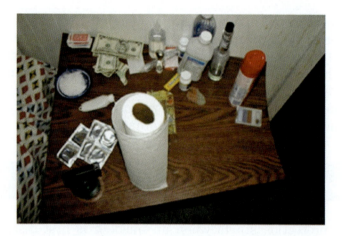

Figure 8.3 Items recovered near a sex-trafficking victim's bed. This table near a sex-trafficking victim's bed contained empty condom wrappers, hand towels, alcohol, rubbing oil, along with cash and other miscellaneous items. The cash she received was from tips given to her by customers. The actual fee for her services had been collected by the trafficker prior to the "john" being allowed to have sex with her. In some instances, victims may be allowed to keep the tips, while in other cases, the tips may be taken by the trafficker (pimp). (Photo courtesy of Lt. George Koder (Ret.), Clearwater, Florida, Police Department.)

has the potential to illustrate a business operation. Detailing that the victim had little furniture or, for example, that her bedside table contained condoms, lubricants, alcohol, rubbing oil, and cash, would certainly suggest, at the very least, a prostitution operation was in progress (Figure 8.3). Photographing that the victim had clothing limited to lingerie or stripper attire that is all contained in one small travel suitcase highlights what is really going on in that person's life.

Another example of the importance of photographs involved one that depicted a brown leather belt hanging from a doorknob in the hallway. This was photographed, but the belt was not collected at the time the crime scene was processed. After repeated interviews with one victim, it was uncovered that she had been beaten by the trafficker with a brown leather belt and buckle. The photograph of the single belt in the hallway outside the victim's bedroom along with photographs of her injuries were invaluable in the prosecutorial process (Figure 8.4).

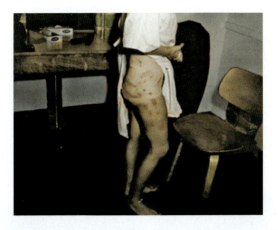

Figure 8.4 Injuries sustained with a leather belt and buckle. Photographs of the injuries sustained by this victim were very important evidence in the prosecutorial process.

Photographs also will support the fact that the primary elements of sex trafficking are present. These would include: (a) lack of consent of the victim, (b) the overriding control of the victim by the trafficker, and (c) showing that there is some type of commercial sex or business operation. Some examples from inside brothels have included a pornography viewing room for men going into the bedroom and stripper poles in the living room for girls to perform exotic dancing. Traffickers often keep calendars and ledgers to keep track of the movement of the victims and how many men have entered the business (Figure 8.5).

The crime-scene technician should record all activity at the scene. This includes evidence seized, photographs, videos, sketches, or measurements made as well as a record of who entered the scene and when they left. Documentation starts with arrival of the first responder at the scene and careful records should be kept of those individuals who enter the scene or what they may have touched or moved. The use of photos or video will show exactly where the exhibits came from. The exhibit should be packaged and labeled. This record of the "chain of custody" of exhibits should continue when the exhibits are passed on for storage or analysis and should continue until the court case is concluded, and (in some cases) after a court case is concluded, in the event there is an appeal.[24]

Figure 8.5 A calendar seized by investigators during a sex-trafficking rescue operation. It had the dates that the victims were going to be transported to another brothel as well as the phone number and name of the driver who would be transporting them to the new location. (Photo courtesy Lt. George Koder (Ret.), Clearwater, Florida, Police Department.)

Collection of Evidence

Appropriate containers should be used in the collection of evidence. The decision on what type of container to use is largely determined by the type of physical evidence retrieved. However, each sample should be sealed with tamper-proof evidence tape, signed by the person sealing it, the date and locations where found, a short description of the evidence, a case number, and evidence log item number.

Managing Exhibits to Ensure Chain of Custody

The main difference between sex-trafficking cases and other cases is that there are potentially a very large number of items that require seizing as exhibits or for forensic examination. This makes a structured approach particularly important.

The "chain of custody" in sex-trafficking cases may be long and complex because sometimes there is a need to transfer exhibits between jurisdictions. Any such transfer should always be done in a way that complies with federal rules of evidence, if the case is going to be tried in federal court, or if being tried in state court, comply with a state's rules of evidence.

Multiple Crime Scenes

In most traditional crimes, there is likely to be a single crime scene, such as a home, where a rape occurred, or perhaps a bank where a robbery took place. However, in sex-trafficking investigations, there is a greater likelihood there will be a number of scenes of interest to investigators and these may require simultaneous management.

In sex-trafficking cases, linked scenes may be found at the source or transit and destination location. Forensic evidence of victims and traffickers is likely to be present in premises in all of these locations. Similarly, there may be evidence linking a person to a transport used in all locations. Advertising, communications equipment, and finance documents are all potentially connected opportunities for forensic examination.

The investigator should always consider what scenes might be linked and where these scenes might be located. The opportunity to examine linked scenes should be explored or a request made that an examination take place. This may not be practical in every case, but there may be local links that should not be overlooked. Even where a scene is in another jurisdiction, an examination may have taken place already and it may be possible to share the results.

Linking scenes may allow the investigator to identify additional victims or suspects, generate intelligence, and present a more robust and comprehensive case at court.

People Present at Locations Linked to a Sex-Trafficking Operation

By definition, there are likely to be people present at locations linked to sex-trafficking operations and this can present a number of difficulties. The people may be "scenes" themselves (as victims or suspects) as will the location. Identifying who is a suspect or potential victim is likely to be difficult, and there may be cross-contamination issues.

Where people have been living or working in close proximity, traces transferred between people may be the result of innocent contact or could be evidence of exploitation.

General Considerations in the Examination of Sex-Trafficking Victims

Upon the first encounter, it may not be clear who is a suspect and who is a victim. Indeed, in many sex-trafficking cases, this may not become apparent for some time. There may be cases where forensic contact evidence alone will prove a victim of sexual exploitation has been assaulted. In many more cases, the forensic evidence will corroborate the account given by the victim or other evidence. The value of examinations of victims may be limited because victims and exploiters (or recruiters and transporters) often have very close, long-term contact with each other. There are particular issues concerning intimate examinations in sex-trafficking cases. For example:

- Showing that a particular individual had sex with or sexually assaulted a victim
- Showing that a particular individual physically assaulted a victim
- Corroborating a victim's account of what happened to her/him
- Establishing how long a person has been victimized
- Establishing the age of the injuries to a victim
- Identifying the victim
- Establishing the age of the victim
- Connecting a victim to a particular location or vehicle
- Identifying any drugs or alcohol administered to or taken by the victim

- Linking a particular piece of equipment or machinery to a victim
- Establishing the scale of the exploitative enterprise
- If physical injuries are present, they should be photographed

Physically Examining Victims: Specific Considerations in Sex-Trafficking Cases

An early decision should be taken by the investigator in consultation with forensic examiners about whether or not a full physical examination should take place (with the victim's consent). Serious consideration should be given by those medical personnel physically examining the victim to using a sexual assault victim examination kit in order to systematically collect physical evidence.

Contents of the Sexual Assault Victim Examination Kit

1. Collection vial (for urine)
2. Collection vial (for blood)
3. Pubic hair combings specimen envelope: Used in the collection of possible foreign material in the pubic hair of the victim.
4. Head hair combings specimen envelope: Used in the same way as pubic hair combings, but for hair on the head of the victim.
5. Vaginal smear slides: Used in the collection of semen fluid for DNA evidence deposited by the assailant in the vagina of the victim. One slide is used for the vaginal area and the other is used for the specimen taken from the cervix of the victim.
6. Smear slides: Used to collect DNA (seminal fluid) from other areas where the perpetrator's DNA may be found on the victim, such as those resulting from the anal or oral penetration of the victim.
7. Swabs: Used in the collection of seminal fluid for DNA evidence that the perpetrator may have left on the victim (anal, oral, or other areas).

8. Vaginal swabs (4): Used to collect seminal fluid for DNA evidence of the perpetrator.
9. Cervical swabs (2): Used to collect seminal fluid from the cervix for DNA evidence of the perpetrator.
10. Saliva standard swabs: Used to collect DNA evidence of the suspect from the victim's mouth.
11. Buccal swab: Used to collect the victim's DNA orally.
12. Extra swabs: To collect possible semen from the suspect wherever it may be found on the victim.
13. Extra swabs: Used to collect saliva left by the suspect from areas that may have been bitten, licked, or kissed.
14. Underwear specimen bag.
15. Genoprobe: Used to screen for *Chlamydia* and gonorrhea. This is taken at the time of evidence collection.

The same kit is used to collect evidence with male victims, but the differences are in the genoprobe that is used in the physical areas of the body from where the evidence is collected. Instead of vaginal swabs, penile as well as anal cultures are collected[25] (Figure 8.6).

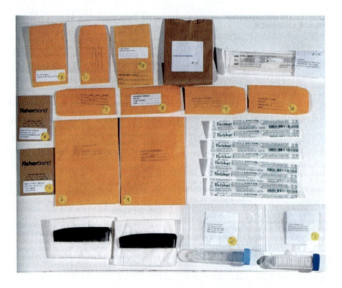

Figure 8.6 Typical contents contained in a sexual assault victim examination kit.

The Need for Knowledgeable Medical Specialists

It is absolutely imperative that the medical specialists taking the samples know what they are required to do and how to do it. An example is the recovery of semen from the higher parts of the uterus, which may allow recovery after an extended time period, but is a difficult process and very invasive. Where it is not possible to conduct a full examination, consideration should be given to undertaking a less intrusive examination. Although this may not prove contact with a specific individual, it may give corroboration of the victim's account, for example; showing visible injuries consistent with what she is saying.

If a full examination is made (with the victim's consent), there is a secondary objective, namely that of corroboration of the victim's account. The presence of semen from many men would be valuable in a sex-trafficking investigation, even if a specific man could not be identified. Within this context, it is important to note that the terms *semen* and *sperm* are not synonymous. **Semen** is a grayish-white fluid, produced by the male reproductive organs, that is ejaculated during orgasm. In liquid form, it has a chlorine-like odor; when dried it has a starch-like consistency. **Sperm** are the tadpole-like organisms that are contained in, and travel through, semen to fertilize the female egg. This distinction is important because the laboratory examinations and tests employed to search for each are quite different. Thus, if the laboratory examines a sample that appears to be semen and finds no sperm, it is very likely that the individual donor was either born sterile or had a vasectomy.[26] However, when sperm cannot be found, a second test may be employed to identify the presence of acid phosphatase, which is an enzyme component in a liquid portion of semen.

Searching for DNA Evidence under Court Order: The Search Warrant

If a search warrant is obtained, and evidence for DNA analysis is sought, the warrant/order should request the seizure of any item on which DNA might be found. A couple of typical items that should appear in the sex-trafficking case on a search warrant are bloodstains and bed sheets where semen stains might exist. Any additional items found that may contain DNA will require the warrant to be amended before seizure.[27] Investigators should work with their prosecutors' office as well as magistrates to be certain they comply with the necessary legal procedures to amend a search warrant when the need to do so arises.[28]

Specific Considerations in the Examination of Sex-Trafficking Suspects

It is likely that the customer of a sex-trafficked women will have biological samples of the victim on his genital area, such as pubic hair, vaginal secretions, possibly blood (as well as on the rest of his body). It also is quite possible that the sex act may have taken place some time ago. Although traces from a customer may have been deposited on the victim's body, they may have also been discharged, degraded quickly, or washed. However, traces of the victim may remain on the custom-ers' body for some time, particularly where he has poor personal hygiene.[29]

Examination of Vehicles for Physical Evidence

Transport vehicles, as well as those in which sexual liaisons may occur, may contain physical evidence that links the sex-trafficking victim to a suspect's vehicle and vice versa. For example, upholstery in cars and other vehicles may contain semen, blood, hairs, and fibers from clothing from both victims and suspects. Also, the victim's fingerprints may be found in the vehicle. Property in vehicles also may offer good opportunities for examination. These can include receipts for gasoline, parking tickets, and so forth. Litter in cars, such as cigarette stubs, condom wrappers, and miscellaneous paper, may offer opportunities for examination. The vehicle may leave tire tracks that are useful in identifying it as having been at a specific location. Plus, the vehicles carry registration and license plates that allow tracing. Even when no vehicle identification number (VIN) is available, it is possible to trace a vehicle. For example, the public VIN on the dash is not the only number that identifies a specific vehicle's body frame or component parts. The location of some of these secondary numbers is not a big secret, but others, referred to as **confidential VINs**, are stamped into frames or bodies in the places supposedly known only to the manufacturer and to law enforcement agencies and officers who are specialists in vehicle identification and auto theft investigation.[30] Vehicles can be removed by law enforcement and kept in a secure location until they are able to be examined in detail. Some vehicles may contain equipment that allows the investigator to track its movements. This can include tacographs (journey recorders) in buses, mobile phones, or satellite navigation systems. However, if the vehicle itself does not have equipment that allows tracking, the people in it may have used or be using mobile phones that can allow tracking.[31]

Examining Vehicles and Crime Scenes for the Transference of Physical Evidence

The following case is a good example of the transference of physical evidence even when the initial assault takes place in a vehicle, but the body is found at another location.

Case

A 16-year-old girl, who was still a virgin, was being transported in a passenger vehicle from one location to another when the driver decided he wanted to be the first man to have sex with her. He drove to a wooded area and when they got there, and while still in the vehicle, he attempted to force her to have sex with him. She resisted and he became very aggressive and started tearing off her clothing. In the process of tearing off her clothing, shredded fibers from her blouse, pants, and panties were being deposited in his vehicle. In addition, once the victim's blouse was pulled up her bra hooks, located at the rear of her bra, became exposed and because she was struggling the hook started rubbing up against the cloth seat covers in the vehicle. The victim was then forcibly dragged from the car, but continued to resist violently. The assailant became angry and frustrated with her resistance and struck her across the head with a metal object he had brought with him. She was rendered unconscious and according to the medical examiner's report, died within one to two hours.

The follow-up investigation led to the suspect and, upon examination of his vehicle, the fibers from the victim's blouse, panties, and pants were found along with her fingerprints. The crime laboratory was able to positively match the fibers in the victim's bra hooks to the fibers from the suspect's cloth seat covers. Because no sexual intercourse had occurred, there was no DNA evidence found. Tire prints found at the crime scene were also positively matched to the suspect's vehicle. The murder weapon was never found. The assailant was subsequently convicted and sentenced to 25 years in prison (Figure 8.7).

Figure 8.7 Exchange of physical evidence. Fibers from this victim's blouse, pants, and panties were found in the suspect's car as he started ripping off her clothes. Her fingerprints were also found in his car. The fibers in her bra hooks were positively identified as coming from the cloth seat covers in the suspect's vehicle. Also, tire tracks left at the crime scene were positively matched to the suspect's vehicle.

Glossary

Biological material: This includes items such as blood, semen, skin, cells, tissues, organs, muscles, bone, teeth, hair, saliva, fingernails, and urine.

Combined DNA Index System (CODIS): The system used in national, state, and local index-system networks to link DNA typing results from unresolved crimes with cases in multiple jurisdictions or persons convicted of offenses specified in the database laws passed by the jurisdictions.

Deoxyribonucleic acid (DNA): The molecules in the body that carry the body's genetic information that establishes each person as separate and distinct.

Forensic science: The part of science applied to answering legal questions.

Latent/invisible prints: These are prints that are unseen or hidden, but which are made visible by the application of fingerprint powder or other chemical processes.

Latent prints: Refers to all categories of prints that have been found at the crime scene or on items of investigative interest.

Mitochondrial DNA (mtDNA): Found in mitochondria, which are organelles. When a sperm and egg join in conception, the new individual gets half of his or her nuclear genetic information from each parent. Conversely, mitochondrial DNA is inherited only from the mother. As it is passed directly from maternal relatives, it serves as a perfect identity marker for those relatives.

Organelle: A specialized part of a cell, analogous to an organ, "the first organelle to be identified was the nucleus."

Patent/contaminated/visible prints: These result after fingers are contaminated with foreign matter, such as soot, oils, face powder, ink, and some types of safe insulation, and then touch a clean surface and leave an image readily visible to the eye.

Plastic prints: These are three-dimensional fingerprints that are molded, indented, or impressed into some pliable surface.

Semen: The grayish-white fluid produced in a male reproductive organ that is ejaculated during orgasm.

Sperm: The tadpole-like organisms that are contained in and travel through the semen to fertilize the female egg.

Review Questions

1. What is forensic science?
2. What are examples of biological material?
3. What is deoxyribonucleic acid (DNA)?
4. What is mitochondrial DNA?
5. What is the function of the Combined DNA Index System (CODIS)?
6. What is a fingerprint?
7. What are latent/invisible fingerprints?
8. What are the most common methods of developing latent/invisible fingerprints?
9. Of what value can document evidence be as it relates to obtaining physical evidence in a sex-trafficking case?
10. What are examples of the types of fibers and micro-trace evidence that can be found in sex-trafficking cases?
11. What steps should be taken to recover and preserve information technology (IT) and electronic communication equipment?
12. What steps should be taken to protect the crime scene in sex-trafficking cases?
13. What steps should be taken in searching for DNA evidence under court order?
14. What specific considerations should be given when physically examining suspects in sex-trafficking cases?

Endnotes

1. *Anti-Human Trafficking Manual for Criminal Justice Practitioners*, Module 7, "Crime Scene and Physical Evidence Examinations in Trafficking in Persons Investigations," (New York: United Nations Office on Drugs and Crime, 2009), 2.

2. Matthew Durose, "Census of Publicly Funded Forensic Crime Laboratories, 2005," *Bureau of Justice Statistics Bulletin* (July 2008). Online at: http://bjs.ojp.usdoj.gov/index.cfm?ty=pbdetail&iid=490 (accessed January 23, 2013).

3. D. Frumkin, et al., "Authentication of Forensic DNA Samples," *Forensic Science International: Genetics* 4 (2) (February 2010), 95–103.

4. "Mitochondrial DNA is passed directly through maternal relatives." Online at: http://www.fbi.gov/kids/dna/dna.htm (accessed July 17, 1998).

5. National Commission on the Future of DNA Evidence, National Institute of Justice, "What Every Law Enforcement Officer Should Know about DNA Evidence," pamphlet (Washington, D.C.: U.S. Department of Justice, no publication date).

6. Theresa F. Spear, "Sample Handling Considerations for Biological Evidence and DNA Extracts" (California Department of Justice, California Criminalistics Institute, June 16, 2003).

7. T. Spear, "Sample Handling Considerations for Biological Evidence and DNA Extracts," and T. Spear & N. Khoshkebarr, "Analysis of Old Biological Samples: A Study on the Feasibility of Obtaining Body Fluid Identification and DNA Typing Results" (California Department of Justice, California Criminalistics Institute, June 16, 2003).

8. Offender Profiles Include Convicted Offender, Arrestee, Detainee, and Legal Profiles at NDIS. Online at: http://www.fbi.gov/about-us/lab/codis/ndis-statistics#DC (accessed April 28, 2012).

9. Ronald Bailey, "Criminal Kinship: Slouching Toward a DNA Database Nation," *Reason Magazine*, May 19, 2006. Online at: http://www.reason.com/news/shows/116487.html (accessed January 23, 2013).

10. Charles R. Swanson, et al., *Criminal Investigation*, 11th ed. (New York: McGraw-Hill, 2012), 93–96.

11. Robert C. Chisnall, "Knot Tying Habits, Tier Handedness, and Experience," *Journal of Forensic Sciences*, 5 (5), 2010, 1232–1244.

12. Swanson, et al., *Criminal Investigation*, 96–100.

13. Brian Yamashita & Mike French, "Latent Print Development," in *Scientific Working Group on Friction Ridge Analysis, Study, and Technology (SWGFAST), The Fingerprint Sourcebook* (Washington, D.C.: National Institute of Justice, September 2010), 7–8, 7–1. The sourcebook has several chapters that are not yet completed.

14. Ibid., 7–4.
15. Barry A. Fisher, *Techniques of Crime Scene Investigation*, 6th ed. (Boca Raton, FL: CRC Press, 2000), 117.
16. Yamashita & French, "Latent Print Development," 7–5.
17. Anti-Human Trafficking Manual for Criminal Justice Practitioners, Module 7, "Crime Scene and Physical Evidence Examinations in Trafficking in Persons Investigations," 7.
18. Ibid., 25–26.
19. The hawala system refers to an informal channel for transferring funds from one location to another through service providers—known as hawaladars—regardless of the nature of the transaction and the countries involved. While hawala transactions are mostly initiated by emigrant workers living in a developed country, the hawala system also can be used to send funds from a developing country to a party in another country, even though the purpose of the funds transfer is usually different.
20. Ibid., 7
21. Ibid., 31–32.
22. Ibid., 9
23. Ibid., 10–11.
24. Ibid., 10.
25. This kit was created by the Florida Department of Law Enforcement and is provided to personnel who are responsible for gathering physical evidence from sexual assault victims.
26. Ibid., 15.
27. Thomas B. Carney, *Practical Investigation of Sex Crimes* (Boca Raton, FL: CRC Press, 2004), 58.
28. Ibid.
29. Anti-Human Trafficking Manual for Criminal Justice Practitioners, Module 7, "Crime Scene and Physical Evidence Examinations in Trafficking in Persons Investigations," 19.
30. For a more detailed discussion on this subject, see the *Passenger Vehicle Identification Manual,* which is published by the National Insurance Crime Bureau. This booklet contains useful information including an explanation of vehicle identification numbers, the Federal Motor Vehicle Theft Prevention Standards, and VIN plate attachment and location.
31. Anti-Human Trafficking Manual for Criminal Justice Practitioners, Module 7, "Crime Scene and Physical Evidence Examinations in Trafficking in Persons Investigations," 23.

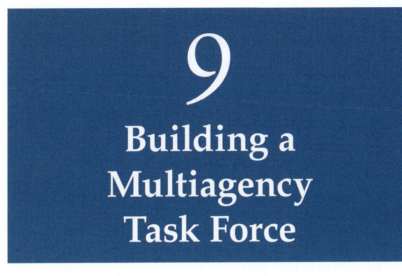

9

Building a Multiagency Task Force

Before this underage girl was rescued by a multiagency task force, she was forced to engage in prostitution with as many as 25 men a day. (Photo courtesy of the FBI.)

Chapter Objectives

1. Understand the importance of building a multiagency task force.
2. Discuss how to gain support for the concept of a multiagency task force with surrounding law enforcement agencies.
3. Explain the role of federal, state, and regulatory agencies; victim services provider; NGOs; and social service agencies working together in multiagency task forces.
4. Understand the importance of the public/media relationship.
5. Describe the most effective ways to create a multiagency membership task force.
6. Understand how to most effectively correct any professional misunderstandings between multiagency task force members.

Introduction

A multiagency sex-trafficking task force is necessary because it is impossible for any single agency or organization to respond comprehensively to the problem of sex trafficking. Traffickers range from opportunistic individuals to sophisticated criminal organizations with multijurisdictional activity. The response to sex trafficking, therefore, is most effective through multidisciplinary and collaborative problem-solving efforts and also increases the likelihood of the crime being discovered, the victims being rescued, and prosecutorial efforts being successful. In this chapter, we will be discussing the most effective ways to maintain a strategic, well-planned, and continuously fostered collaborative relationship among federal, state, and local law enforcement agencies as well as other key stakeholders.[1] We also will be discussing how best to assess the feasibility of formulating a sex-trafficking task force in a given area, the data necessary to assess a sex-trafficking problem and creation of a task force in a given area, how to go about gaining support for a task force, and what elements are needed to make it strategically and tactically efficient and, in the final analysis, successful.

Assessing the Problem

All jurisdictions, regardless of size, are susceptible to any given form of sex trafficking. However, the focus of a task force may differ depending on the characteristics of the area.

In evaluating the utility of forming a task force, the following parameters should be considered:

- The magnitude of the area's susceptibility (socioeconomic, cultural, and demographic factors)
- The proximity to other task force groups
- The historical crime indicators determined from a preliminary assessment

To gain support for the formation of a task force, it is important that the rationale be based on an analysis of available information and an assessment of the experiences of field and frontline personnel in law enforcement and social service organizations.

It is rare that analyses and assessments will reveal a crisis-level problem. The goal of the assessment, instead, is to discover if activity among vulnerable populations or behaviors and practices within suspect locales, establishments, criminal groups, or individuals is indicative of sex trafficking.

Existing task forces have reported that information from advocacy groups and homeless youth services are some of the most informative sources for determining whether sex trafficking may be occurring in a particular area.

Informative Data and Indicators of Sex Trafficking

Informative data and indicators of sex trafficking may come from assessment and analysis of the following sources:

- Booking data from local jails and other correctional institutions
- Census data on population growth in immigrant communities
- Data on teenage runaways and homeless youth
- Geographic indicators (e.g., highways, borders)
- Historical cases
- Historical media reports
- Information provided by former victims of sex trafficking
- Local law enforcement intelligence on criminal group dynamics
- Local law enforcement intelligence on "vice" activities
- Nongovernmental organization (NGO) data on community groups
- Nongovernmental organization (NGO) data on providing services to victims of crime
- Strategic interviews of community members in suspected activity areas

When analyzing the information, it should be done with a broad view of the full scope of sex trafficking in all of its forms. It is important to acknowledge that most forms of sex trafficking occur under conditions that go unnoticed and are significantly underreported to authorities.

Sometimes the most valuable information is received from individuals who have been arrested in multiagency raids. The following sex-trafficking case is an example of this; it also sets forth the investigative steps that were used in building a case for prosecution.

Case

In June 2004, Detective Deborah Scates, who was assigned to the Vice Squad of the Hartford, Connecticut, Police Vice and Narcotics Division, conducted an undercover prostitution sting detail addressing street-level prostitution activity occurring in the City of Hartford. During this operation, numerous females were arrested and charged with prostitution. Detective Scates debriefed all of the accused and obtained information that local suspects ("pimps") were running large-scale prostitution operations throughout the greater Hartford area under the guise of "escort services."

Further investigation, including conducting more detailed interviews with known prostitutes and others, confirmed that the information received was accurate. At this time, Judge Simon of the Hartford Community Court (a municipal court solely responsible for quality of life-type crimes) contacted Detective Scates and informed her that one of the women she had arrested was requesting to speak with her regarding information on these "escort services."

In August 2004, Detective Scates conducted a detailed interview with Victim #1, an 18-year-old female, who gave a detailed account of her experiences during the past year of being held against her will and forced into prostitution through different escort services. Victim #1 was forcibly given heroin and was beaten and sexually assaulted on a regular basis by one of the accused pimps, Brian Forbes, and his associates. Victim #1 identified the person responsible for doing this to her along with others that also were involved in running the same type of escort businesses. It was also learned that some of the people involved with this case were running a bail bonding company that was licensed through the State of Connecticut. The Liberty Bail Bond Company was used as a means to find girls that had been arrested and needed help bonding out. The girls would be bonded out and then informed that they would be required to work off their bonds by working at the escort services as a prostitute. Victim #1 also was able to provide Detective Scates with information regarding other victims.

In September 2004, Detective Scates spoke with Victim #2, also an 18-year-old female. The sworn statement that Victim #2 provided contained the same names and places that had been previously identified by Victim #1. Victim #2 had been lured to Hartford from New Hampshire and, once she was away from her friends and family, she was held against her will and forced into prostitution. Victim #2 stated that one time, when she refused to comply with one of the accused's orders, she was badly beaten, tied up, and rolled up in a rug. She was told that she was going to be given an overdose of heroin and that the accused pimp, Dennis Paris, and his associates were going to throw her body into the Connecticut River. At this point, one of the accused's associates stopped this assault from proceeding any farther stating that they still could make money off of her.

Both Victims #1 and #2 stated to Detective Scates that they had been sold from one pimp and his "manager" (Brian Forbes and Shayana Hicks) to another pimp (Paris) for one thousand two hundred dollars ($1,200) when Forbes grew tired of the victims.

After verifying the victims' statements and initiating an investigation into these allegations, it was recognized that this case investigation would encompass multiple jurisdictions throughout the State of Connecticut and also might include surrounding states. After review of the case by the U.S. Attorney's Office (USAO) District of Connecticut, a decision was made that this case should be prosecuted on the federal level.

This is when a multijurisdictional task force consisting of federal and municipal law enforcement agencies, working under the direction of the USAO, was put in place in September 2004 and an in-depth investigation into the allegations uncovered by Hartford Police Detective Deborah Scates regarding Human Trafficking and Prostitution began.

This task force consisted of Special Agents from the FBI, IRS Criminal Investigation Division, U.S. Postal Inspector's Service, and Det. Scates of Hartford, CT PD. James Genco of the U.S. Attorney's Office, District of Connecticut, Hartford Office, was assigned as the federal prosecutor to oversee the investigation.

Early in the task force investigation, information was obtained that one of the accused (Fanning) had recently been arrested by the Crime Suppression Unit of the Windsor, Connecticut, Police Department and charged with Promoting Prostitution. Investigators met with Windsor police personnel and learned that they had conducted several undercover prostitution sting details that resulted in the arrests of local prostitutes along with their pimps. It was learned that many of the prostitutes who had been arrested by Windsor police had worked or were currently working for several of the task force targets. Officers assigned to the Windsor Police Crime Suppression Unit had conducted interviews and obtained statements from the prostitutes who had been arrested at that time. The statements contained information identifying more accused. As a result of this meeting, Windsor Police Crime Suppression Unit personnel joined the task force investigation.

Investigative Steps/Case Building

From September 2004 to February 2006, the task force conducted an in-depth investigation that included:

- Stationary and mobile surveillance (both in-state and out of state)
- Identifying and locating additional targets/suspects
- Identifying and interviewing victims/witnesses (escorts/prostitutes and associates)
- Identifying and interviewing persons patronizing prostitutes ("johns")
- Arranging for support services to victims including use of federal witness protection programs
- Extensive use of federal subpoenas for bank, credit card, and other financial records
- Extensive use of federal subpoenas for telephone subscriber and toll information
- Obtaining and executing five (5) federal and state search warrants
- Conducting three (3) large-scale undercover prostitution sting operations involving multiagency participation resulting in numerous arrests

- Coordinating a federal warrant sweep conducted by over 50 police personnel from 4 federal law enforcement agencies and 8 municipal police departments
- Interviewing defendants postindictment/arrest with defense attorneys present

This investigation resulted in 11 individuals being identified as owning/operating or working as employees in the illegal running of prostitution rings under the guise of licensed escort services. The accused used these escort services to traffic humans, promote prostitution, launder money, and use interstate facilities to conduct their day-to-day criminal business. The accused would openly advertise their businesses in local newspapers, such as the *Hartford Advocate*, *Xtreme Magazine*, and *Providence Phoenix News*, and also listed their businesses in local telephone books. The accused would operate their businesses out of motels/hotels and also provide services for stag parties. The accused would provide women for "out-calls" to the homes of their customers. Investigators also learned that the accused were taking over motels by renting an entire block of rooms and having the girls stay in the rooms where they could conduct "in-calls" at these locations. The accused would beat, threaten, sexually assault, and intimidate the females in their employ as well as withhold the girls' money in order to keep the girls under their control and to obtain a larger profit from the business. They also would use these tactics on the girls in order to keep them from going to law enforcement.

By June 2007, 9 of the 10 defendants had pled guilty to the offenses with which they were charged. Two of the trafficking suspects, Shayana Hicks and Brian Forbes, each pled guilty to two counts of sex trafficking by force, fraud, and two counts (Hicks) and three counts (Forbes) of sex trafficking of minors, among other charges. The 10th defendant in this case and the third of those charged with human trafficking, Dennis Paris, went to trial and after a two-week trial, he was convicted by a federal jury of all 21 counts including convictions for four counts of sex trafficking (two counts each of sex trafficking by force, fraud, or coercion, and sex trafficking of minors).

All defendants were sentenced by October 21, 2008. The sentences for the conspirators ranged from 12 months and 1 day incarceration followed by 2 years' supervised release to 36 months' incarceration. Of those charged with sex-trafficking offenses, Shayana Hicks was sentenced to 3 years, 10 months' incarceration, while Brian Forbes was sentenced to 13 years' incarceration followed by 3 years' supervised release. Dennis Paris was sentenced to 30 years' incarceration followed by 5 years of supervised release. In addition, Forbes had to pay $16,339 in restitution to the victims, while Paris was ordered to pay $46,116 in restitution to the victims.[2]

Gaining Support

Surveys of existing task forces have indicated that trained law enforcement personnel and direct service organizations need little convincing that collaboration is essential to combat sex trafficking. However, very few frontline personnel in either sector have the authority to commit themselves to a strategic, multidisciplinary, and collaborative effort without the support of their organizational leadership.

To support the usefulness of the task force and validate the urgency of the effort, one strategy is to review the results of the assessment conducted and present the main findings to key law enforcement and victim service leaders.

Ideally, support for the formation of the task force should come from the following offices:

- Chiefs of police or sheriffs
- Executive directors of victim and social service agencies
- Regional specialists and legal service providers with sex-trafficking victim specializations or services
- State attorneys general and district prosecutor offices
- Supervisory agents of federal law enforcement agencies
- The U.S. Attorney's Office (USAO) of the district

The role of the USAO has proved to be a significant factor in the success of task force operations. The USAO is in the unique role of responding to prosecutorial requests from federal, state, and local law enforcement and can enable an array of victim services in the jurisdiction where the case is federally prosecuted.

The U.S. Attorney is in a strong position to assist by emphasizing the importance and benefits of a task force to other key leaders and can be an important mediator when challenges arise. If support from the U.S. Attorney's Office presents a challenge, it is important for a task force to secure the support of a district or state prosecutor.

Core Team Model

Similar to most organizational startups, task force development begins with a small core team building upon a vision for a successful collaborative effort in combating the problem. A core team is needed to create and execute an effective plan for the development of the task force.

While task forces can be successful without such a team, task forces just starting up will benefit greatly from the shared experiences and information provided by the core team as they strategically determine how the task force will operate, the group structure for long-term sustainability, the establishment of strong leadership to manage the operations, and how to foster commitment and a clear purpose for the group.

Most problem-solving initiatives are undertaken by people who have a strong understanding of the problem, high credibility among those to whom they must appeal, and a high level of competence on the likely solution needed. Members of the core team must be committed to fighting sex trafficking and have the authority to commit their organizations and themselves to a long-term relationship with the task force. A reasonable size for a core team is generally five to seven participants.

The startup of any organization is the most challenging stage. Without effective direction of the process, efforts to get the task force under way may be futile.

Core Team Members' Initial Responsibilities

Core team members share the initial responsibilities to:

- research and analyze the feasibility of forming a task force
- develop the framework for the task force structure, operations, roles, and membership
- serve as champions and advocates for the formation of the task force

- seek out funding and other support for task force operations
- ensure that clear, reasonable, and achievable initial goals are set
- select a task force leader
- meet regularly to steer task force development
- plan and coordinate the initial training sessions

It is important to note here that a significant amount of time and human resources are needed to properly develop a task force. Core team members will need to secure the buy-in of their agency's leadership in order to dedicate the time needed to develop a strong task force.

Understanding the dynamics and complexities of sex trafficking is especially important in helping shape a response to the problem. Core team members are not required to be "experts" or "specialists" in sex-trafficking investigations. Most practitioners in law enforcement and victim services are "generalists" across the wide spectrum of problems among the populations they serve. A strong generalist who responds to the sex-trafficking problem should be aware of why the complexities of this problem demand a multidisciplinary, collaborative, and victim-centered response.

A sex-trafficking subject matter expert is, however, an important resource for the task force. The Office for Victims of Crime Training and Technical Assistance Center (OVC TTAC) maintains a consultant database of subject matter experts who are available to provide consultation and training to task forces, law enforcement agencies, and victim service agencies.

Core Team Representatives

Core team members should possess the following characteristics:

- Be visionary and practical: The capacity to plan for a goal and implement reasonable steps to achieve that outcome.
- Have decision-making authority: Possessing representative authority of their agency or organization; having authority to make reasonable commitments.

- Have organizational development skills: General capacity to form a new organization that will likely require fostering nontraditional relationships, synthesizing diverse perceptions of sex trafficking, utilizing a variety of skills, and drawing upon varying disciplines.
- Be resourceful: The ability to tap into human and other value-adding resources.

The most important credential of the core team and members of the task force is a commitment to developing an effective community response to sex trafficking. Many task forces, for instance, have been formed out of local or regional interest without external funding because they believe in the necessity of a coordinated task force response.

The core team should include representatives from:

- Federal Bureau of Investigation
- Federal and/or state Labor Department
- Immigration and Customs Enforcement
- State, county, and municipal law enforcement
- State and/or district prosecutor's office
- U.S. Attorney's Office
- Victim service providers, nongovernmental organizations (NGOs), and social service agencies with expertise in working with victims of sex trafficking

Sources of Leadership in a Task Force

Leadership of existing task forces varies widely, from a single individual within a police department or sheriff's office, to leadership teams composed of individuals from the major agencies on the task force. Successful task forces can be led by a variety of agencies or organizations, and it is up to each task force to determine the leadership that best suits its needs.

Regardless of which agency the individual or individuals who lead the task force come from, it is important to select leadership that the task force membership will respect and follow. In many cases, this individual or individuals will be a ranking law enforcement officer or an experienced assistant U.S. Attorney.

In an ideal situation, the position of task force leader is a full-time commitment. When that is not possible, the leader should have the capacity to give sufficient time to maintaining continuity of task force operations and ensuring a value-added benefit of all functions.

It also is important that leaders are able to find members or co-leaders within the task force to share their duties. Everyone is busy, and participation can be time intensive, creating a burden on already demanding schedules.

Some task forces designate administrators or managers to support leadership and manage operations (sending out emails, coordinating meetings, etc.), while others have created subcommittees focusing on task force administrative management.

Membership/Participation

Various operational structures for membership and levels of participation can be effective for task force efforts. Some groups systematically screen members for participation and others operate in a relatively open forum.

It is recommended that task force operations be conducted with some level of screened participation. Not all organizations add value or contribute to the mission of the task force. Members should have the capacity to actively contribute to the mission, vision, core values, and strategies, and not just attend meetings. Such conditions serve to enhance the focus of the group, develop and build upon key working relationships, and enhance trust and confidence among essential responder agencies and organizations.

In addition to representatives from agencies that are part of the core team, the task force may find it beneficial to include representatives from a variety of agencies and organizations that can expand the capacity of the task force to provide services to victims and bring strong investigations to successful prosecution.

Federal, State, and Local Regulatory Agencies

The regulatory agencies that may serve as task force partners include:

- Alcohol, Tobacco, and Firearms
- Alcohol and Beverage Control
- Department of Public Safety
- Equal Employment Opportunity Commission
- Food and Drug Administration
- Internal Revenue Service
- Licensing departments and regulating bodies (for massage parlors, nail salons, etc.)
- Local government offices
- U.S. Department of State document fraud investigators

Federal, State, and Local Social Service Agencies

Social service agencies that may serve as task force partners include:

- Adult Protective Services
- Child Protective Services or Department of Child and Family Services
- Social Security Administration
- State welfare agencies

Victim Service Providers, Nongovernmental Organizations (NGOs), and Social Service Agencies

Some of the local, state, and national organizations and agencies providing victim services include:

- Antisex trafficking organizations
- Faith-based organizations
- Immigrant advocacy groups and legal service providers

- Law enforcement associations (e.g., state associations, International Association of Chiefs of Police, National Sheriffs' Association)
- Medical professionals including doctors, nurses, and dentists
- Professors, academics, or researchers with an interest and/or specialized knowledge of sex trafficking
- Social and legal services agencies
- Youth shelters and special services providers

Victim service providers bring a diversity of specialized service skills, social resources, and interpersonal and intercultural relationship skills. Through their partnerships and connections with vulnerable populations and people who are difficult for law enforcement to access, victim service providers can create inroads and build bridges with victims and communities for law enforcement partners.

Service provider and law enforcement partnerships are crucial to the provision of a comprehensive and victim-centered response to sex trafficking. Such organizations also may be key partners in reaching targeted populations in culturally sensitive and linguistically correct ways. Victim service providers also can be important consultants to law enforcement on subjects of trauma, emotional bonding, climate of fear, and other circumstances.

An increase in public awareness of the existence of sex trafficking within communities often generates the interest and the benevolence of nontraditional supporters of law enforcement and service provider partnerships. Within many communities, there are networks, coalitions, and groups that share information, create new partnerships, and identify resources, skills, and good practices for enhancing a community response to sex trafficking.

Task forces should collaborate with such groups to create effective community-wide strategies for combating sex trafficking. Participation in a network of supporting partners does not necessitate participation in the primary task force group. Consistent with the necessary vetting of all task force partnerships, these relationships should be evaluated for conformance to task force core values and mission.

Criminal Justice System–Based Victim Assistance

There are many individuals, who work within the criminal justice system to facilitate resources and response for victims, and they are an important asset to the task force. Their role serves as an intermediary between law enforcement and social services, and they can be used as a strong resource for building collaboration and understanding among professional service groups. They can help identify resources for victims and work with NGO case managers or service providers to help identify services to which victims of sex trafficking are entitled by federal statute.

U.S. Attorney's Office Victim–Witness Coordinators

These coordinators are responsible for services to victims and witnesses identified in cases prosecuted by the U.S. Attorney's Office. They provide victims with information and notice of case events, make referrals for social services, and can assist witnesses with all necessary arrangements to facilitate their travel to court. They often act as an intermediary, making certain that all parties involved are communicating effectively. A particular role of the federal victim–witness coordinator is to make sure victims of a federal crime are aware of their rights and privileges as victims of crime. Victim–witness coordinators also can assist with law enforcement trainings, creating victim safety plans, and working with the trial team to address threats to victims' families in their country of origin.

State and Local Victim Coordinators

Some coordinators serve out of the state or district attorneys' offices. Like their federal colleagues, the state and local victim coordinator acts as an advocate and liaison on behalf of crime victims to assure the protection of victims' rights.

These coordinators work as liaisons between victims and prosecutors, accompany victims to hearings and trial, assist with any logistical or language needs, and help prep the victim for appearance in court. This is a particularly important role that demands coordination and cooperation with social service agencies, law enforcement agencies, and community organizations.

FBI Victim Specialists

Each of the 56 FBI field offices has one or more victim specialists who are nonagent support service members of the Bureau. Their responsibility is to assist victims of federal crimes investigated by the division or field office where they work; they also are available to help victims receive information and assistance about their cases and about services in their regions.

The victim specialists are trained in crisis intervention and have backgrounds in specialized victim assistance and diverse exposure to social services available to victims. They are crucial members of the task forces, providing an essential FBI liaison to sex-trafficking victims and should be in contact with victims during the investigation stages of the case.

ICE Victim–Witness Coordinators

The Immigration and Customs Enforcement (ICE) Victim Assistance Program (VAP) is responsible for overall ICE policy concerning victim-related issues, training and technical assistance to Homeland Security Investigations (HSI) Special Agents, as well as information and resource provision to victims encountered in investigations in order to ensure compliance with federal crime victim statutes.

Victim assistance coordinators respond to victims' issues in a wide range of federal crimes, including sex trafficking, child pornography, child sex tourism, white collar crime, and human rights abuse. Victim assistance coordinators provide a critical resource to investigations and criminal prosecutions by ensuring that victims have access to the rights and services to which they are entitled by law as well as the assistance they need to participate actively and fully in the criminal justice process. They routinely make referrals to nongovernmental organizations and community-based service providers for long-term services as well as coordinate emergency medical, mental health, and shelter services in the immediate aftermath of a rescue or other victim identification. ICE victim assistance coordinators also are available to provide technical assistance on issues, such as immigration relief options for foreign national victims of crime.

U.S. Attorney's Office Law Enforcement Coordinating Committees

Each of the 94 U.S. judicial districts has a Law Enforcement Coordinating Committee (LECC), whose purpose is to improve cooperation and coordination among federal, state, and local law enforcement offices. Some districts also have LECC subcommittees or task forces that consist of LECC agency officials working on specialized task forces.

In several task forces, for instance, the Law Enforcement Coordinator (LEC) serves as the main resource person for the group. In multidisciplinary antisex-trafficking task force operations, the LEC may be one of the key sources in coordinating seized and forfeited proceeds among participating law enforcement agencies. The key purpose of the LECC program is to facilitate the identified needs of law enforcement where federal, state, and local agencies work together in furtherance of justice.

Other Important Partners

In addition to the key members who should be a part of a sextrafficking task force in order to conduct effective investigations and provide needed services, there are other important partners who can contribute to the task force efforts and to the identification of victims of sex trafficking and prosecution of traffickers.

Legal Services

In addition to services provided by legal service providers, some attorneys and law firms donate a limited number of hours to community efforts. In certain larger cities, firms may act in association with each other to provide free (pro bono) services.

Task forces may discover through inquiries made to local bar associations or directly to law firms that free legal services are available to assist victims through the processes and legalities encountered in sex-trafficking cases. Attorneys, who routinely represent victims of trafficking, are excellent resources for training and assisting pro bono attorneys, as are law schools and clinics.

It is important to note that expectations and parameters are set when working with these groups to avoid later misunderstandings. For instance, law schools and clinics have high staff turnover and this can be harmful to a case. Attorneys need to know what is expected of them when representing victims of trafficking.

Local Businesses

Local business or industry interest in supporting the efforts against sex trafficking may broaden the resources, create a network of concerned citizens, increase information sources, and expand levels of sex-trafficking awareness. Appeals for support and partnerships may be an appropriate task force outreach effort. Many businesses operate within communities with a commitment to a form of corporate social responsibility that includes support for community-based development and outreach projects. If such projects exist, they often are housed in a company's public affairs office, and it may be useful to contact the individual in charge of these efforts.

Community at Large/Concerned Citizens

Most crime-solving information to be found and accessed comes from the community or region where the violation occurred, not through resources internal to law enforcement. While some task forces include community members and interested citizens as a part of their membership and others do not, the need to engage the community is essential. The community is a primary source of intelligence and a crucial partner in the antisex-trafficking effort.

It also is necessary to manage the public interest and create parameters of involvement to help ensure that interested community members are not engaging in dangerous behaviors by attempting to conduct their own investigations or victim rescues.

The Orange County, California task force provides an example of this with a "letter to the community from the Chief of Police" discouraging citizens from conducting their own investigations and informing them of the national hotline numbers.

Public service announcements (PSAs) are one tool that task forces and their partners use to raise awareness in their local community.

Marketing the Effort

Innovative uses of the Internet can be of significant value to the task force. Creative use of a task force Web site can range from being a source of information to offering a reporting mechanism for members of the community who are suspicious of certain activities they are observing, but hesitant to contact authorities.

Web sites are successfully used to inform the public. An easy way to establish a Web site is to develop a blog using a service, such as Wordpress (www.wordpress.com) or Blogger (www.blogger.com). These services allow an agency to set up a free Web site and include easy-to-use publishing software. Social media sites, such as Facebook, LinkedIn, or Twitter, also offer free and easy-to-use accounts that can assist task forces in publicizing and disseminating information to a wide audience.

A task force may find it beneficial to develop or design a logo to symbolize its efforts. Creating a brand or logo creates a representation of the group's existence, strengthens recognition of the group's efforts, and provides an easy way for people to connect with the group's mission. It also is useful for a task force to create a brochure or information booklet to familiarize citizens on how they, too, can assist the task force in identifying cases of sex trafficking (Figure 9.1).

Figure 9.1 A public information brochure. (Courtesy of Clearwater (Florida) Area Human Trafficking Task Force.)

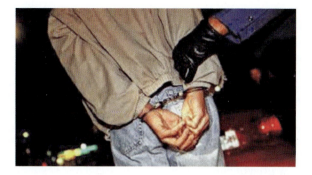

Figure 9.2 Suspect arrested by a multiagency sex-trafficking task force. Twenty-three-year-old Michael Vincent Pree was arrested by the Los Angeles Innocence Lost Task Force and charged with the sexual assault of a minor. He also was involved in an organized sex-trafficking business. (Photo courtesy of the FBI.)

Public media partnerships also can be useful for marketing the task force's efforts. Cultivating a working relationship with interested journalists through frequent personal contact may result in improved coverage of task force events and print news stories that also result in public awareness and public campaigns (Figure 9.2).

In The News

Task Force Arrests Sex Trafficking Suspect

LOS ANGELES—A year-long criminal investigation that was conducted by a multiagency task force into a sex trafficking investigation resulted in the arrest of a local man on Wednesday, December 21. According to a Los Angeles Police Department news release, the arrest of 23-year-old Michael Vincent Pree for sexual assault of a minor was the result of an ongoing investigation by the Los Angeles Innocence Lost Task Force.

During the investigation, police found that Pree allegedly contacted a 12-year-old girl. After bringing the girl to his residence, Pree forced her to engage in sexual intercourse with him on numerous occasions over the course of one week. Investigators also found that Pree was allegedly forcing the young girl to work as a street-walking prostitute over the course of the same week.

After arriving at Pree's residence to arrest him, investigative personnel from the task force served a search warrant and promptly searched the home. The search turned up additional evidence against Pree linking him to his sex trafficking business and was booked into evidence for future court proceedings.

A search on the California Megan's Law Sex Offender Database and the National Sex Offender Public Registry Web sites under Pree's name turned up no records.

The L.A. Innocence Lost Task Force was formed as a part of a multiagency operation that includes the LAPD, the Los Angeles County District Attorney's Office, the FBI, the United States Attorney's Office, and the Department of Homeland Security. According to the FBI's Web site, which is spearheading the operation, the Innocence Lost Task Force was formed in June 2003 to combat the growing problem of the commercial and sexual exploitation of children through prostitution in the United States.

Operating under the Innocence Lost National Initiative, 43 dedicated task forces and working groups throughout the United States, involving federal, state, and local law enforcement agencies, have been created. As of April 2011, more than 1,600 children have been rescued, 719 convictions have occurred, and over $3.1 million has been seized. All of the victims in these crimes were under the age of 18. The investigation is ongoing. (Source: Damian Kelly, *Canyon News* (Beverly Hills, CA), Jan 2, 2012.)

Task Force Operations

A multidisciplinary, collaborative task force operation is significantly less complicated to design than to operate. Their operations demand effective leadership and a unified commitment to the mission and to the team.

Task Force Staffing and Size

Choosing the right members for the task force is just as important as structure. Task forces are encouraged to dedicate law enforcement personnel to this effort through the assigning and funding of one or two full-time investigators who are supported by patrol officers and an intelligence function.

Not all groups have the capacity or resources to dedicate full-time staff. When a full-time staff is not available, assigning formal roles and responsibilities to members of the task force increases the likelihood of effective and consistent operations.

Designation of Key Roles

The designation of the following four key roles can be sufficient to meet staffing needs:

- **Group Leader:** Provides overall task force coordination and coordination of law enforcement; conducts meetings.
- **Group Administrator:** Provides administrative and logistical coordination; may provide grant management support and support to task forces seeking funding.
- **Victim Service Coordinator:** Provides primary liaison and coordination of various victim services that may originate in several organizations.
- **Outreach Coordinator:** Coordinates and leads in the development and delivery of outreach efforts.

Additional Roles

Depending on the size, capacities, and needs of the task force, additional roles may be useful. In some instances, task forces with high demand for community-oriented trainings may choose to designate a training coordinator in addition to an outreach coordinator. The training coordinator may be responsible for developing training material, recruiting individuals to join a speaker pool, and training speakers on key antitrafficking messages.

Community liaison officers with training and language capacity to reach marginalized populations are utilized by several existing task forces and allow for greater law enforcement contact with vulnerable populations.

To maintain a balance in workloads and responsibilities, it may be effective to rotate task force roles and responsibilities on an annual basis. In a more ideal situation where funding and personnel resources are available, it is highly recommended to have a full-time task force leader or administrator.

The appropriate size of a task force depends upon the group's ability to work together efficiently and accomplish established goals. Thus, expanding the group should be a deliberate move to strengthen the task force. Every participant should be expected to contribute actively to meeting the goals of the group.

After Action Debriefing

Bring all members of the team together to include investigators, analysts, prosecutors, and service agency representatives from NGOs immediately to discuss lessons learned during the investigation.

In a nonconfrontational atmosphere, conduct a debriefing with the following goals in mind:

- Identify the strengths and weaknesses in the investigation and prosecution to help streamline and enhance the next investigation.
- Identify any agency policies or procedures that may have unnecessarily hampered information sharing among everyone who had a "need to know."
- The Federal Grand Jury rule limits how much information can be discussed and with whom before the prosecution begins. Investigators should consult with the U.S. Attorney's Office if it is anticipated that the case will be tried in federal court.
- Identify any victim concerns that may not have been fully addressed, and determine if there is a way to meet those needs with future victims.
- Determine victim needs throughout the investigative and prosecutorial process to include the role of the NGO and who liaisons with the victim.
- Draft a report and forward it to all participants involved in the investigation to allow them to comment.
- The report should not contain sensitive information on sources or methods used in the investigation, as well as any information specific to the investigation that may be necessary for the prosecution, because it will become public record.[3]

Memorandum of Understanding

Having a formal Memorandum of Understanding (MOU) among participating agencies and organizations is the first step in defining and understanding expectations. The MOU also is a public statement of commitment and a guide for accountability. The MOU should clearly define roles, responsibilities, and responses to sex trafficking that are within the agency or organization's normal capacity.

It may be tempting to use the MOU to outline the perfect antitrafficking response, but it is best to develop a realistic and achievable response based on the resources and capabilities of each organization.

The simpler the agreements are in their requirements and the clearer they are in expectations, the easier it is for agencies to sign without having to go through layers of legal process and reviews. If an agreement is for purposes of support, then the partner need only express a willingness to assist "to the best of their abilities," and it should be accepted for what is offered.

Many agency leaders hesitate to sign an MOU because the formality of the document may seem to imply a level of commitment with which they are uncomfortable. Some municipalities require that MOUs and other agreements be approved by a larger oversight body, such as a city council, a board of directors, or an organization's headquarters, before they can be accepted.

When there is resistance or discomfort with signing an MOU, the agency executive should be invited to point out those areas of the MOU that present challenges to a successful sign-off and attempt to agree on language and conditions that meet mutual needs.

If an agency or organization is unable or unwilling to sign a formal agreement and their cooperation with the task force is essential, not having the agreement should not prevent them from participation on the task force. In such situations, an unsigned document can be issued to ensure an understanding of the type of involvement that is expected from their participation.

Task Force Operational Protocol

A task force operational protocol is an essential tool for guiding a collaborative response to the trafficking problem. The protocol may include training documents, a resource directory, general guidelines for responding to incidents, procedures for the multidisciplinary response, and investigative and prosecutorial guidelines. A significant benefit of the protocol is that it can be distributed to the participating agencies and organizations to aid in the transparency of the antisex-trafficking effort, foster consistency in the regional effort, and engender patience with the process.

Conducting Meetings

Task force meetings are the cornerstone of the group's development. The meeting is the basis for relationship building, training, exchange of ideas, problem solving, resolution of conflict, innovation, recovery from shortfalls, and celebrations of successes.

When task force members begin to regard the meeting as an assured opportunity to undergo one or more such experiences, then the meeting will have evolved to a gathering of respected colleagues, teammates, and even friends.

The fundamental purpose of the task force meeting is for participants to leave more equipped and enabled to combat sex trafficking. Meetings, therefore, should be planned and purposeful.

The meeting environment should be welcoming, safe for free expression of thoughts and concerns, and offer protection from inappropriate or personal attacks. The meeting should be conducted along a course to achieve its intended purpose, yet not so rigid as to discourage a newly discovered and beneficial area of discussion.

The following are specific recommendations that will assist in accomplishing these objectives:

- *Start and end on time, if not earlier*: Respect the timelines and honor of punctual participants. Those who are routinely late will get the message. Do not allow even an exciting meeting to extend timelines; encourage the excitement to continue on its own healthy energy, and then dismiss the meeting. Early conclusions allow for additional networking time and emphasize that the meeting has met its purpose.

- *Conduct roundtable name, role, and organization introductions at every meeting*: This is especially important in the start-up period of the task force. Contrary to some perceptions, the overwhelming number of meeting attendees prefer this ritual. The ritual validates and honors the individual and the agency they represent.
- *Meet with consistency*: Meeting attendance is more consistent when participants routinely anticipate it at a set time, space, and environment. The frequency of the meeting is determined by established goals and attached timelines to achieve them. In a newly formed task force, it is recommended that a meeting be conducted at least once per month for the first six months with a focus on relationship building.
- *Meetings are facilitated by an agenda; ideas are free-flowing:* A meeting among a multidisciplinary and diverse group of participants that is not facilitated by agenda is akin to chaos. Facilitated meetings are based upon a plan—the agenda. Having an agenda and a facilitator are more conducive to a free flow of ideas than not having one or the other or neither.

A skilled member of the core team or a meeting facilitator is recommended for the initial meetings until a sense of team solidarity is apparent. In time, skilled members from the team may be assigned to this role in rotations. Agenda items should be solicited in advance of the meeting.

- *The preservation of confidentiality is presumed, but never underemphasized*: The level of disclosure among and between task force members is dependent on a number of factors including strength of relationships, the necessity of disclosure, and the purpose of disclosure. One of the corrosives of trust is the breach of confidentiality. Routine reminders of respect for confidentiality as a team value are essential. This is especially true when discussing current cases.

- *Ongoing training is an integral aspect of the team inter-action*: This is true to such a degree that the expression: "I learn something every time I come here," should be commonly heard. Training is both formal and informal. When the task force is envisioned as a continuous learning organization, members look forward to what they will learn at each meeting.

Law enforcement has a tradition of "roll call" training sessions that last from 10 to 20 minutes before deploying a team to duty. This is a good model for the task force. Regular and brief updates require the trainer to get to the point and give the audience just what is needed in order to get out and apply it. Training topics span a spectrum as diverse as the sex-trafficking problem.

Rotating "roll call" training sessions among the task force members gives them the opportunity to share their expertise. This method also fosters a team environment of continuous learning.

- *Sharing information is an integral responsibility of the team members:* Fostering learning is the necessity of sharing. However, it goes beyond necessity to a shared responsibility. Everyone was brought to the table for a reason, so it is important to include everyone in discussions. For instance, victim service providers working closely with the victim may have important knowledge or evidence for the investigation without even realizing it. While it is understood that law enforcement may not be able to share sensitive details of an agency's ongoing investigation, some level of information needs to be shared on all sides so that everyone remains informed.
- *Time set aside for networking is time well spent*: Setting a time for free-flowing and enjoyable team building is important. The midmeeting break is a good time for this. Simple refreshments often help to break the ice and start conversation.
- *The organization that institutionalizes feedback is destined to improve*: Asking: "How are we doing?," frequently and with an intent to refine and develop

based upon the feedback is the hallmark of a learning and improving organization. Ask it of each other often.

- Ensure project and special task accomplishment through subcommittee assignments based on an action plan and a scheduled report-back period: The level of experience and expertise that will exist or eventually be garnered among task force members will become an asset to the team's development and capacity. Training, outreach, and other tasks and projects developed out of an annual action plan are typically progressively improved upon over time.

Intelligence or Vice Operations?

It is important that the task force has an investigative function in order to be truly effective. Choosing where to house the investigative unit is an important decision for law enforcement on a task force. The broader the view of how and where sex trafficking may be occurring, the more likely it will be recognized.

As in all criminal investigations, information and analyzed intelligence are at the core of a good investigation. Investigating sex trafficking may be best centered within an investigative operation that broadly focuses on the collection, aggregation, and analysis of criminal operations. The broader the view of the possibilities, the broader the net that can be cast to draw in sex trafficking operations.

Vice units are typically formed as public order units with a focus on such crimes as prostitution, gambling, and street-level drug crimes. The investigation of sex trafficking greatly transcends this level of focus. Vice units that are assigned to the oversight of sex trafficking cases have a tendency to focus on that area of investigation in which they are trained. Interviews of task forces' members, where the sex trafficking investigations are in vice units, reveal that the majority of those units' investigations are focused on sex trafficking cases.

Understanding the dynamics and the unique aspects of sex trafficking will assist task forces in assigning cases to the most appropriate investigative unit, which will no doubt vary from community to community.

Collaboration

Despite its recent introduction into the U.S. criminal code, sex trafficking is certainly not a new crime, nor is it a recent phenomenon in human history. What is new is the strategic, multidisciplinary, and collaborative response to the problem.

The power of a successful task force collaborative effort is that it can transform the limitations of a singular agency or organization into the strengths of a strategic multidisciplinary team with substantially improved capacity to impact the problem.

The challenge is to become an interdependent team. In the multidisciplinary antisex-trafficking effort, the task force purpose is to have a strategic impact on a complex problem. To be effective, the task force must plan and develop a coordinated multiagency response to the victims and to the criminal justice process.

In uncoordinated and unrelated responses of individual agencies and organizations, attempts to respond to these needs often meet with frustration, inefficiency, increased suffering to the victim, and freedom for the perpetrator. Responding to the victims and conducting the criminal investigation are not mutually exclusive. Effective task force collaboration anticipates these needs and becomes a unified resource for local antitrafficking efforts.

The incentive to remain in a collaborative task force is generally altruistic and all these individuals want to make a greater impact upon the problem. Task forces with effective collaboration have found their partners to be their greatest strength in fighting this crime and a resource to the investigation, rather than an impediment.

Effective collaboration is more easily conceptualized than accomplished; nevertheless, it is essential. Task forces that have worked through initial or longstanding collaboration challenges have found it a difficult, but worthwhile, endeavor.

Professional Misunderstandings

As in any relationship, presumptions, misperceptions, and prejudgments are the core elements of discord and dysfunction. The elements often exist within the same sector (e.g., different law enforcement agencies) and certainly across sectors. Generally, the origins of these barriers can be traced to past experiences and to a lack of understanding of and appropriate regard for roles and responsibilities.

Before a task force can become an interdependent team responding to sex trafficking, the members have to invest in responding appropriately to each other. With the union of groups that have a history of conflict and distrust, specifically among local, state, and federal law enforcement and victim service providers, a systematic way must be found to overcome prejudgments, build trust, and work together as a team.

Tips for Conflict Resolution

- Begin by working to understand the purpose and mission of the represented organizations and how the representatives carry out their role within their organizations.
- Work toward identifying and confronting lingering past and current issues that continue to erect relationship barriers.
- Focus on the issue; do not attack the person.
- Accept responsibility for past failures when it is appropriate.
- Attempt to bring new understanding about organizational dynamics where it is lacking, and work to reach a resolution of differences.

When there is a focus on the issues, well-intended and respectful input from other members of the group can help to resolve the differences and strengthen the group relationship. The common adage "focus on the issue, not on the individual" holds true. In a task force setting, that may need to be expanded to "focus on the issue, not on the agency or organization."

Figure 9.3 A multiagency task force preparing to conduct a raid. FBI agents and other law enforcement officers gather to get briefed before conducting raids on a number of brothels involved in sex-trafficking operations. (Photo courtesy of the FBI.)

All great relationships and organizations are built on trust. It is not readily given nor should it be presumed to exist until it has been earned. The safest presumption that can be made in successfully convening a group to serve as a task force is that the members are there to have an impact upon the problem.

Mutual trust in the group's effort and trust among the members should not be presumed by the level of participation. Convening a group when the only perceived outcome is that a meeting has occurred will quickly lead to dissolution of the group.

Building trust has been recognized by current task force leaders as a necessary part of effective collaboration that takes time. Task force meetings, joint trainings, open discussions, challenges to existing practices, productive debriefings of encountered experiences, and other interactions among task force members all provide opportunities for effective team building (Figure 9.3).

Tips for Building Trust

- Add value to participation by accomplishing measurable results. In many cases, trust is established through the shared experience of working together on one trafficking case at a time, and by communicating or debriefing about the experiences of that case, regardless of whether or not there was a successful outcome.

- Maintain and fulfill commitments made to the team. A most rewarding outcome of participation is in getting out of it what was promised.
- Always work at demonstrating a genuine concern for the furtherance of the cause and for those who will be served by it.
- Respect and support each other. Each participant should become predictable in meeting the good and reasonable expectations that other team members have for them.
- Find nonthreatening ways to facilitate conflict resolution.
- In one task force, the team leader routinely received phone calls during the first year of the group's formation from members with complaints about each other and about other organizations' performances. After a period of weaving those complaints into the meeting discussions in a nonthreatening way that focused on the problem, the leader observed that the members began bringing up their concerns on their own in a similar manner; the group's discussions became more productive and trust among the membership increased.
- Provide opportunities for joint trainings. Several task force leaders conduct joint training sessions with service providers and law enforcement personnel so that they have an opportunity to gain greater understanding of each others' perspectives and build a stronger relationship.
- Strengthen collaboration through social networking. One task force leader simply said that members made efforts to spend social time together, having dinner or drinks, which resulted in stronger working relationships.

Tips for Retention of Task Force Leaders and Members

- Develop at startup detailed member contingency plans and protocol for any necessary member replacement. Turnover is a challenge in the field of law enforcement in general, and that must be acknowledged and prepared for to the degree possible.

- Encourage member organizations to assign more than one person to the task force. These personnel should play a strong liaison role within their own organizations about the activities of the task force.
- Written protocols help to explain the role the agency or individual is to play when new task force members are needed.
- Always keep in mind the mission and purpose of the task force. Several task forces report that having a dedicated staff or a trusted team to share the work helps ease the burden of limited resources and time.

Glossary

FBI Victim Specialists: A nonagent support service member of the Bureau who is responsible for assisting victims of federal crimes investigated by the division or field services where they work.

Foreign national: Generally used to describe a person who is not a U.S. citizen or Lawful Permanent Resident (LPR).

ICE Victim–Witness Coordinators: These are individuals who respond to victims' issues in a wide range of federal crimes including sex trafficking, child pornography, child sex tourism, white-collar crime, and human rights abuse.

Law enforcement: Refers to all federal, state, and local prosecutors, agents, troopers, deputies, and police officers.

Memorandum of Understanding (MOU): A public statement of commitment as a guide for accountability that should clearly define the roles, responsibilities, and responses to sex trafficking that are within the agency's or organization's normal capacity.

Pro bono: Legal services provided by law firms in which they waive their fee for services.

Task Force Core Values: These are the values that express the foundational, consistent, and shared principles that shape the best intentions of the task force.

Task Force Operational Protocol: It may include training documents, a resource directory, general guidelines for responding to incidents, procedures for the multidisciplinary response, and investigative and prosecutorial guidelines.

Task Force Strategy: The strategy that outlines the broad methodology of what will be employed in response to sex trafficking.

United States Attorney's Office (USAO): The individual who is appointed by the President of the United States to prosecute the violation of federal laws in a specific federal judicial district.

U.S. Attorney's Office Law Enforcement Coordinating Committees (LECC): The purpose of this committee is to improve cooperation and coordination among federal, state, and local law enforcement officers.

Victim Service Provider: Service providers in governmental or nongovernmental organizations (NGOs) or representatives whose primary function is to provide services to victims of crime, including victims of sex trafficking.

Victim Witness Coordinator and Victim Specialist: Those who work within the criminal justice system to facilitate the acquisition of resources and responses for victims and serve as intermediaries between law enforcement and community-based victims' services.

Review Questions

1. Why is it necessary for most communities that have a sex-trafficking problem to build a multiagency antisex-trafficking task force?
2. In evaluating the utility of forming a task force, what parameters should be considered?
3. What are the major sources of informative data and indicators of sex trafficking?
4. Ideally, support for the formation of a task force should come from which offices?
5. What are the initial responsibilities of task force core team members?

6. The task force core team members should include representatives from which agencies?
7. What federal, state, and local regulatory agencies may serve as task force partners?
8. What victim service providers, nongovernmental organizations (NGOs), and social service agencies are in a position to provide victims' services?
9. What is the role of the FBI victims' specialist?
10. What functions are performed by the ICE Victim–Witness Coordinators?
11. What are Memorandums of Understanding (MsOU)?
12. What specific recommendations have been made to assure that task force meetings are conducted efficiently?
13. What are some tips for conflict resolution as it relates to members of the task force?
14. What are some of the tips for building trust among task force members?
15. What are some of the tips for retaining task force leaders and members?

Endnotes

1. Anti trafficking Task Force Strategy and Operations e-Guide Bureau of Justice Assistance (U.S. Department of Justice, 2011). This discussion was adapted and modified from this source, pp. 26–39, 42–48, 52–62.
2. *United States v. Dennis Paris* (aka "Rahmyti"), Brian Forbes (aka "B"), Shanaya Hicks (aka "Toni"), et al., United States Attorney's Office District of Connecticut and U.S. Department of Justice (DOJ) Civil Rights Division Human Trafficking Prosecution Unit, Criminal No. 3:06CR64(CFD), pp. 2–5.
3. *Advanced Investigative Techniques of Human Trafficking Offenses*, May 10, 2007, Instructor Guide, Florida Criminal Justice Advanced Course 1166, Criminal Justice Standards and Training Commission Florida Department of Law Enforcement, Unit 2, Lesson 1, pp. 20–21.

10

The Prosecution of Sex-Trafficking Cases

An American prosecutor is a government attorney who initiates the prosecution of an accused person and represents the government at trial. (Photo: Corbis Images. With permission.)

Chapter Objectives

1. Provide a general overview of the role, functions, and decision-making powers of the prosecutor in the United States.
2. Understand the role of the federal prosecutor in sex trafficking cases.
3. Discuss the role played by the Federal Bureau of Investigation (FBI), the U.S. Immigration and Customs Enforcement (ICE), and the Human Smuggling and Trafficking Center (HSTC) in assisting the prosecutorial process of sex-trafficking cases.
4. Identify the resources necessary to train prosecutors to become effective in the prosecution of sex-trafficking cases.
5. Discuss the advantages to law enforcement officers working with both federal and state prosecutors in sex-trafficking investigations.
6. Understand the rules of evidence that must be followed in search and seizure cases involving sex-trafficking cases.

Introduction

Effective prosecution of sex-trafficking cases is an extraordinarily challenging task. Yet, while it is important to examine challenges associated with prosecuting sex traffickers, including the reluctance of victims to cooperate with law enforcement, it is more important to develop innovative prosecutorial approaches. Once challenges have been identified, focus must shift to creative strategies that will lead to successful prosecutions.[1]

In this chapter, we will first provide a diagrammatic overview of the criminal justice process in sex-trafficking cases (Figure 10.1), then go on to discuss the role of prosecutors in general, their decision-making powers, and the specific functions

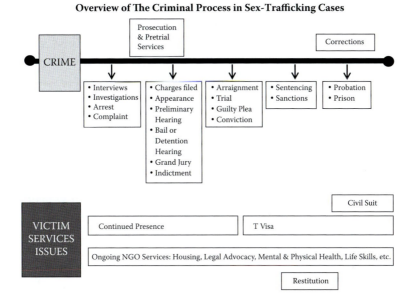

Figure 10.1 Overview of the criminal process in sex trafficking cases. (From: Freedom Network Training Institute, 2013. With permission.)

they are expected to perform. We also will examine the role of federal prosecutors in sex-trafficking cases as well as how they are assisted by the Federal Bureau of Investigation (FBI), Immigration and Customs Enforcement (ICE), and the Human Smuggling and Trafficking Center (HSTC). Since many times a sex-trafficking case can be prosecuted either at the federal or state level, we will discuss the advantages of law enforcement officers working with both federal and state prosecutors and why an ultimate decision may be made to prosecute a sex-trafficking case either in federal or state court. Lastly, we will discuss the rules of evidence as they relate to search and seizure and obtaining search warrants in sex-trafficking cases.

A General Overview of the Role of the Prosecutor in the United States

In the United States, a **prosecuting attorney** is recognized as the legal representative of the government. At the state level, the position is generally titled: district attorney, state attorney, county attorney, or commonwealth attorney. More than 95% of state prosecutors are elected and most are considered the chief law enforcement officer within a state's specific judicial district. Normally, the prosecutor determines which cases will be brought to trial and in what manner they will be disposed of. The prosecutor also determines whether the case presented to his or her office by the police is legally sufficient and, if so, in which court it will be pursued. The prosecutor further decides whether the original charges against the accused will be reduced or even dropped. In many jurisdictions, prosecutors also assist law enforcement agencies in searches, arrests, and investigations of targeted criminal activity.

Across the nation, at the state level, about 2,350 prosecutors' offices handle felony cases in state trial courts and are primarily responsible for advocating for the public in felony cases and in a variety of misdemeanor cases. State law determines the number of chief prosecutors in a state and whether they are elected or appointed.[2]

The Statewide Prosecutor

Some states have even created the appointed position of Statewide Prosecutor. This position is generally filled by the state attorney general and the mission of the Office of Statewide Prosecutor is to investigate and prosecute multicircuit organized crime as well as assist other law enforcement officials in their efforts against organized crime. Sex trafficking certainly falls into this category.[3]

The U.S. Attorney at the Federal Level

At the federal level, there are 94 judicial districts with 93 U.S. Attorneys. Guam and the Mariana Islands share one U.S. Attorney, although they are two separate districts. Thus, with this exception, each judicial district has its own U.S. Attorney. The U.S. Attorney is appointed by the President of the United States, confirmed by the U.S. Senate, and is supervised by the U.S. Attorney General. The U.S. Attorney performs many of the same prosecutorial functions as state prosecutors.

The Prosecutor's Specific Function

Prosecutors serve the government in a number of different ways. They give counsel to law enforcement officers and draft legal opinions on the latest changes in constitutional law to use as a guide to modify future law enforcement procedures. As the government's chief law investigative officer, the prosecutor draws the line when law enforcement officers' conduct infringes upon individual rights.

The Advisory Committee on the Prosecution and Defense Functions of the American Bar Association has pointed out that, unlike any of the other major players in the administration of justice, the role of the prosecutor spans the entire criminal justice process.[4]

Step-by-Step: The Prosecutor's Role

In almost every major step of the criminal justice system, the prosecutor has a number of important roles, namely:

Investigation. During the investigation phase of the criminal justice process, prosecutors assist with the preparation of search and arrest warrants and work with law enforcement officers ensuring that their investigative reports are complete. In some circumstances, either through citizen complaints or suspicion of alleged criminal acts, prosecutors initiate their own investigations, which may be independent of law enforcement activity.

Arrest. Subsequent to arrest, prosecutors screen cases to determine which should be prosecuted and which should be dropped.

Initial appearance. During the first court appearance, the prosecutor ensures that all defendants are notified of the charges against them. Additionally, prosecutors serve as the government's attorney in all cases. They also participate in bail decisions by making bail recommendations to the court. Importantly, prosecutors also can discontinue a prosecution by drafting a *nolle prosequi* (also referred to as *nol. pros*). A *nolle prosequi* consists of formally entering into the record the prosecution's declaration that the government is unwilling to prosecute the case. It is an agreement not to proceed further.

Grand jury. Within the grand jury proceedings, the prosecutor is both the judge and prosecutor and is the only major legal officer in the room when the citizens determine whether or not to indict. The prosecutor alone chooses the evidence that the grand jury will hear and not hear in order to make their decision.

Preliminary hearing. Prosecutors have two functions at the preliminary hearing: (a) to establish probable cause or (b) to not proceed with prosecution. In jurisdictions where they have no initial appearance but proceed directly to the preliminary hearing, prosecutors have the additional task of giving formal notice of charges and participating in bail decisions.

Information and indictment. The prosecutor prepares the information that establishes probable cause and binds an accused over for trial. In jurisdictions that use indictment rather than information, prosecutors establish probable cause before the grand jury.

Arraignment. In this proceeding, prosecutors bring an accused person to the court to answer to the matters charged in the information or indictment. Prosecutors also participate in plea negotiation during this time. Plea negotiation allows defendants to plead guilty to a reduced charge or charges and can occur at any time between formal charging and the reading of the verdict.

Pretrial motions. As representatives of the government, prosecutors draft and argue pretrial motions.

Trial. Prosecutors are the government's trial lawyers and, as such, argue to prove the guilt of the accused beyond a reasonable doubt.

Sentencing. Prosecutors make sentencing recommendations to the judge, usually arguing for more rigid punishment, but sometimes they may recommend that a more lenient sentence be imposed, especially if a defendant has been cooperative.

Appeal. Through written and oral debate, prosecutors ensure that convictions are obtained properly so that they are not likely to be reversed by the appellate courts if appealed.

Parole. In some jurisdictions, prosecutors make recommendations for or against parole for inmates up for review. In most instances, however, prosecutors typically limit themselves to opposing early release of serious offenders, who are likely to recidivate.

Probation and parole revocation hearing. When a probationer or parolee violates a condition of probation or parole, he or she is entitled to a hearing to determine whether probation or parole will be revoked. Prosecutors act as advocates for the government in these hearings.[5]

It is at trial where the prosecutor most fully manifests his or her role as an advocate. This role means that the prosecutor will then present the government's side of the case with passion, vigor, and logic.

If the prosecutor is successful at trial, then he or she also represents the government at the sentencing hearing, which often occurs sometime later. In this hearing, the prosecutor will argue the government's position for the appropriate sentence to give to the convicted felon for the judge's consideration. Although normally, at the state level, the state attorney general's office handles any appeals from a felony conviction, there are times when the trial prosecutor, because he or she is so involved with a case, will want to participate in writing appellate briefs and arguing the merits of the appeal before the appellate court.

The Decision to Prosecute

Deciding whether to prosecute and what the charge will be is the focus of the formal job of the prosecuting attorney. These determinations can legally be made by the prosecutor alone, and the consequences have a great impact, not only on defendants, but also on the other agencies that participate in the administration of justice.

As the due process model emphasizes, a decision to label a citizen a defendant in a criminal action should be undertaken only with full and serious understanding of the consequences. There are clearly negative aspects to being arrested, especially in sex-related cases, but there are even greater penalties attached to being charged with such a crime. Once a suspect becomes a defendant, the entire weight of the criminal justice process is brought to bear on the individual. The government may restrain the person's liberty, and economic burdens are imposed by the requirement that bail be posted and a lawyer hired. There is also the nontangible penalty of damage to the person's reputation; though the public gives lip service to the idea of "innocent until proven guilty," it may also subscribe to the notion that where there's smoke, there's fire.[6]

Prosecutorial Discretion

Under American law, criminal litigation generally does not occur until an action is initiated by a prosecutor. The prosecutor has the power of discretion: the power to decide whether to investigate citizens, order arrests, present one-sided arguments to the grand jury, and recommend sentences to the court. It is also the prosecutor's decision whether a charge will be pursued, reduced, plea bargained, or dropped altogether, and these choices are made with little or no statutory or case law guidance.[7] The duties of the prosecutor are generally not specifically defined by law, other than by state and federal statutes and the respective constitutions that require the "prosecutor to proceed with litigation against those who transgress the jurisdiction's laws," or by case law that describes the prosecutor's duties in equally general terms (see the Landmark Case *United States v. Armstrong*).[8]

Prosecutorial discretion is normally initiated after arrest. Prosecutors receive a copy of the law enforcement officers' reports in their office and screen and evaluate the merit of these reports. The decision whether or not to go forward to trial is called selective prosecution.

In some cases, a prosecutor may simply refuse to proceed. Even after charges are filed or a grand jury indictment is in, the halting of prosecution can be stopped by the principle of *nolle prosequi*. A prosecutor may even ask the court to dismiss the charges. This is singularly the most powerful example of discretionary authority within the criminal justice system.

Although some prosecutor's offices have an internal review for determining whether or not to prosecute a case, many do not. In the final analysis, the government is the victim of every crime, thus, it is the government's right to decide whether to go forward with charges on a crime.

Unethical Procedures and Wrongful Convictions

The large amount of discretion held by the prosecutor creates considerable potential for abuse, such as discrimination, corruption, nepotism, bribery, not prosecuting friends or political cronies, or to accept guilty pleas to drastically reduced charges for personal considerations. On the other hand, overzealous prosecution by the prosecuting attorney seeking heightened visibility in order to support grand political ambitions can be another source of difficulty.

Because, in most cases, state prosecutors are elected by the citizens within their judicial district, politics may exert considerable influence over a prosecutor's decision to prosecute or not prosecute a case. However, gross misconduct by a prosecutor may be addressed by the state supreme court or the state attorney general's office. Short of criminal misconduct, however, most of the options available to either the court or the attorney general are limited. As members of the legal profession, prosecutors are subject to the Code of Professional Responsibility of their state bar associations. Serious violations of the code may result in their being disbarred from the practice of law. The American Bar Association (ABA) standard for criminal justice describes the prosecutor's duty this way: "The duty of the prosecutor is to seek justice, not to merely convict." Hence, a prosecutor is barred by the standards of the legal profession from advocating any fact or position that he or she knows is untrue.[9]

Prosecutorial Diversion

A middle ground between a prosecutor dropping a case and going forward with a full criminal trial is *diversion*. The prosecutors, who use diversion, often believe that the ideals of justice can be better served if they do not seek a criminal trial for a defendant. In the past, the accused were sometimes diverted by requiring them to join the army, join the Peace Corps, or promise never to come back to town. Today, however, diversion has taken on a much more sophisticated meaning. Often the accused receive psychological, social, and medical help to deal with problems thought to be at the root of their criminal behavior. Likewise, if the accused are first-time offenders, these diversions allow them to escape the label of "criminal," thus, giving them a better chance to reintegrate into society.

Adjudication Deferred/Withheld Adjudication

For first-time offenders, as well as youthful offenders, many prosecutors nationwide have determined that, in certain cases, it is in the best interest of society that the adjudication of guilt of such defendants be deferred or withheld. An agreement between the prosecution and defense for a defendant to receive a **deferred adjudication** is usually the result of a plea bargain. Although it is required that the defendant plead guilty or *nolo contendere* (no contest) in these cases, the trial judge does not find the defendant guilty at that time. Instead, the judge defers making a finding of guilt on the issue in question. Afterwards, the defendant is usually placed on probation for a specified period of time and is required to perform some type of community service. If the defendant violates a condition of the probation during this period, the court may then adjudicate the defendant guilty and assess the punishment that would have been imposed before the plea agreement was entered into. However, if the probationary period has expired and the court has not received a violation notice, then the court at a stated future time will enter an order of dismissal for the proceedings against the defendant. This order discharges the defendant.

Normally, a dismissal and discharge under either deferred-adjudication or adjudication-withheld programs may not be deemed a conviction for any purpose within American society. The only exception is upon subsequent conviction of the same state's criminal statutes. This particular tool of the prosecutor affords a valued second chance to people who have made a mistake, have learned their lesson, and probably will never recidivate.

Role of the Federal Prosecutor in Sex-Trafficking Cases

The Criminal Section of the Department of Justice's (DOJ) Civil Rights Division, in collaboration with U.S. Attorneys' Offices nationwide, has principal responsibility for prosecuting sex trafficking crimes, except for cases involving sex trafficking of children. Within DOJ's Criminal Division, the Child Exploitation Obscenity Section (CEOS) are the subject matter experts on the prosecution of sex trafficking of minors and child sex tourism. Over the past decade, the vast majority of sex trafficking cases have been prosecuted in the federal courts by U.S. attorneys. This has occurred in part because of the considerable experience gained by federal prosecutors over the years in prosecuting sex-trafficking cases as well as the availability of enormous federal resources to assist in the development of the cases for prosecution.

Training Prosecutors

In an effort to meet the needs of professionally inexperienced prosecutors, the U.S. Department of Justice, together with the National Association of District Attorneys (NADA), has established a training facility on the campus of the University of South Carolina in Columbia, called the National Advocacy Center (NAC). All training for the Department of Justice employees takes place at the NAC. The NADA also uses the facility to conduct training that covers the entire gamut of criminal law, including areas such as child pornography and sex trafficking.[10]

Human Trafficking Prosecution Unit (HTPU)

Since the U.S. Attorney General created the Human Trafficking Prosecution Unit (HTPU) within the Criminal Section of the Civil Rights Division in January 2007, the HTPU has played a significant role in coordinating DOJ's human trafficking prosecution programs. The HTPU's mission is to focus the Division's human trafficking expertise and expand its anti-trafficking enforcement programs to further increase human trafficking investigations and prosecutions throughout the nation. The HTPU works to enhance DOJ's investigation and prosecution of significant human trafficking and slavery cases, such as multijurisdictional and multiagency cases and those involving financial crimes. The HTPU also provides training, technical assistance, and outreach initiatives to federal, state, and local law enforcement and nongovernmental organizations (NGOs). This training of local law enforcement has resulted in state and local officers being able to assist in the investigation, arrest, and prosecution of sex-trafficking cases at both the federal and state level. The mechanism through which these combined roles have been accomplished is through the collaboration of state and federal law enforcement officers, and through the creation of multiagency task forces (discussed in Chapter 9). The federal agencies, whose activities and responsibilities are very important in the prosecution of sex trafficking cases, are the Federal Bureau of Investigation (FBI), and the U.S. Immigration and the Customs Enforcement (ICE),[11] and the Human Smuggling and Trafficking Center (HSTC).

Role of the Federal Bureau of Investigation in Assisting Federal Prosecutors in Sex-Trafficking Cases

Special agents in the Civil Rights Unit (CRU) at FBI headquarters and in field offices around the country investigate sex trafficking in the United States. FBI Legal Attachés at U.S. embassies around the world support investigations with international links. In addition, FBI agents in the CRU coordinate with agents in the Organized Crimes and Crimes Against Children Units to ensure that cases initially identified as smuggling cases, Internet crimes against children, and/or sex tourism also are identified for potential human trafficking elements.

On August 30, 2005, the FBI began its Human Trafficking Initiative. The initiative involved the FBI's field offices determining, via a threat assessment, the existence and scope of the trafficking problem in their region, participating in an antitrafficking task force, establishing and maintaining relationships with local NGOs and community organizations, conducting victim-centered investigations, and reporting significant case developments to the CRU. To date, the FBI participates in a significant majority of the Bureau of Justice Administration (BJA)-funded human trafficking task forces, as well as other human trafficking task forces and/or working groups. In 2006, the CRU requested that the 56 field offices complete a Civil Rights Program Threat Assessment. A review and analysis of those assessments formed the basis for the National Human Trafficking Threat Assessment, which has been forwarded to all FBI field offices.

In 2008, the FBI opened 132 human trafficking investigations, made 139 arrests, and filed 60 complaints. In 2008, 129 informations/indictments were filed in FBI human trafficking cases and 94 convictions were obtained. However, the FBI does not participate in every human trafficking investigation.

Figure 10.2 Child prostitute rescued. A 14-year-old girl who was being prostituted is taken into protective police custody after being rescued during a coordinated sting operation. (Photo: Brett Myers/Youth Radio. With permission.)

The Innocence Lost Initiative

In June 2003, the FBI, DOJ's Child Exploitation and Obscenity Section (CEOS), and the National Center for Missing and Exploited Children (NCMEC) launched the Innocence Lost Initiative. Their combined efforts are aimed at addressing the growing problem of domestic sex trafficking of children in the United States (Figure 10.2).

The Innocence Lost Initiative brings together state and federal law enforcement agencies, prosecutors, and social services providers. Since its inception, in 2003, the Initiative has resulted in the development of numerous dedicated task forces and working groups throughout the United States with many (as indicated by the following news story) having achieved considerable success.

In The News

99 Suspected Pimps Arrested
in Child Prostitute Crackdown

by *theGrio*
November 9, 2010 at 12:20 PM

WASHINGTON (AP)—More than five dozen child prostitutes have been found in the last three days as part of a nationwide crackdown on the sexual exploitation of children, the FBI said Monday.

FBI spokesman Jason Pack said 69 children were removed from prostitution and 99 suspected pimps were arrested in 40 cities across 30 states and the District of Columbia. Authorities arrested 785 other adults on a variety of state and local charges, Pack said.

All the children found in the last three days have been placed in protective custody or returned to their families.

The children were found during Operation Cross Country, a three-day roundup targeting child traffickers and pimps. The largest group of child prostitutes, 24, was found in and around Seattle, Washington, in the Northwest, according to the FBI.

FBI executive assistant director Shawn Henry said the children found ranged in age from 12 to 17. Authorities are working with the National Center for Missing and Exploited Children to confirm their identities.

Henry said child prostitutes are often recruited by loose-knit groups that seek out kids who may be involved in drugs or runaways looking for a "responsible adult" to help them.

"There are groups of people out there preying on naïve kids who don't have a good sense of the way of the world," Henry said. "Sometimes there's a threat of force, threats of violence. A lot of these kids operate out of a sense of fear."

Since 2003, when the FBI and the Justice Department launched the Innocence Lost Initiative, about 1,250 child prostitutes have been located and removed from prostitution. (From *The Associated Press.* With permission. Online at: http://thegrio.com/2010/11/09/99-suspected-pimps-arrested-in-fbi-prostitution-crackdown/# (accessed May 30, 2012).)

Role of the U.S. Immigration and Customs Enforcement (ICE) in Assisting Federal Prosecutors in Sex-Trafficking Cases

The role of ICE regarding sex trafficking is straightforward: to disrupt and dismantle domestic and international criminal organizations that engage in sex trafficking by utilizing all ICE authorities and resources in a cohesive global enforcement response. Within ICE, oversight of the enforcement of the 2000 Trafficking Victims Protection Act (TVPA) lies with the Human Smuggling and Trafficking Unit (HSTU), ICE Office of Investigations. The responsibility for sex-trafficking investigations within the Department of Homeland Security (DHS) is under the purview of ICE domestic field offices and attaché offices overseas. The ICE Cyber Crimes Center is responsible for worldwide oversight and management of ICE child sex tourism investigations (discussed in Chapter 6). The responsibility for ensuring victim assistance lies with the 350 collateral-duty ICE victims coordinators. ICE agents coordinate cases with DOJ's Civil Rights Division and CEOS as appropriate.

Human Smuggling and Trafficking Center

The Human Smuggling and Trafficking Center (HSTC) serves as the federal government's intelligence fusion center and information clearinghouse for all federal agencies addressing illicit travel, specifically, human trafficking, human smuggling, and the facilitation of terrorist mobility. By co-locating subject matter experts from the participating federal agencies, the HSTC facilitates the exchange of strategic and tactical information in a coordinated manner that supports the U.S. strategy to investigate and prosecute criminals involved in domestic and international trafficking in persons (TIP).

The HSTC Supporting Antitrafficking Efforts

The HSTC supports antitrafficking efforts by monitoring the internal communication and case management systems of its participating agencies, developing leads, and disseminating information relative to the identification of major international trafficking networks. Daily, the HSTC reviews information for potential human trafficking indicators, performs preliminary checks to follow up on that information, and, when warranted, ensures the information is delivered to the appropriate parties for further investigation. This comprehensive review of law enforcement data and collected intelligence assists not only in the identification of domestic and foreign trafficking victims, but also in coordinating international efforts to disrupt trafficking networks. In addition to providing specific case assistance, disseminating intelligence to the appropriate operational components, and assisting domestic and foreign law enforcement, the HSTC analyzes all-source information to identify trafficking trends and identify ongoing international trafficking events. The HSTC conducts studies and prepares strategic reports for U.S. law enforcement and U.S. policymakers.

Strengthening the Prosecutor's Case: Corroborating Evidence in Sex-Trafficking Cases

In any sex-trafficking case, the ultimate goal is corroboration of victims' testimony. This can be accomplished by obtaining and examining the following records.

Phone Records

Phone records subpoenaed from phone companies can reveal crucial details about the identity and location of victims and suspects. Comparison of phone records also may reveal the structure of the trafficking operation. For example, a witness may insist that she does not know the suspected trafficker, yet her phone records may show hundreds of calls to and from him. Phone numbers in the trafficker's phone records may lead to other victims and other perpetrators. Furthermore, investigation may reveal that the suspect is paying for the victim's phones or the victim is living at the trafficker's address.

One investigator reports having interviewed a young woman shortly after a raid. Her phone rang repeatedly during the interview. With each call, she became increasingly agitated and fearful. The woman told the investigator that it was her concerned boyfriend. She gave the investigator permission to examine her phone, and she learned that the repeated calls were coming from the target, her trafficker.

Pimps, traffickers, and madams frequently call victims after a raid in an attempt to control the information victims share during an interview with law enforcement. Surprisingly, most victims will let the investigator look at their cell phone. A cell phone may provide information that the victim would never willingly share, including the identity of her trafficker. Additionally, the victim's contact list may help to identify locations or persons of interest for future surveillance, including the identities of johns.

Prosecutors, however, must obtain the witness's written consent before examining the contents of her phone. Without this document, the prosecution is open to a defense argument that a phone was unlawfully searched and a motion to suppress what may be critical information.

Transportation Receipts

Train, bus, and plane ticket information, obtained via subpoena, can be used not only to track a victim's travel but also to connect the victim to the sex trafficker and to establish the means by which the trafficker obtained control over the victim. This information can verify the victim's account of the story, but it also can elucidate the way the trafficker exercised control by moving the victim from place to place. Records may reveal the victim's departure and arrival points, the identity of the purchaser, and the method of payment. In a recent case, it was found that the trafficker had purchased a ticket for a victim and later demanded that the victim work off this transportation fee and other debts through commercial sexual acts.

Electronic Evidence

Computer information is vital to any trafficking investigation. Like young adults everywhere, trafficking victims often have accounts on Facebook, MySpace, Twitter, and other social networking Web sites. Regardless of whether these pages were created by a young woman before she is trafficked or by her trafficker to promote her image online, they often reveal important details. Posts may include the victim's name, location, nation of origin, activity updates, names of the individuals with whom the victim interacts, and even contact information. These sites also are excellent sources for photographs of the victim, her friends, and locations frequented by the victim and her acquaintances. On occasion, the victim's user profile may even contain information about, or images of, her trafficker/pimp.

Many traffickers post advertisements on different classified ad Web sites for prostitution-related services. They may even post recruitment materials, such as promotional parties and price ranges, to entice girls to come work for them. Sites, such as craigslist.com and backpage.com, charge a nominal fee for each posting in the "adult services" section.[12] A prosecutor can subpoena information relating to a post, including the internet protocol (IP) address used by the creator, the email and street addresses associated with the ad, and the poster's credit card information. IP addresses often can be connected to a region or even an exact location. Credit card numbers and bank account information can be used to investigate a suspect's financial records for evidence of criminal activity and are highly useful in subsequent forfeiture proceedings.

Traffickers often try to increase the demand for their victims by including links to Web sites, where johns rate their experiences with different prostituted women. While the content may be disturbing to investigators, Web sites, such as BestGFE. com and The Erotic Review (http://www.theeroticreview.com), can provide substantial insight into trafficking operations. In one recent post, a customer indicated that the brothel that was being investigated had moved from one location to another. At that time, law enforcement had detectives conducting surveillance, and this tip prevented many wasted hours observing a wrong location.[13]

Photographs

Case law allows photographs to be used to prove elements of crimes or to defeat potential defenses as long as they are relevant[14] and are not offered to "arouse the emotions of the jury and to prejudice the defendant."[15] Pictures of the victim can demonstrate the extent of a sex-trafficking operation by illustrating that traffickers are advertising their victims on escort or adult services sections of Web sites.

Also, photographs of a victim's injuries can be extremely important in demonstrating that the pimp or madam uses violence. Such photographs not only serve as evidence of the use of force against the victim, but also may be used to defeat a pimp's potential defense of consent or to refute the argument that the victim was simply residing with the pimp. Pictures of a victim's injuries and living conditions may be offered; however, only after a proper introduction from a witness (such as a police officer), who viewed the subject of the photograph and who can testify that the image accurately represents the person or scene depicted at the time it was taken.[16]

Surveillance and Crime Scenes

Surveillance, the observation of locations and individuals, can be used to verify the location of a sex-trafficking operation and the identities of those involved in it. Key indicators of sex trafficking include heavy pedestrian flow, predominantly male foot traffic, and the presence of previously identified individuals near the location. This information is particularly beneficial when trying to understand the business patterns: busy times, frequent visitors, and routine activity.

Crime scene investigations (discussed in Chapter 8) also are helpful, particularly since trafficking investigations often involve police raids that bring police inside locations where crimes have been committed. Items found at sex-trafficking crime scenes also need to be included in the search warrant (this will be discussed in much greater detail later in this chapter).

In the absence of consent to search a location of interest, police officers must ordinarily obtain a search warrant. However, an exception to the warrant requirement for exigent circumstances may be applicable.[17] The **exigent circumstances** exception recognizes that a warrantless entry by law enforcement officials may be legal when there is a compelling need for official action and no time to get a warrant. The exception covers several common situations including that a minor on location is in danger, danger of flight or escape, and loss or destruction of evidence.[18]

Wiretaps

Wiretapping is a significant tool for building trafficking cases. By allowing a third party to monitor telephone or Internet conversations covertly, wiretapping enables prosecutors to listen to conversations between a sex trafficker and those involved in the crime. Access to these private conversations grants lawyers insight into the dynamics of trafficking relationships. The intercepted conversations may supplement or even replace the need for a victim's testimony.

For example, in some states, wiretap laws require that a particularly targeted person has committed, is committing, or is about to commit a particularly designated crime.[19] Sex trafficking is among the designated offenses for which wiretapping is permissible.[20] Furthermore, there must be reason to believe that information about a crime will be obtained from the targeted conversation.[21] The applicant also must show that other investigative measures have either not worked, are unlikely to work, or are too dangerous to attempt.[22]

Ascertaining that each of these elements necessary for a wiretap exists is important because without them, there is a danger that the wiretap will be a waste of time and resources, that the risks outweigh the potential gains, or that an innocent person will be wiretapped frivolously. Prewiretap research might include sending detectives into the field to observe the location, interviewing victims and/or individuals arrested at the location, doing surveillance, and corroborating the phone number of the location with prostitution ads on Web sites such as craigslist and backpage.com.

Wiretaps may provide a good deal of information about the trafficking operation, the condition of the victim, or measures taken by traffickers to control the victim. Wiretaps also might intercept conversations with drug providers or record a trafficker inducing a victim into commercial activity by making false statements, demands regarding debt repayment, or threats to harm the victim or her family members. Wiretaps allow prosecutors to avoid risks to victims or compromises to the secrecy of their investigations that direct contact with victims or traffickers might entail. An excellent tool for getting a plea, and thereby avoiding the need for victim testimony, is playing for the defendants the tape catching them in the act, in which case their defense is sunk.[23]

Interpreters

Sex-trafficking cases often require the use of interpreters. For example, during a raid, prosecutors and their investigators may encounter many non-English speaking individuals. To ensure access to statements that could be important evidence during trial, it is of critical importance that interpreters are available from the onset of the investigation. When an interpreter is used to communicate with a defendant, victim, or witness, the interpreter must provide an affidavit of translation, because testimony by the investigator about what the interpreter said that the interviewee said is hearsay.[24]

Business Records

Business records are often key pieces of evidence, but a prosecutor wishing to introduce records, documents, or ledgers as a business record must lay a proper foundation. For example, many states have laws that require that the records be entered in a systematic way, at or near the time the information was received, by someone with knowledge, in the ordinary course of business, and that it was in the regular practice of business to make such entries.[25] Traffickers often keep ledgers with financial data and personal information about their victims or patrons that qualify as business records. These ledgers may contain victims' names and telephone numbers in addition to the names and numbers of customers, and they may be used as evidence to show that the trafficker or pimp was acquainted with the victims or buyers. They also can be used to demonstrate that the customers were committing the crime of patronizing a prostitute.[26]

Expert Witness Testimony

Generally, in many states, expert testimony is admissible when the subject matter is professional, technical, or beyond the scope or comprehension of an average juror.[27] The activities of prostitution rings, the dynamics between traffickers and the women and girls they prostitute, and the complexities of victim trauma are likely to be foreign to average jurors and, thus, suitable for expert testimony.

Expert witnesses can testify generally about psychological phenomena like traumatic bonding, also known as Stockholm syndrome (discussed in Chapter 3). They also can provide insight into the effects of sex trafficking on the psychology of individual victims. While expert testimony cannot be used to prove the occurrence of specific events, the expert's personal observations and interactions with the victim may be used to explain the victim's psychological state. For example, a social worker certified by the court as an expert in counseling sex-trafficking victims may explain to the jury why a victim stayed with the sex trafficker or why a victim's response to law enforcement may have evolved over time. Expert testimony may help jurors understand the dynamics of exploitation and why a sex-trafficking victim might behave in a manner contrary to common sense expectations, especially during the initial encounter with the victim.

Additional Resources That Can Be Used by Prosecutors at the Federal and State Level in Sex-Trafficking Cases

In order for prosecutors at both the state and federal level to be effective, they must be aware of the resources that are available to them and avail themselves of these to maximize the possibility for gaining a conviction of sex traffickers. Many of these resources are identified in Table 10.1.

TABLE 10.1
**Additional Resources That Can Be Used by Prosecutors
at the Federal and State Level in Sex-Trafficking Cases**

Topic	Resource Title	Description
Civil Remedies	*A Guide for Legal Advocates Providing Services to Victims of Trafficking*	In 2004, the U.S. Conference of Catholic Bishops Migration and Legal Services, Catholic Legal Immigration Network, and the Legal Aid Foundation of Los Angeles developed this resource to provide detailed direction for legal advocates working with victims of human trafficking.
	Civil Litigation on Behalf of Human Trafficking Victims	Created by the Southern Poverty Law Center in 2008, this resource is an introduction to basic litigation tools for attorneys representing trafficked clients.
Prosecuting Human Trafficking	*Lawyer's Manual on Human Trafficking: Pursuing Justice for Victims*	This publication, developed through the Supreme Court of the State of New York, Appellate Division, First Department, Judicial Committee on Women in the Courts, provides information, direction, and a variety of resources for working with victims and prosecuting cases of both sex and labor trafficking.
	Prosecuting Human Trafficking: Lessons Learned and Promising Practices	This research paper issued by the National Institute of Justice provides results on a study that examined the effects of existing federal and state legislation from the perspective of the prosecution and identified critical challenges and barriers to successful prosecution of cases.

TABLE 10.1 (continued)
Additional Resources That Can Be Used by Prosecutors
at the Federal and State Level in Sex-Trafficking Cases

Topic	Resource Title	Description
Prosecutor and Legal Service Specific	*Working With Interpreters Outside of the Courtroom: A Guide for Legal Services Providers*	Created by Ayuda, an organization that works directly with victims, this resource provides tips and direction for legal service advocates working with interpreters.
Working with Victims of Labor Trafficking	*Employment Law Guide: Minimum Wage and Overtime Pay*	This resource created by the U.S. Department of Labor provides details on who is covered under the Fair Labor Standards Act in regard to minimum wage and overtime pay.
	Employment Law Guide: Work Authorization for non-U.S. Citizens: Temporary Agricultural Workers (H2A visas)	This resource created by the U.S. Department of Labor provides details on who is eligible for an H2A visa, what is required to obtain the visa, and the employee rights of H2A visa recipients.

Source: Anti-Human Trafficking Task Force Strategy and Operations e-Guide, 2005, pp. 89–90. Online at: https://www.ovcttac.gov/ TaskForceGuide/EGuide/Default.aspx (accessed April 15, 2012).

Federal and State Prosecution in Sex-Trafficking Cases

One of the decisions that has to be made in sex-trafficking cases is whether a prosecution will be conducted in the federal courts or the state courts. For example, the ability to work with both federal and state prosecution varies from district to district. If a case crosses judicial circuit boundaries within the state system, it may be easier to work with the U.S. Attorney's Office (USAO). However, often the process for obtaining subpoenas, search warrants, and Title III (wiretaps, computer monitoring) is simpler and quicker through the State Prosecutor's Office than the USAO.

Sometimes federal agents may prefer that local law enforcement make a probable cause arrest on state charges in order to hold the suspect until the USAO can obtain a federal warrant. Thus, an investigation may begin with state charges, which might also later include federal charges filed in federal court.

A state search warrant can be obtained based solely on a federal felony charge, as advised through the USAO and, if investigative assistance is needed in another jurisdiction, it may be easier and faster to contact that local law enforcement rather than request federal assistance.

Considerations for Additional or Alternative Charges

If a case cannot be prosecuted as a sex-trafficking case, it may be possible to prosecute using other federal charges, such as harboring or smuggling, and/or the Mann Act (discussed in Chapter 2), which involves transporting persons across state borders for the purpose of prostitution. State charges also may be used, such as false imprisonment or sexual battery. However, federal violations can sometimes provide more severe penalties.[28]

Thus, in the final analysis, there is no one right answer as to where a sex-trafficking case should be prosecuted. It depends on the nature of the violation as well as the working relationship and experience level of state and federal prosecutors in the area where the offense has occurred.

The Search and Seizure of Evidence in Sex-Trafficking Cases

It is imperative that law enforcement officers be familiar with the rules of evidence as they relate to search and seizures in sex-trafficking investigations. A failure to understand and comply with the various provisions could result in critical

Figure 10.3 After obtaining a search warrant, investigators retrieved physical evidence in a sex-trafficking-related death case. The photo shows New York City Police Department authorities carrying a container filled with cement and the body of an infant born to an enslaved sex-trafficking victim. The mother of the baby, an illegal immigrant from Mexico, was forced into prostitution. Her pimp viciously abused her and barred her from getting medical care for the infant when he fell ill. The baby died shortly thereafter and was buried in the backyard after being encased in cement. (From: Oates for News. Online at: http://articles.nydailynews.com/2009-11-26/news/17938497_1_ trafficking-ring-trafficking-charges-woman)

evidence not being admitted into the courts for prosecution (Figure 10.3).

The evolution of the law of **search and seizure** illustrates the relationship between federal and state court systems and between the Bill of Rights and its application to the states through the due process clause of the Fourteenth Amendment.[29]

Under early English common law, an illegal search and seizure that produced incriminating evidence was allowed, and the evidence obtained was admissible in court. Surprisingly, federal law enforcement officers in the United States were permitted to follow the same rule until 1914. Up to that time, the search and seizure practices of federal officials had not been scrutinized in light of the wording of the Fourth Amendment.

Weeks v. United States 1914

In 1914, the case of *Weeks v. United States*[30] was decided by the U.S. Supreme Court. Weeks was charged by federal agents with using the mail for transporting materials that represented chances in a lottery. After his arrest for this federal offense, Weeks' room was searched twice without the authority of a valid search warrant. But Weeks had been arrested at his place of employment, not his home. During the search, the agents found and seized various incriminating papers and articles. This evidence was admitted at his trial for the federal violation, and Weeks was convicted. On appeal to the U.S. Supreme Court, the Court established what became known as the "Federal Exclusionary Rule." The Court ruled that any evidence unreasonably obtained by federal law enforcement officers could no longer be admissible in federal prosecutions. The Court made it quite clear that, because this was a federal case, the decision was applicable only to federal law enforcement officers and federal courts and was in no way applicable to the states. But this decision, as do many Supreme Court decisions, left a number of unanswered questions. Out of one question arose what has been called the "Silver Platter Doctrine."

The Silver Platter Rule

The *Weeks* decision prohibited federal officers from illegally seizing evidence, but it did not prevent law enforcement officers of the states from illegally seizing the evidence and handing it over to federal agents on a "silver platter" for use in federal courts. This method of circumventing the Federal Exclusionary Rule remained unchallenged until 1960. That year, in the case of *Elkins v. United States*, the Supreme Court prohibited the introduction in federal courts of all illegally seized evidence obtained by state officers in violation of the Fourth Amendment,[31] which deals with the right against unreasonable searches and seizures.

After the *Weeks* decision, very few states adopted their own exclusionary rule applicable within their own state. It was not until 1949 that a serious attempt was made to seek mandatory application of the exclusionary rule to the states through the due process clause of the Fourteenth Amendment.

Wolf v. Colorado 1949

In *Wolf v. Colorado,*[32] the defendant, a physician, was charged with having performed abortions that were, with very few exceptions, illegal at that time. Based on suspicion of similar prior offenses, officers searched Wolf's office, arrested him, and seized certain documents that were later admitted into trial. Wolf appealed his conviction contending that the unreasonable search and seizure was a denial of due process under the Fourteenth Amendment, as it would be under the Fourth Amendment had he been in federal court. The Supreme Court held that unreasonable searches and seizures by state officials in state cases did not constitute a denial of Fourteenth Amendment due process, but added that the Court did have the authority to rule otherwise if the justices so desired. The interesting point in this case seemed to be that the Court was giving the states fair warning that they disapproved of unreasonable searches and seizures by state authorities and that sooner or later they would rule in favor of incorporating the Fourth Amendment protection in the due process clause of the Fourteenth Amendment. Many states took the hint, but others did not.

Mapp v. Ohio 1961

By 1961, only 18 states had not adopted an exclusionary rule. In that year, the warning that the Supreme Court had given 12 years earlier in the *Wolf* case came to pass. In May 1957, three Cleveland police officers arrived at the residence of Dollree Mapp with information that a person who was wanted for questioning in a recent bombing was hiding out in her home and that there was a large amount of gambling paraphernalia being hidden in the home. The officers knocked on the door and demanded entrance, but Ms. Mapp, after telephoning her attorney, refused to admit them without a search warrant. The officers advised their headquarters of the situation and undertook a surveillance of the house. Some three hours later, the officers, with reinforcements, again sought entrance. When Ms. Mapp did not come to the door immediately, one of the doors was forcibly opened and the officers gained entry. Ms. Mapp demanded to see the search warrant. One of the officers held up a paper that he claimed was the search warrant. She grabbed the paper and stuffed it down the front of her dress. A struggle ensued in which the officers recovered the piece of paper and hand-cuffed Ms. Mapp for her "belligerency" in resisting the attempt to recover the "warrant." A subsequent widespread search of the entire premises disclosed obscene materials. Ms. Mapp was convicted for possession of these materials. No search warrant was ever produced at the trial.

Following Ms. Mapp's conviction and the denial of her appeals in the state courts, her case was appealed to the U.S. Supreme Court. *Mapp v. Ohio,*[33] decided in 1961, established the rule that any evidence unreasonably searched and seized would no longer by admissible in any court—state or federal. The exclusionary rule was now applicable in all courts at all levels.

Among the many unanswered questions created by the *Mapp* decision, the crucial question revolved around the definition of the word **unreasonable**. It did not take the state courts long to find the loophole. In order to avoid applying the decision in the *Mapp* case to instances arising in state courts, state officials merely called previously unreasonable searches and seizures reasonable searches. Because no standards had been set for determining what constitutes a reasonable or unreasonable search, many of the state courts felt free to make their own determination on this issue. In effect, *Mapp* had little impact on these states. However, within two years of the *Mapp* decision, the Supreme Court had the opportunity to rule on this matter. The Court held in *Ker v. California*[34] that the state court judges were still free to determine the reasonableness of searches, but that in making those determinations they would now be guided by the same standards as had been followed in the federal courts, which were established in the line of cases decided since the *Weeks* case in 1914. In essence, the Court said that states would be held to federal standards in search and seizure matters.

Figure 10.4 Implementation of the exclusionary rule in state court. Dollree Mapp. In 1961, the U.S. Supreme Court established a rule that any evidence unreasonably searched and seized would no longer be admissible in any court, state or federal. This became known as the "exclusionary rule." (From: http://www.clevelandmemory.org/legallandmarks/mapp/people.html (accessed April 15, 2012).)

The long line of cases evolving since *Mapp* and *Ker* have essentially revolved around the single issue of what constitutes a reasonable search in instances where law enforcement officers act with or without a warrant (Figure 10.4).

Legal Searches and Seizures

As is true for arrests, the Fourth Amendment also recognizes searches and seizures only by government agents under the authority of a warrant. The U.S. Supreme Court recognizes judicially created exceptions. Thus, legal searches and seizures can be made:

- when a warrant has been issued
- with consent
- incident to an arrest

- of a motor vehicle
- when an emergency (exigent circumstances) exists
- to conduct an inventory
- at border crossing

Search with a Warrant

A **search warrant** is a written order, in the name of the state, signed by a judicial officer, exercising proper authority, and directing a law enforcement officer to search for certain specific property and bring it before the court. To be valid, the warrant must be signed by one who is authorized to sign. Normally, this is a judicial officer. In rare instances, state law may allow a prosecutor or law enforcement officer to sign the warrant to expedite the process, but only after the facts and circumstances have been reviewed over the telephone by a judicial officer, being later subject to that judicial officer's signature. In no case is a prosecutor or law enforcement officer permitted to sign a warrant without that judicial review. The independent impartial review is what provides the warrant with validity.

Probable Cause

A warrant to search must be based on probable cause. In this instance, probable cause can best be defined as facts and circumstances that would lead a reasonable person to believe that the place to be searched and the things to be seized are to be found. The probable cause is established by a written affidavit prepared by the law enforcement officer/investigator, stating all those known facts and circumstances. As is true for an arrest warrant, probable cause in sex-trafficking cases may be established by any number of sources, including information supplied by informants, trafficking victims, customers, and so forth. Once probable cause is established the affidavit is presented to a judicial officer, who independently evaluates it and, if she or he finds it sufficient, issues the warrant. As is pretty evident from the process described so far, probable cause must be established before the warrant is issued. Anything found as a result of the service of the warrant cannot be used to establish the probable cause.

Elements of the Search Warrant

The search warrant must particularly describe the place to be searched. Although the Constitution does not define the word *particularly*, the description must be sufficient to distinguish the place from all others. Normally, one might think of a building on a piece of property as a place to be searched. Using the legal description is not necessary; however, a street address may not be sufficient. There are many appellate cases involving invalid warrants because the address failed to distinguish between two identical numbers on houses on Main Street because one was on North Main and the other on South Main. In addition, numbers may be missing from the house or mailbox, causing problems. What happens when a warrant is issued for 999 Main Street, but the numbers have come loose and flipped over at 666 Main Street and now read 999? Have investigators ever served a warrant at the wrong location? The appellate cases are full of examples. The warrant should contain information, such as the color of the house, the type of floor plan (e.g., ranch-style home); apartment on the third floor, east side of a brownstone tenement; cream colored, vinyl siding, one-story house with green trim, green shutters, bars on the windows; and so forth.

The phrase *particularly describe* also applies to the things to be seized. This governs the extent of the search. The search for and seizure of items typically found in sex-trafficking cases can be pretty extensive. Thus, a carefully crafted search warrant would permit the search of closets, under beds, in dresser drawers, in medicine cabinets, and in kitchen cupboards—and anything found, even evidence of other crimes, may be properly seized and considered admissible (Table 10.2).

Normally, investigators should include in their affidavits, in support of a search warrant, the justification for searching persons found at the place where the warrant is to be executed

TABLE 10.2
Items Typically Included in a Search Warrant for Sex-Trafficking Cases

• Atlas maps	• Gas receipts
• Bed linens	• Journals
• Blood stains	• Large sums of cash
• Bank records	• Leases/Rental agreements
• Brothel tickets	• Log books
• Business cards	• Lubricants
• Calendars	• Luggage tags
• Cameras	• Money-gram receipts
• Cell phones	• Passports
• Computers	• Phone logs
• Condom wrappers	• Photographs
• Condoms	• Residential and cellular phone bills
• Credit card receipts	• Telephone bills
• Drug paraphernalia	• Travel tickets
• Employment records	• Trick book
• Gas/Electric bills	• Victim accounting records

Source: Introduction to Human Trafficking, Student Manual, St. Petersburg College, Florida Regional Community Policing Institute, 2006, p. 44.

and the search conducted. In the absence of such authority in the warrant, persons found on the scene may not be searched unless they are first lawfully arrested.

Once issued, a warrant must be executed within whatever time limits the law requires; time of day/night limits are applicable. In some instances, the warrant may specify that it may be served at nighttime if the probable cause supporting the warrant can justify that the specific criminal activity only occurs at night. Until recently, state laws required officers/investigators executing warrants to knock, announce their purpose and the fact that they were in possession of a warrant, and giving the occupants a reasonable time to answer and open the door. In 2006, the Supreme Court ruled in *Hudson v. Michigan*[35] that violation of the knock and announce requirement for the service of a search warrant will no longer result in the suppression of evidence found during execution of the search warrant. The Court said the social cost of applying the exclusionary rule to knock and announce violations was considerable.

During the search, particularly if several investigators are involved, one investigator should be designated the property custodian. A detailed record must be kept of each piece of evidence, with a specific description, where it was found, and by whom. (For a more detailed discussion, see Chapter 8.) This list then becomes part of the return on the warrant that must be brought back and presented to the judge for review. It, of course, also becomes part of the case file.

In 2005, in *Muehler v. Mena*,[36] the Supreme Court held that officers executing a search warrant of a house, where they were seeking weapons and evidence of gang membership in the wake of a drive-by shooting, acted reasonably by detaining the occupants of the house in handcuffs during the search, especially because there were only two officers to watch over four people.

Search with Consent

One of the most common situations arising today is when a uniformed officer, in encountering a citizen during a traffic stop or other routine activity, asks the person if he/she has any weapons or drugs on his/her person or in the vehicle. Sometimes the person says yes, and that might lead to an immediate arrest. Often the person says no, and the officer may then ask if he/she can search the person and/or the vehicle. If the person gives affirmative consent, the search may be conducted. If the person denies consent, which he/she has the right to do, no search may be made unless there is probable cause to conduct a search under one of the other exceptions to the warrant requirement. A refusal to allow a search, standing alone, does not constitute probable cause to justify any further action.

The crux of a consent search is that the consent must be voluntarily given. It cannot be based on intimidation or threats of any kind.

A person may give consent to the search of his/her home, but in the case where there are roommates living in the same house or apartment and each has his/her own bedroom, an occupant may give consent to the search only of his/her private room and any area shared in common by the roommates, such as the kitchen or living room.

Once consent is given for search of a home, car, office, or any other place, it may be withdrawn at any time by the person who had the authority and gave the consent. When consent is withdrawn, the search must stop. Any incriminating evidence found after consent is withdrawn is illegally seized and is not admissible.

It is always wise to get documentation of the consent to search.

Search Incident to Arrest

The courts have regularly recognized the right of law enforcement officers to search people who have been arrested without a warrant. Such searches are justified for officer safety and to preserve evidence.[37] In 1969, the U.S. Supreme Court limited the scope of a search when it ruled in *Chimel v. California*[38] that a warrantless search of the defendant's entire house, following his lawful arrest in the house on a burglary charge, was unreasonable. This case set the benchmark for searches incident to a valid arrest by holding that such searches may be made of the person arrested and the area under his/her immediate control from which he or she might obtain a weapon or destroy evidence. Initially, searches were reasonable only if conducted in conformity with *Chimel*. Over the years, case law has expanded the allowable area of search following a legal arrest, particularly as applied to automobile searches, but as to searches of an arrestee's home, *Chimel* is still followed closely.

Search of a Motor Vehicle

The search of a motor vehicle, sometimes referred to as the automobile exception to the requirement that a search be conducted with a warrant, really involves two distinct legal issues under modern law. The first can be traced back to a 1925 Supreme Court case. In *Carroll v. United States*,[39] the Court created the "movable vehicle" rule. The Court held that if there was sufficient probable cause to get a warrant, but, because the vehicle was movable, it might be gone if time were taken to get a warrant, a warrantless search was justified. In this case, the vehicle was moving and contained bootleg whiskey during Prohibition. The search of the entire vehicle, including the trunk was justified in this case.

A vehicle search is not reasonable if conducted pursuant to stopping a vehicle for a traffic violation and writing a citation. A citation is not an arrest and no right to search arises. Does the same rule hold true if an officer issues a summons (sometimes called a Notice to Appear)?

Generally, the answer is yes; but consider the case of *Virginia v. Moore*,[40] decided by the Supreme Court in 2008. Moore was arrested for driving on a suspended license. He was searched and cocaine was found on his person. He was charged with the possession of cocaine and convicted. The kink in this story is that Virginia law specified that when officers stopped the vehicle Moore was driving, he should have been given a summons. Had that been done, there would not have been a search. However, when they arrested him instead, they searched incident to the arrest. The Supreme Court held that police did not violate the Fourth Amendment by arresting Moore instead of following state law requiring the issuance of a summons, thereby making the search and seizure reasonable.

Conducting an Inventory

Law enforcement agencies not only have the right but also the obligation to inventory property taken from a person arrested. This includes property taken from the person and from their presence, such as a motor vehicle. The inventory is done for the purpose of protecting the property of the person arrested and documenting what was found with a receipt given to the person arrested. In this manner, law enforcement can prevent accusations of stealing an offender's money or property. Similarly, law enforcement should inventory a vehicle that was impounded pursuant to an arrest. This includes the contents of the trunk. If contraband or evidence of a crime are found by virtue of a valid inventory search, the results are admissible. To justify admissibility of the fruits of an inventory search, the agency must have a standing policy that specifies the inventory in all cases. If such a policy does not exist, but this particular vehicle was inventoried, it will be ruled a pretext for a warrantless search and will be deemed unreasonable.

Plain View Seizures

If an investigator/officer is lawfully in a place and sees contraband or evidence in plain view, the investigator may seize the evidence, and it will be admissible. For example, if in a rescue operation officers observed drugs, drug paraphernalia, and/or illegal weapons at the location, they can seize them and use them as evidence in court even though they may not have been specified as items to be searched for in a search warrant.

Fruits of the Poisonous Tree Doctrine

A final point is necessary to fully comprehend the consequences of an unreasonable search and seizure. The **fruits of the poisonous tree doctrine** provides that evidence obtained from an unreasonable search and seizure cannot be used as the basis for learning about or collecting new admissible evidence not known about before. Not only is the evidence obtained from the unreasonable search and seizure inadmissible, any evidence resulting from the unreasonably seized evidence is also tainted and is not admissible as fruits of the poisonous tree. This doctrine resulted from a 1963 decision of the high court in which a confession was obtained from the defendant after evidence was produced that had been obtained unreasonably.[41]

Glossary

Department of Justice, Civil Rights Division: In collaboration with the U.S. Attorney's Office nationwide, this division has the principal responsibility for prosecuting sex-trafficking crimes, except for cases involving sex trafficking of children.

Deferred adjudication: This process requires the defendant to plead guilty, but the trial judge defers imposing a sentence of guilt as long as the defendant meets certain agreed upon conditions. If the defendant fails to meet these conditions, the judge may then impose the sentence that would have been imposed if a plea agreement had not been reached.

Exigent circumstances: This exception recognizes that a warrantless entry by law enforcement officials may be legal when there is a compelling need for official action and there is no time to get a warrant.

FBI Civil Rights Unit (CRU): Located at FBI headquarters, and in field offices around the country, they investigate sex trafficking in the United States.

Fruits of the poisonous tree doctrine: Evidence obtained from an unreasonable search and seizure cannot be used for a basis for learning about or collecting new admissible evidence not known about before.

Human Smuggling and Trafficking Center: This center serves as the federal government's intelligence fusion and information clearinghouse for all federal agencies addressing illicit travel, specifically human trafficking, human smuggling, and the facilitation of terrorist mobility.

Innocence Lost Initiative: A program that brings together state and federal law enforcement agencies, prosecutors, and social service providers. The Initiative has resulted in the development of numerous dedicated task forces and working groups throughout the United States.

Mapp v. Ohio 1961: The U.S. Supreme Court established a rule that any evidence unreasonably searched and seized would no longer be admissible in court, state or federal, thus making the exclusionary rule applicable in all courts at all levels.

National Advocacy Center: This is a training center developed by the U.S. Department of Justice on the campus of the University of South Carolina in Columbia to train newly appointed, inexperienced prosecutors.

Nolo contendere: This is a plea of guilty or no contest.

Nol. pros.: The abbreviation for *nolo prosecuri*.

Nolo prosequi: This occurs when a prosecutor refuses to proceed with prosecution even after charges are filed or a grand jury indictment is in the process.

Plain view seizures: Applies to law enforcement officers who are lawfully in a place, observe contraband or evidence in plain view, and seize the evidence. Even though the item may not be listed on the search warrant, it can be admitted as evidence in court.

Prosecuting attorney: The legal representative of a state or the federal government with sole responsibility for bringing criminal charges.

Prosecutorial diversion: This is the middle ground between a prosecutor dropping a case and going forward with a full criminal trial.

Search warrant: It is the written order in the name of the government signed by a judicial officer exercising proper authority and directing a law enforcement officer to search for certain specific property and bring it before the court.

Silver Platter Doctrine: The *Weeks v. US 1914* decision by the U.S. Supreme Court prohibited federal officers from illegally seizing evidence, but did not prevent law enforcement officers of the states from illegally seizing the evidence and handing it over to federal agents on a "silver platter" for use in federal court.

U.S. Immigration and Customs Enforcement Cyber-Crimes Center: The center responsible for worldwide oversight and management of ICE child sex tourism investigations.

Weeks v. United States 1914: This ruling of the U.S. Supreme Court established what became known as the federal exclusionary rule and disallowed any evidence unreasonably obtained by federal law enforcement officers to be admissible in a federal prosecution.

Wolf v. Colorado 1949: The Supreme Court held that unreasonable searches and seizures by state officials in state cases did not constitute a denial of Fourteenth Amendment due process, but added that the court did have the authority to rule otherwise if justices desired.

Review Questions

1. What are the prosecutor's specific functions?
2. What does the due process model emphasize as it relates to labeling a citizen as a defendant in a criminal action?
3. What type of discretion does a prosecutor have as it relates to initiating criminal litigation?
4. What does it mean when a case is stopped by a process called *nolle prosequi*?
5. How does the American Bar Association describe the prosecutor's duty?
6. Which division of the U.S. Department of Justice handles the prosecution of sex-trafficking cases of a minor in child sex tourism?
7. What is the mission of the Innocence Lost Initiative?
8. What is the role of the U.S. Immigration and Customs Enforcement (ICE) in sex-trafficking cases?
9. What is the role of the Human Smuggling and Trafficking Center (HSTC)?
10. What resources are available that will strengthen the prosecutor's case and corroborate evidence in sex-trafficking cases?
11. Why would federal agents sometimes prefer that local law enforcement make a probable cause arrest on state charges in sex-trafficking cases?

12. What was the significance of the U.S. Supreme Court decision in *Weeks* v. *United States, 1914*?
13. What was the significance of the U.S. Supreme Court decision in *Wolf* v. *Colorado*, 1949?
14. What was the significance of the U.S. Supreme Court decision in *Mapp* v. *Ohio, 1961*?
15. What is the fruit of the poisonous tree doctrine?

Endnotes

1. Lauren Hersh, "Sex Trafficking Investigations and Prosecutions," in *Lawyer's Manual on Human Trafficking*, ed. Jill Laurie Goodman & Dorchen A. Leidholdt. Supreme Court of the State of New York, Appellate Division, First Department New York State Judicial Committee on Women Courts, pp. 256–257. Online at: http://www.nycourts.gov/ip/womeninthecourts/LMHT.pdf (accessed June 7, 2012).
2. Leonard Territo, James B. Halsted, & Max L. Bromley, *Crime and Justice in America—A Human Perspective*, 6th ed. (Upper Saddle River, NJ: Pearson, 2003), 283–289.
3. The state of Florida provides a good example of how this office of Statewide Prosecutor works. For example, in Florida, the Statewide Prosecutor is appointed by the Attorney General from a list of nominees selected by the Florida Supreme Court, Judicial Nominating Commission. The Statewide Prosecutor then serves a term of four years and acts as the agency head for eight offices stationed throughout the state. The Office of Statewide Prosecutor in Florida was created by the voters in 1986 to counter the expansion of crime in the state. For more information on the State of Florida, Office of Statewide Prosecutor, see online: http://myfloridalegal.com/osp
4. Advisory Committee on the Prosecution and Defense Functions, *Prosecution Functions and Defense Functions* (New York: American Bar Association, 1970), 17–134.
5. Ibid.
6. G. Cole, "The Decision to Prosecute," *Law and Society Review* 3 (1983), 331–343.
7. M. Lewis, W. Bundy, & J. Hague, *An Introduction to the Courts and Judicial Process* (Englewood Cliffs, N.J.: Prentice Hall, 1978).

8. *United States v. Armstrong*, et al., 517 U.S. 456 687 (1996).
9. American Bar Association, *Standards for Criminal Justice: Prosecution Functions and Defense Functions* (Washington, D.C.: American Bar Association, 1993), 18–19.
10. Information provided by Robert E. O'Neill, U.S. Attorney, Middle District of Florida, in personal correspondence, June 1, 2012.
11. Attorney General's Annual Report to Congress and Assessment of U.S. Government Activities to Combat Trafficking in Persons Fiscal Year 2008, June 2009, pp. 35–42.
12. For further information on the posting of adult services, see Craigslist, Backpage, and The Boston Phoenix.
13. Ibid.
14. *People v. Pobliner,* 32 N.Y. 2d 356, 359 (1973).
15. *People v. Wood,* 79 N.Y. 2d 958, 959 (1992).
16. *People v. Carranza,* 306 AD.2d 351 (2d Dept 2003) (mem).
17. Ibid.
18. *United States v. Halloway*, 290 F.3d 1331 (C.A. 11) (Ala.) (2002). See also *Johnson v. United States*, 333 U.S. 10, 14-15 (1948), listing situations falling within exigent circumstances exception.
19. N.Y. CPL § 700.15 (2).
20. N.Y. CPL § 700.15 (8).
21. N.Y. CPL § 700.15 (3).
22. N.Y. CPL § 700.15 (4).
23. Hersh, "Sex Trafficking Investigations and Prosecutions," 267.
24. *People v. Chin Sing,* 242 N.Y. 419 (1926).
25. N.Y. CPLR § 4518(a).
26. Hersh, "Sex Trafficking Investigations and Prosecutions," 268.
27. *DeLong v. Eerie*, 60 N.Y. 2d 296, 307 (1983).
28. Attorney General's Annual Report to Congress and Assessment of U.S. Government Activities to Combat Trafficking in Persons Fiscal Year 2008, pp. 35–42. Online at: http://www.state.gov/j/tip/rls/reports/2009/125631.htm (accessed January 24, 2013).
29. Charles R. Swanson et al., *Criminal Investigation*, 11th ed. (New York: McGraw Hill, 2012), 25–34.
30. 232 U.S. 383 (1914).
31. *Elkins v. United States*, 364 U.S. 206 (1960).
32. 338 U.S. 25 (1949).
33. 367 U.S. 643 (1961).
34. 374 U.S. 10 (1963).
35. *Hudson v. Michigan*, 126 S.Ct. 2159 (2006).
36. *Muehler v. Mena*, 544 U.S. 93, 125 S.Ct. 1465 (2005).

37. *United States v. Robinson*, 414 U.S. 218 (1973).
38. 395 U.S. 752 (1969).
39. 267 U.S. 132 (1925).
40. 553 U.S. 164; 128 S.Ct. 1598; 170 L.Ed.2d 559 (2008).
41. *Wong Sun v. United States*, 371 U.S. 471 (1963).

Appendix: Nongovernmental Organizations and U.S. Government Agencies Available to Assist Sex-Trafficking Victims

NONGOVERNMENTAL ORGANIZATIONS AVAILABLE TO ASSIST SEX-TRAFFICKING VICTIMS

National Service Providers for Commercially Sexually Exploited Individuals

City	Organization	Description	Contact Information	Web Site
		ARIZONA		
Phoenix	Arizona League to End Regional Trafficking (ALERT)	ALERT assists trafficked persons by providing immediate shelter and food for victims and their families, as well as immediate medical attention. ALERT provides assistance in applying for U.S. immigration benefits, or repatriation to the victim's home country, if desired. ALERT further offers mental health counseling and treatment, as well as a bank of on-call translators trained in the issue of trafficking in persons. Through their partners, they also offer long-term assistance finding secure housing and achieving self-sufficiency through employment.	602-433-2441	www.traffickingaz.org

Phoenix	DIGNITY House	Catholic Charities Community Services recognizes prostituted women as victims of sex trafficking and helps them to escape "the life" through DIGNITY (Developing Individual Growth and New Independence Through Yourself). We reach out to sex-trafficked women on the streets and in the jails. Many of the DIGNITY staff have escaped the life and know how to find these women and how to gain their trust.	602-258-2785	www.catholiccharitiesaz.org

CALIFORNIA

| Alameda | The Dreamcatcher Youth Shelter (Foster Youth Alliance) | Alameda Family Services is a human services organization, active in Alameda and the East Bay, whose programs improve the emotional, psychological, and physical health of children, youth, and families. Dream Catcher Youth Shelter is a program of Alameda Family Services that provides emergency shelter to youth ages 13 through 18. Other services include case management for CSEC individuals. | 510-629-6300 | www.fosteryouthalliance. org/partners/dreamcatcher.htm |

continued

National Service Providers for Commercially Sexually Exploited Individuals (continued)

City	Organization	Description	Contact Information	Web Site
Los Angeles	Coalition to Abolish Slavery and Trafficking (CAST)	CAST's social services goal is to help clients recover from years of abuse and trauma so they may become self-sufficient, thriving members of our community. These services include: access to food, shelter, and job training; intensive case management (information, assistance and legal education; mental health and wellness services (counseling, art therapy, peer support); alternative non-Western healing therapies that are culturally appropriate; education and life skills training (English as a Second Language, computer and financial literacy). Other services include shelter and legal advocacy.	213-365-1906	www.castla.org

Los Angeles	Children of the Night	Assisting children between the ages of 11 and 17 who are forced to engage in survival sex. Services include shelter, rescue from pimps, counseling, GED preparation, ticket to go home, medical appointments, and court appearances.	818-908-4474	www.childrenofthenight.org
Oakland	Banteay Srei	Offers court advocacy, family services (they have networked with organizations that can help translate for Mien-, Vietnamese-, and Cambodian-speaking families) and referrals for housing, health services, and peer services. Due to the high intensity and amount of time we dedicate to working with our young women, can only work with young Southeast Asian women and girls.	Asian Health Services c/o Banteay Srei 818 Webster St. Oakland, CA 94607	www.girlsempoweringthemselves.com

continued

National Service Providers for Commercially Sexually Exploited Individuals (continued)

City	Organization	Description	Contact Information	Web Site
Oakland	MISSSEY: Motivating, Inspiring, Supporting, and Serving Sexually Exploited Youth	Provides direct services to CSEC victims through the SACEY program, which includes a drop-in recovery center. They also provide CSEC victims with client advocacy, case management, and additional recovery and transition services.	510-267-8840	www.misssey.org
Sacramento	Opening Doors, Inc.	Assists underserved members of the Greater Sacramento Area to find greater opportunities within the U.S. social and economic system, to become self-sufficient, and to realize their dreams of a better future. Our programs help those escaping sex trafficking and newly arriving refugees to restart safe and healthy lives. They provide tools for immigrants, refugees, and low-income citizens to build or grow small businesses, and to gain greater control over their personal finances.	916-492-2591	www.openingdoorsinc.com

continued

		They do this with a very hardworking multicultural staff and group of volunteers that respect the cultural identities and individual goals of our clients.	
San Diego	Bilateral Safety Corridor Coalition (BSCC)	Advocacy for prostituted and trafficked girls and women. Assistance in providing a comprehensive, multifaceted network offering wrap-around services to women, men, and children who have been victimized by traffickers and held as slaves. Services include case management, housing, legal advocacy, and immigration relief.	Hotline 619-666-0797 www.bsccoalition.org
San Diego	San Diego Youth and Community Service (SDYCS)	This nationally recognized agency offers emergency services, safe places to live, and long-term solutions for kids "on their own" by providing shelters, group homes, foster homes, community centers, and transitional housing.	619-221-8600 www.sdyouthservices.org

National Service Providers for Commercially Sexually Exploited Individuals (continued)

City	Organization	Description	Contact Information	Web Site
San Francisco	SafeHouse	While at SafeHouse, a woman receives clothing, food, shelter, and supportive services. She receives intensive case management and access to resources to help heal mind, body, and soul. A woman may reside at SafeHouse for up to 18 months—giving her time to heal emotionally and physically, gain life skills, and save money, while building her self-esteem. Other services include job mentorship, mental health services, and medical treatment.	415-643-7861	www.sfsafehouse.org

| San Francisco | SAGE Standing Against Global Exploitation Project | The Standing Against Global Exploitation Project—or SAGE Project—is a nonprofit organization with one primary aim: bringing an end to human trafficking and the commercial sexual exploitation of children and adults (CSEC/CSE). SAGE contributes to this goal by raising awareness about trafficking and CSEC/CSE issues and by providing treatment services for survivors.

SAGE is committed to improving the lives of women who are survivors of sexual exploitation, violence, and prostitution. The services they offer include peer support, referrals, day treatment programs, clothing assistance, massage, acupuncture, community education, and legal advocacy. | 415-905-5050 | www.sagesf.org |

continued

National Service Providers for Commercially Sexually Exploited Individuals (continued)

City	Organization	Description	Contact Information	Web Site
South Gate	Mary Magdalene Project	The Mary Magdalene Project's Mission is to provide a long-term residential rehabilitation program for women who want to leave prostitution. Other services include food, clothing, medical care, individual and group counseling, and job training for 18 months to 2 years.	818-988-4970	www.mmp.org
		COLORADO		
Denver	Prax(us)	Addresses the root causes of exploitation by creating systemic change and providing direct services through a comprehensive street outreach program. They conduct street outreach through a harm-reduction lens that supports youth agency and facilitates access to resources. They achieve systemic change through community organizing, collaborative relationships, community education, and policy work.	303-974-2942	www.praxus.org

CONNECTICUT

Clinton	The Barnaba Institute	The Barnaba Institute is a nonprofit organization whose mission is to raise awareness about human trafficking as it pertains to sexual exploitation through education and media; to provide professional training courses on how to identify human trafficking victims; and to provide support, guidance, and care to sexually exploited and trafficked youth and adults. Services include transportation and street outreach.	860-447-2060	www.barnabainstitute.org
Westbrook	The Paul & Lisa Program, Inc.	The Paul & Lisa Program, Inc., focuses on four concepts through their programming: Prevention, Assistance, Redirection, and Support. They contract with the State of Connecticut Judicial Branch to administer an alternative to incarceration program for women arrested on prostitution charges in the Waterbury and Hartford Community Court System.	800-518-2238	www.paulandlisa.org

continued

National Service Providers for Commercially Sexually Exploited Individuals (continued)

FLORIDA

City	Organization	Description	Contact Information	Web Site
Statewide	Florida Coalition Against Human Trafficking (FCAHT)	FCAHT works closely with community service providers to provide victims with emergency food and shelter, medical and psychological treatment, and other services as needed to help these individuals restore their lives and their freedoms.	727-442-3064	www.stophumantrafficking.org
Miami	Kristi House	Kristi House provides a healing environment for all child victims of sexual abuse and their families, regardless of income, through prevention, treatment, and coordination of services with their community partners. Services include housing, case management, and medical treatment.	305-547-6800	www.kristihouse.org

GEORGIA

Atlanta	Center to End Adolescent Sexual Exploitation (CEASE)	CEASE was created by the Juvenile Justice Fund to raise community awareness and offer advocacy and prevention services for CSEC survivors and youth at risk of exploitation. Angela's House is their main source of housing for CSEC survivors and serves about 18 girls annually.	404-224-4999	www.juvenilejusticefund.org
Atlanta	iCAtlanta	The International Center of Atlanta is dedicated to the promotion of universal human rights for all persons regardless of ethnicity, origin, culture, religion, or legal status. We implement our mission by educating in regards to and advocating for human rights. We join in coalition with other organizations that, and individuals who, advocate for universal human rights. Together we shall help create the awareness needed among the peoples, communities, governments, and nations of the world to deliver the promise of universal human rights for all.	1-888-373-7888	www.icatlanta.org

continued

National Service Providers for Commercially Sexually Exploited Individuals (continued)

City	Organization	Description	Contact Information	Web Site
HAWAII				
Honolulu	Sisters Offering Support (SOS)	SOS's mission is to provide prostitution prevention and intervention through education and awareness. Services for CSE individuals include individual counseling and peer group support, referral to community resources, a crisis line, and community education.	808-941-5554	www.soshawaii.org
IDAHO				
Boise	Idaho Coalition Against Sexual & Domestic Violence (ICASDV)	The Idaho Coalition Against Sexual & Domestic Violence is a statewide nonprofit dual coalition that advocates on behalf of victims of domestic violence and sexual assault. Incorporated in 1980, the ICASDV has grown to become a statewide membership network of over 80 shelter programs, counseling programs, law enforcement, victim witness units, prosecutors, and allied professionals, advocating for the		

safety and rights of victims of domestic violence and sexual assault. The Coalition is governed by a board of directors elected by the membership and consists of representation from each region of Idaho.

ILLINOIS

| Chicago | PROMISE Salvation Army | PROMISE, developed by The Salvation Army, includes a task force that engages in initiatives that address the PROMISE provisions of awareness, prevention, intervention, and service delivery. Strategies for implementing the provisions are developed by members who represent the social service, education, legal, judicial, healthcare, law enforcement, and other government sectors, thus ensuring a comprehensive and holistic approach. | 312-291-7916 | www.sapromise.org |

continued

National Service Providers for Commercially Sexually Exploited Individuals (continued)

City	Organization	Description	Contact Information	Web Site
Chicago	STOP-IT Salvation Army	The STOP-IT Program attempts to build relationships with suspected trafficked persons through street outreach, and assists persons currently victimized, as well as survivors through service referrals and ongoing support.	877-606-3158	www.sa-stopit.org
Chicago	The Dreamcatcher Foundation	The Dreamcatcher Foundation reaches out to girls and young women between the ages of 12 and 25 with the hopes of igniting confidence, courage, independence, and inner strength within them. As a not-for-profit organization, The Dreamcatcher Foundation seeks to improve the lives of Chicago's most disadvantaged and disenfranchised young women through education, empowerment, and prevention of sexual exploitation. Services include education, counseling, and health services.	312-458-9615	www.thedreamcatcherfoundation.org

continued

MARYLAND

Baltimore	You Are Never Alone (YANA)	The mission of YANA is to reach out in love to women and girls involved in prostitution and human trafficking, offering alternatives to those seeking change and compassionate support for those exploited by any aspect of the life. Their mission is accomplished through street outreach (daytime and evening/night); drop-in services (food, clothing, personal items, and support offered in a homelike setting); trauma counseling; medical services (through Health Care for the Homeless), and advocacy.	410-566-7973	www.yanaplace.org

National Service Providers for Commercially Sexually Exploited Individuals (continued)

City	Organization	Description	Contact Information	Web Site
		MASSACHUSSETTES		
Arlington	Germaine Lawrence	Germaine Lawrence provides the highest quality residential treatment services in New England for adolescent girls. They offer a comprehensive continuum of services that helps girls reduce destructive behaviors, develop age-appropriate social skills, and make enough progress to enable them to live at home or in the community safely again. Services include clinical services, counseling, healthcare services, education, and housing.	781-648-6200	www.germainelawrence.org

| Boston | The My Life, My Choice Project | MLMC provides a unique continuum of prevention, victim identification, and intervention services. MLMC offers provider training, prevention groups, case coordination, and survivor mentoring to victims of exploitation. Since 2002, MLMC has reached over 500 girls and over 2,000 providers in Massachusetts and nationally in a variety of locations including group homes, juvenile detention facilities, child protective services offices, schools, and other community-based settings. | 617-779-2179 | www.jri.org/mylife |
| Boston | Roxbury Youthworks | Roxbury Youthworks Inc. combats the roots of juvenile delinquency in the inner city neighborhoods of Boston by providing innovative support services to court-involved and other youth up to 21 years of age. RYI provides Boston's only Life Coaches that work with victims of commercial sexual exploitation. Services include education, counseling, and advocacy. | 617-427-8095 | www.roxburyyouthworks.org |

continued

National Service Providers for Commercially Sexually Exploited Individuals (continued)

City	Organization	Description	Contact Information	Web Site
		MICHIGAN		
Detroit	Alternatives for Girls	Alternatives for Girls helps homeless and high-risk girls and young women avoid violence, teen pregnancy, and exploitation, and helps them to explore and access the support, resources, and opportunities necessary to be safe, to grow strong, and to make positive choices in their lives. AFG accomplishes this mission through three key services: AFG Prevention, the AFG Shelter/Transition to Independent Living Program (TIL), and AFG Outreach.	313-361-4000	www.alternativesforgirls.org

MINNESOTA

Minneapolis	The Freedom and Justice Center	The Freedom and Justice Center promotes a comprehensive, collaborative, and systemic approach to prostitution to provide prostituted women with the level of service they deserve. Services include medical treatment, mental health services, housing, case management, and legal advocacy.	612-721-6327	www.angelfire.com/mn/fjc
Minneapolis	Prostitution to Independence, Dignity, and Equality (PRIDE)	PRIDE is a nationally recognized and highly successful program to help women get out, and stay out, of prostitution. PRIDE is based on self-help, advocacy, and support for women. We also offer outreach and assistance to the children of prostitution victims. Outreach, court advocacy, community presentations and services occur at the Family & Children's Service Lake Street Branch, in jails, correctional facilities, district courts, and other agencies.	612-728-2062	www.everyfamilymatters.org

continued

National Service Providers for Commercially Sexually Exploited Individuals (continued)

City	Organization	Description	Contact Information	Web Site
St. Paul	Breaking Free	Breaking Free was established in October 1996, by Vednita Carter, founder and executive director, as a nonprofit organization serving women and girls involved in systems of abuse, exploitation, and prostitution/sex trafficking. Its mission is to educate and provide services to women and girls who have been victims of abuse and commercial sexual exploitation (prostitution/sex trafficking) and need assistance escaping the violence in their lives.	651-645-6557	www.breakingfree.net

MISSOURI

| Kansas City | VERONICA'S Voice | VERONICA'S Voice educates and provides resources to help clients with options to assist them in leaving a life of prostitution, sexual exploitation, drug addiction, and violence, and to transition into new lives free from abuse. Survivors direct the programs and work with the clients at the VERONICA'S Voice SAFE Center. Services include housing, court advocacy, and education. | 816-483-7101 | www.veronicasvoice.org |

continued

National Service Providers for Commercially Sexually Exploited Individuals (continued)

City	Organization	Description	Contact Information	Web Site
St. Louis	St. Louis Rescue and Restore Coalition	The intent of the Rescue & Restore campaign is to increase the number of identified trafficking victims and to help those victims receive the benefits and services needed to live safely in the United States. The first phase of the campaign focuses on outreach to those individuals who most likely encounter victims on a daily basis, but may not recognize them as victims of human trafficking. We hope to encourage these intermediaries, as well as the general public, to look beneath the surface by recognizing clues and asking the right questions because they may be the only outsiders with the chance to reach out and help victims.	314-773-9090	www.elaurins@iistl.org

NEBRASKA

Omaha	Salvation Army Wellspring Program	TSA operates the Wellspring program, which provides support, education, and advocacy for women, men, and children affected by sex trafficking and prostitution. The services provided at Wellspring are designed using a holistic approach that includes group therapy, case management, individual and family therapy, limited material assistance, monthly outings, transportation, and referrals. Wellspring also provides care and support for the children of prostituted persons.	402-898-5900	www.usc.salvationarmy.org/usc/www_usc_western.nsf

continued

National Service Providers for Commercially Sexually Exploited Individuals (continued)

City	Organization	Description	Contact Information	Web Site
		NEVADA		
Las Vegas	Anti-Trafficking League Against Slavery (ATLAS)	ATLAS is comprised of federal, state, and local law enforcement, prosecutors, victim social services programs, community stakeholders, and community supporters. The goals of the task force are to: increase public awareness, train to identify victims/situations of human trafficking, train to investigate and prosecute cases of human trafficking, rescue victims, and prosecute traffickers. They offer social services to CSEC victims.	702-828-0237	Las Vegas Metropolitan Police Department PIO@lvmpd.com

continued

| Las Vegas | WestCare | Services include substance abuse and addiction treatment, shelter for homeless and runaway youth, domestic violence treatment and prevention, and mental health programs. These services are available to adults, children, adolescents, and families; they specialize in helping people traditionally considered difficult to treat, such as those who are indigent, have multiple disorders, or are involved with the criminal justice system. | 702-385-2090 | www.westcare.com |

NEW JERSEY

| Newark | Polaris Project | The NJ TIP provides case management services to victims to address the lack of specialized services available in New Jersey. Services provided include emergency, short-term and long-term case management services for victims of trafficking. Services provided through case management include crisis intervention, criminal justice advocacy, court accompaniment, locating resources and referrals, interpretation, emotional support, and more. | 973-624-5454 | www.polarisproject.org |

National Service Providers for Commercially Sexually Exploited Individuals (continued)

City	Organization	Description	Contact Information	Web Site
		NEW YORK		
Hudson Valley	My Sister's Place	My Sisters' Place (MSP) strives to engage each member of society in our work to end domestic violence so that all relationships can embrace the principles of respect, equality, and peacefulness. Since 1978, we have advanced this mission in Westchester County and the surrounding region through advocacy, community education, and services to those harmed by domestic violence.	800-298-7233	www.mysistersplaceny.org

continued

| New York City | Girls Education and Mentoring Services (GEMS) | Girls Educational & Mentoring Services (GEMS) is the only organization in New York State specifically designed to serve girls and young women who have experienced commercial sexual exploitation and domestic trafficking. GEMS was founded in 1998 by Rachel Lloyd, a young woman who had been sexually exploited as a teenager. GEMS has helped hundreds of young women and girls, ages 12–24, who have experienced commercial sexual exploitation and domestic trafficking to exit the commercial sex industry and to develop to their full potential. GEMS provides young women with empathetic, consistent support and viable opportunities for positive change. | 212-926-8089 | www.gems-girls.org |

National Service Providers for Commercially Sexually Exploited Individuals (continued)

City	Organization	Description	Contact Information	Web Site
		NORTH CAROLINA		
Asheville	Hope House: Eagles Wings Ministries	Their mission is to provide a place of seclusion, restoration, and healing for domestic minor sex-trafficking victims (U.S. girls under 18). Services include education, case management, spiritual mentorship, life skills, and counseling.	877-276-8023	www.hopehousenc.com
Chapel Hill	The Carolina Women's Center at the University of North Carolina at Chapel Hill	The Carolina Women's Center at the University of North Carolina at Chapel Hill works toward eradicating sex trafficking in the state and worldwide through policy and advocacy efforts. The Center helps to generate research and knowledge about trafficking practices. We raise awareness, both on campus and in the community, about the human rights violations trafficking causes, including the mental and physical effects on its victims and the impact on communities.	919-962-8305	www.womenscenter.unc.edu

continued

The Center is a member of two statewide antitrafficking coalitions: the North Carolina Coalition Against Human Trafficking, comprised of direct service providers, law enforcement, policy and legislative advocates; and NC Stop Human Trafficking, the focal point for individual and community group advocacy and activism.

OHIO

| Cincinnati | YWCA of Greater Cincinnati | In 2001, the Legal Aid Society of Greater Cincinnati formed the Alliance for Battered and Abused International Women, now called the Alliance for Immigrant Women, to respond to the increased number of immigrant women who were seeking services or injured as a result of domestic violence. Over 20 agencies have joined to develop prevention and intervention programming and to coordinate services for immigrant/non-English speaking victims in the community to ensure they have access to necessary resources. | 513-361-2134 | www.ywcacincinnati.org |

National Service Providers for Commercially Sexually Exploited Individuals (continued)

City	Organization	Description	Contact Information	Web Site
Toledo	Second Chance	Second Chance is a social service program located in Toledo that provides comprehensive services to victims of domestic sex trafficking and prostitution. Services include case management, counseling, education, and CSEC support groups. Second Chance Mission is there • to offer supportive services to women and youth affected by or at risk for involvement in sex trafficking or commercial sexual exploitation, as they reclaim lives of choice; • to raise community awareness about the issues of sex trafficking and the commercial sexual exploitation of children and to work diligently to end the exploitation and victimization of women and youth; and	419-244-6050	www.secondchancetoledo.org

- to advocate with women and youth throughout the country to secure and provide resources for treatment and services for victims of sex trafficking and exploitation.

OKLAHOMA

| Oklahoma City | The Salvation Army | In Oklahoma City, The Salvation Army provides shelter, feeding programs, senior citizen programs, social services, disaster services, youth programs, drug and alcohol rehabilitation, transportation, clothing assistance, Christmas cheer programs, and worship programs. CSE services specifically include clothing, transportation, and shelter. | 405-246-1100 | www.salvationarmyokcac.org |

continued

National Service Providers for Commercially Sexually Exploited Individuals (continued)

OREGON

City	Organization	Description	Contact Information	Web Site
Portland	Lola Greene Baldwin Foundation	The mission of the Baldwin Foundation is threefold: To help people escape the life of prostitution, survive, and recover from its long-term effects. To provide education about the effects of the sex industry on those used in it, and its effects on the larger community. To educate actual and potential users of prostituted persons about the meaning and consequences of their behavior. Services include crisis intervention, case management, and legal advocacy.	503-236-7244	www.prostitutionrecovery.org
Portland	Sexual Assault Resource Center (SARC)	Their mission is to provide immediate response and support to sexual assault survivors and empower them to heal and regain control of their lives. To minimize the aftermath of harm by providing advocacy, information, and referrals to the survivors and their families.	1-888-640-5311	www.sarcoregon.org

		To educate and create awareness surrounding sexual assault to members of the community. Services include case management and mental health services.		
Portland	Transitions Global—Project Every Girl	Transitions provides comprehensive restorative aftercare for girls rescued from sex trafficking. Each girl at Transitions receives personalized care to heal her past and provide opportunities for her future. A girl who finds her home at Transitions finds a new beginning. She finds hope, and with holistic trauma therapy, life skills, and sustainable career training—she finds a dream for her future. We help girls transition, through the power of a dream, from darkness to light, from victim to survivor to world changer.	513-898-9372	www.info@transitionsglobal.org

continued

National Service Providers for Commercially Sexually Exploited Individuals (continued)

City	Organization	Description	Contact Information	Web Site
		PENNSYLVANIA		
Philadelphia	Philadelphia Anti-Trafficking Coalition (PATC)	The Philadelphia Anti-Trafficking Coalition (PATC) aims to coordinate an appropriate response to the needs of victims and seeks to make available a wide range of services by creating a network of agencies that can properly assist them. Chaired by Covenant House Pennsylvania, the coalition was founded in 2005 and convenes several times each year to discuss the efforts to fight Human Trafficking.	215-951-5411	www.horgan@covenanthousepa. org
		PATC's main focus currently centers on the increased out-reach efforts toward vulnerable populations as well as training events for those likely to encounter or provide services to victims. Other projects include protocols, a language bank, and a resource guide for trafficking in Philadelphia.		

continued

TEXAS

Dallas	LETOT	Letot Center is a co-educational, short-term residential facility that provides assessment, crisis intervention, emergency shelter care, foster care, nonresidential counseling, and referral services for status offenders. The facility has a shelter capacity for 40 youth in residential care. Programming is designed to reunite runaways with their families whenever possible and to prevent youth from committing criminal offenses or from entering the Juvenile Justice System. Individualized treatment plans for each youth and his/her family are designed to increase healthy protective factors and decrease risk factors associated with delinquency.	214-357-0391	www.dallascountywanted.com
Houston	Houston Rescue and Restore Coalition	HRRC exists to prevent and confront modern-day slavery by educating the public, training professionals, and empowering the community to take action for the purpose of identifying, rescuing, and restoring trafficking victims to freedom.	713-874-0290	www.houstonrr.org

National Service Providers for Commercially Sexually Exploited Individuals (continued)

City	Organization	Description	Contact Information	Web Site
		WASHINGTON		
Seattle	New Horizons Ministries	The staff of New Horizons, both paid and volunteer, establish relationships with youth through street outreach as well as by providing meals, clothing, and other emergency services. New Horizons also provides case management, relational counseling, recreational activities, job mentoring, life discovery classes, and a comprehensive referral system. All of these services are designed to equip youth with the life skills, confidence, and sense of community that are vital for them to successfully exit street life.	206-374-0866	www.nhmin.org
Seattle	YouthCare Safe House	YouthCare Safe House provides services specifically for CSEC survivors. Services will include case management, legal advocacy, counseling, housing, and education.	206-694-4500	www.youthcare.org

WASHINGTON, D.C.

| District of Columbia | Courtney's House | Courtney's House is committed to providing a safe space and loving home environment—in a therapeutic and emotionally healing atmosphere—for domestic sex-trafficked girls between the ages of 12 and 18. Courtney's House is dedicated to the mission of ending domestic sex trafficking and commercial sexual exploitation of all children. They focus efforts on providing long-term group home residency and providing direct services, which include housing, street outreach, and case management. | 1-888-261-3665 | www.courtneyshouse.org |

continued

National Service Providers for Commercially Sexually Exploited Individuals (continued)

City	Organization	Description	Contact Information	Web Site
District of Columbia	FAIR Fund	FAIR Fund approach combines preventative education workshops, outreach to exploited youth, and art therapy for girl survivors. FAIR Fund provides comprehensive care and services to teen girl survivors of human trafficking and sexual violence. Our model art therapy and economic empowerment program, JewelGirls, supports victimized girls as they transition into being independent young survivors.	202-265-1505	www.fairfund.org
		HIPS was founded in 1993 by a coalition of service providers, advocates, and law enforcement officials as an outreach and referral service. HIPS' mission is to assist female, male, and transgender individuals engaging in sex work in Washington, D.C., in leading healthy lives.		

continued

| District of Columbia | Helping Individual Prostitutes Survive (HIPS) | Utilizing a harm reduction model, HIPS' programs strive to address the impact that HIV/AIDS, sexually transmitted infections, discrimination, poverty, violence, and drug use have on the lives of individuals engaging in sex work. Services include legal assistance, emergency housing, and street outreach. | 202-232-8150 | www.hips.org |
| District of Columbia | Polaris Project | Polaris Project operates the Greater DC Trafficking Intervention Program (DC TIP) to combat human trafficking in the District of Columbia, Northern Virginia, and Southern Maryland. Launched in 2002, DC TIP works to create an effective community-based response to curb local human trafficking network activity. DC TIP provides comprehensive services to foreign national and U.S. citizen victims in the Washington, D.C., metro area and works toward long-term, systemic change. | 202-745-1001 | www.polarisproject.org |

National Service Providers for Commercially Sexually Exploited Individuals (continued)

City	Organization	Description	Contact Information	Web Site
District of Columbia	Restoration Ministries	RM provides a prostitution intervention/prevention program at the youth detention center five times a month to girls 11 to 17 who have been trafficked or who are at a high-risk of being trafficked. RM hosts a weekly therapy group at the District Jail for adult females who have been incarcerated for solicitation charges. RM also provides mentoring services and job mentorship.	202-544-1731	www.restorationministriesdc.org

WISCONSIN

| Madison | Project RESPECT | Project RESPECT is a women's center that provides advocacy, case management, counseling, crisis intervention, transitional housing, and peer support group services for women with prostitution histories that have changed or want to change their lives. We provide a safe and nonjudgmental place to meet and talk with other women with similar histories. We assist women to have increased options available to them and reach their goals. Women served include survivors of domestic violence, sexual assault, childhood sexual abuse, women with chemical dependency, and vocational issues. | 608-278-2300 | www.arccommserv.com |

Source: National Service Providers for Commercially Sexually Exploited Individuals, available at: http://g.virbcd n.com/_f/files /28/FileItem-175887-Nationalserviceprovidorsfinal.pdf; accessed, October 17, 2012.

U.S. GOVERNMENT AGENCIES AVAILABLE TO ASSIST SEX-TRAFFICKING VICTIMS

Department of Health and Human Services (HHS)

HHS leads the Rescue and Restore Victims of Human Trafficking public awareness campaign, funds organizations to conduct outreach to foreign and U.S. citizen victims, funds comprehensive case management, and support services for foreign victims in the United States, and certifies foreign victims of a severe form of sex trafficking to be eligible to receive federal benefits and services to the same extent as refugees. A range of programs also assist youth at-risk of trafficking, including Runaway and Homeless Youth Program.

HHS also funds the National Human Trafficking Resource Center that provides a nationwide 24/7 hotline at **888-3737-888.**

Rescue and Restore Coalitions

U.S. Department of Health and Human Services, Administration for Children & Families, The Campaign to Rescue Victims of Human Trafficking

Location of Coalition	Name of Coalition	Lead Organization	Contact Name	Email	Phone Number
Maryland Human Trafficking Taskforce, Victim Services and Public Awareness Committee	Maryland/ Statewide Coalition	None	Melissa Snow Lisa Carrasco	msnow@turnaroundinc.org mhttf.awareness@gmail.com	410-377-8111
Baltimore City and surrounding counties	Maryland Rescue & Restore	The Samaritan Women	Chris Spoonire	cspoonire@ thesamaritanwomen.org	410-207-1283

Location	Organization	Contact	Name	Email	Phone
Maine, New Hampshire, Connecticut, Massachusetts, Rhode Island	Northeast Coalition Against Trafficking	The Trauma Center Brookline, MA	Cynthia Kennedy	ckennedy@jri.org	617-232-1303 ext. 322
New York City	Empire State Coalition of Youth and Family Services	Empire State Coalition of Youth and Family Services Brooklyn, NY	Margo Hirsch	mhirsch@empirestatecoalition.org	718-237-2722
Philadelphia, Pennsylvania	Philadelphia Rescue and Restore	Covenant House Pennsylvania	Hugh Organ	horgan@covenanth ousepa.org	215 951 5411 ext. 2118
Columbus, Ohio	Central Ohio Rescue and Restore Coalition	The Salvation Army in Greater Columbus	Trisha Smouse	Trisha.Smounse@USE.SalvationArmy.org	614-358-2614
Cincinnati, Ohio	End Slavery Cincinnati	YWCA of Greater Cincinnati	Debbie Porter	escoordinator@ywcacin.org	513-479-2772
Toledo, Ohio	Lucas County Human Trafficking Coalition	none	Celia Williamson	info@lchtc.org	419-530-4084

continued

Rescue and Restore Coalitions (continued)

Location of Coalition	Name of Coalition	Lead Organization	Contact Name	Email	Phone Number
Dayton, Ohio	Abolition Ohio, the Rescue & Restore Coalition in the Miami Valley	Abolition Ohio	Anthony Talbott	Anthony.talbott@udayton.edu	937-229-4326
Kentucky/ Statewide coalition	Kentucky Rescue & Restore Coalition	Catholic Charities of Louisville	Marissa Castellanos	mcatellanos@archlou.org	502-636-9263
Nashville, Tennessee	Nashville Rescue and Restore	Free for Life International Nashville, TN	Colette Bercu	info@freeforlifeintl.org	1-888-335-8835
Northeast Tennessee	No Silence Now	No Silence Now Blountville, TN	Amber Smith	amber@nosilencenow.org	423-946-8511
Chattanooga, Tennessee	Greater Chattanooga Coalition Against Human Trafficking (GCCAHT)	Second Life of Chattanooga	Terri Self	tself@secondlifechattanooga.org	423-994-4857

North Carolina/Statewide coalition	NCCAHT North Carolina Coalition Against Human Trafficking	Legal Aid of North Carolina Raleigh, NC	Caitlin Ryland	caitlinr@legalaidnc.org	919-856-2180 ext. 113
Georgia/Statewide coalition	Georgia Rescue & Restore	Emory University School of Law, Barton Child Law Policy Center Atlanta, GA	Kirsten Widner	kwidner@emory.edu	404-712-1233
Orlando, Florida	Orlando Rescue and Restore Coalition	Florida Coalition Against Human Trafficking Clearwater, FL	Tomas Lares	OrlandoRRC@gmail.com	407-495-5846
Tampa, Florida	Tampa Bay Rescue and Restore	Florida Coalition Against Human Trafficking Clearwater, FL	Giselle Rodriguez	Grodriguez96@yahoo.com	727-442-3064
Sarasota County (Florida)	Sarasota Rescue and Restore Coalition	Florida Coalition Against Human Trafficking Clearwater, FL	Giselle Rodriguez	Grodriguez96@yahoo.com	727-442-3064

continued

Rescue and Restore Coalitions (continued)

Location of Coalition	Name of Coalition	Lead Organization	Contact Name	Email	Phone Number
Manatee County, Florida	Manatee County Rescue and Restore Coalition	Florida Coalition Against Human Trafficking Clearwater, FL	Giselle Rodriguez	Grodriguez96@yahoo.com	727-442-3064
Brevard County, Florida	Space Coast Rescue and Restore Coalition	Florida Coalition Against Human Trafficking	Tomas Lares	spacecoastrrc@gmail.com	407-495-5846
Greater Birmingham and northern Alabama	Freedom to Thrive	Southeastern Network Birmingham, AL	Tammy Hopper	thopper@senetwork.org	865-521-7131
Baton Rouge and New Orleans, Louisiana	Rescue and Restore Coalition	Healing Place Serve	Claudia Berry	claudia.berry@healingplacechurch.org	225-753-2273
Oklahoma/ Statewide coalition	Oklahomans Against Human Trafficking Humans (OATH)	Oklahomans Against Human Trafficking Humans (OATH) Oklahoma City, OK	Mark Elam	Markelam07@yahoo.com	405-523-3508

Houston, Texas	Houston Rescue and Restore Coalition	Houston Rescue and Restore	Maria Trujillo	maria@houstonrr.org	713-874-0290
Chicago, Illinois	Illinois Rescue & Restore	Illinois Department of Human Services	Lisa Fedina	Lisa.fedina@illinois.gov	312-793-0014
Detroit, Michigan	Michigan Rescue and Restore Coalition	Global Project for Hope, Help, and Healing	Pamela Hudson	michiganrescueandrestore@gmail.com	313-205-7300
Minnesota/Statewide coalition	Rescue & Restore Coalition	Civil Society St. Paul, MN	Linda Miller	office@civilsocietyhelps.org	651-291-0713
Wisconsin/Statewide coalition	Wisconsin Rescue & Restore	Practical Strategies, Inc. Milwaukee, WI	Mary Jo Joyce	mjj@practical-strategies.com	262-334-1821
St. Louis, Missouri	St. Louis Rescue and Restore Coalition	International Institute of St. Louis	Suzanne LeLaurin	lelaurins@iistl.org	314-773-9090 ext. 150
Central Missouri	Central Missouri Stop Human Trafficking Coalition	Central Missouri Stop Human Trafficking Coalition Columbia, MO	Deb Hume	deb@stophumantraffickingmo.com	573-884-3757

continued

Rescue and Restore Coalitions (continued)

Location of Coalition	Name of Coalition	Lead Organization	Contact Name	Email	Phone Number
Idaho/Statewide coalition	Idaho Coalition Against Sexual and Domestic Violence	Idaho Coalition Against Sexual and Domestic Violence Boise, ID	Kelly Miller	kmiller@idvsa.org	208-384-0419
Portland, Oregon	Oregonians Against Human Trafficking	Catholic Charities Portland, OR	Chris Killmer	ckillmer@ catholiccharitiesoregon.org	503-542 -2855 ext. 40
Pacific Northwest (Washington, Oregon, Montana, Alaska, Northwestern Idaho)	Northwest Coalition Against Trafficking (NWCAT)	National Women's Coalition Against Violence & Exploitation (NWCAVE)	Michelle Bart	info@nwcave.org	626-644-3472
Washington/ Statewide	Washington Anti-Trafficking Response Network	International Rescue Committee Seattle, WA	Kathleen Morris	Kathleen.morris@theirc.org	206-623-2105

Las Vegas, Nevada	Network of Emergency Trafficking Services (NETS) of Las Vegas	Salvation Army Las Vegas, NV	Lauren Hermosillo	Lauren_Hermosillo@usw.salvationarmy.org	702-649-8240 ext. 230
Colorado/Statewide coalition	Colorado Network to End Human Trafficking (CONEHT)	Colorado Organization for Victim Assistance (COVA) Denver, CO	Lauren Croucher	lauren@coloradocrimevictims.org	303-996-8087
New Mexico/statewide coalition	New Mexico Rescue and Restore Coalition	New Mexico Organized Against Trafficking Humans	Dr. Susan Travis	travis@nm-oath.org	575-937-0294
San Francisco, California	San Francisco Rescue & Restore	SAGE Project, Inc. San Francisco, CA	Mollie Ring	mollier@sagesf.org	415-358-2737
Fresno, California	Central Valley Against Human Trafficking	Fresno County Economic Opportunities Commission Fresno, CA	Ronna Bright	ronna.bright@fresnoeoc.org	559-268-1045 ext. 103

continued

Rescue and Restore Coalitions (continued)

Location of Coalition	Name of Coalition	Lead Organization	Contact Name	Email	Phone Number
Contra Costa County (California)	Contra Costa County's Zero Tolerance for Human Trafficking Coalition	Contra Costa County Martinez, CA	Juliana Granzotto	jgranzotto@ehsd.cccounty.us	925-313-1591
Sacramento, California	Sacramento Rescue & Restore Coalition	Sacramento Employment & Training Agency (SETA)	Mary Jennings	mjenning@delpaso.seta.net	916-263-1555
Southern California	California's Key-2 Freedom Alliance	Coalition to Abolish Slavery and Trafficking (CAST) Los Angeles, CA	Vanessa Lanza	vanessa@castla.org	213-365-1906
San Diego, California	San Diego Unity Coalition	Bilateral Safely Corridor Coalition San Diego, CA	Marisa Ugarte	info@bsccinfo.org	619-336-0770
Puerto Rico	Coalicion del Caribe contra la Trata Humana	Florida Coalition Against Human Trafficking	Karla Gonzalez	karlafchat@gmail.com	787-528-1550

Source: Available at: http://www.acf.hhs.gov/programs/orr/resource/contact-information-for-coalitions; accessed, October 17, 2012.

Index

E

F

G

V

W

Y